KIN, KILTS AND KOLONIE

Also by G. Roger Knight

Colonial Production in Provincial Java: The Sugar Industry in Pekalongan-Tegal, 1800–1942 (Amsterdam: VU University Press, 1993)

Narratives of Colonialism. Sugar, Java and the Dutch (New York: Nova, 2000)

With Ulbe Bosma & Juan Giusti-Cordero (eds), *Sugarlandia Revisited: Sugar and Colonialism in Asia and the Americas, 1800 to 1940* (with a preface by Sydney W. Mintz) (London & New York: Berghahn Publishers, 2007)

Commodities and Colonialism. The Story of 'Big Sugar' in Indonesia, 1880–1940 (Leiden & Boston: Brill 2013)

Sugar Steam and Steel: The Industrial Project in Colonial Java, 1820–1885 (Adelaide: The University of Adelaide Press, 2014)

Trade and Empire in Early Nineteenth-Century Southeast Asia: Gillian Maclaine and his Business Network, 1816–1840 (Woodbridge: Boydell & Brewer, 2015)

KIN, KILTS AND KOLONIE

Scottish Sojourners in the
Dutch Empire in Asia

G. Roger Knight

Published in the United Kingdom by Amaurea Press
Amaurea Press is an imprint of Amaurea Creative Productions Ltd.
London, United Kingdom
www.amaurea.co.uk

Copyright © 2026 G. Roger Knight

The moral right of G. Roger Knight to be identified as author of this work has been asserted by him in accordance with the Copyright, Designs and Patents Act 1988.

All rights reserved. Apart from any fair dealing for the purposes of criticism or review, as permitted under the Copyright Acts, no part of this book may be reproduced, copied or transmitted in any form or by any electronic or mechanical means, including information storage and retrieval systems, without permission in writing from the publisher.

ISBN 9781914278938 (hardback)
ISBN 9781914278945 (eBook edition)

This edition © 2026 Amaurea Press

British Library Cataloguing in Publication Data
A catalogue record for this book is available from the British Library

Printed and bound by CPI Group (UK) Ltd., Croydon, CR0 4YY

Cover, book design & typesetting by Albarrojo
Cover photo courtesy of Richard MacNeill, Melbourne

For Jarran Zen

Contents

List of Illustrations	ix
Preface	xiii
Introduction: To the Ends of the Earth – and Back	1
1. From the 'Land o' Cakes'	11
2. *Tempo Doeloe* and Highland Homecomings	29
3. The Kilted Dancer and an Antipodean 'Ardtornish'	53
4. Islay and the Wealth of the Indies	75
5. Death in Bournemouth and a Surrogate Scotland	97
6. Good Steady Scotsmen	113
7. Aberdeen, Antwerp and the Indies	137
8. Sugar, Sheep and an Empire Family	173
9. Gathering the Clan, Advancing the Empire and the Lure of London	197
10. A House Built from Sugar	219
11. Upper Deck and *Indisch*	237
12. Expatriates and Survivors	263
Conclusion: Scotland's Diaspora Refracted Through the Lens of the Indies	287
Endnotes	293
Bibliography	339
Index	361

List of Illustrations

1.1: Map of Java	10
1.2: Gillian Maclaine	12
1.3: Johannes van den Bosch	14
1.4: Edward Watson	19
1.5: Rudolphina de Sturler	22
1.6: Cipanas, the Governor-General's country house	23
2.1 to 4: Batavia's European Quarter, c.1850	30
2.5: John Pryce's House, Koningsplein, Batavia	34
2.6: Tjepiring Sugar Factory, c.1870	37
2.7: Willem van der Hucht, Adriaan Holle and Nata di Lagaa, 1861	41
2.8: Victoria and Albert's Scottish Baronial palace	47
3.1: Donald Maclaine, partner in Maclaine Watson, in later life	54
3.2: Willemskerk, Batavia's Protestant Church	57
3.3: Donald Maclaine and Emilie Vincent and family's Batavia house	58
3.4: Map of Mull and Morvern	60
3.5: Lochbuie House, ancestral home of the Lochbuie family	61
3.6: Wall plaque commemorating Margaret Maclaine-Pryce	63
3.7: Ardtornish House, Morvern, Scotland	65
3.8: Ardtornish, South Australia	66
3.9: Donald Maclaine photographed in 1862, a year before his death	70
3.10: Murdoch Gillian Maclaine	71
4.1: Lachlan McLean	76
4.2: Map of Islay	77

4.3: Maclaine Watson's Batavia Office, c.1865	78
4.4: John MacNeill	79
4.5: Laggan Farm, Islay	81
4.6: Kilchoman Free Church	82
4.7: Islay House. Leased by Lachlan McLean	88
4.8: The widow, Elizabeth Cameron McLean, and five of her children	93
4.9: Elizabeth Cameron	94
5.1: Death Notice of Alexander MacNeill	98
5.2: Alexander MacNeill	98
5.3: Freemasons' lodge in Surabaya	99
5.4: Bordlands House	101
5.5: Neil MacNeill	105
5.6: Elia MacNeill	108
6.1: View of Singapore in the 1830s	115
6.2: Park Square East, Regent's Park, London	123
6.3: Carte-de-visite of Lewis Fraser and his wife Sophie Cumming	124
6.4: Oxford Square, north of London's Hyde Park	125
6.5: Lewis Fraser	127
7.1: Mongewell House, c.1893	140
7.2: Boompjes, Rotterdam	141
7.3: Alexander Caspar Fraser	142
7.4: Arthur Fraser	146
7.5: Alec Fraser	150
7.6: One of the Indonesian artist Raden Saleh's paintings	151
7.7: Julia van Citters	153
7.8: Fraser in the Scottish Borders, Hartrigge House	154
7.9: 3 Craven Hill, Hyde Park	160
7.10: Henriette Fraser, 1897	163
7.11: Henriette Fraser-Bankes as chatelaine of Kingston Lacy	164
7.12: Kingston Lacy	165
7.13: The Drucker-Frasers	168
8.1: A sugar factory in Java, c.1860	174

8.2: A wool-shed in Australia, c.1890	175
8.3: Donald McLachlan	180
8.4: James McLachlan	181
8.5: Mientje van der Hucht	182
8.6: Donald McLachlan	183
8.7: James and Mientje McLachlan's Holland House in Cheltenham	184
8.8: James McLachlan in Retirement in Cheltenham	186
8.9: John Forrest	187
8.10: Cheltenham Ladies' College	188
9.1: Neil McLean as president of the Clan MacLean Association	198
9.2: Islay-born Neil McLean	200
9.3: Breda House	204
9.4: Neil and Elizabeth McLean in their later years	206
9.5: London High Society. 'Presented at court', 1932	210
9.6: The 'party-going' Isobel McLean, early 1930s	211
9.7: Isobel and Terence Skeffington-Smyth, 1935	212
10.1: William Loudon MacNeill's Shennanton in Wigtownshire	220
10.2: William Loudon MacNeill	220
10.3: Barbados in Wigtown	221
10.4: William Loudon MacNeill and fellow golfers in Surabaya, 1890s	224
10.5: Everyone for tennis. Java, c.1890s	226
10.6: Marriage of William Loudon MacNeill's grandson	232
11.1: SS *Burgemeester den Tex*	238
11.2: Wilhelmina Johanna Couperus	240
11.3: Koninginnegracht, The Hague, c.1900	244
11.4: Richard Mac Neill amidst his extended family, The Hague, c.1903	245
11.5: Arabella Mac Neill and Gijsbert van Tienhoven	247
11.6: Hubner and the Mac Neills, 1909	249
11.7: Johanna Bezoet de Bie and Alexander Mac Neill, 1897	250
11.8: Johanna Mac Neill-Bezoet de Bie and her first child, c.1900	250
11.9: The *tuan besar*, the *nyonya besar* and their children, c.1905	251
11.10: Oemboel Sugar Factory, Probolinggo, East Java, c.1904	252

11.11: Eugenie Jackson in the swimming pool at Oemboel 254
11.12: Children's bath-time at Oemboel, c.1904 255
11.13: Interior of Mac Neill and Bezoet de Bie's house at Oemboel 256
11.14: Party scene at Oemboel, c.1900 256
11.15: Bezoet de Bie in kabaya and sarong at Oemboel 257
11.16: Johanna Bezoet de Bie and friends in Bandungan, Central Java 261
11.17: Back in the Hague, c.1938 – Bezoet de Bie and grandchildren 261
12.1: Advertisement for concert starring Lili Kraus, October 1940 262
12.2: A concert artist in her prime: pianist Lili Kraus, c.1939 264
12.3: The wedding of Callum McLean and Betty Lydall, Dec. 1935 273
12.4: Kayun, Surabaya, c.1940 279
12.5: Enjoying the Concert, Surabaya, October 1940 280

Preface

HOW ON EARTH did an Englishman long settled in Australia come to conceive of a book about Scots living in what was then the Dutch Southeast Asian colony of Java? The answer – one which engages with long-established narratives of Scotland's diaspora – is less puzzling than might appear. Over the years (there were many of them!) the Englishman in question gradually became an 'authority' on a commodity (sugar), which the colony concerned had once manufactured and exported in huge quantities. As it turned out, moreover, for a century or more one of the biggest European firms involved in that export bore the name (Maclaine Watson) of the Scot and the Londoner who had co-founded it back in the 1820s. The Londoner's interest in the business ended fairly rapidly after a decade or so, but Scottish associates of his erstwhile 'spouse commercial' Gillian Maclaine, a Highlander from the Western Isles, kept the firm going long after the latter's death at sea (together with his wife, children and the entire ship's crew) somewhere in the Indian Ocean in April 1840. My research journey into the lives of Maclaine himself and of the people (and their descendants) who ran the business for more than a century after its co-founder's death took me to places where I'd never been before (both literally and metaphorically) or only 'knew' in a quite different dimension.

Not least of the outcomes of the tragedy of April was that Maclaine's surviving kin in Scotland – above all his younger brother the Reverend Angus Maclaine – sought (very effectively) to keep his memory alive through the conservation of the many letters Maclaine had written primarily to his mother, Marjorie Gregorson-Maclaine, in the years before her death in 1836, and subsequently to Angus, who by that time was a minister in the Church of Scotland. It was in the Reverend Angus's study that I first saw this archive in the house that he had built for himself on the banks of Loch Gilp on the West Coast of the Scottish Highlands on his return from a lengthy sojourn as a substantial farmer in the Antipodes. The year would have been 1967, and I had no idea that I, too, would shortly be Australia-bound. Nor did I have much idea that the vistas into the Scottish diaspora that his brother's letters had opened would many years later come to engage me so completely.

That engagement effectively began in the wake of my book about Gillian Maclaine's mercantile career (*Trade and Empire in Early Nineteenth-Century Southeast Asia*, 2015), and was no doubt fuelled by the fact that in the northern suburbs of Adelaide, the South Australian city where I had worked for almost half a century, there still existed the house (much added to) in which the Reverend Angus had lived back in the 1840s. Angus, backed by the 'Java' money that he had inherited from his late brother, had prospered by rearing sheep on land from which its Kaurna 'First Nation' people had been driven off and decimated at least as effectively as in any of the Highland Clearances that played (and maybe still does play) so large a part in the story of Scotland's diaspora. The visitation of the Antipodes by a plague of sheep and the managerial role played by Scottish sojourners (and settlers) of the 'gentry' rather than crofter class, was nonetheless only a lesser dimension of my growing interest.

For the core of my investigation came to focus not on Britain's occupation of the 'Great South Land' but on what the Dutch invariably referred to as 'the Indies', and in particular on the island of Java, some month or more's sea-voyage to Australia's north-west. Among other things, it quickly became apparent that the story of the Scottish diaspora in 'the Indies' was not exclusively one about business and businessmen. Far from it. The Dutch colonial communities on Java and elsewhere in the Indonesian archipelago, it turned out, were heavily marriage- and family-oriented, so that although almost all the Scots who arrived on the island were single males, a significant number found wives there or, alternatively, wed while 'on leave' in Scotland and brought their partners back to Java with them. As a result, my investigations brought into focus wives, mothers and daughters to an extent that quite belied any notion that overseas sojourners – people, that is to say, who always intended to return home, hopefully enriched, after their time in 'the East' – were pre-eminently unmarried men who postponed matrimony until they returned home.

But what also came to fascinate me were the returnee afterlives of families – many of them established in the Indies and often extending over several generations – that played out not only in Scotland but also in England, and what they no doubt referred to as 'the Continent'. I was, of course, at a serious disadvantage in this regard, not having at my disposal anything comparable to Gillian Maclaine's voluminous letters home. But, along with all the plethora of information-locating advantages of the digital age, I was delighted to find that I had at my disposal the support of a number of people whose ancestors were among the Scottish associates who continued to run the Maclaine Watson business on Java after the death of its co-founder. Invaluable contacts were made for me; letters and photographs, above all ones detailing diasporic life in the Indies, were generously made available; and on one unforgettable occasion back in Scotland, I was taken on a voyage of discovery by car and ferry to the island of Mull, there to be given morning tea in the first floor drawing room of the mansion where one of 'my' mid-nineteenth-century sojourners must himself have sat, with his Indies-born wife, during the family's repatriate years.

It is the life stories of this particular couple, together with those of a number of their contemporaries and their descendants, that propel the present book. Among the latter, over the years I have been the beneficiary of the enthusiasm and generous hospitality of James and Janet Greenfield, whose collaboration turned what might simply have been a task into a pleasure. In the same context must also be mentioned the late Lord Crickhowell and Lady Crickhowell, as well as the late Ian Macpherson, Lorne Maclaine, Nicolas Maclaine, Giles Forrest and Iain Thornber. Likewise, the late Richard Mac Neill in Melbourne and his Australian son and daughter-in-law, Richard MacNeill and Nora van Waarden; Elizabeth del Court Konig van Essen in The Hague; and Michael McNeill and Charlie McNeill in Wigtownshire in the far south-west of Scotland. I should stress, however, that the opinions expressed in the following pages, and the conclusions reached, are those of the author alone, to whom must also be sheeted home sole responsibility for any mistakes and errors.

Outside the circle of the families concerned, Tom van den Berge and Marieke Bloembergen, at the University of Leiden, offered much-appreciated support; while in The Hague the late Peter Christiaans of the CBG-Centre for Family History gave unstintingly of his encyclopaedic knowledge of the Indies Dutch, and Alexander Claver was always ready to share his unique files on the Indies' premier financial institution. Not to be forgotten, either, is the encouragement and commentary provided by James Hammerton in

Melbourne, whose parallel investigations most recently bore fruit in *Love, Class and Empire* (Cambridge University Press, 2025). Likewise, warmly remembered are longstanding friends: the late Pim van der Meiden and Joke de Wit in The Hague, Heather Sutherland on the Prinsengracht in Amsterdam and the late Frans Husken and Cora Govers in their '*buitenhuis*' on the edge of the Hooge Veluwe National Park, together with Colin Brewer and Adam Bakker on London's Bankside – all of whom kindly provided much-appreciated home-from-home for an itinerant researcher. My profound thanks also go to Jonathan Curry-Machado, my indefatigable editor and publisher at Amaurea Press; and, here in Adelaide, to the unflinching help in matters of manuscript preparation of William Woods, scholar and gentleman. No acknowledgements would be complete, nevertheless, without a deeply affectionate reference to Jarran Zen, my companion and carer over the last decade, to whom this book is dedicated.

KIN, KILTS AND KOLONIE

Introduction

To the Ends of the Earth – and Back

IN THE MIDDLE months of 1822, an 18-year-old Scots woman, Jean Steuart Fraser, together with her recently wed husband, John Robert Turing, sailed down the Atlantic and rounded the Cape of Good Hope into the Indian Ocean. Their destination, more than 14,000 miles away by the route they took, was Batavia (present-day Jakarta) on the north-west coast of the island of Java, at the heart of what is now the Republic of Indonesia. For although the 'Kin' and 'Kilts' of the book's title were indubitably Scottish, the *'Kolonie'* was Dutch, the sprawling archipelagic empire in Southeast Asia that its colonial hegemon simply referred to as 'the Indies' (invariably omitting the anglophone 'Dutch East' prefix). Fraser-Turing, who spent the better part of a decade there, was a woman about whom we know little. Her marriage – to outward appearances a 'dynastic' one arranged between two Scottish mercantile families based in Aberdeen, Antwerp and Rotterdam – looks nonetheless to have been companionate. Something of the kind, at least, is implied by the fact that she accompanied her husband when Turing, who had set up on his arrival in Batavia as a wholesale trader in local and imported commodities, subsequently embarked on two lengthy, business-related sea-borne journeys to the Indian subcontinent and to what Europeans were apt to call the 'China Coast'. In 1826, however, his business, which included the management of a large 'up-country' estate for a Scottish firm based in Bombay, went bankrupt. Eighteen months later, scarcely 35 years old, Turing himself was dead.

His widow, left destitute on Java with two young children while still in her mid-twenties, subsequently made her way back to Europe, where she lived initially in her younger, unmarried sister's household in her native Aberdeen, in the north-east of Scotland, before accompanying her now adult clergyman son south of the Border and eventually to Cambridge. It was there that she herself died in 1870, at the age of 66, after a lengthy repatriation lasting for a little over four decades.[1] Meanwhile, through their sister's agency, two of Fraser-Turing's siblings sought their fortunes in 'the East' – a great deal more successfully than had been the case with her late husband – and her own immediate descendants became part of the Scottish 'contingent' in England, where her great-grandson, *the* Alan Turing, was to achieve international fame as a pioneer of the proto-computer.[2]

To the Ends of the Earth

To the Ends of the Earth[3] is the title of a magisterial survey of the diaspora of which Fraser-Turing and her kin formed part, its appropriateness underscored by the observation of another leading authority that 'the Scots have always been a restless people, "wonderful at living anywhere but in Scotland"'.[4] Over the centuries, beginning around 1600 or even earlier, a significantly higher proportion of Scots appear to have left their homeland for overseas destinations than was the case with their English contemporaries. Indeed, between the middle of the nineteenth century and the inter-war Depression of the 1930s, only Ireland and Norway exported a greater proportion of their people. Early Scottish migrants went mostly to other destinations in continental Europe; but by the nineteenth century the flow (upwards of some two-and-a-half-million people) was directed to the wider world – primarily, but far from exclusively, to North America, southern Africa and Australasia. As such, it constitutes a significant part of the exploration of the country's recent and not-so-recent past. During recent years, moreover, against a background of renewed interest in separation from the United Kingdom, identification as a diaspora has brought 'the great Scottish exodus' firmly under a rubric that links it with a global meta-narrative of compelling resonance.[5]

Even so, the concept of a 'diaspora' associated with the overseas movement of peoples from the British Isles in general – Scotland included

– still has its problems. To be sure, it 'carries a sense of somewhere else into multiple . . . destinations and ways of being', at the same time 'challenging the "monogamy of place"' and 'destabilising our understanding of "home"'.[6] Yet, as the leading authority on the Scots in Australasia observed, 'the very word releases hares in all directions,'[7] while its twentieth-century journey from Judaic and Biblical studies into an altogether broader context has not been an invariably happy one. As another keen student of the subject has wryly noted, 'like so many words that become more and more fashionable, mushiness in meaning was a prerequisite for popularity';[8] and yet another has remarked on 'the semantic instability around the term'.[9] More than that, 'an uncritical use of the term "diaspora" has broader issues than semantic quibbles'. Rather, with reference to Scotland, it risks obfuscating the heavily segmented character of an exodus that had multiple dynamics, and which was far from homogeneous in character.[10] Not least, it was a phenomenon that extended far beyond the tragic stories of the Highland Clearances and forced emigration. Likewise, too much emphasis on 'the presence of a "Scottish community" to support emigrant Scots arguably clouds assessments of Scottish *integration* into host communities abroad'.[11] Indeed, it is arguable that only a minority of overseas migrants who subscribed (or still subscribe) to the notion of 'clubbing together' as Scotsmen and women, whereas most migrants eschewed manifestations of national identity in favour of assimilating into their host communities.[12] Perhaps in recognition of this, it has recently been postulated that we should restrict the term to 'a form of social and cultural organisation, in which not all migrants . . . are straightforwardly diasporans';[13] and to apply it only to those of the dispersed who had a 'desire to remain connected to their own homeland and to maintain their ethnic identity'.[14]

But there is something else at stake here: something that relates to a tendency in diasporan studies toward a sealing-off of Scotland from a broader history of the British Isles in a way which impoverishes rather than enriches. As has been argued regarding the Scots' role in the British Empire in general, the discourse that has grown up around the diaspora has tended towards a 'highlighting of Scottish distinctiveness rather than similarities or connections with England'. As such, it risks misstating the nature and extent of the demarcation between Scotland and its southern neighbour and becoming a manifestation of Celtic national isolationism,[15] while at the same time fostering a quite false impression that there is (or historically was) a single 'Scottish Identity'.[16]

There are, in short, a multiplicity of issues relating to Scotland's diaspora that call for both elucidation and disentanglement – something which this book approaches in the context of the empire of a European power whose metropole lay across the North Sea from the British Isles and whose prime *kolonie* lay in maritime Southeast Asia. For similar diasporic currents to those that propelled the Turing-Fraser couple to the Indies early in the nineteenth century subsequently carried not only two of her siblings but also several score of their fellow countrymen and women: together, they constituted the nucleus of the cohort of families – there were around ten such – that forms the basis of the present group biography. As such, they were people whose combined histories demonstrate critical insights into the narrative of the Scottish diaspora to be gained by attending to the story of a small contingent of Scots located, albeit not at 'the ends of the earth' but most definitely in a spot remote from the main bastions of the British imperial presence.

Commodity Chains and Gains

The cohort in question gravitated, over several generations, around a major mercantile business first established in Batavia in the 1820s and known throughout its lengthy existence as Maclaine Watson. Whereas Robert Turing failed in business, Maclaine Watson (after a rocky start) made a great success of it as a wholesale trader in a multiplicity of 'colonial' staples, but eventually above all else in the export of sugar – something that made the Maclaine Watson partners and their families not only rich but sometimes even very wealthy indeed. Accordingly, one of the big questions posed by their activities in this regard relates to a growing body of revisionist analysis of the provenance of diasporan wealth and of its deployment after repatriation. In following the 'commodity turn' in historical studies,[17] it explores more rigorously than was once the case the critical linkages between production, commerce and consumption. In so doing, among other things, it provides a critique of older heroic narratives surrounding 'the Scots Abroad': 'Did Slavery make Scotia Great?' is the plaintive title of one recent contribution to debate about the fortunes made through the exploitation of enslaved African workers in the British Caribbean.[18]

To date, however, analysis of wealth originating in Asia rather than the Americas has played a distinctly secondary role in this revisionist project, despite a growing recognition of Asia's integration into 'a wider imperial system in which the Atlantic and Indian Ocean worlds were both entwined and mutually sustaining'.[19] Apart from a timely emphasis on the role played by military conquest and the concomitant accumulation of what was quite literally loot,[20] identification of (limited) parallels with what took place in the Atlantic Zone, without slipping into the morass of 'equivalence', has focused largely on the trade in opium from the Indian subcontinent to China that played a big part over several decades in the creation of wealth for Scottish business people.[21] Nonetheless, opium's broad designation as a 'debilitating drug' in all the wide circumstances of its use remains an open question,[22] and preoccupation with it obfuscates a comprehensive approach to the circumstances of capital accumulation by diasporan Scots throughout 'the East' in general. Against this background, analysis of the commodity chains and gains associated with Maclaine Watson's long-term role in the trade in colonial Indonesia's massive output of cane sugar (its industry came to rank with that of Cuba at the apex of world commerce in the commodity) adds an important dimension to the narrative of Scotland's diaspora.

Sojourning – and Repatriate Afterlives

That narrative remains, despite a keen awareness of emigrant returnees,[23] predominantly one of dispersal and resettlement. As such, however, it is complicated and potentially disrupted by an evolving emphasis on sojourning – identified as until recently 'the Cinderella of diaspora studies'[24] – and its corollary of repatriation. Admittedly, it has been objected that 'transiency or sojourning' are incompatible with diaspora since the term 'should be confined to movements that involve a long-term separation from an imaginary or real homeland'.[25] Yet familiar and seasoned usage dictates otherwise. So too does recognition that the two groups in question are not so easily differentiated, above all because a large number of Scottish *soi-disant* migrants (an estimated third or more during the period 1860–1914) subsequently made their way back to Britain.[26] But intent matters, and one important category among diasporan Scots, exemplified in the present context by Jean Fraser-Turing's two brothers who sailed to the Indies in her wake, comprised 'career emigrants . . . [whose] mobility was predicated upon the making of a fortune and returning home with the means to secure or enhance the sojourner's social status'.[27]

As such, sojourning has potential implications extending well beyond the immediate histories of the families concerned in this book: witness the argument recently advanced by Andrew Mackillop about Scotland's 'pathway to empire and globalisation'. Envisaged as something contingent (given its scarcity in *monetary* form) on the export of *human* capital, it focuses on the departure overseas of 'high-value' individuals who returned to Scotland with accumulated repatriable wealth on a scale totally disproportionate to their numbers.[28] Their ability to do so, moreover, was based on the capacity for essentially local networks to hook themselves onto global counterparts, in a 'glocalisation' which involved the 'tack[ing] back and forth between and among various territorial levels ... in which the local, regional, national, trans-national and global are mutually implicated'.[29] It was these combined developments that played a critical role in what has been termed the 'proto-globalisation' stage of Scotland's modern history, a stage that began late in the seventeenth and culminated in the opening decades of the nineteenth century. The present book builds on this and similar foundations to carry kindred issues surrounding sojourner repatriation late into the same century and well beyond, during a period in which our knowledge on this score remains rudimentary.

Consequently, the book's attention to repatriation and its aftermath is far more than a matter of completing the story (intrinsically interesting as that may be). Rather, it stems from a conviction that the history of returnee afterlives – which, in the case of the Maclaine Watson cohort, were often remarkably lengthy – is as crucial to an understanding of the Scottish diaspora as are exodus narratives and accounts of time spent overseas. As such, it informs a holistic approach that reflects the extent to which the New Imperial History 'has united "home" and "away" into a single conceptual category',[30] and raises issues relating not only to what the cohort's repatriation meant for Scotland in a social, cultural and economic sense, but also (and critically) to what 'Scotland' in its several evolving guises meant for them. At the same time, the histories told here make clear the ambiguity and complexity inherent in the concept of repatriation envisaged solely or even predominantly in terms of 'Back to Caledonia'.

Networks and Networkers in a Trans-Imperial Setting

Jean Fraser-Turing and her husband were a newlywed couple dispatched to the Indies by a mercantile network based in both Aberdeen and the Low Countries, after which Turing himself operated a business based in Dutch Batavia, which had strong commercial and financial ties with British interests in the Indian subcontinent and linkages of some sort to the Celestial Empire to its distant northwest. In short, the couple's history draws attention to the lives of people 'at home in multiple imperial settings' whose significance has been marginalised by an exclusionary focus on empire as a pre-eminently national concern.[31] To be sure, any such reckoning needs to take account, among other things, of the formidable Scottish presence, beyond the formal British imperial sphere, among the Shanghailanders of the 'China Coast' and among the British element settled in nineteenth-century Argentina.[32] Yet the situation of the Maclaine Watson cohort, of which the Turing-Frasers were precursors, was and remained singular, in so far as its members were located at the Asian heart of another *European* colonial empire rather than in notionally autonomous parts of the world. As such, their stories go some way towards addressing a recent complaint that we 'know very little about what people at the heart of British-owned enterprises thought they were doing in regions that were not subject to [British] . . . imperial control'.[33]

Most immediately, however, the cohort's claim to our attention stems from its position as a classic instance of the kin-based mercantile networks that played a critical role in 'Unlocking the World' during the long nineteenth century's 'Age of Steam',[34] and whose strength came mainly from the 'loyalty that existed within the family core, from intermarriage between family members and from the hierarchical structure and "patriarchal" authority exercised by the head of the family'.[35] Within this global frame, the focus of the present book – neither a business history nor even the history of a business – is not on networks themselves but on the social actors who made up the network's lived reality, and is attuned to the argument that 'kin relations provide an especially useful optic for historians' and constitute not only 'the crucial *human* dimension of [the British] empire', but also of the Scottish diaspora with which that empire was famously imbricated.[36]

Consequently, the chapters that follow form an actor-centric history – one interlaced with that of the money trail critical to it – that highlights lives spent both 'out East' and, however notionally, 'back home' by mothers, wives, and daughters as well as by fathers, husbands and sons. As such, it draws on a rich crop of research-based studies on 'colonial women', domesticity and kindred subjects,[37] while seeking to expand their remit. In the case of the Indian subcontinent, for example, although the *memsahibs* have a well-established place in narratives of the British Raj, that historiography remains concentrated – with only a few exceptions – on their presence in official rather than business circles.[38] In this context, Jean Fraser-Turing's 'pioneer' history is a starting point for discussion, ground-breaking in the case of the Indies, of the 'role of women in the business networks of men',[39] and for the crucial inclusion in diasporic narratives of 'the birthscapes of empire [that] hinged vitally on women's reproductive work ... and on the socialisation and careful placement into gainful employment or marriage of children'.[40] As we shall see, moreover, the singular colonial social milieu of the Indies possessed, among other things, a rich potential for local matrimony that challenges a recent hypothesis that Scottish sojourners throughout Asia formed 'a transient group for whom marriage and family were not the top priorities'.[41] The stories of the cohort's sojourners and repatriates also illuminate a further dimension: one in which women's agency is envisaged not only in terms of being in the service (in whatever shape or form) of family and mercantile networks, but also of women's capacity for developing different agendas, and for opting out or breaking away when and if the circumstances were propitious.

An Archaeology: Recovery, Reconstruction and Significance

Accounts of Scotland's diaspora in 'the East' – *The Scottish Experience in Asia* is a recent prime example[42] – have little or nothing to say about the Indies, presumably a result of the relatively few people involved, combined with the difficulty of dealing with the Dutch language sources in which some of their history is inscribed. In consequence, reconstructing the stories at the heart of this book has involved a kind of archaeology. With the notable exception of the extensive correspondence of Maclaine Watson's co-founder, evidence in the shape of what cultural historians have taken to describing as 'ego documents' (memoirs, letters, photographs and suchlike) exist only in fragmentary form. Even so, they provide insights, however fleeting, into the diasporic aspect of what the British economic and social historian

Emma Rothschild has eloquently referred to as 'the inner life of Empires',[43] something that cannot be comprehended from the public record alone.

That record, nonetheless, has undergone such a radical transformation in recent years that it is now plausible to speak of new directions in family research, ones made feasible by the massive digitalisation of data of births, deaths and marriages, along with a similar processing of census records, marriage registers, ocean-liner and aeroplane passenger lists and the like, as well as, very importantly, colonial and metropolitan newspapers. Not to be forgotten amongst these and suchlike developments, however, are the labours of generations of genealogists – and the great bulk of materials 'buried' in the official imperial and domestic archives of the states concerned.

Admittedly, despite this wide range of newly searchable information, dimensions of the present inquiry remain deeply frustrating, not least because of the limitations still imposed by the nature of the materials. Yet that inquiry has been energised by the assumption that 'rich rewards' (as one recent writer in an entirely different field has remarked) are indeed attendant on 'the painstaking recuperation of ephemera, [and] facts on the ground'.[44] Accordingly, what follows is written in the conviction that we can learn a great deal about the Scottish 'dispersal' by applying what we know of the experiences of individuals and families whose stories might initially appear marginal to its key narratives but which, in fact, serve to significantly enhance and productively complicate them.

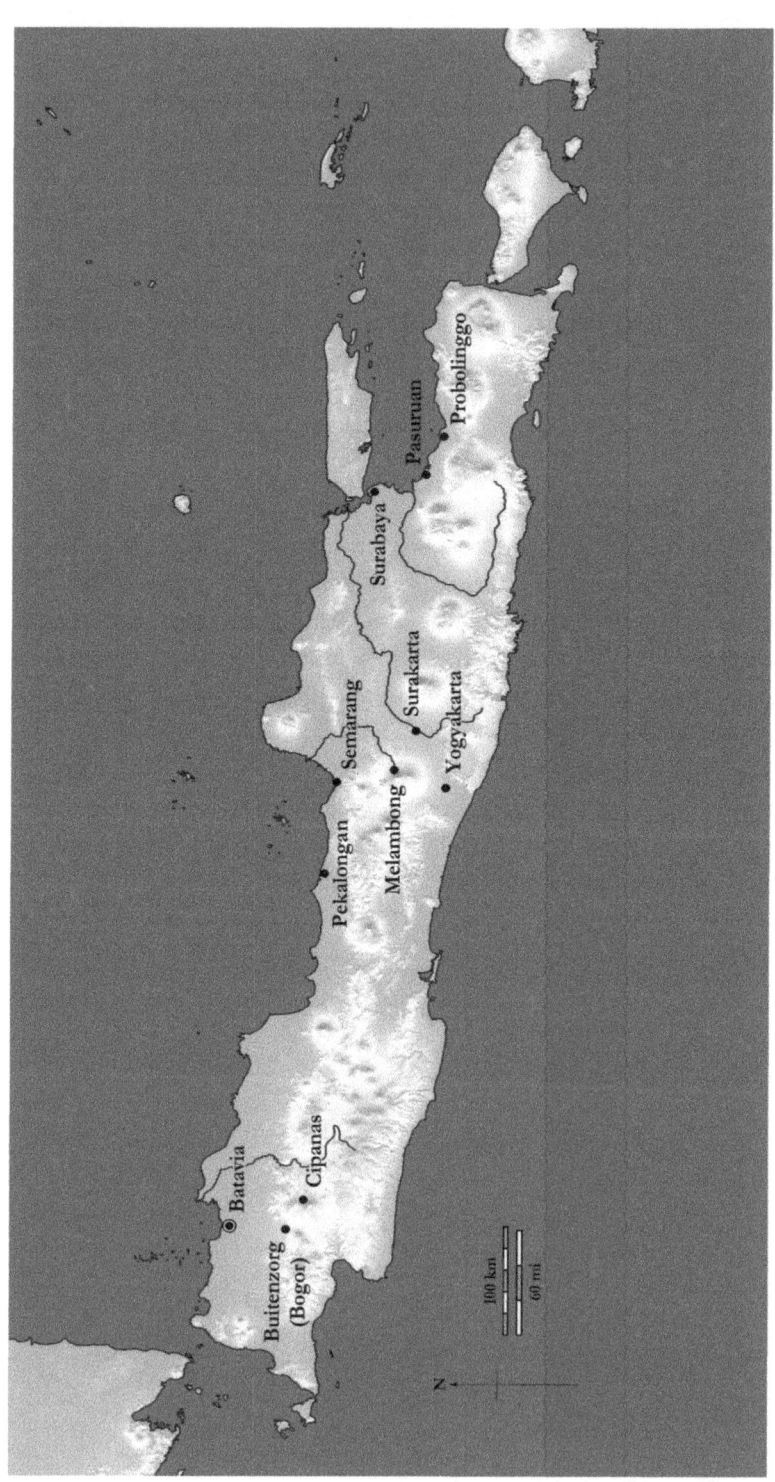

Figure 1.1: Map of Java (Collection of the Author)

1

From the 'Land o' Cakes'

It must have been a boisterous evening. After some fourteen toasts and accompanying musical interludes – among them, by way of a poetic reference to their homeland, was a toast (courtesy of Rabbie Burns) to 'The Land o' Cakes', followed by a rendition of *Auld Lang Syne* – the party only broke up at two-thirty the following morning. The year was 1838 and the occasion, reported quite extensively in what was at that time the colony's only newspaper, was a gathering of the city's small contingent of Scots (and their many Dutch guests) who had sat down to celebrate St Andrew's Day with an elaborate dinner in Batavia, the prime colonial city on Java and capital of the Dutch East Indies (Figure 1.1).[1] It is a gathering that provides a cue for the stories of the ten or more families who gravitated around the Batavia-based firm of Maclaine Watson from the 1820s through to the Second World War and beyond, and as such recounts the arrival of sojourning Scots and other Britons and Irish at the heart of the Dutch empire in Asia during the opening decades of the nineteenth century. Primarily engaged in mercantile pursuits, their history is epitomised in the story of co-founder Gillian Maclaine and the Dutch woman, Catharina van Beusechem, whom he married in Batavia in 1832. The pages that follow explore how the Maclaine Watson cohort integrated into the Dutch colonial system through marriages, business acumen and their ability to navigate between British and Dutch imperial spheres. It emphasises that these Scots were not merely interlopers but became integral to the colonial project in Southeast Asia.

Figure 1.2: Gillian Maclaine (KITLV / University of Leiden)

The dinner in question was perhaps the first formal event of its kind to be held anywhere in the Indies, and as such the local precursor of something (celebrated annually on 30th November) that became a staple of the Scottish diaspora worldwide. The Indies was no exception. Quintessential manifestations, such dinners have been described by one recent writer on the theme of 'Haggis in the Raj', as 'well-attended, ritualised events' that were instrumental in confirming, constructing and romanticising identity, as well as in 'promoting oneself in potentially profitable ways by playing up one's affinity for things Scottish'.[2]

That 'affinity' was, of course, fully explicit in the toast in question, the evening's fourth. It had been proposed by Gillian Maclaine (Figure 1.2), born on the Scottish Inner Hebridean island of Mull and co-founder more than a decade earlier of the Batavia-based commodity-trading firm of Maclaine Watson – the business concern that became the centre of gravity for the cohort of families whose stories form the substance of this book. A successful and increasingly wealthy individual among the Scots on Java, whose marriage to a young Dutch woman had brought him into the heart of the Indies' colonial elite, he was the number-two figure presiding over the dinner and the proposer, later in the evening, of a further toast to 'The Memory of Burns and Scott' – both poet and novelist were already well on their way to becoming the twin paragons of the cultural focus of the diaspora.

The evening's sequence of such acclamations had been launched by the dinner's presiding figure, the Aberdeen-born John Davidson. His origins among the mercantile element in north-east Scotland's major port served as a reminder that although some of the Scottish contingent on Java, including members of the Maclaine Watson cohort, were Highlanders, a significant number of them were not. Scion of a family evidently wealthy enough to send him to his native city's Marischal College, north-east Scotland's leading educational institution, he had first arrived on Java via the South Asian city of Bombay. By the 1830s he was a veteran of several mercantile partnerships in Batavia, and was a principal figure among the city's Freemasons, where he was an inaugural member of Batavia's 'Star in the East' Lodge, founded in 1837, but incorporating brethren from two earlier lodges in the same city.[3]

Freemasonry worldwide has often been depicted as one of the signifiers of a specifically *Scottish* identity, not least because Scots 'so frequently established lodges wherever they went'.[4] In the Indies, however, the prior existence of a network – dating in some cases from the final decades of the eighteenth century and underlining the extent to which the Brotherhood had gained in traction not only in the Netherlands but also in its distant Asian colony[5] – meant that instead of confirming any sense of Scottish separateness, the Brotherhood formed a bridge between arrivals from Scotland and the colonial society in which they were located. This was reinforced by a history of Anglo-Dutch co-operation centred on a shared espousal of Freemasonry during the British occupation of the island between 1811 and 1816.[6] Admittedly, they would have noted some marginal differences. In particular, what has been described as the 'subtle mixture of European and Asian influences' in the material culture of the Indies lodges may have given them an unfamiliar appearance to Scots initiates.[7]

Yet they would also have been fully cognisant of the essentials of the Indies lodges' rituals and ceremonies as well as of Freemasonry's cosmopolitan ideals, in addition to the more mundane benefits of financial and social support for the deracinated who found themselves separated from both kin and country in far-flung parts of the world.

Hence, Scottish arrivals found themselves in what was a familiar cultural environment – and one shared by the highest ranks of the colonial establishment, among them Jan Michiel van Beusechem who was not only the Grand Master (successively) of the Batavia lodges 'La Virtueuse' and the 'Star in the East', but also the old and close friend of the erstwhile Governor-General Johannes van den Bosch (Figure 1.3), an individual whose adherence to Freemasonry dated from an earlier sojourn in the Indies, where he had first arrived in 1798, before returning there three decades later as the Dutch monarch's representative.[8] Appropriately, the St Andrew's Day festivities continued with toasts to 'The King of the Netherlands' and 'The Civil and Military Authorities'.

Figure 1.3: Johannes van den Bosch (Collection of the Author)

Nor, however, were 'The Ladies of Batavia' forgotten, in a toast proposed by the youngest Scot present: Gillian Maclaine's cousin, the 22-year-old Donald Maclaine of Lochbuie, who had arrived in the colony only two years earlier. According to his not always amused relative, whose house guest he was, the young man had 'a most unfortunate trait of falling in love'.[9] Indeed, around this time he had written home to his dissolute elder brother, boasting that 'I am happy as the day is long, in town all day making money and in the country in the evening making love'.[10] The 'Ladies of Batavia', whatever connection they may have formed with Donald 'Lochbuie', were none of them present at the dinner, but a goodly number of their menfolk most certainly were. Indeed, the Scots in attendance would have been greatly outnumbered by their Dutch guests whose 'Health and Prosperity' were the subject of a toast halfway through the evening, and a further one to 'The Land We Live In', followed by 'appropriate music', presumably Dutch in inspiration. In short, the event was a far from exclusive affair: as well as being part of the glue that stuck diasporic Scots communities together, St Andrew's Day celebrations also had the effect of consolidating their ties with their 'host' community and of helping further strengthen the networking that was an essential ingredient of commercial success.

Even so, the emphasis was heavily on Scotland and on things Scottish. Hence 'The Memory of Wallace and Bruce' was celebrated, followed by a rendition of 'Scots Wha Hae', and, after a further toast to '[Thomas] Campbell and Living Poets', the dinner concluded with one to 'Auld Reekie' (Edinburgh). Of course, outward appearances, no less than sentiment, mattered, and although the newspaper only alluded to the fact that the Scots guests wore 'distinctive apparel', reports of similar events towards the end of the colonial era were more forthcoming: on one such occasion, for example, a Dutch guest observed that 'a Scot is not a Scot without his national costume' and recorded that the haggis was borne in 'by a splendidly outfitted individual', accompanied by others similarly attired.[11] This was almost a century later, and allowance might need to be made for the passage of time, but there can be little doubt that back in 1838 Donald 'Lochbuie' would have appeared in the same 'full Highland dress' in which he had appeared at a masked ball given at Government House fairly soon after his arrival in the colony.[12]

Small But Perfectly Formed: Scottish Arrivals in the Indies

Thirteen Scottish men participated directly in the 1838 St Andrew's Day Dinner as proposers of toasts (Gillian Maclaine was a proposer twice over, bringing the total of toasts to fourteen). How representative this number was of the total of Scottish males present in the city and its environs at that date is a matter of guesswork, since contemporary Dutch record-keepers had little interest in distinguishing between English and Irish people and those born north of the Border. In the mid-1820s, the British presence on Java numbered around fifty individuals, with approximately fifteen bearing recognisably Scottish names. Official residence permit records spanning fifty years from 1819 suggest that no more than 120 Scots were domiciled on Java during this period, amounting to less than a quarter of the total British presence. It seems unlikely, in short, that the number of Scots in Batavia at the time of the dinner significantly exceeded the thirteen proposers of toasts, and that the total Scottish contingent on the island likely did not surpass a couple of dozen at any given time in the 1820s and 1830s.[13] Small as the contingent may have been, however, it was 'perfectly formed' in respect to its elevated social and substantial economic position in the colony.

How did they come to be there? In the case of John Davidson, the presiding figure at the dinner, he had arrived there almost a quarter of a century earlier as part of the British expeditionary force that had seized Java in August 1811. For some of the numerous Scots (civilians as well as people in uniform) who had made a landfall in the Indies, their stay was only a short-lived one. Literally so, in the case of Lieutenant Hector Maclean. A Highlander from the Inner Hebrides, he died within twelve months of his arrival, from the wound he received – inflicted, it was said, by a court lady whom he was attempting to carry off – during the successful storming of the Sultan's *kraton* (palace complex) in Yogyakarta, one of the Principalities of South-Central Java (Figure 1.1).[14] Others of his compatriots were luckier. The Shetland-born John Deans, for example, who went on to become a close associate of Gillian Maclaine, had also taken part in the storming of the *kraton* and carried off a sufficient share of loot to set himself up in business on the island. Among other things, it was a business geared to the import and sale of opium on Java, either illicitly or through contract with the government, for whom revenue from the sale of the drug was a major source of income.[15]

The British invasion that brought Davidson, Maclean, Deans and their ilk to Java had been launched from Calcutta rather than London, and represented a venture in which the English East India Company (EIC) was deeply involved. The trans-imperial connection established thereby between the Netherlands Indies and British interests on the subcontinent continued potent after the British forces withdrew in 1816, when some of the British (Deans among them) stayed on in the Indies and were subsequently joined by others of their countrymen, including Gillian Maclaine. What ultimately motivated them was related to broad developments in the worldwide trade in industrial and agricultural goods that extended far beyond the Indies, while also making the Netherlands' great Asian colony a particular focus of mercantile attention. In the specific case of the 22-year-old Maclaine, however, we can safely say that the immediate cause of his being there was a broken arm.

Not *his* arm, but that of a fellow Scot who was already established on Java. The plan had been a simple one. In February 1820 Maclaine took passage from the Thames Estuary to the Indies on the ship *Mary Anne*, in charge of a cargo of cotton 'piece goods' (rolls of British-manufactured plain cloth and bales of colourfully dyed material) being exported by his employers, the London-based firm of the brothers Duncan and Patrick McLachlan, whose business, centred on trade with 'the East Indies', was rapidly expanding during the commercial boom that followed the ending of the Napoleonic Wars in 1816.[16]

His destination was Batavia – but it was not intended that he should stay there for long. Instead, he was to hand the McLachlans' share of the cargo over to their agents there and then proceed to Calcutta, where he was expected to take up a position in the office of another Scot, Donald Macintyre – an entrepreneur who shuttled between Britain and the Indian subcontinent, while concurrently in partnership with the McLachlans. As it was, matters turned out rather differently. Having sailed on the *Mary Anne* into Batavia in July 1820, Maclaine found that neither of its cargo's putative consignees were available. An accident to his arm had immobilised Thomas Anderson, a Glaswegian who had arrived in the Indies via Calcutta a couple of years earlier, while his business partner, William Menzies (another attendee and toast-proposer at the St Andrew's Day Dinner some eighteen years later) was away in Bengal and not expected back for some time.[17]

Accordingly, with the warmly acknowledged help of other Scots already established there, Maclaine himself set about hawking the cargo around the city, presumably to the big Indies Chinese (Sino-Indonesian) merchants who dominated the island's wholesale trade. 'I felt considerably at a loss also from not being able to speak Malay, which is the language used in business all over the island,' he reported, but 'this is however so easily acquired that I can already manage to drive a bargain in it!'[18] Having thus cleared what he could of the *Mary Anne*'s cargo in Batavia, he then sailed on to Semarang, some 450 kilometres to the east (Figure 1.1), and repeated the procedure in what was the commercial gateway to the densely populated interior of South-Central Java, a part of the island that was to feature prominently in Maclaine's subsequent history.

Meanwhile, back in Batavia, it was Menzies, following a timely return from Bengal, who had been a key figure in prompting Maclaine's decision to remain on Java and to ignore his London principals' instructions to proceed to the subcontinent. Menzies himself, according to Maclaine, was 'a complete Highlander in appearance and manners. . . . I never knew a person give a more regular Highland [hand] Shake'.[19] Born in Perth, he appears initially to have made his living as a saddler, after which he 'found his way to London' and then relocated to the subcontinent where 'McIntyre saw his talent for business, took him into his employ and sent him down here with a large investment of cotton goods'.[20] Keenly aware that his family back home might suppose that he had been led astray, Maclaine was careful to assert the credentials of his new-found friends. Anderson (the man with the broken arm) was singled out as 'one of the steadiest young men I have seen in Java. Notwithstanding the ridicule of several of his acquaintances he maintains his strict Presbyterian principles'. He also made it clear how disadvantageous for his future career the move to Calcutta was likely to be.[21] His London employers, meanwhile, were far from happy with his impromptu arrangement and there began an often-acrimonious relationship between Maclaine on Java and the McLachlan brothers in London, with their partner McIntyre acting as a doubtfully honest intermediary. This continued for the rest of the decade, during which Maclaine added the role of coffee planter to that of the head of his own small commodity-trading firm, Gillian Maclaine & Co., in Batavia itself.[22]

Later that same decade, and in poor health, Maclaine made a sudden decision to return temporarily to Great Britain, where he was not only successful in getting well again but also in reviving the fortunes of his Batavia business – now known as Maclaine Watson after he had gone into partnership with his former head clerk, the Londoner Edward Watson

Figure 1.4: Edward Watson (KITLV / University of Leiden)

(Figure 1.4). Hence it was in a buoyant mood that he subsequently sailed back to the Indies from the Dutch port of Rotterdam, on a four-month voyage on which he first encountered, together with the rest of her migrating family, the woman who was to become his wife. He arrived back in Batavia in June 1832, and three months later, the now 34-year-old was a married man whose bride, the 18-year-old Catharina van Beusechem, provided an entrée into the colony's top circles of government courtesy of her uncle Jan van Beusechem's long-standing friendship with Governor-General Van den Bosch and through marriage ties with his successor. The upshot, as Maclaine remarked somewhat jocularly to his mother, 'my interest . . . at court is just as great as a merchant requires'.[23]

It was, nonetheless, an exogamous match – and he was at pains to allay the fears of his family in Scotland that 'marrying a Dutchwoman may estrange me from my native Country'. In fact, he assured them that 'I consider a Dutch girl less a foreigner than an English girl', while remarking that among the advantages of his spouse was that 'her religion is the same as mine'.[24] The Presbyterianism of the Church of Scotland, in which he had been brought up, was a close relation in terms of theology and practice to that of the Reformed Church to which the majority of the Dutch subscribed: both churches were staunchly Calvinist in doctrine. Admittedly, there were differences. Sailing back to Java on a Dutch ship, Maclaine was prepared to allow that the piano might be open on the Sabbath, something that was evidently not acceptable in the Western Highlands at the time. Even so, he felt justified in admonishing the womenfolk of the upper deck about the inappropriateness of bringing their embroidery to the religious service that was a regular feature of shipboard life.[25] For the most part, however, he was evidently more at ease with attendance at the 'Dutch Calvinist Church' than at what he described as the city's 'English chapel': 'The service was at night and the administration of the Sacrament by candlelight in a *Protestant* Church, though new to me, was most solemn and impressive.'[26]

A sympathetic cultural milieu, moreover, evidently chimed with Maclaine's susceptibility to a young woman – 'she being only 18 and I alas! nearly 34' – who had 'a sweet expression & countenance, indicating much modesty and good sense, her face when animated strikingly beautiful – her figure tall and handsome . . . a mild, retiring feminine disposition'. Moreover, his apprehension that 'taking the most favourable view of things, I have not a chance of settling myself in Scotland before my 40th year – a period of life I consider too far advanced for marrying', was allied to more prudential calculations. Not the least of these was the advice of the widower John Deans (shortly to become Deans-Campbell following an advantageous marriage of his own), who had just lent him a considerable sum of money to help relaunch his career[27] – that 'as a man of business [marriage] will increase rather than diminish my credit', and that the married state would, he presumed, 'make me a better and steadier man' and 'keep me out of the noisy roaring bachelor parties at Batavia, which I always detested – & save me expenses even in my house keeping'.[28]

Catharina van Beusechem's only surviving comment as to her feelings about being uprooted from the Netherlands and her relatives and friends comes in a letter to her mother-in-law:

The remembrance of all that took place in the year 1832 is not of little importance for me; my departure from my native land, and all the dear relations, and friends, of whom I must take leave to go to a foreign country, where all was strange and new to me, was a grievous *époque* and gives us much pain; but all that became much softened, through the pleasant and fortunate voyage that we made, and our good and safe *arrivement* to the place of our destination; there I now, in my union with the best of all men, make me, also here in Java, the happiest of all mortal beings.[29]

'Higher than Ben Nevis', Roses and Hot Springs, and a few words in Gaelic

The newly-weds' honeymoon jaunt – their little party included 'my old and faithful servant Radin and my wife's maid Mina, a Javanese'[30] – got underway by horse-drawn carriage early in September 1832 and the first stop was in the foothills to the south of Batavia. There they stayed on an estate part-owned by William Menzies, his old friend and business associate, who was to be one of the toast-proposing guests at the St Andrew's Day Dinner held in the city some six years later. Maclaine and his wife left their 'complete Highlander' and embarked on the next stage of their jaunt, one which took them southwards into the mountains of the Priangan ranges that dominate the volcanic interior of West Java. On the steeper gradients:

> our carriage was drawn by four horses and six Buffaloes, assisted by several natives. . . . [T]he country . . . is truly magnificent – hills much higher than Ben Nevis, wooded to the top.

Catharina van Beusechem, now Catherine Maclaine, having been born and brought up in a country not celebrated for its high altitudes, 'was quite in raptures with the scenery . . . so different from what she was accustomed to in the *Pays Bas*' – so much so, indeed, that 'she wrote her mother a letter from the very summit of the mountain, in a small bungaloe where we halted for breakfast'.[31] The mother in question, Sara Justina Renaud, had wed Nicolaas Philippus van Beusechem in 1813, and her husband, from an equally 'good' patrician Dutch family,[32] was a municipal officeholder who had spent most of his adult life in the city of Gouda.[33] Aged 54, and facing an uncertain financial future with five young offspring, he opted to relocate to the Indies, where the extensive Van Beusechem clan already had a long history – and where he had a wealthy relative prepared to look after him and his family.³⁴ Moreover, in migrating he presumably expected that his three daughters would eventually find well-to-do husbands among the Indies colonial elite.³⁵ If this was his calculation, his eldest daughter fulfilled his expectations admirably, albeit perhaps a little earlier than anticipated, and with a foreigner rather than a Dutchman.

That daughter and his newly acquired son-in-law's destination on this leg of their jaunt was Governor-General Van den Bosch's 'summer' palace, high in the mountains at Cipanas, some 100 kilometres from Batavia (Figure 1.6). It was not the first time that Catherine Maclaine (though possibly not her husband) had met Van den Bosch and his (second) wife, Rudolphina Wilhelmina Elisabeth de Sturler (Figure 1.5), for when they first arrived on Java, her family had 'lived for some time with the Governor-General and were received by his Excellency with the most marked attention',³⁶ no doubt

Figure 1.5: Rudolphina de Sturler, the second wife of Van den Bosch (Collection of the Author)

Figure 1.6: Cipanas, the Governor-General's country house (Collection of the Author)

in consequence of the latter's long friendship with her uncle. That 'attention' was now further manifest in the warmth of their reception at Tjipanas, and on their departure, the Van den Bosch couple personally threw roses and other 'exotic' flowers into their guests' carriage.[37] The connection to the centre of power that Maclaine's newly forged nexus with the Van Beusechem family brought in its train extended, moreover, to Van den Bosch's successor: the latter was 'a fine fellow', Maclaine informed his mother, 'and a relation by marriage to my wife's family,' in consequence of which 'my interest . . . at court is just as great as a merchant requires'.[38] It was a theme to be reiterated in the stories of subsequent members of the cohort later in the century.

Once on their way again, the couple travelled along the great Post Road out of the mountains and more than 300 kilometres eastward along the island's north coast, to be greeted by another Scottish connection. Gillian Maclaine must have come to know Alexander Loudon during their time together on Java in the 1820s, and it was an acquaintance that was most likely deepened when Loudon, who had been born a few miles outside Dundee on Scotland's east coast, visited Maclaine in the Western Highlands during the latter's own brief return home at the beginning of the 1830s.

When they next met, it was back in the Indies in the very different setting of Loudon's newly built 'splendid house', one set among 'grounds laid out with much taste' and in which there were 'apple trees in fruit and hedges of European roses and citron . . .' in the hills south of Pekalongan, on the north coast of Central Java (Figure 1.1).[39] Its proprietor was, Maclaine reported, 'doing well' as a contractor manufacturing sugar and the dyestuff indigo for the Indies government.

Loudon's success owed a great deal to his family connections with the Dutch colonial establishment on Java. He arrived in the Indies on a British ship late in 1811 with no other immediate prospects than 'a view to being advanced to a purser in the Navy', but marriage on Java to a very young Dutch woman (Susanna Gaspardina Valck) enabled him to expand his horizons. The Valck family included several high-ranking colonial officials, and his bride appears to have been related through her mother to Jean Chrétien Baud – the same man whom Gillian Maclaine counted as an influential relative through marriage. A key figure in Dutch colonial circles during the middle years of the nineteenth century, Baud was successively both Governor-General and Minister of Colonies, and subsequently a renowned *éminence grise*. It was he, moreover, who acted *in loco parentis* to Loudon's orphaned children when their father died prematurely in The Hague in 1839. One of those children himself became Governor-General, and another scion of the Loudon family was, at a somewhat later date, one of the leading lights in what became Royal Dutch Shell, while several of Loudon's descendants, Caledonian-Dutchmen with footholds on both sides of the North Sea, were subsequently prominent in the Maclaine Watson partnership.[40]

That was some time off in the future, however, and in 1832 Gillian and Catherine Maclaine's host was as yet no more than one among the several Scottish sojourners whom the newlyweds visited on their 'jaunt' through Java, and on leaving his establishment in Pekalongan they travelled some 100 kilometres further east to Semarang, the Central Java port at which Maclaine had first called very shortly after he had arrived in the colony more than a decade earlier, there to meet with another Highlander with whom Maclaine would appear to have been associated since his earliest days in the colony. Together with an Indonesian population estimated around the middle of the nineteenth century to be about 30,000 strong, Semarang housed a largely creole Dutch community of several thousand men and women, along with a variety of other non-indigenous groupings, primarily Chinese and Arab. The port was important not simply as the locus of colonial power in Central Java, but also because it was the main point of access to the fertile and densely populated interior to its south, which not only produced coffee but also substantial quantities of sugar for the island's export trade, while at the same time constituting a significant market for cotton goods imported from the Indian subcontinent and from British and other European centres of manufacture.

It was, in short, potentially a very good place to do business, and no doubt the reason that John MacNeill (the man who greeted the couple on their arrival there) had settled in the port shortly after he 'went out' to the Indies around 1819. The mercantile business that he established there, MacNeill & Co., operated in conjunction with Gillian Maclaine's similar enterprise in Batavia. 'The son of a small Argyllshire Laird,' he hailed from Islay in the Inner Hebrides and, according to his guest, was 'a fine sterling fellow of most gentlemanly feelings and possessed of very excellent abilities and tact as a man of business.'[41] Business, however, was not the sole subject of conversation on this occasion, and 'at dinner MacNeill delighted at hearing Catherine speak a few words of Gaelic'.[42]

Echoes of home were also very much a feature of the couple's final destination at Melambong, among the volcanic peaks of South-Central Java where, almost a decade earlier, Maclaine had set up as a novice coffee planter and named his little settlement there 'Morvern',[43] in celebration of that part of Scotland's Western Highlands in which he had spent much of his early youth, in the mansion at Ardtornish of his mother's brother, John Gregorson, a wealthy sheep-farmer and local administrator.[44] In writing to him as well as his mother, Maclaine professed himself to be quite enchanted by the beauty of the scenery and fairness of the climate. 'It is situated I believe about three thousand feet above the level of the sea and is surrounded by gigantic mountains, not one less and many double the height of Ben Nevis.'[45]

A rich larding of similar references reflected not only his own nostalgia and sense of identity but also his determination to make the Indies legible to his family back home in Scotland. Hence even his reception by an Indonesian aristocrat was recorded as having 'nothing Javanese . . . [about it,] it was perfectly Highland. . . .'[46] It was an encounter explained by the fact that the Melambong venture had brought Maclaine into contact with the Javanese elite at the court of the Susuhunan of Surakarta, one of the four Principalities of the island's South Central region, and with the individual from whom he leased the land on which his coffee bushes were to be grown: 'The expense of labour is so trifling,' he explained to his family, 'and the advance of capital so little, there being no Sink of money for an Estate, slaves etc. as in the West Indies.'[47] The sole Indonesian to appear as other than a servant or a labourer in Maclaine's accounts of his twenty years on Java, *pangeran* Buminata ('my Landlord, the good Prince Boeminotto') was a younger brother of the Susuhunan and known as a devout Muslim who warmly supported the cause of Islam. What he had in fact conferred on Maclaine was not only land but labour, in the form of corvée transferred to the lessee by the Javanese appanage-holder concerned. Payments to workers may indeed have taken place – as Maclaine asserted was the case – but they took place in a broader context of the compulsion inherent in 'traditional' relations between lords and peasants throughout the island.

The *pangeran* (according to Dutch sources 'the best educated and most intelligent member of the Surakarta court')[48] was instrumental in protecting Maclaine's enterprise at Melambong when it was threatened during a major colonial war waged by the Dutch between 1825 and 1830. The war claimed the lives of thousands of Javanese, hundreds of Dutch troops – and the life of Maclaine's agent in Semarang, John McMaster, who had ridden out with a squad of regular troops and volunteers to 'put down' what they appear fondly to have supposed was a raggle-taggle 'rebel' band. Instead, he and his companions suddenly found themselves confronted by a formidable and well-organised foe. In the resultant rout, McMaster was among those who did not make it back to the safety of the port but was slaughtered, along with a score of others, among the villages and rice fields of the surrounding countryside.[49]

Maclaine himself escaped the war unscathed, though undoubtedly shaken by the death of McMaster, a fellow Scot from his own Highland neighbourhood who had been his companion while living at the 'bungaloe' he had taken at the hill-town of Salatiga, a few kilometres from his plantation, in the early days of its establishment: there they had conversed in Gaelic, 'recalling to mind many anecdotes of the happy days we spent together in the "Land of the ... Heather"'.[50] By September 1832, however, the Java War had been over for more than two years and the area around his coffee plantations at Melambong effectively pacified. And this time, of course, he had a female companion:

> We ... spend our time most agreeably. Ride out together morning and

evening, for you must know that your daughter in law rides most gracefully. She rode with me the day before yesterday ten miles on horseback before breakfast. I am very proud of her, so would you be if you saw her. We enjoy the best of health and I am delighted to observe that the climate agrees with her as well as with me.[51]

Following the round of convivial visits over the preceding weeks, Gillian and Catherine Maclaine's stay in her husband's old haunts up in the 'highlands' around Melambong was presumably a quiet and private one. Leastways, apart from the summary account sent to his mother, there is little other surviving record of the couple's time there. Nor is there one of how Gillian and Catherine Maclaine returned from South-Central Java to their marital home in Tanah Abang, in the foremost European quarter of mid-nineteenth-century Batavia. It is to the mid-nineteenth-century Maclaine Watson cohort's way of life there, and that of their Dutch colonial 'hosts', along with the provenance of their wealth, that we can turn in the chapter that follows.

2

Tempo Doeloe and Highland Homecomings

WHEN GILLIAN AND Catherine Maclaine (as she now was) returned from the highlands of Java in October 1832, they settled into the same house in Tanah Abang in which Maclaine himself had already been living for some years, at an address immediately to the west of the *Koningsplein* – the huge square which lay at the centre of the new European sector of Batavia, expansively laid out early in the nineteenth century, when the affluent among the colonists finally abandoned the mosquito-ridden old Dutch town that existed to its north (Figures 2.1-4). As a woman who had hitherto spent most of her life within the tightly packed confines typical of a provincial town in the heart of the Netherlands, his wife would no doubt have found the experience as novel as were the mountains through which she had recently passed. The nearest we can come to an impression which this affluent part of the city made on new arrivals, however, is a report not from her but from her brother-in-law, Gillian Maclaine's sole sibling, the Reverend Angus Maclaine, who visited the city in 1846.

By that date, his brother had been dead for six years: on his way back to Britain from Java in 1840, he, his wife, and their two young children were lost at sea, together with Catherine Maclaine's mother and her two unmarried sisters, when their ship went down in a storm somewhere off Mauritius. His sibling (and sole heir) had arrived in the city on a steamer that had brought him from Singapore on a leg of a long journey that was taking him back to his sheep farm in Australia (where we shall meet him

Figures 2.1 to 4: Batavia's European Quarter, c.1850 (Collection Scott Merrillees, Melbourne)

again in a subsequent chapter) from a lengthy stay in Scotland. What had brought him there was the need to finalise arrangements, complicated by the undocumented circumstance of his brother's death, for the transfer of his inherited capital from the business partnership that continued to bear his late brother's name.

Evidently the Reverend Maclaine was much taken with the spaciousness of the residence – quite possibly the very same that Gillian and Catherine Maclaine had occupied a decade earlier – which he shared with his temporary host, the Londoner John Lewis Bonhote. The son of the head clerk under whom Maclaine Watson's co-founder had worked in London before he had shipped out to the Indies in 1820, Bonhote had joined the firm early in the 1830s, and by the time the Reverend Maclaine encountered him – and found him 'exceptionally contentious and sometimes difficult to do business with' – he was senior partner and evidently lived in an appropriate style.[1] To be sure, grand colonial dwellings such as his were hardly unique to Java: after all, the top British officials and business people in the main cities of the Indian subcontinent likewise lived in a grand manner. Even so, for someone like the Reverend Maclaine, who had been to neither Calcutta, Bombay nor Madras, the wealthy European quarter of Batavia was literally something to write home about: the more so since his own rural farmhouse and urban cottage in South Australia, where he had been domiciled (in part) since the beginning of the decade, offered nothing remotely similar in scale or in the way of the everyday life lived there:

> [Its main] apartment [is] filled in the style of a drawing room, sixteen feet in height as is the whole house, and more than 60 feet by 30 feet in area. . . . The doors are open Venetian from about 4 feet from the floor, as are also the shutters of the windows – and these airy halls are lighted by handsome lamps suspended from the ceiling or equally handsome . . . lamps on stands. . . . In front is the veranda running along the whole breadth of the house, about 90 feet within walls and about half that in its breadth. . . . In the morning, which is always cool and pleasant, we meet [there] a little after 6 and have a cup of tea or coffee – and I often smoke a cigar – walk about the grounds, lounge or read as we feel inclined for an hour or two. Dress between 8 and 9 and breakfast at 10. After Breakfast . . . I employ myself reading, writing and sleeping until near five. Then I dress, ride, drive or walk until dark. Dine at 7 – at eight either make calls or return to the veranda . . . until 10, a friend sometimes dropping in to pass an hour. In

the country they regularly sleep during the heat of day. This is the routine of Java life and this house may be taken as a good sample of respectable European residences.[2]

Among those 'routines of Java life' – for himself as a man of the cloth, but also for many of his contemporaries – would have been church attendance. On a steamer crossing the Mediterranean, on his way to the Indies, he had encountered 'a native of Madras, an Indian black, going back as a Minister of our Scottish Church', while 'on Sunday the Captain read prayers to us all, assembled in the Cabin, and read them uncommonly well'.[3] Transhipping in Singapore prior to boarding the Java-bound steamer, he had taken the opportunity of going to church:

> for we were in good time for the morning service. The church was handsome and commodious and the congregation most respectable, but I have heard better sermons. The Minister is, however, well-liked and respected.[4]

Whether Maclaine subsequently relished any sermons during his stay in Batavia is not evident from his surviving correspondence, but he may well have attended what was described at that time as the 'British Church' or (by his late brother) as the 'English chapel', a place of worship built in 1831 and at this stage in its history said to be multi-denominational.[5]

The mid-nineteenth-century colonial order in the Indies, in which British arrivals like the Reverend Maclaine found themselves, has subsequently been designated (and romanticised) as a *Tempo Doeloe* – literally a 'time past' in the Dutch transcription of a Malay phrase, but better understood as 'the Good Old Days'. Leisured and lordly, it came to be seen as the antithesis of subsequent, late colonial bourgeois 'modernity' and its concomitant self-consciously middle-class 'European' identity – and as such constituted a purportedly somewhat 'orientalised' social order that had drifted some distance from its Western moorings.[6] Nonetheless, the Reverend Maclaine's late brother, at least, may have viewed it rather differently: 'I believe,' he wrote to his Uncle Hector, 'there are few places in the Indies more agreeable and more European than Java at present. Twice a week French Operas, Concerts and Balls every fortnight, races twice a year etc., etc.', together forming a milieu in which his and his young wife's participation was 'sufficient to rub off tropical rust and keep up a sufficient quantum of polish for the "home market"'.[7] The Reverend Maclaine himself, writing a decade later, was struck by something else, something apparent at an official reception that he attended immediately on his arrival in Batavia in July 1846: 'the utter contempt for the climate' shown by high-ranking officials, clad from 'head to toe in black with stocks and straps, [aligned to] perfect European stiffness and correctness of costume'.[8]

Moreover, for all its notionally Asiatic characteristics, *Tempo Doeloe* might well be better considered an Indies equivalent of the equally chimerical Antebellum American South, itself likewise a subsequently 'lost world'.[9] Some of the more resplendent photographic images of colonial life in mid-nineteenth-century Batavia and other of Java's main urban centres do indeed support that characterisation. One mansion in particular, in the very centre of the European quarter – owned by the proprietor of an auction and import business, and leading member of the island's British contingent, the Anglo-Welsh John Pryce – was a massive construction with a pillared front gallery, reminiscent of a stage-set for *Gone with The Wind*. Echoes of the Antebellum South were also present with respect to hospitality. A contemporary who was a frequent visitor to the Pryce household – where the chatelaine would have been Margaret Maxwell Maclaine-Pryce, a cousin of the Reverend Maclaine's who had become widower John Pryce's second wife in 1858 – was evidently awed by the scale and lavishness of the regular entertainments held there.[10]

It is the image of the Pryce mansion itself, however, as reproduced from a contemporary photograph in one of the latter-day celebrations of *Tempo*

Figure 2.5: The Anglo-Welsh business man, John Pryce's House, Koningsplein, Batavia (KITLV/University of Leiden)

Doeloe (Figure 2.5), that is most revealing: not least for the fact that before its grand façade, together with its proprietor and his Dutch business partner and brother-in-law, Willem van der Hucht, are stationed two dozen or so retainers and their children.[11] Until the 1860s, they might well have been household slaves, the presence of whom in the Batavia mansions of the Dutch colonial elite – it was reported that one such house was entirely run by as many as fifty slaves[12] – fitted awkwardly with the sensibilities of at least some European newcomers. In fact, before slavery was abolished in the Indies in 1863, there were nearly seven thousand slaves to be found in Batavia and on the landed estates of its hinterland,[13] many of them, presumably, captives brought from the islands of what is today Eastern Indonesia.

Commodity Chains and Gains: Sugar and Peasant 'Serf-itude'

Yet parallels with the Antebellum South only extend so far. In the Southern states prior to emancipation at the end of the Civil War in 1865, enslaved African workers formed the economic foundation of the 'Good Old Days', whereas in mid-nineteenth-century Java the source of the riches accruing to the Indies' colonial overlords was of a different order. From around 1850 onwards, the Dutch colony developed into Asia's prime sugar colony, exporting huge amounts of the commodity to Western Europe, destinations within Asia itself, and (for a brief interlude) North America. As such, well before the century's end, the island rivalled first Brazil and subsequently Cuba at the apex of the international sugarcane economy.

It was not the exploitation of enslaved African workers, however, that underpinned this development: instead, servility of a different kind prevailed. Generally, chattel slavery on the Atlantic model – played a markedly subsidiary role in the commandeering of (mostly) rural resources in those parts of Asia impacted on by Western imperialism. In its place, there existed a mosaic of coercive, controlling arrangements – many of them involving locally settled 'peasantry' rather than workers imported from elsewhere – characterised as 'a pattern of obligation to labor without wages for a patron, lord, creditor, or king'.[14] Such coercive arrangements varied substantially over place, time and opportunity: indeed, under the aegis of European and North American rule and reflecting capitalism's capacity to 'cannibalise the old to construct the new',[15] they were modified and adapted to suit locally particular purposes.

In the specific case of mid-nineteenth-century Java, Dutch colonial officials, and the sugar manufacturers who operated in cahoots with them as government contractors (Gillian Maclaine's friend Alexander Loudon was an early example), worked through the intermediary of an intimidated and accommodated Javanese aristocratic-bureaucratic elite inherited from the pre-colonial state, and on this basis set peasants to work growing cane and processing it into sugar in scores of proto-industrial factories embedded among the densely-settled villages and irrigated fields of extensive tracts of lowland Java (Figure 2.6). As such, it was a formula for exploitation without direct expropriation, and meant that anything akin to the New World model of barrack slavery was unnecessary in Java, even had it been feasible. In short, while in the Atlantic Zone the demand from highly industrialised societies for sugar, cotton and other suchlike commodities led, in the case of Brazil, Cuba and the North American South, to a reinvigorated 'Second Slavery',[16] a very different kind of coercion was elaborated in Southeast Asia by a colonial government responding to similar commercial incentives.

Under the auspices of what came to be called the 'Cultivation System' (*Cultuurstelsel*), inaugurated under Governor-General Van den Bosch at the beginning of the 1830s and reaching its florescence around mid-century, peasant labour (under the 'feudal' rubric of *corvée*) was commandeered on a grand scale. At the same time, large tracts of peasant farmland were requisitioned for the cultivation of cane on a rotational basis with the elaborately irrigated rice that remained the mainstay of peasant agriculture. To be sure, varying degrees of duress, combined, when necessary, with brute force, were softened round the edges by the cash payments and by consumer goods (opium, cotton cloth) whose increased circulation lubricated compulsion for some of those caught up in it.[17] Yet for all its complexities, until late in the nineteenth century, this form of 'serf-itude' remained at the heart of the production of the commodity from which the Maclaine Watson partners made their money. Not that it greatly concerned them. Drawing explicitly on information supplied in conversation in Batavia with a leading figure in the firm's mid-century cohort – and reflecting the latter's seeming indifference to the existence of coerced labour – the visiting 'colonial expert' J. W. B. Money assured his readers that, despite Dutch demands on his land and labour, the 'Java peasant ... [is not] visibly sensitive to the exactions he is supposed to endure'.[18]

Settling In: Familiarity, Marriage and the Family

That money afforded them access to the upper echelons of Dutch colonial communities that had been established on Java (and elsewhere in the Indies) since the seventeenth century. Although not a 'colony of settlement', the island most certainly became a colony with settlers: rather a lot of them, in fact (albeit perched asymmetrically astride a largely indigenous Asian society that outnumbered them by at least two hundred to one). As such, the Indies came 'to form a European enclave' – one which by the 1850s already numbered well over 10,000 adults – 'that was quite extensive in comparison to the number of British or French settlers who lived and worked in other Asian locations'.[19] Too few to form a discrete community of their own, Scottish arrivals in the Indies – among whom the Maclaine Watson partners featured prominently – associated, in varying degrees of proximity and intimacy, with their much more numerous Dutch colonial counterparts.

Figure 2.6: Tjepiring. A Sugar Factory on the north coast of Central Java, c.1870 (KITLV / University of Leiden)

Not that those counterparts were totally alien – indeed, quite the contrary. Gillian Maclaine's remark to his family back home in Scotland apropos his Dutch bride-to-be that 'her religion is the same as mine' alluded, as we have seen, to the close theological ties between the Scottish Kirk of which he was an adherent and the Calvinism of the Dutch Reformed Church to which most of Java's Dutch colonists would have belonged. Likewise indicative of shared proclivities (at least among the males concerned) was a mutual espousal of the brotherhood of Freemasonry, something illustrated by the histories of some of the Scots present at that boisterous 1839 St Andrew's Day dinner documented in the preceding chapter. In turn, this reflected centuries-long, well-honed connections across the North Sea between Scotland and the Dutch metropole that had bred a degree of social and cultural familiarity[20] – some at least of which transferred to the colonial setting.

In another respect, nonetheless, the situation in which Scottish newcomers found themselves was somewhat less familiar, at least outside colonies of settlement. Writing about early nineteenth-century Jamaica, at that date a prime exemplar of the sugar colony that Java was subsequently to become, the British cultural historian Catherine Hall remarked that the island was essentially an 'outpost', where British colonial transients, including a goodly number of Scots, led often irregular social lives far removed from the middle-class norms of the metropolis: 'England was for families,' she suggests, while 'Jamaica was for sex.'[21] By way of contrast, what British arrivals (the Scots contingent prominent among them) encountered in the Indies were colonial communities in which, though sex was hardly off the agenda, marriage, regular domesticity and family formation flourished among strongly kin-oriented colonial communities, some of whose members had been domiciled in the Indies for several generations.

As such, they were a demographic success story – something substantially dependent, in turn, on a ratio between men and women that, although skewed, was not grossly disproportionate. Around the mid-nineteenth century, colonial enumerators counted (along with around 8,000 children) some 6,115 adult male Europeans and 4,577 adult females, a ratio of less than three to two.[22] In short, new arrivals in the nineteenth-century Indies found themselves in a colonial social terrain where they might reasonably hope to find a marital partner and start a family well in advance of any projected return to patria. It was a potential which, among other things, greatly complicates any notion, tentatively formulated regarding Scottish sojourners throughout Asia, that they formed 'a transient group for whom marriage and family were not the top priorities'.[23]

Admittedly, the Reverend Maclaine's host in Batavia in 1846 was a single man who evidently postponed finding a wife until after repatriation – when he married, in 1849, the 24-year-old Margaret Still Fraser, a woman of Scottish ancestry who outlived him by more than three decades.[24] Others among Bonhote's mid-nineteenth-century contemporaries, however, followed the lead of the firm's co-founder and 'married out' to women from the Dutch community while still on Java. In short, in a reversal of Catherine Hall's formulation of the situation facing British sojourners in the Caribbean, in the Indies it proved possible both to make a fortune *and* to enjoy a regular family life. Indeed, the two might well be not only contemporaneous but crucially symbiotic.

It was a context in which the welcoming comforts and companionability experienced on Java by the Scottish contingent encompassed a close association with Dutch counterparts with whom they were, quite literally, on speaking terms. A rare British 'tourist' in mid-century Java might remark that 'Dutch is not a language for which we have any particular fondness or that we would take much [*sic*] pains at any time to acquire',[25] but his sojourner contemporaries clearly begged to differ. Individual Scottish diasporans and diasporic communities had established themselves in the Low Countries from at least the sixteenth century onwards – and some early members of the Maclaine Watson cohort had come to Java via their families' lengthy sojourns there. For others, acquiring Dutch was something that only commenced when they disembarked. In 1852, for example, one newly arrived tyro was placed, not in a Scottish household in the great port of Surabaya, but in an hotel, with the specific purpose of encouraging him to learn to speak Dutch.[26] In short, there is every reason to assume such fluency was de rigueur and widespread. Later in the same decade, for example, Norbert P. van den Berg – a man with a great career ahead of him in colonial and metropolitan business circles – remarked of a British companion (on a mountain jaunt the pair were about to make) that he spoke 'perfectly good Dutch'.[27]

A shared penchant for the equestrian combination of racing and hunting also had a part to play here. Race meetings themselves (as indicated by Gillian Maclaine's listing of the things that purportedly gave life in Batavia such a 'European' aspect in the late 1830s) were a significant part of the social calendar of the upper echelons of a colonial community where fine horses and horsemanship were prized possessions and attributes. It could well have been the British who introduced horse racing into the Indies and, in any event, their involvement in the sport was unmistakable: evidenced, for example, by the appearance in the 1850s of English as well as Dutch copy (something otherwise unknown) with respect to the racing news in the colonial capital's new weekly paper, the *Java Bode*.[28] It was nonetheless a Dutch colonist, Willem van der Hucht, who was the key figure: he was the person standing next to John Pryce in front of the latter's porticoed, 'Gone with the Wind' Batavia mansion described earlier (Figure 2.5), and it was he who became the father-in-law of James McLachlan, one of the leading lights of the Maclaine Watson cohort during the third quarter of the nineteenth century.

The nexus with Van der Hucht also helped consolidate the British arrivals' entrée into the labyrinthine, strongly matriarchal family networks that characterised the upper levels of 'old' colonial society in and around Batavia until late in the nineteenth century – as indeed they had done for the better part of a century prior to that.[29] One such individual, Jan Casimir Theodorus van Motman, was described by Van der Hucht as one of his 'best friends'. He also remarked, however, that this colonial-born scion of a family established on Java since the late eighteenth century, who owned a string of estates in the hinterland of the colonial capital, had not spent any time in Europe.[30] He pointedly observed that although he is 'a fine and upright fellow, bear this in mind, so don't go by the surface only'.[31] It was a shortcoming nonetheless addressed in the next generation of his family: early in the 1860s, Maclaine Watson's Batavia office informed their Amsterdam correspondents, the well-known firm of Van Eeghen, that two young Van Motman boys (their fathers are 'intimate friends of ours') were off to the Netherlands in the charge of a 'governor'.[32]

Together with others of his kin, Jan van Motman himself was a partner with Van der Hucht in several plantation ventures, in tandem with Karel Frederik Holle, a prominent pioneering tea-planter related to the Van Motmans through marriage.[33] Naturally enough, both families were keen on breeding horses as well as on racing them. Indeed, one 'up-country' Holle was said to have had as many as one hundred on his property.[34] It was among these people that members of the Maclaine Watson cohort such as James McLachlan and his older brother Donald were able to pursue an enthusiasm for the turf that they had most likely acquired during an earlier sojourn in the Antipodes – where racing fever was endemic. Moreover, as members of the appropriately named Nimrod Club, they roamed the high country of West Java hunting deer, wild boar and other more exotic species – and did so in the company not only of leading individuals from Batavia's Dutch colonial community but also of members of the local Indonesian elite, as evidenced, for example, by a contemporary photograph (in the context of the hunt) of Van der Hucht and one of the Holle family in company with Nata di Laga, a Sundanese *Wedana* or (aristocratic) district head (Figure 2.7).

As such, Nimrod provides one of those occasions in the narratives of the Maclaine Watson cohort when the 'invisibility' of Indonesians – in this case the Sundanese people of Western Java – gives way, however momentarily, to something more illuminating, complementing co-founder Gillian Maclaine's apparently cordial relations with 'the good prince' Pangeran Buminata. At the same time, moreover, what in modern parlance would be styled as 'race relations' in mid-nineteenth-century colonial Java took on a

Figure 2.7: Willem van der Hucht, Adriaan Holle and the Sundanese minor aristocrat Nata di Laga, West Java, 1861 (Van den Berg & Wachlin, Album voor Mientje)

further and very significant dimension from the long-term incorporation into the Dutch communities with whom Scottish arrivals associated of large numbers of individuals of mixed European-Asian heritage.

The Kilt and the Sarong:
Identity, Race and Ethnicity in a Creole Terrain

The story of 'being "Dutch" in the Indies' centred on 'a history of creolisation and empire'.[35] 'Creole' itself is a term that unleashes a plethora of issues, ranging from Homi Bhabha's much-quoted aphorism of 'almost the same but not white',[36] through to mundane questions as to its embrace of all colonial-born colonials or only those of mixed race. Indeed, it was the latter – creoles with varying amounts of Asian ancestry – who were much to the fore at virtually all social levels in the Dutch colonial communities on Java and elsewhere in the archipelago, among whom there existed a broader understanding of who might be categorised as 'European' than came, over time, to be common among their counterparts in the British imperial sphere in Asia. In the Indies, contrary to what held good in the bastions of the British imperial presence in 'the East', a father's formal recognition of Eurasian offspring (mothers were excluded from this process) conferred on them, assuming he himself enjoyed European status, the same European legal standing (and social recognition) as that enjoyed by locally born 'white creoles' and by *totoks*, as the Europeans 'born elsewhere' came to be termed (generally with reference to their Netherlands origin).

By the late nineteenth century, for Scots (and Britons in general) increasingly divergent notions about ethnic mixing ('miscegenation') came to influence their perceptions of the Indies Dutch. Indeed, it has been argued that:

> many English-speaking visitors felt uncomfortable in the hybridised social setting of Dutch colonialism in Java, because they were alarmed by the visible results of several centuries of intermarriage and interracial reproduction.[37]

Nonetheless, how far this held good for mid-nineteenth-century contemporaries remains questionable. Gillian Maclaine's friend Alexander Loudon was perhaps a little ahead of his time when, in the 1830s, he confided to his journal that he found people of mixed race physically repulsive and 'the perspiration from . . . half-caste and black hides insufferable'.[38] Loudon, it seems, took care to have as a 'housekeeper' at his widower's establishment in provincial Java a woman – one Jane Fyfe – whose 'pure' Scottish credentials were as impeccable as his own. His case, however, was an exceptional one. Far more commonplace was the implication of the information, delicately imparted by an observant British contemporary in the 1830s, about the widespread practice among male 'foreign residents . . . [of placing] a Javanese woman at the head of their establishments', and that, in the colonial capital at least:

> the situation of the individual thus selected is not very apparent, and a stranger might take up his abode in a mansion at that place for some time without being aware that any body was invested with authority over its domestic concerns besides the master.[39]

The mid-century Scots-Javanese offspring of one such far-from-transient encounter, 'recognised' by his father and sent off to the Netherlands for a good education and seasoning as a Dutchman, went on (as we shall see in a subsequent chapter) to become a leading partner in Maclaine Watson and to establish, late in the century, a family among the bourgeoisie of the 'alternative metropole' across the North Sea. A similar point was made by Gillian Maclaine's old friend – he and his newly-wed wife had stayed with him on their honeymoon 'jaunt' in 1832 – William Menzies, who had likewise used his family and business connections back home (this time in Britain rather than the Netherlands) to ensure that his mixed-race offspring would receive the kind of social conditioning and education that would equip them as Europeans and enable them to settle successfully in their adopted country. Two of them (a third appears to have remained on Java and become his heir)[40] he not only acknowledged (and hence legitimised according to Indies law and custom) but also sent to Britain to join the family of his brother, Robert Menzies, who worked as a surgeon in Lambeth, a largely lower-class area of London immediately south of the Thames.[41] In fact, both Eurasian young people (a boy and a girl) became 'wards' of Gillian Maclaine's erstwhile business partner, Edward Watson. When he and his British-born wife, Margaret Barugh, repatriated in 1837, they took the boy with them; and although Alexander Anderson Menzies, a student of civil engineering at Putney, succumbed to tuberculosis at the age of 17, his sister, Mary Menzies, lived into full maturity. She had been enrolled alongside two of Watson's own children at a school in Hemel Hempstead run by Watson's sister, less than 25 miles north of the Watson family home in Hampstead.[42] It was from the latter address in 1864 that she married the 35-year-old Thomas Denne, a surgeon who was perhaps a young professional acquaintance of her uncle's or a contemporary of her cousin, Robert Bunn Menzies, who was also trained in medicine.[43]

Their Scottish parent, meanwhile, had become one of those arrivals on Java who 'came and stayed' (as the Dutch put it), instead of repatriating. Not that the 'Old Country' was entirely forgotten, for when Menzies' household effects were put up for sale after his death in 1854, along with a collection of 'Native weaponry', they included armaments of a somewhat different kind in the form of a bound set of the *Illustrated London News,* complete from its first issue in 1842.[44] There were indeed other settlers like him. Established in East Java in the 1820s, Donald MacLennan never returned to his native Kintail, in Wester Ross in the north of Scotland, and, full of years, wealthy and a 'well regarded' member of the local Freemasons' Lodge, he died in 1863 in the sugar town of Pasuruan, some 50 or so kilometres eastwards along the coast from Surabaya.[45]

Nonetheless, stories like these were not representative. Instead, for all that the Scots in question found themselves in a quasi-settler colonial society in which home comforts were available to new arrivals in a milieu characterised by a close association with their Dutch 'hosts', it remained the case that, along with the British contingent in general, most members of the Scottish diaspora in the Indies – certainly those who, like the Maclaine Watson partners, were rich enough to do so – repatriated once they had 'served their time in the East'. To be sure, this did not necessarily represent a severing of ties for, as with the Empire Families of the British Raj,[46] sons and nephews often replaced repatriating fathers and uncles – a process that did not invariably exclude daughters and nieces, who might bring new blood into the firm through marriage – to take their 'turn' in the Indies as (eventual) partners in the Maclaine Watson mercantile business. Even so, the presumption of returning home after serving their time in 'the East' remained paramount. Just *why* it did so is something that subsequent chapters set out to explain. What is clear from the outset, however, is that an inextinguishable loyalty to Scotland, though it may have explained the behaviour of a few individuals, does little to explain that of most members of the Maclaine Watson cohort. Not least, because Highland Homecomings per se were only part of the story. It is, nonetheless, to what was perhaps the best-documented of them that we can first turn.

Highland Homecomings, Repatriate Afterlives and the Meaning of 'Scotland'

We owe to serendipity a contemporary account of the homecoming of a mid-nineteenth-century sojourner from the cohort that affords us a unique glimpse of the actual moment of return from the Indies of Donald Maclaine of Lochbuie, who as a young man had been an attendee at the St Andrew's Day dinner some two decades earlier, where he had proposed a toast to 'The Ladies of Batavia', and who had subsequently become a partner in the firm. On the final stage of his passage back to his native Inner Hebridean island, quite by chance, he travelled on the same vessel, making its way from Glasgow to Oban and beyond, as the celebrated Scots geologist and explorer Roderick Impey Murchison. It is Murchison's biographer who tells the story:

> In their northward journey, the steamer, which usually holds her course straight through the Sound of Mull, turned aside into one of the inlets on the southern shore of that mountainous island, to land there Maclean of Loch Buy, who, after a successful life abroad, had come back and repurchased the lands of his ancestors which he was now about to re-occupy. In his journal Murchison refers to this event thus: 'The gratification I experienced was great in seeing the happy disembarkation of the rich man from Java, with his wife, many children, a Malay woman, and all sorts of traps. Not to be forgotten that thirty-two years ago Sedgwick and I danced with our nailed shoes in the halls of Loch Buy, then belonging to the old laird who was ruined. Property now regained by eldest son. Guns saluting... numerous boats.[47]

Lochbuie was only 39 at the time of his and his family's disembarkation on Mull. Other, subsequently repatriating members of the cohort, stretching well into the twentieth century, were as young (or only a very little older), meaning that, potentially at least, they enjoyed quite exceptionally long afterlives as returnees. Not in Lochbuie's case, to be sure (he was destined to die a few days short of his forty-seventh birthday) but certainly in those of many of his repatriating contemporaries and successors – something that, in turn, has major implications for a holistic understanding of the diaspora since it throws the spotlight not only on sojourning but also on its aftermath. Most immediately, repatriation and the attendant theme of 'Back to Caledonia'[48] raises questions about what 'Scotland' meant for returnees such as those of the Maclaine Watson cohort – a question less easily answered, perhaps, than the more usual question of what returnees (and their wealth) meant for Scotland itself. For while large tracts of the Scottish Lowlands had been transformed into an industrial landscape, the Highlands and Borders were themselves experiencing a transformation of a different kind. Most obviously, it was a transformation that reflected an Anglo-Scottish project for the reimagining of Scotland as the haunt of a landed gentry and aristocracy, whose predilections for stalking quadrupeds were catered for by an exponential growth of deer forests, and whose taste for Highland malts went hand in hand with a fashion for shooting game birds en masse – something that led, in turn, to a sharp increase in the extent of grouse moors and the concomitant nurturing of birds in huge numbers prior to their annual ritual slaughter.

Yet there was more. When the Lochbuie family arrived on Mull in the mid-1850s, they disembarked, as Murchison's biographer tells us, from a *steamer* that had brought them from Glasgow at the end of a lengthy sea voyage and rail journey that had begun in Batavia three months or more earlier. Their mode of transport was hardly a novelty – paddle steamers built on the Clyde had begun plying this route in the 1820s[49] – but it was nonetheless a reminder that, beyond Lochbuie's native Highlands and Islands, the country to which he was returning had evolved since the late eighteenth century into one of the most heavily industrialised (and urbanised) countries in Western Europe, characterised by the growth of factories, foundries, shipyards, mines, and their attendant workers' quarters and middle-class suburbs.[50] In terms of manufacture, Glasgow and Clydeside were fully a match for the industrialised conurbations that had grown up south of the Border, while within Scotland itself the new urban-industrial economy extended to east-coast Dundee and as far north as Aberdeen.

And then there was Edinburgh.[51] Though already overtaken three decades earlier by industrialising Glasgow as Scotland's largest city, Edinburgh in the 1850s remained the nation's capital and the headquarters of its professional classes, who lived in or nearby the New Town's Georgian squares and terraces, on the city's northern and windswept flank, and were

Figure 2.8: Victoria and Albert's Scottish Baronial palace (Collection of the Author)

separated from the much older – and generally less socially desirable – southern districts by the crest of the great hill that runs eastward from the castle down to the Palace of Holyrood, forming the dominant feature of Edinburgh's cityscape. As such, 'Auld Reekie' – as it had been fondly designated in one of the toasts proposed at the St Andrew's Day dinner in Batavia in 1838 – its legendary pall of smoke, now circumventable by the affluent, was a magnet for returnees, among them several of the Maclaine Watson cohort.

By the middle decades of the nineteenth century, however, beyond the urban-industrial districts of the central and eastern Lowlands, Scotland was being reinvented, and heavily romanticised under the impress of Victorian-era 'Highlandism'. As such, it formed part of a broader cultural makeover that 'looked to Highland "traditions", landscape and legend to define Scottish nationality'.[52] Moreover, the purchase of Highland property itself had further implications: 'Highland acreage,' as one recent discussion paper argues, 'had a cultural attraction and value to those with imperial fortunes' and carried with it 'connotations of "ancient" and "authentic" [that] were the antithesis of transient and unstable commercial wealth.' In short, 'acquiring land changed both the owner and the nature of their money.'[53]

In turn, this was a context in which Highlandism came to embrace built form – in the shape of the Scots Baronial variant of Revival Gothic – that may itself have served, in part, to mask the origins of the capital invested.[54] Popularised by (though scarcely epitomised in) the castellated mansion at Balmoral in Aberdeenshire (Figure 2.7), erected by those celebrated monarchs of the glen, Queen Victoria and her Prince Consort, rampant 'Balmoralism' overlapped with the cult of the kilt and the concomitant 'clanscaping', not only of Scotland itself, but also of large tracts of the diaspora. Indeed, it was in diasporic communities that late nineteenth-century clan revivalism, and the establishment of tartan-heavy clan associations – predicated on the notion of the primordial consanguinity of those who shared the same patronym – took on its ripest form. Yet alongside, and infusing its easily parodied dimensions ('a wee dram of bonnie Scotland'), was a Highland revivalism of a qualitatively different kind: one that sought to preserve and reinvigorate, and which had roots going well back into the eighteenth century.[55] How these differing scenarios played out in relation to the repatriates of the Maclaine Watson cohort is something exemplified – and complicated – in the stories that follow. Moreover, repatriate returns to *Scotland*, in whichever of its guises, were only part of the story.

The Lure of London, the English Provinces and Sea Air

Instead of returning to their native turf in the Highlands and Islands or the north-east of Scotland, a significant number of the cohort's returnees chose to exploit an alternative option: that of taking up permanent domicile south of the Border. Recent research has done much to deepen our understanding of the phenomenon encapsulated in Dr Johnson's famous quip about the 'high road ... to England' as the desideratum of any ambitious Scot, through analysis of what has been described as the 'near diaspora' in a southern metropolis which had long been a favourite resort for wealthy (and not-so-wealthy) Scots – not least because of what it had to offer in terms of sociability, combined with openings in the professions and in business, as well as ready access (after 1707) to the British Parliament and its attendant spoils of office.[56] In consequence, returnees from the diaspora would be sure of finding themselves in a place where sizeable Scottish communities counted among their number occasional visitors, people who regularly moved back and forth, those who led a parallel existence in both

Scotland and England, and individuals or families who were permanently domiciled there.

Along with informal Scottish clubs meeting in inns and coffee houses, London also came to possess a small number of institutionalised forms of specifically Scottish association – notably the charitable Scottish Corporation (founded 1665) and the Highland Society (1778). There followed, in the first half of the nineteenth century, the Caledonian Society (1837), instituted 'to promote good fellowship and brotherhood, and to combine efforts for benevolent and national objects connected with Scotland, and to preserve the picturesque garb of "Old Gaul"',[57] while by the mid-nineteenth century, a London-based Scot of good social standing might well be found in attendance at such functions as the 1854 grand fancy-dress ball in aid of the Caledonian Society that took place at Willis's Rooms in the heart of the West End. Patronised by 'the usual brilliant and numerous assemblage of the Scotch and English nobility and beau monde', many of whom were 'dressed in Highland garb', it was an event at which 'carriages commenced arriving just after ten o'clock and continued to set down, in one unbroken line, until past one o'clock, by which time there were nearly a thousand persons present'.[58]

It was an urban landscape, moreover, in which there was a multiplicity of ever-expanding 'Londons'. Gillian Maclaine's London, when he first arrived there from the Highlands at the end of 1816, was an East India 'counting house' in the City itself, and lodgings at Hatton Garden, then a mixed residential and artisan district, a short walk to the City's north-west, where he lived with two of the firm's partners in an apartment carved out – 'a house within itself' he called it – of a larger property.[59] By the mid-century, however, his successors in the cohort, in addition to having what was now a 'city office', had established themselves some three or so miles to the west, in the elite district north of London's Hyde Park – a former royal hunting ground, turned into a public space during the seventeenth century, and much improved during the following one. The predominantly stuccoed terraces and squares of this newly built sector of the city quickly filled up with rich and influential people. Although its easternmost sector was designated as 'plutocratic' – comparable in wealth though not in blue blood to the aristocratic Belgravia district immediately south of the Park – the whole area attracted both old and new money. Repatriates from 'the East' in general were to be found in appreciable numbers in this new part of fashionable London during the second half of the nineteenth century, people for whom, among the more specific attractions of London for those arriving back from overseas, was the presence of other similarly repatriated veterans from Asia and elsewhere.[60]

Even so, London was not the sum of 'the South' for the returnee families who made up the repatriate sector of the cohort. Far from it. Even prior to his time in the Indies, Gillian Maclaine (on the way to stay with a wealthy uncle and aunt who lived near the major port city of Bristol) had visited Cheltenham, some 100 miles to the west of the metropolis, in agriculturally rich Gloucestershire, and reported back to Scotland on a town whose spa was still much frequented by fashionables intent on 'taking the waters':

> I was much struck by the bustle that appeared about the streets even at so late an hour as 10 o'clock at night. The Assembly Rooms were lighted up and crowds, carriages, chairs etc. about the entrance. It required only half an eye to see that it was solely a place of amusement. I put up at the inn the coach stopped at and soon after my arrival went to bed.'[61]

Although, as 'a place of amusement', its fame subsequently faded, it evolved (as we shall see in detail in a subsequent chapter) as a major node on British imperial circuits: a haunt for colonial repatriates and a nurturing ground for 'empire families', who were attracted there by the excellence of its schools and its somewhat uneasy pairing of piety and horse racing. And then there were the resort towns of the South Coast of England, chosen as places of domicile, so it would seem, because of the health-giving promise held out to the sick by their mild winter climates and clean air. Something very similar also held good for locations in continental Europe, likewise much favoured by at least some of the Maclaine Watson cohort's returnees.

Indeed, given what we know about their repatriate afterlives, it looks very much as if the concept of 'Back to Caledonia', in any literal sense, covered the afterlives of only a small minority of the members of the Maclaine Watson cohort and their immediate descendants. What is altogether more intriguing in this context are the questions that this raises relating to issues of cultural and ethnic identity – issues that form a continuing counterpoint in the diasporan dialogue. How far, for instance, are the cohort's stories illuminated by the concept of a gradual but cumulative 'shedding of Scottishness', as postulated in an investigation of a Scottish family's 'becoming English' over the course of several generations?[62]

Howsoever that may be, the chapters that follow are grounded in the argument that a holistic, comprehensive approach to Scotland's diaspora needs to focus not only on overseas sojourning but also on repatriate afterlives, lived out over several generations and in many and diverse locations.

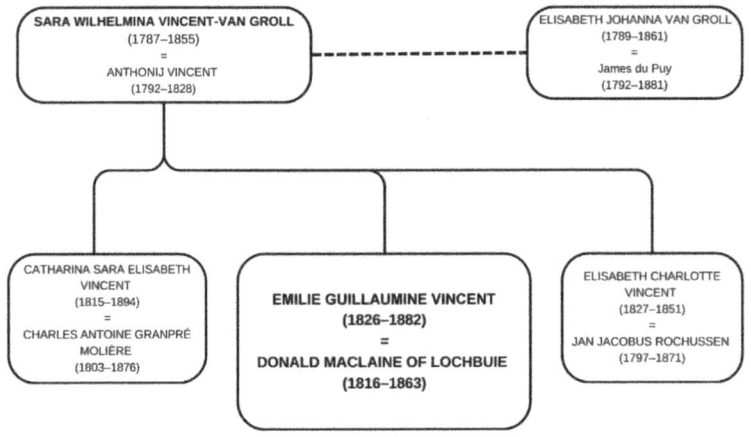

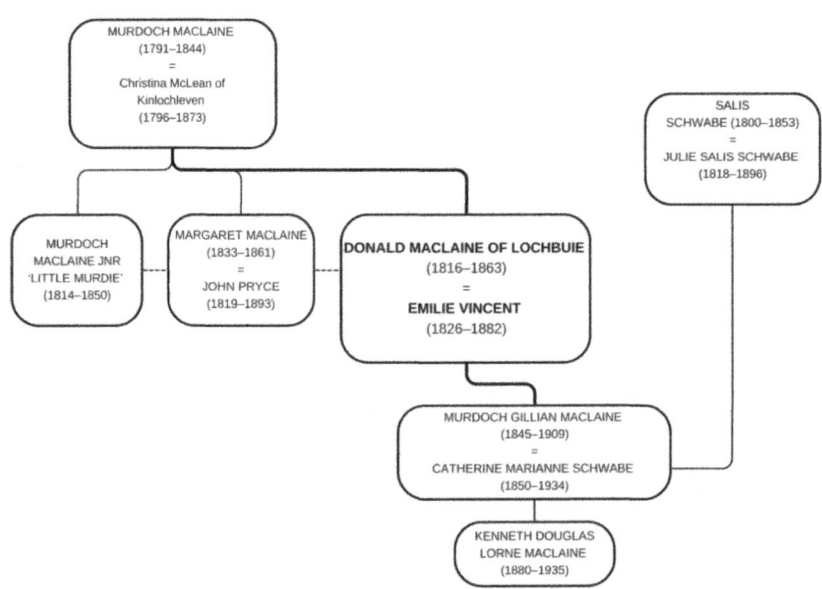

3

The Kilted Dancer and an Antipodean 'Ardtornish'

'I INTRODUCED HIM at Government house,' Gillian Maclaine wrote of his recently arrived cousin Donald Maclaine of Lochbuie where the 21-year-old 'appeared in full Highland costume at a masked Ball... A great favourite among the Dutch, he galloped away... with the Governor's Lady and afterwards with my old acquaintance Mrs General Nahuys.'[1] It is a scene that opens vistas onto the infiltration of elite colonial circles on Java by members of the nascent Maclaine Watson cohort during the lifetime of the firm's co-founder. The new arrival evidently developed from very modest beginnings ('his education has not been so carefully attended to as it ought to have been – as he himself is now well aware')[2] – into an astute and successful businessman. 'Donald Lochbuy pleases me very much,' Maclaine recorded early in 1837, after the young man had been on the island for only a matter of months, 'and in the course of two years more will I trust be a useful assistant to the firm. His obliging temper has gained him many friends & he seems quite happy and delighted with the climate and place. I really am very much gratified by having so warm hearted and trustworthy a young countryman with me.'[3] His tone, moreover, subsequently became even more positive: 'I am much pleased with Donald,' he wrote to his brother some eighteen months later in August 1838. 'He is most attentive to business and one of the steadiest young men I have seen on Java.'[4] Nonetheless, being

Figure 3.1: Donald Maclaine, partner in Maclaine Watson, in later life (KITLV/ University of Leiden)

'attentive to business' was only one dimension of becoming rich in a commercial environment in which success was also predicated on having the right personal contacts, both in the business world of the Indies and in the official circles of a colony in which the state bureaucracy held (sometimes literally) the whip hand. However fortuitously – and there may indeed have been an element of happenstance in what eventuated – Donald Lochbuie scored highly in this respect (Figure 3.1).

Not least, because he made what turned out to be an exceptionally 'good' marriage when he wed the 18-year-old Emilie Guillaumine Vincent in Batavia in October 1844.[5] Ten years younger than her husband and destined to outlive him by almost two decades, Emilie Vincent had been born in the Dutch Residency town of Padang, on the West Coast of Sumatra, where her father, Anthonij Vincent, held an official post as *Secretaris*, the Resident's right-hand man. He had died there, however, when she was less than two years old, and the pivotal figure in the story that follows was her mother, the widowed Sara Wilhelmina Vincent-Van Groll. Born in the town of Zwolle in the eastern provinces of the Netherlands, her family background was in the waterborne world of the Dutch East India Company (VOC) and its land-based trading settlements in Africa and Asia, while she herself had taken as her husband a man who hailed from the Americas. Her father, Gerhardus van Groll – an old VOC hand born in Cape Town, at that time still a Dutch possession – had subsequently found his way to Java before relocating to the Netherlands. It was from there that he returned to the Indies in 1814, together with his 17-year-old daughter and the 22-year-old Antonij Vincent, who became his son-in-law when the two were wed at the Cape en route to Batavia. It was, it might be suspected, an unfortunate alliance.

Far from being the wealthy Amsterdam businessman of Clan Maclaine legend,[6] Vincent was the Demerara-born offspring of a Dutch sugar planter of uncertain fortune operating on the Caribbean coast of Suriname, who had made his way to the Netherlands before embarking for Java. He subsequently enjoyed a mixed career in semi-official employment in Batavia – at one time he was under arrest, accused of dishonesty[7] – before finding a middle-grade position in the colonial service in the relative obscurity of Padang. It was there that he died, insolvent, at the age of 36 in 1828. At this point, his widow took the family fortunes in hand. Initially, she remained in Padang; and it was there that her eldest daughter, the 16-year-old Catharina Sara Elisabeth Vincent, married Charles Antoine Granpré Molière, who was the local agent of the Netherlands Trading Society (Nederlandsche Handel-Maatschappij or NHM). Then scarcely out of its foundational stage, the Trading Society subsequently evolved into the Indies' dominant commercial and banking concern, first as an arm of the Indies government and subsequently as a 'free-standing institution' that in terms of power and influence was second only to that of the colonial authorities themselves.[8]

Vincent-Van Groll evidently had ambitious plans for her remaining offspring – whom she subsequently shipped back to Java, where her younger sister, Elisabeth Johanna van Groll, was married to the London-born, naturalised Dutchman James du Puy, an individual who was consolidating a successful career in the Indies bureaucracy that culminated in a position on the Council of the Indies, the Governor-General's key advisory body and the ultimate goal of any ambitious civil servant. As such, he provided a valuable entrée into the realm of the colony's all-powerful Dutch officialdom. Indeed, as early as the 1820s as Resident of the West Coast of Sumatra, he had been the same uncle who probably pulled the strings necessary to secure an official appointment for his seemingly hapless nephew. On stepping down from the Council, moreover, instead of repatriating, Du Puy remained on Java as a person of influence, while enjoying the post-retirement spoils of office as a contractor to the Indies government, supplying them with sugar from a factory in the island's Eastern Salient.[9]

After relocating to the colonial capital early in the 1830s, the widow Vincent-van Groll's subsequent history highlighted the extent to which the Dutch communities in the Indies had deep-rooted antecedents centred on regular family formation and intermarriage among well-established Dutch colonial populations. Creole (that is to say, colonial-born), they also took good care to maintain family and associated cultural ties with the metropole, so that they and their social peers in the Netherlands retained an organic connection.[10] The widow was no exception. At the close of 1833 she left Batavia for Holland with five of her children – together with her sister and brother-in-law and *their* six children.[11] Her family remained in the Netherlands or thereabouts for the next six years before returning to the Indies in March 1841.[12] In the interim, the children – perhaps the girls in particular, who were said also to have had the advantage of strikingly good looks[13] – would have acquired the kind of European 'polish', both in terms of formal education and from living among their metropolitan kin, that greatly enhanced their chances of finding 'suitable' marriage partners back in the Indies.

And 'suitable' partners were indeed what they found. Some three years after her family's return from the Netherlands, Emilie Vincent married Donald Lochbuie – not entirely coincidentally, it might be suspected, some months *after* he had been admitted as a partner in the Maclaine Watson business.[14] Business did indeed figure prominently: his eldest sister-in-law's husband, Granpré Molière, after his modest beginnings in Padang, had risen to be one of the key figures in the NHM's Batavia branch; while another sister-in-law, Rosalie Antoinette Vincent, cemented existing ties with the Du Puy family by marrying James du Puy's second (surviving) son, P. J. G du Puy – for good measure, the young man was taken into the Maclaine Watson partnership. Nor were Vincent-van Groll's sons neglected in this peerless demonstration of matchmaking. Most immediately, the widower Charles Pahud, one of their fellow passengers on board the ship that had brought the family back to Batavia in 1841[15] – a man whose career in government service culminated in his appointment as Governor-General

– was evidently happy for one of her 'boys', Anthonij Willem Adriaan Vincent (he rose to the rank of *Resident* in the government service before his career was prematurely terminated by his murder while at his post in South-Central Java) to have the hand of a cherished daughter, Antoinette Catharina Pahud.[16] Subsequently, another son, Edward James Elize Vincent, wed Anna Catharina Hofland, the daughter of Java's foremost and probably wealthiest landowner, the co-proprietor of the colony's largest estate, Pamanoekan and Tjiasem (Pamanukan and Ciasem), of which his son-in-law became *administrateur* or general manager. A property that covered about 200,000 hectares, stretching from the Java Sea up into the Preanger Mountains to the south, it had an Indonesian peasant population of over 100,000.[17]

Even allowing for her other successes in this respect however, the greatest day of Vincent-van Groll's life must surely have been 2nd September 1848, when her youngest child, Elisabeth Charlotte Vincent, became the spouse of Governor-General Jan Jacobus Rochussen (Figure 3.2). The fact that the groom, a widower with six children from his first marriage, was some thirty years older than his bride would have mattered far less than his vice-regal standing and parentage among the *haute bourgeoisie* of his native

Figure 3.2: Willemskerk, Batavia's Protestant Church, where Donald Maclaine's sister-in-law married Governor-General Rochussen (KITLV/ University of Leiden)

Rotterdam.[18] As reported in what was still the colony's only newspaper, the day's proceedings began around 5.30 in the evening with a statutory civil ceremony at which the marriage was registered, with her uncle Du Puy and brother-in-law Granpré Molière acting as the bride's witnesses. It was followed by a church service, replete with choral renditions of several apposite psalms, in Batavia's foremost place of Christian worship, the *Willemskerk,* situated not far from Donald Lochbuie's house on the Koningsplein, in the heart of Batavia's European quarter (Figure 3.3). His marriage, in short, had brought rich rewards in terms of the colonial circles into which he had been introduced.

His mother-in-law, the widow Vincent-van Groll, no doubt kept in close contact with him for she lived on the 'road to Tanah Abang',[19] a little to the west of the Koningsplein itself – admittedly a public space so big that it swallowed a whole racecourse without undue difficulty – and in late July 1854 it was in his company and that of her daughter and their children that she sailed from Batavia to Singapore aboard the steamer *Macassar.*[20] Once arrived in the Lion City the family party transferred to another steamer to continue on a journey that terminated in locations more than 10,000

Figure 3.3: Donald Maclaine and Emilie Vincent and family's Batavia house (Collection Scott Merrillees, Melbourne)

kilometres distant that were, to varying extents, familiar to all the adults in the party: both Donald Maclaine and his mother-in-law and her offspring had last been in either Scotland or the Netherlands only a little over a decade earlier. Even so, the conditions under which sojourners like themselves travelled were changing, most dramatically in relation to the voyage between the Indies and the ports of Western Europe. Although the opening of the Suez Canal in 1869 did much to speed up and regularise the transport of people and goods between Asia and Europe, for those who could afford it, the qualitative leap had taken place in the 1840s, with the development of the so-called Overland Route via the Red Sea, Cairo (reached initially by a bumpy ride across the intervening desert), and a boat trip down the Nile to Alexandria followed by a further voyage by steamer to Marseille, Genoa, Trieste or Southampton.[21] Going in the opposite direction in 1846, the Reverend Angus Maclaine – brother of the co-founder of Maclaine Watson – had arrived this way in Batavia (via Singapore) on a journey that had taken him fifty-one days.[22] About the norm around the mid-century, this represented a reduction by at least half on the sailing times logged in for the sea voyage down around the Cape of Good Hope.

On their arrival in Europe (in the absence of any surviving itinerary), we can only assume that the Maclaines and the widow Vincent-van Groll first travelled overland from Marseille, presumably by recently opened railways on much of the route south of Paris and likewise northwards towards Belgium, before finally arriving in the Netherlands, where there would have been relatives aplenty for the family to visit. Maybe, indeed, for Vincent-van Groll herself this was the point of the journey: a return to her native land before she died – which she did in mid-August 1855, in the German spa-town of Kleve, just over the border with the Netherlands, a few months short of her sixty-ninth birthday. By that date, Donald Lochbuie and his family were in Scotland, but the widow had not been alone at the time of her death. Rather, she had been joined there by another of her sons-in-law, the leading ex-Indies businessman Granpré Molière, who had himself repatriated earlier that same year. At least, it was he who signed the death notice (dated from Kleve) that appeared in Dutch newspapers.[23]

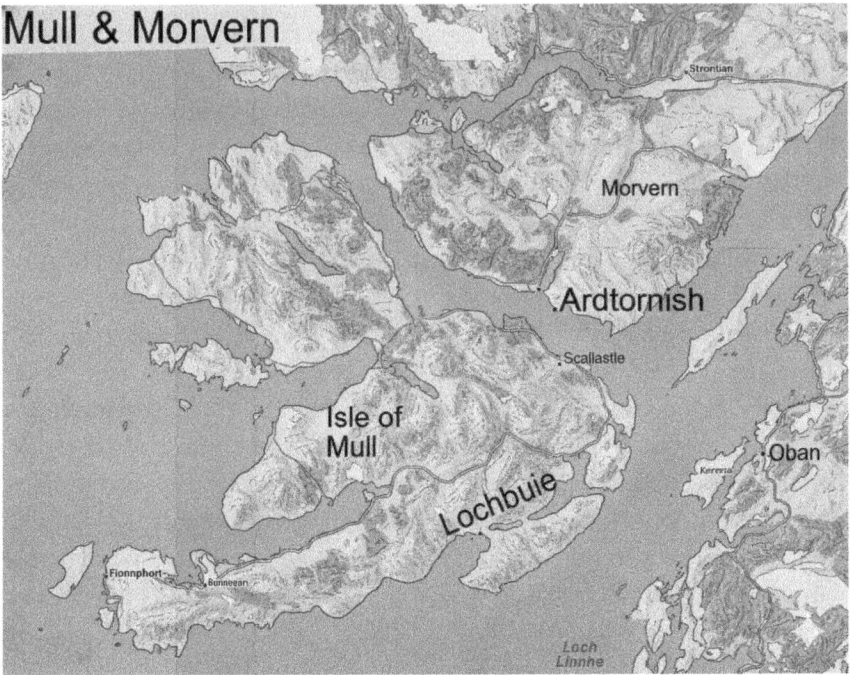

Figure 3.4: Map of Mull and Morvern (Collection of the Author)

A Patrimony Regained

On Java, marriage into an elite Dutch colonial family had smoothed Donald Lochbuie's way within a community in which ramifying ties of this kind were the key to status, influence and wealth. His situation vis-à-vis his Scottish kin on the Inner Hebridean island of Mull, however, was radically different (Figure 3.4). His immediate family (and it was a large one) was saddled with an extensive and not particularly productive estate, little capital, and a feckless heir whose (prospective) patrimony was comprised of a large Georgian mansion, a ruined castle and more than 10,000 hectares of arable land, sheep runs, and predominantly wild moorland located in mountainous country bordering on the southern reaches of the Sound of Mull and the Atlantic Ocean (Figure 3.5). Its early nineteenth-century proprietor, the well-regarded Murdoch Maclaine, the 20th Laird, died suddenly in August 1844 – an attendee recorded that he 'had seldom seen a funeral where the deceased was so much regretted as that of the late Lochbuy'[24] – leaving his distraught widow, Christina McLean of Kinlochleven, with eleven children, ranging in ages between 12 and 30. The Lochbuie estate passed into the hands of Donald Maclaine's elder brother, also Murdoch Maclaine, the 21st Laird, who was distinguished from his father by being known as 'Little Murdie'. He was also known, however, as a heavy drinker and gambler who ran up liabilities said to be in the region of £10,000. 'A coarse and vulgar-minded man to the very core,' he took little practical interest in the property, instead spending his time in Edinburgh and making plans to go to the Caribbean. In 1850, however, only six years after he became the Laird of Lochbuie, 'Little Murdie', presumably sodden with drink, died bankrupt with his estate taken over by assignees appointed by his creditors.[25]

His inheritance compromised by debt, for Donald Lochbuie the immediate task on his return to Scotland was to use his Indies money to literally retrieve the family fortunes: which he did at auction in Edinburgh in September 1855 by repurchasing the alienated part of the Lochbuie estate for a sum approximating to the 'upset' (reserve) price of £30,835.[26] His resumption of his hereditary lands was, in turn, the occasion for an impressive celebratory banquet in November 1855, on his thirty-ninth birthday, an event widely reported in the Scottish newspapers under the heading of 'Rejoicings at Lochbuy':

Figure 3.5: Lochbuie House, ancestral home of the Lochbuie family (Collection of the Author)

Mr MacLaine entertained at dinner a large company of his relations and friends at Lochbuy House; and in a ball room fitted up and decorated for the occasion, the whole of his numerous tenantry and dependants sat down to a most substantial dinner. Both in the mansion house and ball room the health of the Laird of Lochbuy was drunk with Highland honours, amid the roar of cannon from the castle, the ancient residence of his ancestors. In the evening, dancing was kept up for a considerable time to the stirring strains of the pibroch.[27]

Alluding to what was taking place elsewhere in the Highlands, where, 'by the middle decades of the nineteenth century, over two thirds of . . . estates had changed hands',[28] the newspaper also editorialised:

[i]t was, in these days of change, a most gratifying and cheering sight to see a Highland chief, the representative of one of the oldest Highland families, with his amiable lady and children, surrounded by so many relatives and . . . Tenantry . . .[29]

In keeping, no doubt, with the shouldering of responsibilities inherent in his new situation, the 22nd Laird had joined the Highland and Agricultural Society on returning to Scotland and become involved in a project, designed to promote the economic welfare of the region by ending its isolation, to build a railway from Glasgow to Oban,[30] the main urban centre of the Western Highlands, where the new laird also bought property, including the town's main hotel.[31] In the short run, indeed, his capital outlays on his return from 'the East' – they included, along with the redemption of Lochbuie itself, paying off his late brother's personal debts and buying (for £10,200) the adjoining Kinloch estate, a property that had been owned by his grandfather[32] – look to have been substantial enough to have driven him to return temporarily to the Indies in an effort to consolidate his finances.

Once back on Java, where he remained a partner in Maclaine Watson, Lochbuie assumed the position of British consul at Semarang,[33] before subsequently relocating to Batavia, and to the house that he had lived in prior to his departure for Europe in 1855. Along with his immediate family, he had taken back with him to the Indies his youngest sister, Margaret Maxwell Maclaine,[34] the last-born of his siblings and a penurious single woman with no obvious prospects. That was about to change, however, for early in 1858 she married the widower and businessman John Pryce,[35] the proprietor of a successful auction house in Batavia and owner of a grand mansion on the Koningsplein just a few doors down from Donald Lochbuie's own residence. Appropriately enough when, a few months later, the family were on the move again, this time permanently back to Scotland, it was his recently-acquired brother-in-law who conducted the usual 'prior to departure' sale of their effects – which included furniture, coaches, horses and 'several good milking cows'.[36]

At the latest, the family were back in Scotland by late July 1858, when 'Donald Maclaine of Lochbuy' was recorded as one of the visitors at the Edinburgh Academic Examinations.[37] In October, there followed in the pages of the *North British Mail* a report of Maclaine's prowess in bringing down 'as large a stag as has been killed on Mull in many years' – it was the first shoot that he had attended since his return 'from the East' – and it concluded with the observation that 'we trust that it is an omen of his taking a place among the deer stalkers of his native land'.[38] Margaret Maclaine-Pryce, as she now was, followed her brother and his family to Scotland with her husband less than three years later. The denouement,

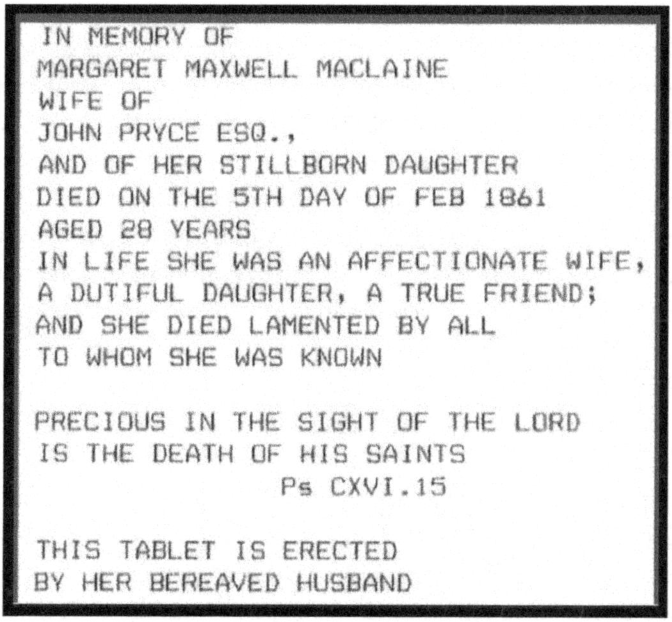

```
IN MEMORY OF
MARGARET MAXWELL MACLAINE
WIFE OF
JOHN PRYCE ESQ.,
AND OF HER STILLBORN DAUGHTER
DIED ON THE 5TH DAY OF FEB 1861
AGED 28 YEARS
IN LIFE SHE WAS AN AFFECTIONATE WIFE,
A DUTIFUL DAUGHTER, A TRUE FRIEND;
AND SHE DIED LAMENTED BY ALL
TO WHOM SHE WAS KNOWN

PRECIOUS IN THE SIGHT OF THE LORD
IS THE DEATH OF HIS SAINTS
            Ps CXVI.15

THIS TABLET IS ERECTED
BY HER BEREAVED HUSBAND
```

Figure 3.6: Wall plaque commemorating Margaret Maclaine-Pryce, youngest sister of Donald Maclaine (Collection of the Author)

however, was a melancholy one: Maclaine-Pryce gave birth to a stillborn child in Edinburgh on 4th February 1861 and died there herself the following day (Figure 3.6).[39] Her bereaved husband stayed with the Maclaines at Lochbuie House in the months following her death,[40] before returning briefly to the Indies. Another, somewhat later visitor, was perhaps less welcome.

The Antipodean Ardtornish and the Reverend Angus Maclaine

Alexander Campbell Maclaine, the individual in question, was the next-to-youngest of Donald Maclaine's brothers, and one whose case evidently became urgent after the death of his father in 1844 and the accession of his ne'er-do-well eldest brother. His Java-based sibling's initial response was to find him a niche in the family business on Java, for which purpose the gangling 18-year-old (he was at least six-foot-four) was first dispatched to Antwerp to gain some commercial experience (probably in the office there of James Mathison Fraser, whose younger brother was one of the Maclaine Watson partners) and then sent on to the Indies, where he arrived sometime in 1846.[41] After that, however, things appear not to have gone according to plan and Alexander Maclaine's subsequent history (to which we shall return shortly) was that of a prototype of the 'global nomad'.[42] Beyond demonstrating a certain footloose propensity, his trajectory also highlights unexplored dimensions of the Maclaine Watson cohort's stories: for the next stage of this diasporan history was played out neither in Britain nor even in the Indies but on the Australian continent to their southeast, where migrant and sojourner communities of Scots had been in existence since the earliest days of European settlement late in the previous century[43] – and where the key actor in this particular instance was Donald Lochbuie's cousin, the Reverend Angus Maclaine, the younger sibling of Maclaine Watson's co-founder.

Having previously resigned his Highland parish and in the wake of his brother's death at sea in 1840 (when his ship went down with all hands in the Indian Ocean), the Reverend Maclaine had become a landed proprietor near Adelaide in the newly occupied colony of South Australia, established in 1836 on the fertile fringe of the Great Australian Bight.[44] With a sailing time of weeks rather than months from the Indies, and in common with the other main centres of British settlement in the Antipodes, it offered an outlet for Java's commodities, sugar and rice above all, and a potential for landed investment. The point had not been lost on the Reverend Maclaine's elder brother: 'I believe I formerly mentioned to you that I have a ship engaged in the trade between this and Australia, which we find a rather profitable one,' Gillian Maclaine confided some eighteen months prior to his premature demise. 'We dispatched the *Justina* last month with our friend [Alexander] Loudon on board as passenger, for Hobart town and Sydney – with liberty to call at the new Settlement of S[outh] Australia.' It was on the strength of this reconnaissance that the elder Maclaine had purchased land near Adelaide with some of the capital that he had accumulated in the Indies and placed it eventually under his brother's management. In writing to that brother about his intentions, Maclaine added:

> I have requested Loudon to make particular inquiries respecting the new Settlement, and even authorized his investing 2000 pounds – if he thought favourably of the purchase of land there, he himself also advancing a like sum of 2,000 pounds – thus making a joint purchase of 4,000 pounds. For every 100 acres of land we buy, I believe that we have the right of getting out free of expense 12 emigrants, but I will give you all the particulars when Loudon comes back. He has sold his Sugar Plantation and is now a man

Figure 3.7: Ardtornish House, Morvern, Scotland. The home of Gillian and Angus Maclaine's uncle, John Gregorson, where the boys spent much of their youth (Collection of the Author)

of 25–30,000 pounds property, and having nothing to do, I advised his making a voyage in the 'Justina'. . . . I have some plans, very unformed as yet, in view by which we (that is, you and I) can do good to some Highlanders and benefit ourselves.[45]

'Unformed as yet,' the plans rapidly came to fruition, in the form of a 640-acre landholding named 'Ardtornish' in homage to the property owned in the Highlands by the Maclaine brothers' maternal uncle, John Gregorson, in a part of Scotland, the Morvern Peninsula mid-way up the west coast, where sheep-runs became as ubiquitous as they were becoming in the Antipodes (Figure 3.7): indeed, the arrival of ungulates of this kind in Scotland and the Antipodes was virtually contemporaneous,[46] giving rise to parallel histories that blurred the distinction between metropole and colony. An erstwhile *tacksman* of the Duke of Argyll, Gregorson was the proprietor of an extensive sheep farm on the Peninsula; and it was there, at Ardtornish House, that, along with their mother, the two siblings had spent much of their childhood and early youth.[47] With its First Nation Kaurna inhabitants driven off or otherwise 'dispersed', Gregorson's nephew repopulated the *other* Ardtornish with sheep from New South Wales, well over a thousand kilometres to the east, together with a score or more of

Figure 3.8: Ardtornish, South Australia - the house built near Adelaide by Angus Maclaine, younger brother of Gillian Maclaine. Photographed in the late 20th century (Collection of the Author)

impoverished Highland families recruited from his former parish of Ardnamurchan, on Morvern's bleak north-western coast (Figure 3.8).[48] The upshot was to open the possibility for Donald Maclaine of Lochbuie, the Reverend Maclaine's cousin now established in the Indies, to use South Australia as a convenient destination for his own indigent and in some cases unruly kin.

This was certainly the case with Alexander Maclaine, the most immediately needy of Donald Lochbuie's younger brothers, who had initially been destined (so it would appear) for employment of some sort on Java but for whom his sibling (on his arrival there) quickly sought an opening instead on the Reverend Maclaine's sheep station near Adelaide. Writing to his cousin Donald in January 1847, the latter remarked that:

> If Alexander, your brother, comes here, let him forget all the habits of India. Here he must look sharp after every sixpence — and live roughly, do everything for himself that the boys do for you in [the Indies], at least he need not look for personal attendance. Yet if he possesses a high spirit, he will learn to like the country well.[49]

The Reverend Maclaine himself had evidently cut something of a figure in Adelaide's colonial community, not least at what might well have been the city's inaugural St Andrew's Day dinner in 1841. This appears to have been a rather sombre and sober affair, in which the majority of the sixteen toasts that marked the occasion were heavily focused on giving an uplifting public message about the financially precarious state of the colony, while the Reverend Maclaine's contribution to the gaiety of the evening took the form of a description of the 'measures which the General Assembly [of the Church of Scotland] had adopted for the promotion of Christianity among the colonies', something which he 'detailed at some length'.[50]

It was around this point in time that the narrative becomes entangled in that of another of Donald Lochbuie's penniless siblings, John Campbell Maclaine, the third oldest of the late Murdoch Maclaine's bevy of sons. Rather than opt for Java under the wing of his elder brother, he was initially employed, around 1842, in South Australia by his cousin, who was evidently somewhat sceptical of his staying-power: 'though he has not shown any flinching yet,' the Reverend Maclaine reported back to Mull, 'if John does not resolve to go through with it, the sooner he leaves the better.'[51] In fact, it looks as if he may indeed have resolved *not* to go through with it, since in 1844 he was thought to be with his brother Donald Maclaine on Java.[52] Even so, he was back in Adelaide in November 1846 – having accompanied his cousin who was returning from Europe, via the Indies, to his South Australian property.[53] Subsequently, a large flock of his cousin's sheep was 'under his charge' – and remained so when the Reverend Maclaine himself repatriated some six months later in mid-1847.[54] By 1852, however, the young man was back again in the Indies, where an overseer's job had been found for him at a sugar factory on the north coast of Central Java, in which Maclaine Watson had a financial interest.[55] How long he remained on Java is not clear: he was presumably still there in 1858, when his elder brother (on the verge of repatriating) lent him £1,000, adding to a debt of £371 incurred some five years earlier (the total debt was subsequently regarded as unrecoverable by Lochbuie's executors).[56] What is certain, however, is that he eventually found his way back to the Antipodes – though not to South Australia but to the neighbouring colony of Victoria, where, still apparently a single man, he died in the rural town of Coleraine in 1885, leaving an estate valued at just over £100.[57]

His elder brother, Alexander Campbell Maclaine, meanwhile had also found himself a marriage partner in Adelaide – Marian Palmer Sands, the English-born daughter of Adelaide settlers David Sands and Marie Austier Winterbottom – and it was in the vicinity of that city that the first two of the couple's children were born. By the mid-1850s, however, they had left South Australia for Horsham in the neighbouring state of Victoria, where they appear to have been living with yet another of Donald Lochbuie's siblings, Allan Maclaine – an individual about whom little seems to have survived in the public record, other than that he died at Sale in the Gippsland district of Victoria (where he would appear to have been a farmer) some two decades later.[58] Long before that, however, in June 1859 his brother Alexander had shipped out of Melbourne on his way back to Scotland,[59] where his arrival prompted the caustic comment from one of his brother's old business associates on Java that:

> I am amused to hear of the return to Lochbuy of Alexander Maclaine. . . . As he has come home without his wife, I fear that his Australian experiences have not improved him.[60]

The wife in question did reappear, nonetheless, and their third offspring was born in Scotland in 1863, some eleven years after their last.

Their older brother, the 22nd Laird of Lochbuie, died in Edinburgh in October of the same year, a development which may have prompted the couple to get on the move again – allied, perhaps, to a fear that his late brother's executors would demand repayment of a loan well in excess of £2,000.[61] By 1865 Maclaine and his wife were farming in Massachusetts, New England, while a year later they had relocated north of the United States border to Montreal, where a fourth child died in infancy. A final move (though there was a short interlude back in Adelaide) brought them to New Zealand, around 1868, and it was there, in or near Christchurch on South Island, that Alexander Maclaine died in 1885, predeceasing his wife by some four years.[62]

Well before this, however, there had been a further, sad pendant to Lochbuie's attempt to use his position on Java and connections in the Antipodes to benefit his siblings. His youngest brother, Colquhoun Maclaine, came out to join the family on Java, probably sometime in the first half of 1853. By late August of that year, however, he was dead at the age of 24, having succumbed – as the brief death-notice placed in several newspapers took care to explain – to a fever that had carried him off in only a few days.[63] However, the place where he died (Plantungan, in a remote spot in the mountains of Central Java, about 60 kilometres south-west of the major port of Semarang) was a small hospital set up by the colonial army in the middle of the previous decade – primarily, it would seem, because the mineral content of the adjoining hot springs was considered efficacious in the treatment of syphilis.[64] It is likely, therefore, that the recent youthful arrival had been sent there for a cure, and had instead fallen victim to some more specifically tropical affliction.

A True Highlander – and a Patrimony Lost Again

Donald Lochbuie's death (Figure 3.9), leaving a 37-year-old widow and five children ranging in ages from 7 to 18, had taken place only a few days short of his forty-seventh birthday and scarcely four years after his family's definitive return to Scotland.[65] In that all too brief interim, the 22nd Laird's commitment to the country of his birth was absolute. His widow, Emilie Maclaine-Vincent, does not appear, however, to have shared in her late husband's devotion to the Highlands. Indeed, having spent her formative years in the Indies and the Netherlands, she had no reason, beyond respect

Figure 3.9: Donald Maclaine photographed in 1862, a year before his death (Collection of the Author)

for her husband's memory, to be enamoured of Scotland. Within a few years his widow, well provided for in her husband's Will, had relocated south of the Border to a large terrace house in an eminently respectable part of central London, where the household of which she was head included her younger son, Anthony Vincent Maclaine, a married daughter and son-in-law (Frederick Campbell), and their baby.[66] Subsequently, Campbell and Maclaine, who had been in business together in the importation of 'East Indies' produce, went bankrupt after what appears to have been a promising beginning, and decade later,[67] presumably forced into cheaper accommodation on account of this, Lochbuie's widow was no longer in London but living in a boarding house in the South Coast resort of Eastbourne, which is where she died (intestate) in 1882.[68]

Long before that, however, the elder of her two sons, Murdoch Gillian Maclaine, had embarked on a very different trajectory, one that amplified his father's allegiances to no little extent.[69] To be sure, a childhood spent in the Indies – such as his had been – would seem an unlikely start to the life (as described in his obituary) of 'a true Highlander' who 'always wore a kilt' and was 'devoted to everything traditionally Highland . . . [where] every ancient custom was something to be carefully preserved'.[70] Yet such was indeed the case. The half-Dutch 23rd Laird – who proudly designated himself in the Census of 1871, though he was living near London at the time, as 'a landed proprietor of 28,000 acres in Argyllshire' – initially looked destined for a military career, but within a very few years sold his commission and settled instead for civilian life, together with a wife, Catherine Marianne Schwabe, who was a scion of a Jewish-German family that had migrated to Britain in the middle of the century and established themselves very successfully as manufacturers in the 'Cottonopolis' of Manchester, where they counted among their friends the celebrated free-trade advocate Richard Cobden.

Figure 3.10: Murdoch Gillian Maclaine (Collection Lorne Maclaine)

Notwithstanding these cosmopolitan bourgeois connections, the 23rd Laird of Lochbuie pursued a career dedicated to his heritage on Mull – and to devising ways to make that dedication financially feasible without further recourse to the wealth of the Indies. For unlike his father (and possibly at the urging of his mother) he never 'went out East'. Instead, he concentrated his efforts on making the Lochbuie estate attractive as a stalking, shooting and fishing holiday destination for wealthy southerners. Adding a further and important dimension to such pursuits, moreover, was also his long-term commitment to the promotion and preservation of Gaelic literature, music and domestic industries in the Highlands.

At the same time, Murdoch Gillian Maclaine's and his wife contrived to mingle in London High Society – where the laird was, it appears, often mistaken for the Prince of Wales, such was the similarity of their beards and builds. The two aspects of his life were in a sense complementary, in so far as his profile – literal and metaphorical – in the metropolis served to drum up business for Lochbuie. And business needed to be drummed up, because the couple's outlays appear continually to have pressed hard on their income. Indeed, when the 23rd Laird died in 1909, debts and death duties left his heir – who pushed his father's role as a 'true Highlander' to what was perhaps its logical conclusion by appearing on New York's Broadway as 'the Maclaine' – with insurmountable financial problems that culminated in the loss of the Mull estate to his less-than-scrupulous creditors. Meanwhile, the 24th Laird's widowed mother, though evidently a woman of spirit who described herself on the 1911 Census as a 'Globe Trotter', ended her days, in 1934, in a modest cottage near Bournemouth on the south coast of England, leaving an estate valued at less than £700.

Within three-quarters of a century, in short, Donald Lochbuie's work on restoring his family's patrimony had come completely undone. His story had been richly illustrative, nonetheless, of the extent to which colonial wealth, in tandem with global connections, might become the basis for restored fortunes back home, while also demonstrating its precarious nature. At the same time, it points up diaspora's role in shaping nineteenth-century Scottish identity, revealing how seemingly local Highland histories depended on (trans-)imperial connections. In so doing, it highlights the complex interplay between Scottish, British and colonial identities while illustrating broader patterns of sojourning, wealth accumulation, and repatriation. One such illustration, taking the form of an analysis of the ties that linked the

Inner Hebridean island of Islay to the wealth of the Indies, is to be found in the next chapter.

THE ISLAY NETWORK

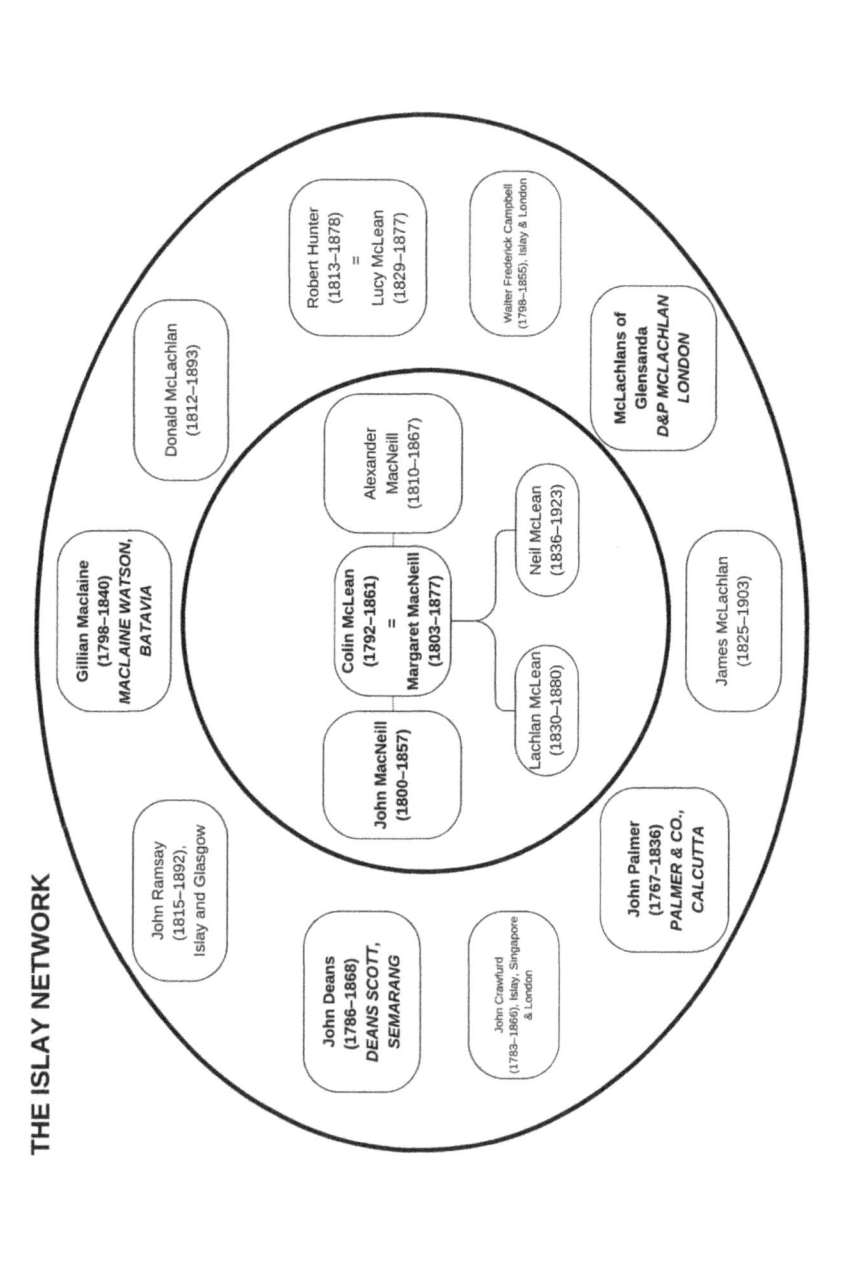

4

Islay and the Wealth of the Indies

Your nephew Lachlan McLean arrived per Salatiga at New Year and is now hard at work in the office under Von Laer in the bookkeeping department. He is a fine quiet gentlemanly lad with good manners, and I am much pleased with him. He writes a capital hand, is willing and steady, which is all that is required. He is doing his best to learn Dutch which I am pleased to find. I placed him at the Hotel for the same reason that I had with my brother at Semarang viz.: that in this way [he will] become more a man of the world and learn Dutch speedily. Next month he and [another employee] take a small house . . . close to me. At present he has . . . 150 [guilders] a month but [this] will increase . . . so that he can live as a gentleman without being extravagant. However, he looks to be a careful laddie like most of his countrymen.[1]

THE 22-YEAR-OLD Lachlan McLean (Figure 4.1) had sailed to the Indies from Rotterdam early in September 1852 on the maiden voyage of the Dutch barque *Salatiga,* launched from a Dutch shipyard in April of that year. It took McLean to the great East Java port of Surabaya, the biggest and busiest in the archipelago, where he landed at the very beginning of 1853, after a four-month voyage down the Atlantic, around the Cape of Good Hope and through the Indian Ocean. His father Colin McLean – himself an old 'Indies hand' who had no doubt dispatched him there – was evidently somewhat taken aback by the reception accorded his son on his

Figure 4.1: Lachlan McLean, Islay-born partner in Maclaine Watson (KITLV/University of Leiden)

arrival. To be sure, the young man had already left the parental home by 1851 and had most probably been installed by his father as a junior in a lawyer's office in Glasgow. Yet there was a world of difference between a boarding house run by a respectable widow in a 'good' part of Glasgow and the hazards and temptations of hotel life in Surabaya. As a result, the elder McLean had to be reassured that although 'I certainly expected that [Donald] McLachlan [the Maclaine Watson partner who had met the young man off the boat] would have taken Lachlan to live with him', on thinking over the question, 'I am just as well pleased that he has been thrown on his own resources at once.'[2]

From Islay to the Indies: Building a Network

Lachlan McLean's sojourn in the Indies, which lasted (with a short break) for the better part of two decades, was integral to the establishment there of a small diaspora from Islay, the sizeable, southernmost island of the Inner Hebrides (Figure 4.2). As an informal mercantile network originating among two of the island's socially elevated families, it exemplified a trend for kin from the financially relatively poor rural societies of Britain's Celtic 'fringe' to export *human* capital on a small scale, something that nevertheless paid very substantial dividends (both literally and metaphorically) in terms of (eventually) repatriated wealth. The key to their doing so, moreover, lay in the facility with which such essentially local networks were able to hook themselves onto global counterparts that enjoyed a far greater geographic and commercial reach. In this sense 'glocalisers' to the manner born, the McLeans and MacNeills, over the course of several generations, beginning quite early in the nineteenth century, fulfilled these several preconditions with a rare determination and degree of success. What that transfer of wealth from the Indies meant for either Islay itself or Scotland in general, nonetheless, remains altogether more problematic.

The foundational figures in bringing together the Islay network and securing its global affiliations were Lachlan McLean's father and his mother, a woman who brought critically important family connections to the nascent network. As the captain of what was termed a 'Country Ship' operating exclusively in Asian waters, Colin Mclean himself would have become well-versed in doing business in the Indies during the second and third decades of the nineteenth century. He was closely associated with Gillian Maclaine, co-founder of the Maclaine Watson concern (Figure 4.3), and with another likewise Indies-based mercantile house, Deans Scott & Co., whose co-partner, John Deans, was to become a close associate of Gillian Maclaine later as well as agent on Java for John Palmer, 'Prince of [British] Merchants' in Calcutta.[3] But he also enjoyed close relations with the island's Sino-Indonesian and Armenian merchant communities and, more than coincidentally, played an intermediary role in shipping opium from the

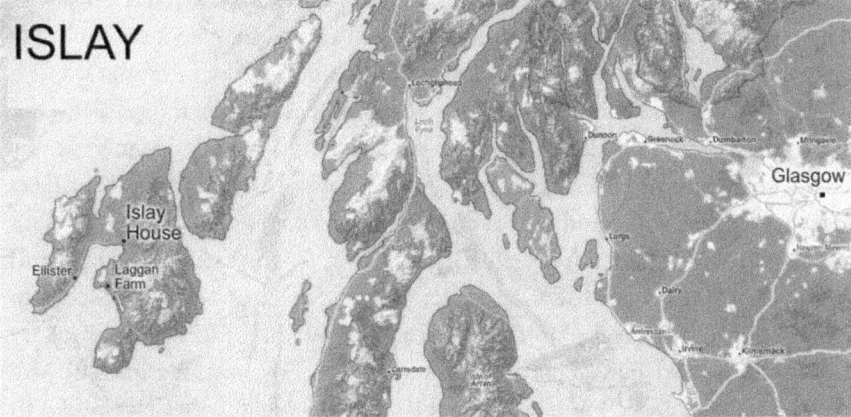

Figure 4.2: Map of Islay (Collection of the Author)

Figure 4.3: Maclaine Watson's Batavia Office, c.1865 (KITLV/University of Leiden)

Indian subcontinent into the Indies and elsewhere in maritime Southeast Asia and to the ports of southern China. As one of Deans' 'Country Captains', Colin McLean was doubtless involved in this: indeed, a 'Country' vessel that he commanded was identified as an 'opium ship' as early as 1819, at a time when the trade was in its relative infancy.[4]

As to the subsequent development of the Islay network itself, following his return from the Indies late in the 1820s, Colin McLean was aided and abetted by his wife, Margaret McLean née MacNeill, and *her* two brothers, scions of an erstwhile tacksman family at Ellister on Islay's Rhinns Peninsula. The elder of the two men, John MacNeill (Figure 4.4), arrived on Java a year or so prior to Gillian Maclaine himself, and was subsequently closely associated with him as the founder of MacNeill & Co. at Semarang – a 'sister firm' of Maclaine Watson for the next century or more. Together with those of his considerably younger brother Alexander MacNeill, his family connections offer clues as to how a network of kin based on Islay came to gain national and global connections. Meanwhile, Colin McLean's marriage to Margaret MacNeill forged a link to another West Highland family, the McLachlans of Glensanda and of Salachan – on the Morvern Peninsula some 100 miles or more by sea to its north.[5] Indeed, a relationship briefly alluded to by Gillian Maclaine – 'By the by, you can inform Mrs McLachlan Salachan that her nephew [John] MacNeill is well'[6] – proved to be a critical pivot.

It was three brothers from this same Highland family, under the leadership of Patrick McLachlan, who had established a thriving 'East India' mercantile business in London around 1813. Trading as D. & P. McLachlan, and in close association with another fellow Scot, Donald MacIntyre ('one of the sons of the British General John MacIntyre through his white mistress'),[7] they carried on an initially highly successful trade in British cotton goods to the Indian subcontinent and Southeast Asia. It was they who dispatched Gillian Maclaine to the Indies in 1820 and thereby launched him on his business career. Even before that, however, the McLachlan connection appears also to have provided a similar link (likewise from the Hebrides to the Indies) for the Islay-based MacNeills. Further ramifications of the Islay network were manifest around the mid-century when additional kin, the brothers Donald and James McLachlan, became partners in the Maclaine Watson business. Meanwhile, the direct Islay connection was further strengthened by the probable participation of yet another (adoptive) islander, John Ramsay of Kildalton, an Islay distiller and Glasgow businessman, who was said to have 'an interest in the fast-sailing ships trading with the East Indies'.[8] In combination, their operations, carried out across several continents, were an early manifestation of the trans-imperial networks seen throughout this book.

Figure 4.4: John MacNeill, elder son of Colin and Margaret McLean and friend of Gillian Maclaine (KITLV/University of Leiden)

Colin McLean, Laggan, and Mid-Century Islay

Colin McLean, the patriarch of the Islay connection to the Indies, had settled permanently back on his Hebridean island after returning from 'the East'. Not much is known about his antecedents, other than that he hailed from Kilchoman in Islay's bleak north-west.[9] A modest propertied background of some sort was implied by the fact that his wife's family had been tacksmen on Islay. Even so, observed Gillian Maclaine, who otherwise spoke highly and warmly of his 'good honest friend' and of his 'sound judgment, honourable feelings and firm principles', he was a man who 'in his early days did not have the benefit of a good education' and whose 'looks and address are not in his favour'.[10] Something more of his background and character can be imputed from the fact he remained a tenant farmer on Islay, albeit a substantial one, rather than a gentleman proprietor for the more than three decades that he spent there after his return.[11] As such, he leased 800 acres at Laggan on the island's west coast, where he employed, in 1861, the last year of his life, eight labourers, four herdsmen and a boy.[12] As an old photograph demonstrates (Figure 4.5), Laggan was a sizeable farmhouse complex, complete with the attendant yards and outbuildings of a working farm.

With four live-in domestics, McLean senior's establishment on Islay may not have been a grand one, but he and his wife evidently knew some rather grand people. Among them (he described himself as a cousin and was himself born on Islay)[13] was the celebrated John Crawfurd. Based during the 1820s as Resident in the recently established British entrepôt of Singapore, Crawfurd was the nonpareil of experts on, and lobbyists for, the colonial cause in maritime Southeast Asia through to his death in London more than forty years later.[14] Crawfurd wrote to McLean in 1854 requesting hospitality on Islay for his son and daughter who were about to visit the island and were curious 'to see what the earth is like from which their father was unkenneled half a century ago'.[15]

Even grander in terms of connection and influence, however, was Walter Frederick Campbell. A near kinsman of the Duke of Argyll, Campbell was the county of Argyll's long serving (if frequently absentee) Member of Parliament from 1822 until his retirement in 1841.[16] Above all, however, he was by far the largest of Islay's landed proprietors and the resident owner of Islay House itself prior to his spectacular bankruptcy in the late 1840s.

Figure 4.5: Laggan Farm, Islay. Home of Colin McLean and his wife Margaret MacNeill (Collection of the Author)

One sympathetic contemporary concluded that 'unfortunately, Mr Campbell was no man of business'.[17] Nevertheless, Campbell and Colin McLean were evidently on sufficiently good terms for their friendship to survive financial catastrophe and Campbell's flight to the Continent: McLean was among his lesser creditors, having lent Campbell the far from trivial sum of £1,000 back in 1837.[18] 'My dear Laggan,' as Campbell's son, John Francis Campbell invariably styled McLean, was 'the only one of my father's peers in the island who has shown him any kindness in his misfortunes,'[19] and was the only person on the island to whom his son wrote with the grim tidings on the day of father's death in Normandy in 1855. He asked McLean to pass on the news 'to any of his old friends you may happen to meet' because he is far too busy to write himself.[20]

Campbell's bankruptcy was symptomatic of an agrarian crisis throughout the Highlands and Islands that impacted on the great proprietors as well as on tenants and cottars. McLean's own verdict, penned at the request of Campbell's son in 1852, drew attention to the fate of the tenant farmers: 'the Islay tenants generally ... have not been in a prosperous state for some years back,' McLean reported, 'many ... have been sequestered and sold out during the last two years (their lands still tenantless), and I fear that many more will [soon] share the same fate.' 'I cannot help saying,' he concluded, 'that I despair of ever again seeing a numerous, well-doing and thriving tenantry in Islay.'[21] Among other things, potato blight (the same that ravaged contemporary Ireland) savagely reduced the output of the main staple of food production. Meanwhile, what was until the mid-century an ever-increasing population put pressure on agricultural resources which, for whatever reason, were not sufficiently developed to cope with an agrarian crisis exacerbated by the collapse of kelp gathering and processing (in the face, among other things, of cheap imports of the ash to which it was burnt for use in the manufacture of glass and soap), low prices for cattle, poor cereal harvests and inadequate links to markets on the mainland.[22]

In short, the specific background to Lachlan McLean's 'going out' to the Indies in 1852 combined the dire social and economic conditions of mid-century Islay with his own immediate family history. His father's financial standing was not such as to enable his heirs to have any expectation that they could live off inherited wealth: indeed, when he died in 1861 Colin McLean's 'fortune', including the Laggan farm stock and implements, amounted to no more than £4,000.[23] His connection with the Maclaine Watson mercantile network in both the Indies and Great Britain, however, had offered a ready solution.

Meanwhile, four years after his father's death and some twelve years after his own departure from Islay, his elder brother, Lachlan, had returned briefly to his native turf. Already a partner in the Maclaine Watson concern

Figure 4.6: Kilchoman Free Church, where Lachlan McLean married Elizabeth Cameron in 1865 (Collection of the Author)

of some four years standing by that date, in the middle months of 1864,[24] the by now 34-year-old was wealthy enough to have been able to make a relatively speedy journey home by the so-called Overland Route, via the Red Sea and the Mediterranean. For those who could afford it and for the mails which it carried, it had a transformative effect unmatched until the arrival of civilian air travel in the 1920s. For Lachlan McLean and his ilk, some sixty or more years earlier, it meant that they could take 'home leave' without having to endure a return journey eight months or more to do so. In his case, moreover, it gave him the opportunity to make a truly endogamous marriage: indeed, that may have been his prime object.

His bride was Elizabeth Cameron, an Islay-born woman some fifteen years his junior and the younger of the two daughters of the Reverend Alexander Cameron of Kilchoman and his wife Mary Cameron née Stiles. Having joined the strongly evangelical, breakaway Free Church at the time of the Great Disruption in the Church of Scotland in 1843, Cameron and his wife were obliged to leave the grand manse and nearby church in Kilchoman township – where he had been the pioneering first incumbent nearly two decades earlier – and relocate to Port Charlotte, some eight miles away on the shores of Loch Indaal, where an altogether humbler Free Church and manse were erected.[25] It was there that McLean wed the minister's daughter in July 1865 (Figure 4.6),[26] shortly before returning to the Indies with his bride. Nearly five years were to elapse before they returned (this time permanently) to Scotland.

Over the course of those years, Elizabeth McLean, as she now was, became integrated into the network linking Islay to the Indies not only as a marital partner and child bearer, but also as the bringer into the enterprise of an older brother, Alexander Patrick Cameron. Recast from his role as a humble clerk in a Glasgow sugar warehouse into a prominent figure in what had become one of the biggest sugar-trading concerns in Asia, Cameron repatriated in 1899 (after almost a quarter of a century as a partner in Maclaine Watson), bought a grand house in London's West End, as well as large country house back in Scotland.[27]

Doing Well: Sugar and the Sugar Trade

Once back on Java, Lachlan McLean set about consolidating his financial position – one that was strong enough by the close of the 1860s for him to retire from an active role in the firm and repatriate while not yet forty. A vital clue as to how he (and his contemporaries in the cohort of families that gravitated around Maclaine Watson) managed this emerges from the surviving fragments of his and his wife's correspondence. While the couple were still in the Indies, in August 1867, Elizabeth McLean wrote from Batavia to one of her relatives in Scotland that her husband was currently away on business 'up country', inspecting some sugar factories[28] – something indicative of the larger context in which McLean made his money, for by the time that he became a partner, sugar was the commodity that played the dominant role in Maclaine Watson's dealings. In several of the colony's key production areas, indeed, they enjoyed a virtual monopsony, based on the partnership's position as the unique buyer in a field of many sellers. Among other things, around 1870 the firm was reputed to have a stranglehold on the sugar output of a sizeable tract of coastal West Java and of much of the island's Eastern Salient,[29] and a little over a decade later they were reliably reported to have cornered around 40 per cent of the colony's entire sugar export. Any more precise calculation is precluded by the fact that most of Maclaine Watson's sugar was not bought on the open market but came directly from factories in which 'it had an interest':[30] for although the firm owned only a handful of Java's factories it evidently had contractual arrangements with scores more, which were supplied with capital in return for delivery of their output.

That output, in turn, was contingent on the 'serf-itude' of Java's peasantry whose land and labour – commandeered under the aegis of the Cultivation System – underpinned the exponential growth of an industry whose exports of sugar increased in volume between 1830 and 1885 by well over fifty-fold, from scarcely 7,000 metric tonnes annually to something approaching 400,000 tonnes, equivalent to around 10 per cent of the world's recorded output of the commodity.[31] Indeed, even by the time that Lachlan McLean exited the colony permanently in 1870, Java was already well on the way to becoming the 'Asian Cuba' – the oriental equivalent of the Caribbean Island that was already beginning its rise to become the leading world exporter of cane sugar. For Maclaine Watson itself, minimal outlay on land and labour inputs combined with sound investment in advanced manufacturing technology – in conjunction no doubt with canny business dealings – meant that the partners were able, over the decades, to make very good money.

An important insight into the actual extent of their profits comes from a minute, dating from April 1872, in the archives of the Java Bank (DJB), the Batavia-based institution that was Maclaine Watson's long-term and principal financier. A record of interview with one of the firm's senior partners, it reveals that their recent net profits, averaged over the years 1869–71, gave an annual return on capital of more than 25 per cent. It also transpired that one of McLean's predecessors had left the partnership less than a decade earlier with a capital of around £67,000 (approximately £10 million at today's prices) – while the share one of McLean's co-partners in the firm's 1871 net profits apparently amounted to £38,000 (reflecting the increased scale of the firm's sugar business over the previous decade). To be sure, both men were senior in the partnership hierarchy to Lachlan McLean himself and can therefore be assumed to have enjoyed a significantly larger share of the annual take. Nonetheless, their wealth provides some index to what even a junior partner might have been worth.[32] The partner concerned here – no longer junior by that date and firmly settled back in Scotland – observed to his younger brother in the middle of 1875 that although the 'results of last year' had not met the latter's high expectations, 'they are still very handsome' and that he was hopeful that the outcome over the next four years from the current agreement for profit sharing among the partners 'will be equally good'.[33] The point was one of some significance in relation to the issue of how repatriates deployed wealth acquired in this 'far-flung' part of the diaspora.

In the case of Lachlan McLean, the repatriate money trail, as is clear from the inventory of his assets made after his death,[34] was of a kind that would have been increasingly common among sojourner returnees of his ilk. Apart from a modest £2,000 in shares of Caledonian Railway Company, the great bulk of his capital (nearly £137,000) had been placed overseas. It was a far cry from the situation of less than a century earlier, when Scottish sojourners who had grown wealthy in 'the East' had ploughed their capital back into their native soil.[35] It was, however, very much in keeping with a broad trend, already in evidence well before the end of the nineteenth century, for wealthy Scots (returnee sojourners among them) and for wealthy Britons in general to invest abroad rather than domestically.[36] A very substantial tranche of this particular returnee's capital (around £53,000) took the form of deposits in one or other of three London-based mercantile banks that did their business virtually exclusively in Asia and the Antipodes: the Oriental Banking Corporation; the Chartered Mercantile Bank of India,

London and China; and the Chartered Bank of India, Australia and China.[37] It is curious that a further £20,000 of McLean's capital was tied up in bond issues of the Portuguese, Spanish, Chilean, Argentinian, Egyptian and Japanese governments. Even so, the far larger sum of £50,000 had not been repatriated at all, but instead had been left where his expertise was undoubted: it was booked by his executors as 'the deceased's interest in the business of Messrs. Maclaine Watson & Company, Merchant, Batavia, in the island of Java'.

As this suggests, although based on Islay, the repatriate had evidently maintained a keen watch on those of his assets that continued to be in the Dutch colony. Indeed, one of the things he did during the first months after his return was to make a trip to Holland (among other places on the Continent),[38] where he would no doubt have been in contact with the leading Amsterdam mercantile firm of Van Eeghen (they had been Maclaine Watson's commercial associates in that city since the 1850s),[39] and visited his firm's Netherlands-based present and former partners. Among the latter would likely have been the Amsterdam-born Johannes Jacobus Blanckenhagen and his Indies-born wife, Dorothea Elisabeth Sebo, who had relocated to the Netherlands a couple of years earlier,[40] after having spent their last weeks in the Indies with the McLean family before taking 'the English Mail' to Europe.[41] Business, under these circumstances, might well be combined with pleasure. Hence while McLean was holidaying in Cannes with his wife and family in March 1880, he was also getting information on the 'very satisfactory' outcome of some dealings in sugar evidently conducted in cooperation with another of Maclaine Watson's Netherlands-based partners, Frederick Bogaardt, who, together with *his* family, was holidaying further east along the Riviera at Nice, whence the McLeans went to join them, staying at the Hôtel de France.[42] These happy times were destined to last for only few more months.

Homecoming to a 'Princely Residence'

Lachlan and Elizabeth McLean had arrived back on Islay in mid-1870 (this time permanently) with their two Java-born offspring. Their return would have reunited them with their surviving parents. The Reverend Cameron and his wife, Mary Cameron-Stiles, were still in residence at Port Charlotte, where her father remained Kilchoman's Free Church minister, and at the time of the 1871 Census their grandson, the 4-year-old, Java-born Colin Alexander McLean Jnr, was recorded a 'visitor' to their household.[43] Lachlan McLean's own father had died in 1861, a full decade after his elder son's departure for the Indies and some two years after his younger son had sailed in the same direction. Indeed, the older man's will concludes with a poignant little codicil, penned only ten days before his passing, containing the observation 'that there is [now] no likelihood of either of my sons Lachlan and Neil returning from Java before my death'.[44]

Their mother, the widow Margaret MacNeill-McLean, on the other hand, was very much alive. After her husband's passing, she had moved from Laggan farm to Newton House near Bridgend – together with a complement of furniture and silver plate valued at £200. Living a mile or so from where her repatriated son and daughter-in-law had subsequently taken up residence, in early in the 1870s, she maintained a household that employed three servants, and included her youngest daughter, Flora McLean, and an infant grandchild, Rennie Ballingal – the only child of her middle daughter Annabella McLean-Ballingal, who had died some four years earlier.[45] The widow herself died – 'suddenly', according to the death notice inserted in several newspapers – at the beginning of April 1874. The placement of those notices is itself revealing. For although at least one was in a Scottish newspaper, two others were in publications in the metropolis, the *London Evening Standard* and the *Pall Mall Gazette*.[46] As such, they were presumably placed by her London-based eldest daughter, Lucy McLean, and her husband Robert Hunter – a City insurance broker who had formerly been active in business of some kind in Calcutta and whose incorporation through marriage into the Islay network was a further illustration of the way in which the 'womenfolk' of the family contributed to those linkages that connected the local to the national and the global.[47]

In the case of his mother-in-law, moreover, the London connection hinted at a social profile at some remove from that of an 'obscure' widow 'immured' in the Inner Hebrides. The presumption must be that at various times after her daughter's marriage on Islay in 1855, and after she was widowed six years later, Margaret MacNeill-McLean had travelled south to visit the Hunter-McLean couple and their growing family, and that as a result she was well-enough known among their acquaintances in the capital for news of her death to be circulated there. Clearly not a *wealthy* woman (her late husband had not been rich man), on her death she still left a small portfolio of shares which, together with a bank deposit, were worth a little over £2,000. It was a mere pittance, nonetheless, in comparison with what her elder son had accumulated in the Indies and who had deployed a modicum of it to set up in some considerable style on Islay: a style, indeed, far removed from that which either he or his wife had known there previously.

As has been remarked of mid-nineteenth-century diasporan returnees to the Western Highlands and Islands in general, the acquisition of an estate – even a leased one, as was the case here – was indeed 'a material and symbolic moment',[48] and social elevation was clearly high on Lachlan McLean's agenda. Even before he had returned from Java, he had paved the way for his family's repatriation, by taking a long lease on Islay House, by far the island's largest and most impressive property (Figure 4.7). Located on the west coast, near the village of Bridgend, and set in extensive and well-laid-out grounds, it was, as one contemporary described it, a 'Princely residence'.[49] After the financial collapse in the late 1840s of its previous owner, Walter Frederick Campbell, the great house, along with much of the island itself, had found a buyer in the English multimillionaire businessman James Morrison, who had paid £451,000 for it in 1853.[50] His family and heirs had multiple properties elsewhere in Britain, and were evidently happy to find a wealthy tenant. The estate, as described later in the century in *The Field*, covered more than 40,000 acres, while the mansion itself boasted 'three public rooms' and a billiard room, as well as 'about twenty bedrooms ... besides kitchens and ample servants accommodation',

Figure 4.7: Islay House. Leased by Lachlan McLean (Collection of the Author)

complemented by stabling for six horses and two coach houses.[51] Lachlan McLean, in short, was installed on Islay in a far more opulent style than his father had ever been at the working farm at Laggan some six or so miles away; there was, of course, a farm on the Islay House estate, but it was a physically quite separate enterprise, based around a courtyard well away from the main residence.

As the master of Islay House, McLean was unquestionably the foremost figure in the island's social hierarchy, following in the footsteps of four generations of patriarchal Campbell proprietors who had relinquished their position (and mansion) on Islay scarcely two decades earlier, and well within the living memory of many of the Island's older inhabitants. In September 1870, for example, when he had been back on the island for only a few months, 'Lachlan McLean Esq., Islay House, kindly consented to act as commodore' at the Islay Regatta, where the stewards included his brother-in-law Robert Ballingal and his younger brother Neil, currently 'on leave' from the Indies.[52] How great McLean's prestige really was, of course, is not easy to judge. At the British general election of 1880, Neil McLean (who had himself repatriated some five years earlier) wrote to his holidaying elder brother urging him to use his influence in the Conservative (or Unionist) cause by writing a letter for circulation on Islay in support of their candidate, Lieutenant-Colonel John Wingfield Malcolm. Although modestly declaring that 'I am afraid that you greatly overstate my influence politically . . . whatever little I might possess in person would avail nothing in a letter', the older man nonetheless promised such a missive if his brother would send him a draft[53] (since Malcolm subsequently lost the election, McLean's modesty may not have been misplaced).

Islay Transformed

Lachlan and Elizabeth McLean's social elevation on Islay had taken place in significantly changed local circumstances. For her, the big house with its elaborately laid-out grounds, commanding views down the loch, along with a bevy of live-in servants to manage (there were nine at the time of the 1871 Census, including a butler and footman) must have given life a quite different aspect from that of the modest Free Church manse, four miles away, in which she had grown up.[54] Even so, another aspect of her new life on Islay was less novel, in the sense that it involved a continuation of the role which she had already begun to play while on Java: that of child bearer for this branch of the Islay diasporan network, a key facet of her life that was highlighted by the presence in her new household of a wet nurse and a nursemaid, the former recruited locally and the latter hired from south of the Border.[55]

Whatever degree of change Cameron-McLean experienced in her personal circumstances, however, might have been matched by what both she and her husband could hardly have failed to observe about the island world to which they had recently repatriated. The wealthy man to whom she was married, fifteen years her senior, might well have been more aware than his wife of the extent to which Islay had been denuded of people since his boyhood there in the 1830s,[56] when its recorded population peaked at around 15,000. Thereafter, emigration either to the Scottish Lowlands or, increasingly, across the Atlantic to Canada, promoted and financed by several newly installed proprietors, culminated in the 1860s, by which time perhaps one quarter of Islay's population had departed the island. At the same time, in developments that had their origins late in the eighteenth century, Islay's remaining population was heavily concentrated in new townships where they found employments including fisheries and distilling.

To be sure, Islay around the mid-century was not completely tamed. Nor were the spirits consumed there exclusively of local provenance. Indeed, in May 1859 a drunken affray, involving several hundred people, had taken place on the island's northern shore, when a wrecked ship had been looted — much in line with the traditions of British coastal dwellers generally[57] — of many cases of alcohol. Two policemen who attempted to intervene were driven off by the mob and one of the leaders, a fisherman said to be the biggest and strongest man on Islay, was later found literally dead drunk on the beach.[58] Even so, the incident was, by that date at least, sufficiently unusual for it to be widely reported in Scottish newspapers as far away as Inverness, and the secular trend, in tandem with the culling of the population, was towards the 'Highlandism' of the shooting and stalking fraternity. It was no accident, therefore, that the same advertisement in *The Field* (which dated from the early 1890s) that listed the attributes of Islay House, itself also drew attention to the fact that the estate had 'fair salmon and sea trout fishing' and had 'plentiful grouse, blackgame [a kind of grouse], partridges, woodcock, snipe, duck etc., besides hares and rabbits'. Indeed, some forty years earlier, an attempt to lease the mansion by Campbell's Trustees in

1849 had likewise lauded the rich potential of its 'shootings' and the 'superior' opportunities for fishing, along with the promise of 'numerous roe deer'.[59]

Evidently, none of this had been lost on McLean during his tenancy beginning two decades later: 'went last week to the lighthouse for a couple of nights,' he wrote his younger brother, Neil, in October 1871, and 'we were pretty successful, having bagged about 35 brace of grouse and black cock.'[60] During the course of the decade that followed it looks as if, at Islay House as elsewhere in the Highland and Borders, the pursuit of game became a more formalised affair, centred on the 'Glorious Twelfth' [of August] when the grouse shooting season opened. Admittedly, there is no reason to suppose that Lachlan McLean indulged in the grotesque, large-scale massacres of feathered birds that were such a feature, later in the century, of large, landed estates, both in Scotland and England – a development that took place under the ultimate patronage of no lesser a well-rounded figure than the future Edward VII. Even so, it can be reasonably assumed that an invitation to join the shoot would have been a warmly anticipated event in the calendar of McLean's acquaintance. Who else were those 'around twenty bedrooms' meant to house? Sadly, those visitors, no doubt arriving early August 1880, would have been greeted with the news of (or actually witnessed) the sudden expiry (he died at Islay House on the 9th from acute appendicitis) of their host, scarcely fifty years old and the survivor of nearly twenty years in the ostensibly death-dealing tropics.[61]

The Flight Southwards

Elizabeth Cameron-McLean was only 35 when her husband died – and she was to outlive him by some 55 years (Figure 4.8). A story handed down in the family is that she was so devastated by his death that she fled to the South and never returned to her native Scotland. And it was indeed in the South that this resourceful widow, now the sole parent of seven children ranging in ages from 2 to 14, brought up her now fatherless progeny: something materially assisted by her late husband's solicitude in leaving her the income from £40,000 worth of investments which would have assured her of an annual £1,600 or more and made her a substantially wealthy woman.[62] Even so, not everything went well: in 1899, her youngest son died in wretched circumstances while still in his mid-twenties. He had made something of a hash of setting up (somewhat prematurely) as a country gentleman in the English county of Norfolk, and was planning to relocate to Argentina when he was killed in a freak railway accident in the south-west of Ireland whilst out walking with his fiancée.[63]

Almost twenty years before that calamity, his mother had taken a house in the Blackheath-Greenwich area on London's south-eastern fringe, where her eldest son initially went to Blackheath School (he was later an undergraduate at Brasenose College, Oxford) and her eldest daughter quite possibly went to its 'sister school' opened in 1880 'to provide a standard of education for the young women of Blackheath, comparable to that of the boys'.[64] Sometime later in the decade, however, the family moved to Hampstead on the city's salubrious northern heights, to Fitzjohn's Avenue, a grand, recently developed tree-lined boulevard studded with large houses, described by *Harper's Magazine* in 1883 as 'one of the noblest streets in the world'.[65] Cameron-McLean's household there was soon joined by her newly-wed eldest son Colin Alexander McLean, an army officer, and his wife Dora Georgina Rivers Thompson, the daughter of a colonial official whose career had culminated in his appointment as Lieutenant-Governor of Bengal.[66]

It was from this same address that in 1896 the widow's eldest daughter, Mary Stiles McLean, wed the London-born stockbroker, fellow Hampstead resident, George Percy Howard. The McLean household was still in Fitzjohn's Avenue at the beginning of the new century, although Cameron-McLean herself was not in residence; instead, she was staying in the Branksome Tower Hotel, near the resort towns of Poole and Bournemouth in south-west England, together with her youngest daughter Elizabeth Nora McLean.[67] It may have been at the Branksome Tower that the 23-year-old first met her future husband, Harold Whiteman Woodhall, an engineer whose father was a wealthy industrialist from Liverpool,[68] and who (as the Census reveals) was also staying at the hotel with his father and two of his sisters. The 'Branksome', it is worth pointing out because of what it implies about Cameron-McLean's social standing (and aspirations) was no simple seaside boarding house. Rather, it was a grand hostelry, established in 1892, sited majestically on a cliff-top and, as 'one of the most luxurious and well-appointed hotels on the South Coast', had an international reputation and was frequented by people of quality, among them (it was claimed) aristocrats, diplomats, and royalties.[69] Whatever the precise circumstances of their meeting, it was Woodhall whom she wed in July of the same year. After war service in 1914–18 that saw the husband rise to the rank of

Figure 4.8: The widow, Elizabeth Cameron-McLean, and five of her children (Collection Ann Crickhowell, London)

Lieutenant-Colonel, the couple retired to rural Dorset, latterly to a picturesque manor house some five miles from the county town of Dorchester – a well-heeled location reflected in the fact that the Colonel's widow left an estate worth over £76,000 when she died in 1959.[70] In these different matrimonies there were two salient facts in common: in the first place, none of the marital partners concerned were themselves Scots; and, secondly, all the couples remained domiciled well south of the Border. Islay itself was a long way off.

A similar pattern of total physical severance from the family's Scottish roots was discernible in the life-story of Cameron-McLean's second son. Born in the Indies, Alexander McLean returned there, following in his late father's footsteps, as a partner in the Maclaine Watson sugar business; but, unlike the older man, 'married out' to a Dutch woman (Francina Henriette Gill) born in the colony[71] – and on repatriation lived in affluent retirement with her in a villa in Roehampton, immediately to the south-west of London.[72] Only his one surviving male sibling deviated from the norm of his generation. Colin Alexander McLean took a commission in a regiment with strong links to the Highlands and, once he had resumed civilian life, became Chief Constable of Inverness-shire in Scotland's north. Even so, although he died in Edinburgh in 1937 and his widow remained north of the Border until her own death almost a quarter of a century later, she herself was a woman of solidly English rather than Scottish ancestry.[73]

By the second decade of the twentieth century Elizabeth Cameron McLean (Figure 4.9) no longer had a household in Hampstead (the family had grown up and mostly moved away) and in 1911 at the age of 66 she was living, together with her daughter, Lucy (who had remained a single woman) and two maids, in the recently opened and luxurious Great Central – 'among the grandest of the London railway hotels' – in London's Marylebone.[74] A decade later, mother and daughter were still domiciled in central London, where they shared a house in a 'good' part of Paddington, a little to the north of Hyde Park, which is where Cameron-McLean seems to have remained until her death in 1935.[75] Lucy McLean herself died, still in London, in 1953, eighteen years after her mother and having outlived all but one of her siblings.[76]

Figure 4.9: *Elizabeth Cameron, who outlived her husband Lachlan McLean by 55 years (Collection Ann Crickhowell, London)*

Conclusion: Islay and the Diasporan Trail from the Indies

Lachlan McLean and his younger brother (Colin McLean's two Islay-born sons) were by some margin the richest of the Islay contingent active in the Dutch colony during the third quarter of the nineteenth century, and in neither case did their money flow back as investment to their Hebridean birthplace – or to anywhere else in Scotland. Instead, their Indies-made fortunes were either not repatriated at all and remained on Java as capital for the sugar-trading partnership in which they had spent their sojourning years, or else (and this was the case with the greater part of their funds) were deployed in ways that made them available, virtually exclusively, for investment abroad. It might well be said, of course, that they were doing no more than a following the trend which characterised the British economy in general from the mid-nineteenth century onwards, and that they were simply maximising the profits that were ultimately returned to Scotland from the diaspora.

Yet, in so far as can be judged, the actual situation was a good deal more complicated than this might suggest. Above all, this was because the diasporan fortunes amassed by Lachlan McLean and his brother appear largely to have been expended on promoting and sustaining their family's social elevation – something that also came to involve locational shifts that raise, among other things, questions about 'Scottishness' and identity that cannot be easily answered. What can be said with some certainty, however, is that after Lachlan McLean's untimely death, the nexus between Islay itself and the wealth of the Indies was decisively broken. His widow took her family down to London where they all contracted exogamous marriages and, with one exception, remained domiciled south of the Border. It was likewise with virtually all the family of another foundational member of the Islay 'network', Alexander MacNeill, and it is to his story, and that of his wife and their offspring, that we can now turn.

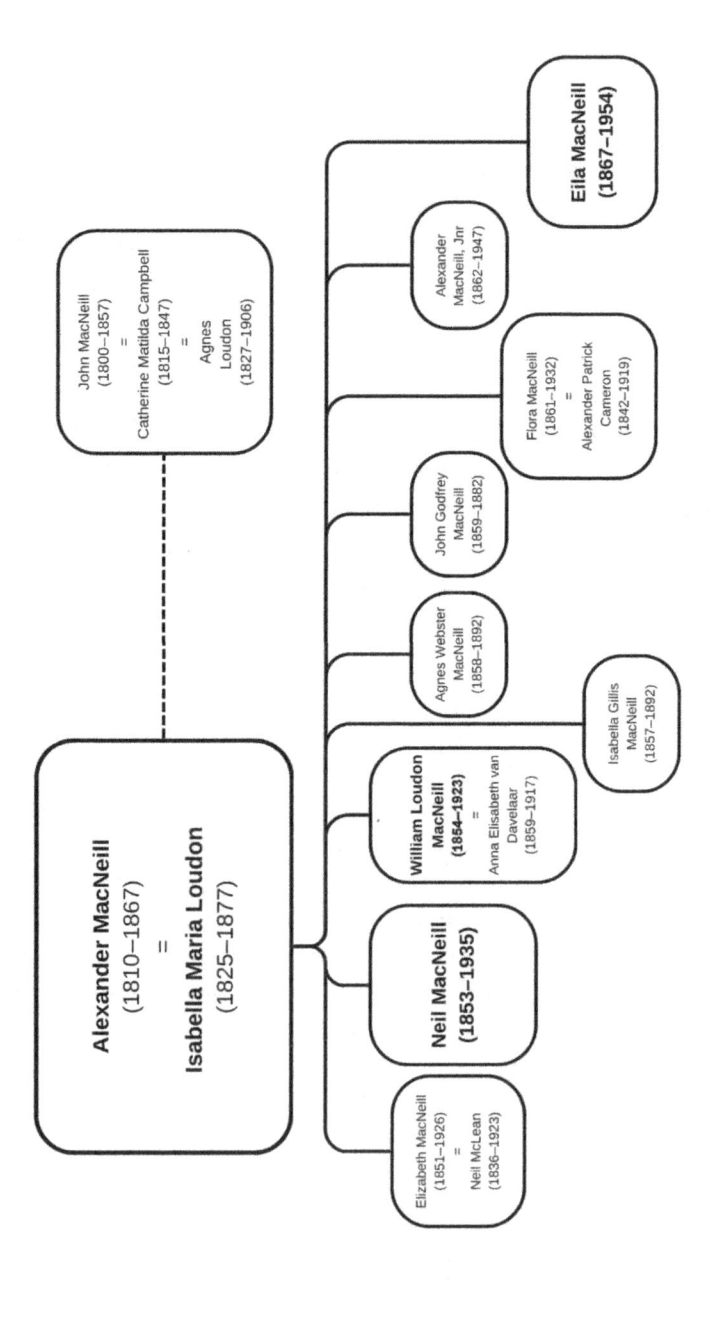

5

Death in Bournemouth and a Surrogate Scotland

ALEXANDER MACNEILL, 'late of Java', died in Bournemouth on 13th April 1867, two days after his wife had given birth to their ninth child (Figure 5.1).[1] He was 57 and Isabella Loudon, as she had been before their marriage in Edinburgh in 1850, was his junior by 15 years. Almost certainly stricken with tuberculosis, he had brought his family south to Bournemouth, an English coastal resort that was fast becoming 'an invalid's Paradise', famous not only as 'a metropolis of bath chairs' but also as the locale of a grand sanatorium, which boasted more than ninety beds 'for consumptive patients and for those suffering other diseases of the chest'. 'They come here to die,' wrote the man who laid out the gardens by the pier: 'Let us make death beautiful.'[2]

MacNeill's death was a pivotal moment in the family history recounted in this chapter, one that focuses on his transition from colonial businessman to Scottish landowner and on the life stories of his immediate *British* descendants. For during Alexander MacNeill's sojourn in the Indies, he had co-habited with a Javanese woman whose son went on to become a leading figure in Maclaine Watson before settling with *his* family not in Britain but in the Netherlands (we shall return to his story later in the book). Repatriated on the other side of the North Sea, meanwhile, Alexander MacNeill established a further lineage whose commercial connection with the Southeast

Asian archipelago lasted into the mid-twentieth century but whose ramifying histories presented in total a picture of great diversity. While emphasising the global connections that underpinned even seemingly local histories and the complex interplay between Scottish, British and colonial identities during the late imperial era, they complicate to a degree our understanding of the diaspora in question. In this broad context, what follows develops two major themes: the first concerns repatriation and its associated money trail

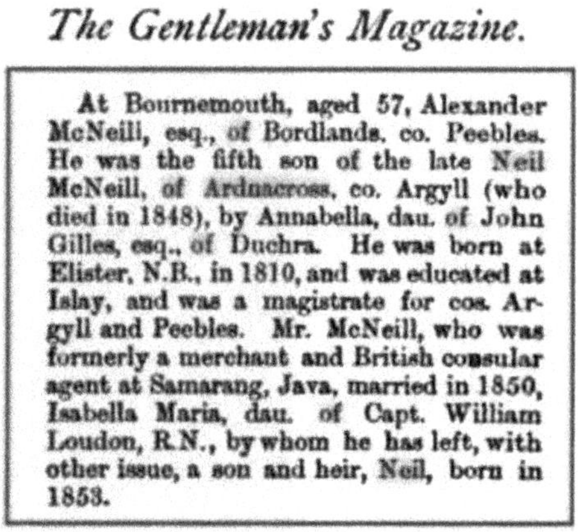

The Gentleman's Magazine.

At Bournemouth, aged 57, Alexander McNeill, esq., of Bordlands, co. Peebles. He was the fifth son of the late Neil McNeill, of Ardnacross, co. Argyll (who died in 1848), by Annabella, dau. of John Gilles, esq., of Duchra. He was born at Elister, N.B., in 1810, and was educated at Islay, and was a magistrate for cos. Argyll and Peebles. Mr. McNeill, who was formerly a merchant and British consular agent at Samarang, Java, married in 1850, Isabella Maria, dau. of Capt. William Loudon, R.N., by whom he has left, with other issue, a son and heir, Neil, born in 1853.

Figure 5.1: Death Notice of Alexander MacNeill, who died in Bournemouth – aged 57 (Collection of the Author)

Figure 5.2: Alexander MacNeill, partner in Maclaine Watson and husband of Isabella Loudon (KITLV / University of Leiden)

and the second (interwoven with this) relates to an evolving relationship to 'Scotland' on the part of MacNeill's British descendants.

Alexander MacNeill himself had arrived on Java from Islay in the mid-1830s (Figure 5.2) to join his considerably older brother, the same John MacNeill whom Gillian Maclaine and his bride had visited on their honeymoon jaunt through the island a few years earlier. The pair were key actors in a 'glocalising' commercial network that linked Inner Hebridean Islay to the archipelagic Dutch empire in Southeast Asia from the 1820s onwards. Trading from Semarang as MacNeill & Co. (a business that remained operating in Semarang until the eve of the Second World War) the brothers engaged in the import-export trade that flourished between the north coast port and its hinterland beyond the mountains in the agriculturally rich and heavily populated, volcano-strewn plains of South-Central Java. As such, they were people of some standing among the Dutch colonial communities among whom they found themselves, one indicator of which was the degree of their involvement in Java's network of masonic lodges. Presumably already initiated into the brotherhood before leaving their native Scotland (where the lodges also held considerable sway), John MacNeill was credited with helping revive Semarang's La Constante et Fidèle Lodge, first established in 1798, during his lengthy sojourn in the port, while his younger sibling was likewise at various times a member of this Lodge and of its counterpart, De Vriendschap, in the great East Java port of Surabaya (Figure 5.3).[3] Unlike

Figure 5.3: Freemasons' lodge in Surabaya, of which Alexander MacNeill was a member (KITLV/ University of Leiden)

many of their colonial counterparts in the Indies, however, they were not people who (as the Dutch phrased it) 'came and stayed' – and by the late 1840s, Alexander MacNeill, after less than a decade-and-a-half on Java, appears to have made enough money to follow his elder sibling back home to Scotland.

'MacNeill of Bordlands': Repatriation and Marriage

The MacNeill family hailed from Ellister on Islay's Rhinns Peninsula, where their immediate ancestors had been 'tacksmen' (tenants in chief), and the eldest male was formally designated as 'of Ardnacross'. The youngest of four brothers, however, Alexander MacNeill did not inherit the family honorific, nor any of the proprietorial standing that putatively went with it – something that was held successively by his three older siblings.[4] Instead of his native Islay, on repatriation at the end of the 1840s he joined his elder brother in Edinburgh, where John MacNeill, after *his* repatriation earlier in the decade, had settled – at the same time describing himself as a 'landed proprietor'.[5] And it was while in Edinburgh that the younger man – still only in his late thirties when he returned to Scotland – met his future wife when, towards the close of 1849, he went to pay his respects to the brother of a fellow Scot, one whom he would have known quite well from their time together in the Indies.

The widower William Loudon and his daughters lived at Backhill House in Inveresk near Musselburgh, only a short ride to the east of Edinburgh.[6] He was a retired naval officer who, as far as we know, had never been to the Indies. His deceased younger brother Alexander Loudon, however, most certainly had. Among other things, he had been a great friend of Gillian Maclaine and would doubtless have encountered the MacNeill brothers on Java during the 1830s, since his sugar factory on Java's central north coast was within easy reach of their base in Semarang. It was Alexander's niece, Isabella Maria Loudon, whom Alexander MacNeill married in Edinburgh in July 1850 in what looks to have been a happy union of families: at least, his elder brother, John, by then a widower, wed his sister-in-law, Agnes Loudon, five years later.[7]

Within a year of their marriage, Alexander and Isabella MacNeill had bought a country property, Bordlands, in Peeblesshire, some 20 miles south-west of Edinburgh, where they set about transforming the existing

Figure 5.4: Bordlands House, Scottish home of Alexander and Isabella MacNeill (Collection of the Author)

'dwelling house in the cottage style with all the conveniences for a genteel family'[8] into a small Scottish Baronial mansion (Figure 5.4). Underwriting these new credentials, MacNeill joined the Highland and Agricultural Society and was present in 1859 when its annual meeting in Glasgow was chaired by the Duke of Atholl, a Scots grandee (and fellow Freemason).[9] Bordlands, though agriculturally highly productive, was a minnow in the waters of Scots proprietorship, covering at most 370 acres.[10] The new house itself was likewise modest: though possessing a 'double reception room' it had no more than five bedrooms.[11] Nor did it boast much in the way of the gentlemanly pursuit of game. Indeed, a couple of years after taking over there, its proprietor was reduced to applying through his brother-in-law, the Islay-based Colin McLean, to 'take a shot at a Partridge or a Hare' on the adjoining Neidpath estate of the Earl of Wemyss, whose nephew, John Francis Campbell, was an old acquaintance of McLean. The reply came back that the Earl (who had only inherited the property very recently) was himself resident there at the present time, and that any request 'would certainly meet with a refusal', though when he was absent, 'he might perhaps allow a day or two, but he is such a fell sportsman that I doubt it'.[12]

It was possibly a refusal that reflected MacNeill's relatively lowly status among the local gentry and aristocracy. Bordlands itself, nonetheless, may well have been no more than the family's alternative or even secondary home: at least, the 1861 Census found them in Edinburgh, solidly established, together with eight live-in servants, in a substantial terrace located on the western fringe of the fashionable New Town.[13] His now deceased elder brother had lived nearby but, in establishing himself there socially, it is likely that his wife and her family also played a significant role in making this repatriated, ex-Highlander feel at home among Edinburgh's close-knit elites. It was a fine place to settle, not least because it lacked the relative remoteness of the Inner Hebrides where MacNeill had been brought up. Indeed, by the time that they established themselves there, among other things the city was already well connected by railway – initially to Glasgow and, by 1848, to London and then northwards to Aberdeen two years later in 1850.

Some of Alexander MacNeill's Indies money, of course, had been spent on setting himself up as a minor country gentleman, but his outlays in this respect were quite limited. Late in the eighteenth century, several Scots returnees from 'the East' – among them retired General Patrick 'Tiger' Duff and Sir Hector Munro – as landed entrepreneurs, had invested wealth accumulated in the diaspora in ventures designed to transform the productivity of (and hence income from) Scottish agriculture. They had invested heavily, among other things, in drainage, in deep working of the soil (thereby bringing to the surface the rich subsoil hidden beneath gravel and clay), in crop rotation and stockbreeding.[14] MacNeill's Bordlands, on the other hand, at the time of his purchase was already a well-developed estate with extensive 'grass parks' – advertised as 'among the finest in the country' – on which sheep and cattle were bred or fattened for the Edinburgh market,[15] and the bulk of his fortune (at the time of his death in 1867 he was worth upwards of £55,000) went elsewhere than into agricultural improvement. Instead, it was deployed in ways that underline the complexity of assessing the impact on Scotland of diasporan homecomings. A little over half of his personal estate was accounted for by landed or urban property, most of it located in his native country, whereas the remainder took the form of shares and debentures, only somewhat less than 10 per cent of which was invested in enterprises north of the Border – mainly in a modest portfolio of shares in railway companies. His late brother John's money had likewise been invested in railways: indeed, by far the greater part of *his* repatriated capital had been placed with railway companies operating exclusively in England.[16]

Similarly exogenous investment characterised his younger sibling's portfolio, although it was structured rather differently: some 43 per cent or more of his 'free' capital had been placed with several London-based banks and finance companies whose virtually exclusive sphere of operations was overseas, while his single most substantial investment (amounting to more than 20 per cent of his total holdings in shares, debentures and stock) was in government securities of the Australian colony of Victoria.[17] MacNeill's predilection for the overseas rentier placement of capital in turn reflected the fact that, from the mid-Victorian era onwards, Scottish wealth was increasingly being diverted away from the domestic front to the Empire, and elsewhere.[18] 'Repatriated' wealth only reached Scotland in very modest amounts and was channelled, via City of London banks, brokers and finance companies, into share and bond holding, usually with a strong overseas component. To be sure, some part of the family's wealth (as we shall see shortly) went into setting up in a 'surrogate Scotland' in rural England, but it amounted to no more than a modicum.

North of Hyde Park: The MacNeill Family in London

Alexander MacNeill's widow, 'formerly of Bordlands in North Britain but late of 77 Gloucester Terrace, Hyde Park, London', only survived him by a decade, despite being fifteen years his junior.[19] Her eldest daughter, Elizabeth MacNeill, married her cousin Neil McLean[20] – thereby consolidating ties between two Inner Hebridean families who were foundational members of the Maclaine Watson cohort – and her repatriate afterlife with her husband and their seven children was spent almost exclusively in the north of Scotland. Eventually, moreover, another of the siblings and his wife moved back north of the Border after many years in London, though not to the Highlands.

The remaining MacNeill siblings, however, opted – as did their mother – for domicile in the South. Which is not to say that 'Caledonia' was forgotten: rather, it was the case that Highland pursuits, in one form or another, were now played out in the context of afterlives spent in the metropolis and in the southern counties of England with which it was closely and conveniently connected. No doubt more than coincidentally, the widow Isabella Loudon-MacNeill had settled in a part of London – the newly built stuccoed terraces and squares of Hyde Park, Paddington and Bayswater, immediately north of the Park itself – that was becoming much frequented by other returnees of the Maclaine Watson cohort, at addresses ranging from Inverness Terrace in its westernmost sector through to Oxford Square in the east, taking in along the way such prime locations as the free-standing mansions in Craven Hill (a rarity in this part of London) and the grandeur of Westbourne Terrace.

It was in this last location, at number 57, that Isabella Gillis MacNeill, the second of Alexander and Isabella MacNeill's five daughters, was living at the time of the 1891 Census.[21] A single woman aged 34, she was identified as the head of a household that included, along with six female domestics, a bevy of her kin, among whom was her youngest brother, Alexander MacNeill, Jnr, whom we shall meet again shortly. On the distaff side of the household were three of her sisters – all single themselves at that point in time – along with their Dutch sister-in-law, Anna Elisabeth van Davelaar-MacNeill. Together with her husband, William Loudon MacNeill and their four children, she was evidently staying there on a visit from Java, where the family were to remain domiciled for another six years.[22]

Within less than twelve months of the 1891 Census, however, calamity struck the household at number 57, when Isabella Gillis MacNeill and her younger sister, Agnes (both of them still in their mid-thirties), died within a fortnight of each other in January of the following year, probably from influenza. The *British Medical Journal* reported that the influenza epidemic of 1892 in London had 'culminated in the third week of January' and the statistics show a considerable number of younger people among the fatalities.[23] We know little about the pair otherwise – the Census identified both women simply as 'living on own means' – though the fact that a death notice for Agnes was placed in *The Gentlewoman*, a weekly journal started only two years earlier and already with a reputation for good writing, suggests that they were individuals of some cultivation as well as relative wealth. The journal had, in some respects at least, a feminist agenda: in 1893 it launched a campaign against 'tight-lacing', the fad for ever-smaller waists created by very tight corsets, which it described as 'this modern madness' and 'this pernicious habit', and in the following year its editor founded the Society of Women Journalists.[24] The two women were survived, among other family members, by their two sisters, the younger of whom, Eila MacNeill, never married and subsequently joined two of her likewise unwed male siblings, Neil MacNeill and Alexander MacNeill, Jnr, in a household based both in London and in the English county of Norfolk, some hundred miles or so to its north-east. Their story throws yet more light on how wealth gained from the sugar trade in the Indies was deployed by repatriates and their immediate descendants.

A Surrogate Scotland

The oldest of Alexander and Isabella MacNeill's four sons, Neil MacNeill (Figure 5.5) had 'gone out' to Java to join Maclaine Watson as a very young man early in the 1870s; was subsequently admitted as a partner; and, after nearly two decades spent mostly in Batavia, in April 1891 embarked on a leisurely voyage of repatriation via China, Japan and the United States.[25] Once back in Britain, together with his similarly unwed siblings, he had established himself in the heart of London's West End, at successive Mayfair addresses, where the below-stairs housekeeper of his bachelor establishment was Jane Craik, a woman now in her seventies who had been in service with the MacNeill family for more than fifty years, assisted by five other live-in servants.[26]

Figure 5.5: Neil MacNeill, eldest son of Alexander and Isabella MacNeill. Partner in Maclaine Watson, who retired first to London, and then to a country house in Norfolk. (KITLV/University of Leiden)

Neil MacNeill's business activities (he remained a partner in Maclaine Watson until 1917) appear to have played no more than a subsidiary role in an exceptionally lengthy repatriate afterlife that extended for well over four decades following his departure from the Indies. As was commonly the case among the returnees of the Maclaine Watson cohort, his money was productively 'invested' primarily in underpinning a genteel mode of life in both town and country (in tandem with a modest amount of local philanthropy) and the purchase of the requisite real estate, backed by a rentier portfolio of worldwide investments – managed presumably by a first-rate broker, since he was worth well over £600,000 at the time of his death in 1935.

His wealth enabled him, in addition to a Mayfair townhouse, to become the owner of a substantial country property – The Lodge, Gooderstone, near King's Lynn in deeply rural Norfolk. With its great tracts of open country and fenland, the county constituted a surrogate Scotland in respect, at least, to its suitability for replicating the Highland pursuit of feathered game, a point not lost on the Prince of Wales (the future Edward VII) when he turned his Sandringham estate into one 'of the finest shoots in England',[27] and the centre for the ritual slaughter of game birds on an epic scale that exceeded anything known north of the Border. One keen and well-heeled devotee, a long-term friend of the King, was reputed to have shot more than half a million game birds during the course of his life, which ended, appropriately enough, in the butts, at the age of 71. In his prime, he was said to have brought down twenty-eight birds in a mere sixty seconds.[28] MacNeill's own Norfolk estate, which he purchased in 1901 when the 'large freehold agricultural and sporting property of 1,367 acres' came up for sale,[29] was an altogether more modest affair, and its annual head count of dead birds likewise presumably much smaller.

It was at his Norfolk seat, rather than in London, that the eldest of the MacNeill trio died in 1935. 'Many mourners at the funeral of Mr. Neil MacNeill,' ran the headline in the *Yarmouth Independent*; and it was evident that although the deceased may have begun his career as a Scottish businessman in 'the East', he had ended it as an English country gentleman – yet one who was, nonetheless, buried in a tartan-draped coffin. It was as such that he was escorted to his grave in Gooderstone's Anglican churchyard by, among others, Sir Henry Edward Paston-Bedingfeld of neighbouring Oxburgh Hall. Along with Bedingfeld and in company with MacNeill's tenantry, teachers from the local school that he had supported and a bevy of his kith and kin, the chief mourners included Sir Thomas Leigh Hare of Stow Hall (one-time MP for South-West Norfolk and subsequently High Sheriff), Admiral Richard Morden Harbord-Hammond (one-time Deputy Lieutenant of Norfolk) and Colonel John Patrick Villiers-Stuart of Beachamwell, adjacent to Sandringham (a distinguished soldier and scion of an old aristocratic family).[30] In short, the late Mr MacNeill had evidently been well-connected among establishment figures of some note in a part of England that was well-provisioned with their kind.

An Oxford Man Returns from Exile

Neil MacNeill had been followed to the Indies not only by his next younger brother William Loudon MacNeill, but also by the youngest of his male siblings. Not yet five years old when his father died in Bournemouth in 1867, Alexander MacNeill Jnr had been expensively educated near Edinburgh at Loretto School, one of the foremost in Scotland, and subsequently became the only family member of his generation to attend university – in England rather than his native Scotland. This Oxford man arrived in Java early in the 1890s but was never admitted to the partnership. Instead, he was dispatched to manage a remote, 'up-country' plantation in East Java, in the extensive hinterland of Surabaya, where Maclaine Watson's sister firm of Fraser Eaton was based. Perhaps he had no head for business, for this was a familiar way of disposing of a useless relative. Back in the 1830s, co-founder Gillian Maclaine had located an unwanted kinsman (an uncle's natural son) in a similar fashion.[31] Situated in the Tengger Mountains and more than 16 miles from the nearest railway station on one of the many branch lines that criss-crossed Java by the end of the nineteenth century, Alexander MacNeill, Jnr's place of exile was a coffee-growing enterprise (along with some tea and chinchona), employing predominantly local Javanese wage labour.[32]

It was there, at Alas Bezoeki, that (following his own father's example) he started an 'Indies' family, his partner identified only as 'the Javanese woman Kasminah'. MacNeill, following standard Dutch colonial practice, legitimated their offspring before repatriating around 1908. There was a boy, Edward Henry Mac Neill who subsequently worked as a chemist and then as a production manager in the sugar industry on Java,[33] and a girl, Ann Jeanne Mac Neill. Moreover, having given them his family name, albeit

Figure 5.6: Eila MacNeill, youngest daughter of Alexander and Isabella MacNeill – who lived in Norfolk for much of the later part of her long life (Collection of the Author)

in its Dutch two-word variant, their 'bachelor' father evidently took responsibility for their education – though appears to have done so in the Netherlands rather than in Britain, possibly because any stigma attaching to their mixed Asian-European ancestry was very much more muted there. Howsoever that might be, he evidently kept up contact: when his and Kasminah's daughter married a teacher at a Dutch religious school in Groningen in the north-east of the Netherlands in 1920, the 22-year-old was able to identify her father as living in Piccadilly in London's West End.[34]

In fact, by that date the individual in question had been living jointly for a decade or more in both neighbouring Mayfair and in his Norfolk mansion, and it was there that he died in 1947, leaving an estate worth almost £50,000. Whether he had been gainfully employed since his return from Java almost forty years earlier seems unlikely – a brief obituary in a local Norfolk newspaper could only draw attention to the fact that in his youth he had been an 'Oxford Blue'[35] – and the available evidence from the public record merely shows that he had a taste for travel, among other things making frequent trips by sea to destinations in the Mediterranean, Portugal and Canada. Returning from one such trip in 1932, he declared himself to be an 'artist' – but as the declaration was made on the First of April this may well have been a joke.[36]

His younger sister, Eila (Figure 5.6), survived her brother Neil by almost a decade, before dying (likewise at Gooderstone) in April 1956, shortly before her eighty-ninth birthday, leaving an estate valued for probate at over £24,000.[37] Memorialised in her obituary as 'Sister of the Squire of Gooderstone', she was evidently much more than just that. Remembered as a woman who, 'after her London home was blitzed,' settled permanently at The Lodge, she subsequently became much involved in village affairs. Among other things, she was the first President of the newly founded Gooderstone Women's Institute, the local branch of a community-based national organisation dating, in England, from 1915. In the words of its most recent historian, over the decades its members played a significant role 'in the moulding of modern Britain', through 'a long tradition of activism' focused on rural women, inter alia, by encouraging women to take part in public life; promoting adult education and skills enhancement; and, not least, by pushing for equal pay for equal work.[38] MacNeill was also a member of the church-affiliated Mothers' Union, 'a most devout Christian' and financial supporter of the parish church; added to which she was on the managerial board of the local school, where, among other things, she paid for the installation of 'modern sanitation'.[39] Her funeral, though hardly as grandly attended as that of her eldest brother ('the squire') two decades earlier, was still a socially impressive one, with her near neighbour Sybil, the widowed Lady Paston-Bedingfeld, listed prominently among the mourners.

Matters of Identity

Lives spent in Mayfair and Norfolk suggest a degree of severance from things Scottish. To an extent, however, such a conclusion may be misleading. For the likes of Neil MacNeill and his siblings, Norfolk itself was a surrogate Scotland, well provided with at least some of the appurtenances of gentry life in the Highlands, above all an abundance of the wherewithal for the shooting parties that had come to form such an essential part of 'Highland' life. Moreover, the history of Alexander and Eila MacNeill's sister and brother-in-law, Flora MacNeill and Alexander Patrick Cameron, likewise points to a social milieu characterised by the complementarity of England and Scotland in the lives of the people concerned: two halves of a single homogenous whole rather than alternate or divergent ones.

Having 'gone out' to the Indies as a raw recruit to the Maclaine Watson business in the 1860s, Cameron went on to make a fortune on Java – he died in 1919 worth more than £200,000. Not for him, it would seem, an Indies marriage like some others of the Maclaine Watson cohort. Instead, it was in 1891, after repatriation and at the age of nearly 50, that he married the 30-year-old Flora MacNeill at Christ Church, Lancaster Gate,[40] in the wealthy Bayswater-Hyde Park area of West London, and finally started a family. A decade later the couple and their three children (all girls, with another in the offing) – supported by a domestic staff of seven servants, three of whom were also Scots – were settled in an imposing stuccoed terrace house in Cleveland Square, a little to the north of the Park itself, and no more than a couple of miles away from their near-relatives' townhouse in Mayfair.[41] It was not a bad outcome for the son of a Free Church minister who had been turned out of his grand manse on Islay back in the 1840s at the time of the split in the Church of Scotland (and obliged to find much humbler quarters), and who himself had been taken to Java as a needy young man of 22 by his well-to-do brother-in-law.[42]

Outliving her husband by more than a decade, sometime after his death the widow Flora MacNeill-Cameron, in company with her daughter Bridget, had retreated from London to the Highlands – to the twelve-bedroom Ardsheal House near Kentallen on the eastern shore on Loch Linnhe, some twelve miles south-west of Fort William.[43] It was a mansion which, together with its 770-acre estate, her husband had bought earlier in the century (perhaps encouraged by the fact the railway had arrived in its vicinity around 1900) and immediately greatly extended and remodelled, albeit in an architecturally haphazard style.[44] It was at Ardsheal that MacNeill-Cameron herself died in 1932, leaving an estate valued for probate at just under £10,000 (the bulk of Cameron's fortune had presumably been disbursed among his other legatees in a successful attempt to avoid further death duties). She was buried alongside her late husband at Ballachulish, about six miles from their Lochside home, at a location in which (weather permitting) they would both have enjoyed a fine view of Ben Nevis, Scotland's (and Britain's) highest mountain.[45]

In short, though partly domiciled in the metropolis, Neil MacNeill's younger sister and brother-in-law had nonetheless staked out a claim, both in life and in death, to their native Scotland. On the assumption, moreover, that intra-family visiting had been a regular feature of their *repatriate* afterlife, then they would appear to have established a network of well-heeled leisure that ran between London, rural Norfolk and various locations in Scotland. Oddly enough, the one place their itinerary did not embrace was their ancestral turf on Inner-Hebridean Islay itself. For some members of the Maclaine Watson cohort, however, as we are about to see, the umbilical cord notionally connecting them to Scotland was cut, apparently decisively, by people who remained more-or-less exclusively domiciled in London after repatriation and whose offspring made exclusively exogamous marriages.

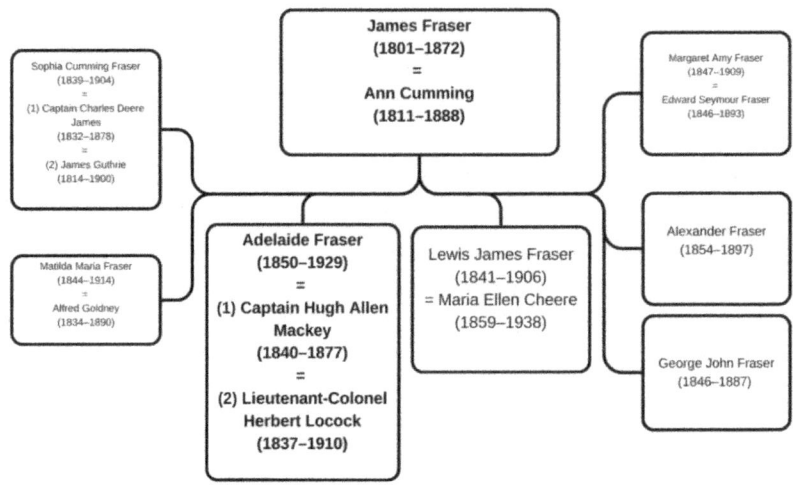

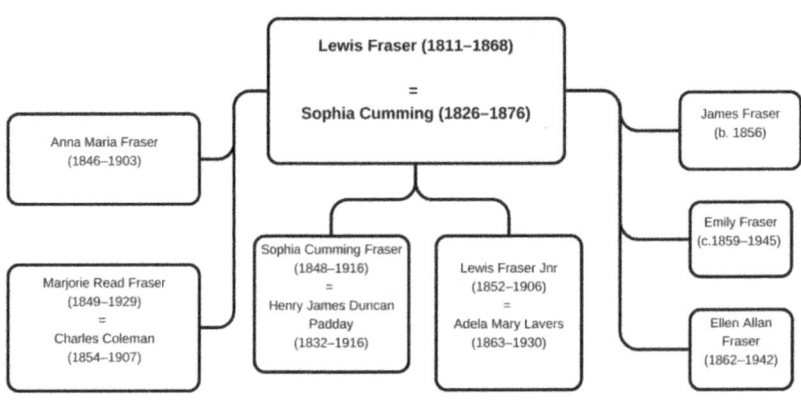

6

Good Steady Scotsmen

A 'GOOD STEADY SCOTSMAN' was the verdict of the Reverend Angus Maclaine, younger brother of Maclaine Watson's co-founder, on the compatriot with whom he stayed briefly in Singapore in June 1846:

> I had my tiffin with Frazer of Maclaine, Frazer & Co, but immediately thereafter the mail brought intelligence to Mrs Frazer of the death of a brother, a fine young man who was doing uncommonly well [as a medical doctor] in Rio [de Janeiro]. . . . I therefore would not dine at the house, then a house of mourning, and re-joined my fellow passengers at the Hotel. I slept, however at Frazer's and breakfasted with him next day . . .[1]

His hosts, Lewis Fraser and Sophia Fraser née Cumming were long term sojourners in the island-entrepôt, where the husband had arrived around a decade earlier to join his brother James Fraser in a mercantile firm that was the Singapore outlier of Maclaine Watson's Java-based business. At the time of Reverend Maclaine's visit, the as yet childless couple, their hospitality clouded by news of a family tragedy that underscored the far-flung character of the diaspora to which they belonged, were living at a large house on the Singapore foreshore;[2] and remained in the colony another seven years, before 'repatriating' to London in 1853, together with their four Singapore-born children. Their arrival in the metropolis, where they stayed for the rest of their lives, must have had the aspect of a family reunion, since James and Ann Fraser née Cumming and their family had already been settled there for the better part of a decade. Their joint history, however, and that of their descendants, while encompassing both the Lion City and London, is one that begins in the north of Scotland in the opening decade of the nineteenth century and terminates in the south of England in the 1940s.

One crucial segment of that history unfolds in a location that, while part of the British Empire, was also a trans-imperial hub that connected that empire not only to the Dutch imperium to its immediate south and west but also to the Chinese imperial realm much further to its north-east. To that extent, the part played by Singapore in James and Lewis Frasers' story highlights the connections *between* empires and across imperial boundaries (Figure 6.1). At the same time, however, it is also a story of the repatriate afterlife of diasporan families and their fortunes 'back home' over two or more generations. As such, it raises issues, already familiar from preceding discussion but raised here in an unfamiliar setting, relating to the money trail and to the larger context – one central to an understanding of the evolution of the Scottish diaspora in general – of identity, ethnicity, class and social aspiration.

Most pressingly, however, the Frasers' 'careering' over several decades and in several locations raises the question of how it all began: not least, because the north-east of Scotland may seem an unlikely location from which to connect with 'the East'. In fact, the contrary was the case. Places like James and Lewis Frasers' hometown of Forres, on the Moray Firth, some 25 miles east of Inverness, had a long history of commercial connections not only with Europe and the Americas but also with Asia. As early as the 1680s, for example, a certain James Brodie from Forres worked (as did other Scots) as a ship's surgeon for the (English) East India Company, and as such must have journeyed several times to South Asian ports, where he would no doubt have been dealing in modest supplies of trade goods (as allowed by his employers) as well as in broken bones and sick bodies. A century later, another family member, Alexander Brodie, Member of Parliament for the neighbouring seat of Elgin Burghs, was a 'nabob' who 'had amassed great wealth in India', both working for the Company and as a private merchant in Madras, before his return to Britain around 1783.[3] Meanwhile, in the town of Elgin itself, a little over 12 miles across easy country from Forres, the potential for making a fortune in Asia was prominently on display in the shape of an agglomeration of proud civic buildings paid for in part by a retired general of the Company's army.[4] Nor was he a lone figure. Back in Forres, Alexander

Figure 6.1: View of Singapore in the 1830s at the time when both James and Lewis Fraser were in business there in association with Maclaine Watson (Collection of the Author)

Falconer, brother of the town's most illustrious son, Hugh Falconer – among other things, an internationally famous geologist and botanist who spent more than two decades on the Indian subcontinent – also made a substantial mercantile career for himself in Calcutta almost contemporaneously with that of the Fraser brothers.[5] In short, there was nothing untoward for young men like these to have sought their fortunes in the places in which they later found themselves.

Singapore: Cloth, Guns and Opium

Initially, it was not in British Singapore but in Dutch Batavia that the elder of the two brothers settled on his arrival in 'the East' in 1823 and where he took up a position in the office of Gillian Maclaine, whose business affairs had not yet evolved into the Maclaine Watson partnership. Only a relatively recent arrival himself, Maclaine informed his mother that: 'Our establishment here musters strong. I have lately got out two fine young men as assistants, a Mr Frazer and a Mr Bain, both Scotchmen, to whom I have given a room each at my house, which makes our society *un peu mieux*.'[6] Most likely, therefore, it was Maclaine's own Scottish patrons and erstwhile employers, the McLachlan brothers and Donald MacIntyre, partners in the London East India House of D. & P. McLachlan, who had provided that 'connection' in the mercantile world that was absolutely necessary for even the most ambitious and enterprising.[7]

After less than three years in the Dutch colonial capital, however, Fraser was dispatched to join his firm's branch in the recently established port of Singapore. It was a location distant from Java not only in the literal sense (it was some 900 kilometres to its northwest) but also in respect to its society. In addition to being the legatee of cultural affinities and commercial ties that had long characterised relations between Scotland and the Netherlands, on Java Fraser would have found himself among a large quasi-settler colonial Dutch community many thousands strong. In Singapore, on the other hand, he was placed in an outpost that was in many ways distinctly alien. To be sure, it was a *British* outpost – a point not lost on Maclaine when he visited there in 1824 and reported (keenly aware that he had crossed an imperial frontier) that 'the sight of the old British flag displayed on Government Hill refreshed me not a little, having never seen it, at least flying, on terra firma since I left home'.[8] But it was there that familiarity largely ended. Above all, Singapore was a location at which, much more obviously than was the case in Batavia, a tiny group of diasporan Scots, along with their English and Irish counterparts, intersected with a vastly larger and altogether more ancient diaspora.

The flag to which Maclaine referred was British, but the population of the town over which it flew was predominantly Chinese. Members of their wealthy mercantile elite were to be found in the city's Chamber of Commerce and in its municipal government – and played host to visiting British colonial dignitaries of the highest rank.[9] By the 1860s people of Chinese origin accounted for around 65 per cent of the colony's inhabitants, the remainder being composed of Indians and Malays and others from elsewhere in Southeast Asia. Even by that stage – when the port had been operating as a mercantile hub for over four decades – the European population numbered no more than 330, among whom the gender balance was skewed heavily in favour of men, who outnumbered women by at least two to one. When James Fraser first arrived there, around 1826, the numbers were much smaller – only 70 to 80 individuals, who were primarily traders, government officials and military or naval officers[10] – and the gender disparity very much greater.

It was against this background that James Fraser – still only in his thirties and within less than a decade of his arrival there – gained a prominence in the affairs of the Lion City that would have been unthinkable 'back home' or, quite probably, in Batavia or elsewhere on Java. In 1835, for example, he was a trustee of the Raffles Institution, newly established to celebrate the memory of the modern city's founder, while in the following year he was listed in the *Singapore Free Press* among those protesting a proposal emanating from the India Office (under whose jurisdiction Singapore fell until 1867) to impose duties on goods passing through the port.[11] He also became one of the original subscribers to 'the establishment of theatrical performances' in the city. Among other things, it helped provide an opportunity for his fellow businessman (and recent arrival) William Henry Macleod Read to tread the boards in drag as 'the leading lady in most amateur theatricals' – in this instance in the persona of Charles Dickens's Miss Petowker, something for which he was well qualified by virtue of having, as well as a petite figure, 'the smallest waist and smallest feet of any in Singapore'.[12]

Meanwhile, Lewis Fraser – the same 'good steady Scotsman' with whom the Reverend Angus Maclaine briefly lodged in Singapore in 1846 – had arrived there to join his elder brother in business. He became a partner in the mercantile firm, now known as Maclaine Fraser, in 1839;[13] but well before that he had already thrown himself into the colony's civic and social life. In so doing, moreover, he evidently paid his dues to the Scottish diaspora that accounted for his presence there. If we accept the argument that 'clubbing together along ethnic lines' was one of that diaspora's defining characteristics,[14] then it is significant that the younger Fraser was a steward at a 'Scotch Dinner' held in Singapore in 1837 to celebrate St Andrew's Day,[15] and that some years later he was among the stewards at the city's inaugural 'St Andrew's Day Ball and Supper'.[16] Nevertheless, his participation in the social life of the colony was not limited to occasions on which the colony's Scots might be expected to collaborate. Perhaps the more outgoing of the two brothers, in February 1843 for instance, he was one of the stewards at a ball held after Singapore's first race meeting; while in the following year he was among the subscribers involved in setting up a library in the Raffles Institution.[17]

What had brought the Fraser brothers to Singapore, however, and what kept them there, was neither horse racing, amateur theatricals nor civic eminence: rather, it was the mercantile business that was the Lion City's lifeblood. Unlike Java, where the Maclaine Watson concern was based, Singapore did not have a richly productive hinterland that provided the foundation for a lucrative commerce. Instead, it was an entrepôt in which commodities from elsewhere were bought and sold. Leaving aside such minor lines of business as the trafficking in women and girls from all over

Asia – something which helped account for the Lion City's sobriquet of 'Sin Galore' – the main items traded during the Fraser brothers' time there included cotton goods, guns and opium. As such, they were all branches of mercantile activity that had a largely trans-imperial character: goods that originated in one empire found markets in another, and products originating outside the borders of empire were channelled to imperial consumers. Above all, in the case of Singapore, the port was a major node on commodity chains that took only passing cognisance of territorial frontiers of any description.

Foremost among the commodities in question were the dyed, patterned and plain cotton materials – which, in the British Empire, fell under the generic term 'Manchester', by way of recognition of their presumed origin in the damp, noisy and smoke-ridden 'Cottonopolis' of England's industrial north-west and its satellites (though they might well also have originated further north in Glasgow and its environs). Taken together, they were the prime manufacturing node along a global chain that began with the labour of enslaved African workers in the cotton fields of the southern United States and terminated among markets and consumers not only across the Atlantic but also on the other side of the world.[18] It would have been the prospective sale to locally based Chinese traders and other so-called 'middlemen' of British cotton goods – or their counterparts manufactured in the Indian subcontinent – that took James Fraser from Batavia to Singapore to join Maclaine's agent there, John Argyll Maxwell, and which probably remained a vital part of the Singapore business.

It was not, however, the only part. Armaments, of North American and British or European origin and sold to virtually anyone who had the wherewithal to purchase them, quickly became a key item in the port's stock-in-trade. Along with other destinations (and underscoring the trans-imperial dimensions of Singapore's business) large quantities were exported to China around the mid-century – where the Taiping Rebellion (1850–64) no doubt created a ready market – and it was said that 'there is scarce a mercantile firm in the place, English or foreign, that does not import largely guns, small arms, military stores and ammunition'.[19] The port's reputation in this respect was presumably high among the reasons for the arrival there, in December 1863, of the infamous Confederate cruiser *Alabama*.

The American Civil War had broken out two years earlier, and with scores of captured and burnt vessels and drowned sailors to its credit in the Atlantic, this Liverpool-built scourge of Union shipping had then evaded pursuit by sailing into the Indian Ocean – and eventually steamed into Singapore in search of repairs, coal and other provisions. The latter were provided – no doubt at a handsome profit as well as at the risk of some obloquy, since Great Britain and its colonies were supposedly neutral – by an erstwhile Singapore partner of the Frasers, Hugh Rowland Beaver.[20] Described by the *Alabama*'s captain as 'a clever English merchant [who] came on board and offered to facilitate us all in his power in the way of procuring supplies', Beaver featured in both Captain Semmes's own memoirs and in those of one his officers. Suitably resupplied, the *Alabama* then went on to prey on any American ships not flying the Confederate flag in Southeast Asian waters.

Then there was opium. For much of the nineteenth century, Singapore was Southeast Asia's 'Opium Central'.[21] Its importance to the port's cosmopolitan mercantile community was undoubted, particularly with respect to intra-regional trade. Opium, most of it originating in the Indian subcontinent, passed through (or by) Singapore on its way to China, where the burgeoning market from the 1810s onwards made the fortunes of a number of diasporan Scots firms, with the 'China Coast' smuggling business of Jardine Matheson very much to the fore.[22] Yet appreciable quantities of opium were also sold in Southeast Asia itself, both in the Indies, where the Dutch colonial government's monopoly on the sale of the commodity was constantly subverted by an extensive and lucrative smuggling trade, and in the string of Chinese mining and plantation settlements running southwards along the coast from Bangkok to Singapore.[23] Indeed, during the period when James and Lewis Fraser were active there, opium was placed second only to cotton among the Lion City's recorded exports to destinations in the neighbouring region; and, on the Malay Peninsula itself, where there were many settlements of Chinese labourers, opium was the principal import.[24]

In these circumstances, it is a fair assumption that the Frasers and their business associates sought to profit from engagement in a trade with which they were demonstrably fully conversant. As was revealed by his evidence to a British Parliamentary Committee after he returned home at end of the 1820s, James Fraser's one-time principal in Singapore, John Argyll Maxwell, was well-informed about opium, and had himself travelled to Canton, at that time the sole destination for the opium clippers sailing to China, at least once. Meanwhile, back on Java, Gillian Maclaine himself was sufficiently au fait with the trade to petition the Dutch colonial authorities in the mid-1830s to contract his firm to supply the quantities needed to provision their lucrative business of making the drug available to selected Indies-Chinese wholesalers ('Opium Farmers') who then organised its retail sale throughout Java and elsewhere in the Indies.[25]

Nonetheless, from the mid-century onwards it was another of the Lion City's key trade staples that featured most prominently on the Frasers' balance sheet. This was rice. By the mid-century, Singapore had become the linchpin of the Southeast Asian rice trade 'as entrepôt, distribution centre, and intermediary between Southeast Asian producers and consumers both inside and outside of the region'.[26] For the Frasers, it was a commodity that undoubtedly brought them into a close relationship with one of the city's leading Chinese businessmen, Tan Kim Ching. In addition to being the owner of two steamers, Tan possessed rice mills in Saigon and in Bangkok, where his close connections with the Thai court presumably strengthened his hold over the latter port's rice trade.[27] To be sure, Tan's greatest days were still before him during the period in which the Frasers were operating in or trading with Singapore. Indeed, he only reached the apogee of his commercial career post-1870 – his steam-driven rice mill in Bangkok dated from 1872 – but his commercial importance in Singapore, and that of his father Tan Tock Seng, dated from some decades earlier.

Something of the extent (and character) of the Fraser brothers' dealings with him is evidenced by the fact that when one of their partners, Simon Fraser Cumming, retired to the UK late in the 1860s, he left 10,000 Spanish dollars (around £2,500 sterling) with Tan, secured by a mortgage 'on certain *godowns* or warehouses in Singapore'.[28] Meanwhile, the Frasers themselves, after relocating to London, did a considerable business in imported Southeast Asian rice – a commodity which, while finding favour among the middle classes as a 'nutritional complement or supplement' and enjoying a ready sale as 'a versatile and cheap dietary staple' for the underprivileged, was also sold extensively for animal feed and for industrial use in the starch and paper industries.[29]

Local Liaisons and a 'Wee Wifie' from Back Home

Of course, life in Singapore was not exclusively about commerce. Both Fraser brothers, a decade apart, had arrived in the colony unwed and without the financial resources to contemplate marriage. When those resources did become available and the business in Singapore had become a paying concern, they opted for endogamous marriage: in contrast to some, at least, of their counterparts in the Indies, they sought wives 'back home' in Scotland. It was, indeed, with a touch of wry amusement that in 1836 the exogamously-wed Gillian Maclaine (he had married a young Dutch woman in Batavia some four years earlier) wrote to his mother that his Singapore business partner – a man of small stature whom he invariably referred to as 'the Bodachan' (a diminutive character from Gaelic mythology) – had left for Scotland with a view to finding 'a wee wifie' in his hometown.[30]

Before that, however, James Fraser had already established an 'unofficial' family in Singapore, where what looks to have been a long-term liaison with a locally born, presumably Eurasian, woman produced four 'natural' children. Fraser took three of them dutifully home with him to Forres in 1837 and left them there with his parents to complete their education. Two of them (James Maclaine Fraser and John Ellis Fraser), both said to be 'born overseas', were at his parents' house at the time of the 1841 Scots Census. Their sister Annie Fraser, likewise born in the Lion City, was not present for the Census, but subsequently married in Forres in 1857 to the architect William James Audsley. In acknowledgement of the wife's heritage, the couple's eldest boy, born 1863, was given the Christian names Maclaine Fraser.[31] James Fraser himself evidently remained in contact with his Singapore-born offspring, since he remembered his daughter in his will, in which she was left £900, while her surviving sibling was slated to receive £300, later reduced by a codicil to £100 (possibly because his father had advanced him the balance in the interim).[32]

These sums were, nonetheless, mere pittances in comparison to the assets, valued for probate at something under £60,000, that James Fraser left on his death to his widow and the children of his 'regular' marriage back in Forres in April 1838, where he wed the 27-year-old Ann Cumming.[33] Her father, the late John Cumming, had been a banker in Forres, and its 'sometime Provost', and the marriage may well have been a significant step up the social ladder for a man – arriving back newly enriched from the 'the East' – whose own father had been a stone mason.[34] Cumming himself had been the agent in Forres for the British Linen Company, and as a banker would presumably have been much involved in the financing of local flax production.[35] By the 1830s, however, that industry was in decline, something that may help explain why several of his children followed James Fraser to Singapore after he had returned there with his bride late in 1839.

Howsoever that might be, James Fraser's sister-in-law, Sophia Cumming (the Reverend Maclaine's hostess in the Lion City in the following year) had 'gone out' to marry Fraser's younger sibling there in 1845,[36] and three of her brothers arrived in her wake: in partnership with her husband and with several other Scots, they continued to do business in Singapore during the mid-century decades.[37] Meanwhile, another of the siblings, Marjory, had also made her way to the Lion City; and it was there, in 1846, that she married the businessman-thespian W. H. Read – by then a partner in the firm of A. L. Johnson & Co. Sadly, however, within three years of her marriage, the young bride herself was dead: probably already a sick woman, she had returned alone to her native Scotland, and it was in Forres in 1849 that she died, aged just 21.[38]

But marital ties and commerce were not the only things connecting these Singapore Scots: all the menfolk were also heavily involved among Singapore's nascent brotherhood of Freemasons. Read's prior credentials in this respect are unknown, but both the Frasers had come to the colony from a strong background in Scottish Freemasonry, where members of the family had been prominent in the Lodge St Lawrence in Forres since the time of its inception in the 1770s. Indeed, James Fraser himself had been inducted into the brotherhood as a very young man in 1820, before he sailed to 'the East'. Established in Singapore in the early 1830s, moreover, as a newly wealthy trader, he had contributed five guineas to the fund for erecting a new masonic lodge in his home town;[39] while in the decade that followed his younger brother played a major role in establishing and supporting the colony's Zetland-in-the-East Masonic Lodge, of which his brother-in-law (and business partner), James Bannerman Cumming, became secretary and treasurer and subsequently Worshipful Master.[40] It was no accident, therefore, that when Lewis and Sophia Fraser themselves departed permanently for Europe early in 1853, the festivities were marked by the members of the same Lodge giving:

> a ball and Supper in the Assembly Rooms as a farewell token of their regard.... The assembly was numerous, and the rooms were most tastefully decorated with various masonic emblems. The Military band was in attendance, and everything went off in excellent style. At supper, Mr Read, the present Master of the Lodge, proposed the toast of the evening in a short but appropriate speech, and after it had been drunk with masonic honours as well as the hearty cheers of the uninitiated, Mr. Fraser made a

Figure 6.2: Park Square East, Regent's Park, London – home of James and Ann Fraser and their family early in the 1850s after their return from Singapore (Collection of the Author)

suitable reply. After the company left the supper table, the dancing was resumed and kept up with great spirit to an advanced hour.[41]

A London Locale and a Community of Scots

In choosing a locale for their repatriation, neither of the Fraser brothers opted for their native Scotland, let alone the town in the country's north-east where they had been born. Instead, they both chose London. After leaving Singapore in the mid-1840s James and Ann Fraser lived initially at the southern end of Regent's Park in one of the city's more affluent areas, where, by the time of the 1851 Census, they occupied a grand stuccoed terrace – part of Park Square East – built some quarter of a century earlier to the plans of the great Regency architect and entrepreneur John Nash (Figure 6.2). A few years later the family moved to similar accommodation on the east side of nearby Park Crescent, which is where they remained until after James Fraser's death in 1872.

A similar social milieu – one heavy with the households of high-ranking individuals in commerce, finance, government and the professions – characterised the Hyde Park district, north of the eponymous Park itself,

Figure 6.3: Carte-de-visite of Lewis Fraser and his wife Sophie Cumming, whom he wed in their hometown of Forres in 1838 (National Portrait Gallery, London)

where Lewis and Sophie Fraser (Figure 6.3) and their young family first settled in a large Victorian terrace on Oxford Square (Figure 6.4) before moving to the equally affluent Montague Square a little to its east. Both couples were well provided with servants – and presided in this latter respect, at least, over distinctly Scottish households. In 1851, for example, three of James and Ann Fraser's five live-in servants at Park Square, including the butler and a mature nurse, were Scots; while ten years later his brother Lewis's household in Oxford Square counted eight live-in servants, including both a governess and a nurse, five of whom (among them the nurse) were Scots.

James Fraser also maintained a house – known appropriately as Singapore Cottage, it was 'an elegant and commodious dwelling house, two storeys high, slated and in good repair' – in his native Forres.[42] Nonetheless, Scotland itself appears otherwise to have been physically somewhat remote for the Fraser brothers: joint summer holidays were spent at resorts on the fashionable Isle of Wight rather than in Scotland.[43] Even so, in London itself, both kept up the Scottish connection. Back in the mid-1810s when Maclaine Watson's co-founder first arrived in London from the Western Highlands, he had found himself among self-consciously fellow countrymen who, among other things, took the young man along not only to a resplendent private party at which a Highland Scots theme was the dominant motif of the evening's entertainment, but also to a grand public dinner given in aid of the city's Scottish Hospital.[44] That same charity was also patronised some four decades later by 'J. Fraser Esquire', who was among the two hundred or more attendees at a Scottish Hospital Dinner to celebrate St Andrews Day at the Freemasons' Tavern in central London, under the 'presidency of Reverend Norman Macleod' – a leading figure in the Church of Scotland and a popular writer on religion.[45]

Yet, their attendance at gatherings such as these should not be taken as an indication that James and Lewis Fraser (and their families) moved exclusively or even largely among fellow Scots. Indeed, the record of their business affairs in London in the 1850s and 1860s suggests that quite the contrary was the case. The 1851 Census data includes James Fraser's self-description as a 'retired East India merchant': subsequently, however, he was anything but. Once established in London, both Frasers kept up (or re-invigorated) their links to the Lion City by running a trading company, J. and L. Fraser & Co., from premises in Mincing Lane, the hub of the City's 'East Indies' commercial quarter. Judging by the advertisements appearing in various of the London newspapers, the firm began operations sometime in the late 1850s and dealt, as brokers, in several colonial commodities –

Figure 6.4: Oxford Square, north of London's Hyde Park, where Lewis Fraser and his family lived during the 1860s (Collection of the Author)

above all in rice imported from a variety of Southeast Asian locations.⁴⁶ At the time of his death in 1872, James Fraser still possessed *godowns* (warehouses) in the colony;⁴⁷ and one of his sons continued in business there for a decade or more thereafter.

Meanwhile, the brothers also set about building a profile in the City's financial as well as commercial circles. 'The availability among the growing group of returned merchants . . . of men with local experience which they were willing to trade for a directorship' was a significant element in the City of London's mid-century location at the epicentre of global commerce and finance.⁴⁸ This was certainly the position in which the Frasers found themselves after repatriation, when they withdrew some of their capital from Singapore and reinvested in the newly incorporated merchant-banking and insurance companies that sprang up in London in the early 1860s in the wake of far-reaching government deregulation.⁴⁹ In so doing, they largely bypassed the British *domestic* capital market: instead, most of the boards on which the Fraser brothers sat as directors were those of companies that had an overseas, often imperial focus.

The most significant of the companies in which James Fraser, the elder of the two, was involved – at least in terms of its global reach and long-enduring character – was the Chartered Bank of India, Australia and China (eventually part of the still-extant Standard Chartered combine). Founded in 1853, it established offices throughout Asia, including one in Singapore in 1859, around the same time that Fraser joined its board. He was still one of its directors at the time of his death in 1872.⁵⁰ But this was not the only City financial venture with which he became associated: among the others were the English and Swedish Bank, the London Financial Association and the London Chartered Bank of Australia.⁵¹ Lewis Fraser had likewise found a niche in City financial circles sometime after his family returned from Singapore, and from around 1860 onwards began to take up a string of City directorships, including ones in the Bank of British Columbia, the Union Bank of Ireland, the Merchant Banking Company of London (Figure 6.5), and the Home and Colonial Insurance Company.⁵²

Admittedly, some of the businesspeople with whom the Fraser brothers associated in London were fellow Scots, among them William Nicol and William Rennie. Aberdeenshire-born, Nicol was the founder of the Bombay firm of William Nicol & Co., and after repatriation became Member of Parliament for Dover.⁵³ Rennie, of Scottish birth but likewise eventually domiciled south of the Border, was a partner in Cavan, Lubbock & Co., a

> **THE MERCHANT BANKING COMPANY**
> of LONDON (Limited).
> Offices, 23, Cannon street, E.C.
> Subscribed Capital, One Million sterling.
> DIRECTORS.
> CHAIRMAN—JOHN PATERSON, Esq.
> DEPUTY CHAIRMAN—THOMAS STENHOUSE, Esq.
>
> Richard Henry Browne, Esq.   William Pearce, Esq.
> Charles Butler, Esq.   Felix Pryor, Esq.
> J. H. Reynell De Castro, Esq. James Adam Smith, Esq.
> Alexander Fraser, Esq.   Henry Thurburn, Esq.
> Lewis Fraser, Esq.   Harrison Watson, Esq.
> James M'Master, Esq.   Edward Weston, Esq.
> John George Megaw, Esq.
>
> J. O. Megaw, Esq., Director in attendance.
> B. O. Gray, Esq., Deputy Manager.
> BANKERS.—The Alliance Bank of London and Liverpool.

Figure 6.5: Lewis Fraser, younger brother of James Fraser, sat on the board of the London-based Merchant Banking Company after his return from Singapore at the end of the 1850s (Collection of the Author)

London-based firm with extensive sugar interests in the West Indies.[54] There was also John Paterson. An Aberdonian who initially went overseas as a schoolteacher, Paterson became one of the leading British businessmen-politicians in southern Africa; followed by a lengthy sojourn in London, where he became foundational chairman of the London-based board of the Standard Bank of British South Africa.[55]

Even so, the Scottish connection was not paramount. Indeed, an important aspect of James and Lewis Fraser's repatriate afterlives was the extent to which they rubbed shoulders on the boards of City companies with 'Sassenachs' – and others. To cite but one prominent example, James Fraser (one of its founding directors)[56] was the sole Scot on the board of the London Financial Association, where his co-directors included John Borradaile and John Hackblock, both of them London-born. The former's family originally hailed from Cumberland in England's north-west and he himself was a returnee from Calcutta, where, along with mercantile interests, he had also been chairman of the Calcutta and South-Eastern Railway.[57] Hackblock's career, meanwhile, was at least as remarkable in 'self-made' terms as that of the Fraser brothers themselves: a cockney from Shoreditch (an impoverished part of the city), he made enough money to retire to a Thames-side mansion to the immediate south-west of the capital, became the owner of broad acres in Ireland and died worth something 'under £120,000'.[58] Another of Fraser's fellow directors at the Association was William Turquand, co-founding partner in Coleman, Turquand, Young &

Co. (one of the City's most enduring accountancy firms) and likewise a native of London and its environs.[59] Also on the board was another individual from the professional classes (albeit only a recent arrival among them): fellow board member Henry Paull was a London-born barrister and MP whose father had been a businessman with commercial interests in the West Indies, where he was involved in the ownership of enslaved Africans.[60] Yet another director, however, was neither Scottish nor English. Literally the child of another of the great global diasporas, Michel E. Rodocanachi was the naturalised scion of a wealthy Greek mercantile family and had been born on the Aegean Island of Chios but, having escaped the murderous ethnic cleansing that had taken place there in the year after his birth, subsequently spent most of his adult life in London.[61]

It would be a mistake, in short, to assume that, as City businesspeople, James and Lewis Fraser moved exclusively among fellow Scots, or that the diasporic Scots communities in London were hermetically sealed or sufficient unto themselves. Instead, the picture was of two newly arrived, diasporan Scots who parlayed their decades-long experience in 'the East' into membership of a metropolitan business elite that was engaged in overseas financial dealings of considerable substance, some of them trans-imperial in character. That substance, however, was about to be tested in an extreme fashion: by a deep-seated and enduring financial crisis in the City, which began in May 1866 with the collapse of Overend Gurney, the City firm whose activities were central to the discounting of the bills of exchange that formed the lifeblood of international commerce (much of it centred on London) in the mid-nineteenth century. There followed an infamous 'Black Friday' as City commuters read the confident prediction in *The Times* that the shock of Overend Gurney's failure the previous afternoon 'will, before the evening closes, be felt in the remotest corners of the kingdom'. In the City itself, meanwhile, there was: 'Great confusion all day, the streets were crowded and almost impassable . . . a day of the most intense excitement and panic . . . in fact such a day as has never been experienced, it was said at the time, in the memory of anyone.'[62]

Whatever their losses – which were likely to have been substantial – the brothers were hardly left destitute. On his death in 1868 (perhaps hastened by the stress of the previous 18 months) Lewis's estate was still valued for probate at 'less than £20,000',[63] which evidently enabled his widow and their children to continue to live comfortably. By the time of the 1871 Census the family had moved out of Montague Square – but socially all was far from lost, since they were still living, with a modest complement of three servants and a governess, in salubrious York Terrace,[64] very near to James Fraser and his family. The elder Fraser had presumably survived financially rather better than his late brother, and left an estate valued for probate at 'under £60,000'. To be sure, some of his contemporaries in the City were substantially better off, perhaps because they had weathered the meltdown of 1866 rather better than the Frasers. Hackblock, for example, one of his fellow directors on the board of the London Financial Association died worth almost twice as much as the elder Fraser. Nonetheless, the latter was evidently moderately wealthy by the standards of mid-Victorian England, his younger sibling rather less so.

The Colonel's Wife: Adelaide Fraser's Story

The relative affluence of the ex-Forres, ex-Singapore Frasers was reflected in the social history of their immediate families. In turn, its history enhances our understanding of a 'near diaspora' that notionally embraced Scots who settled south of the Border, and of the role of repatriate afterlives in the history of the Scottish 'dispersal' in general. The essential point is that, for all their own apparently robust sense of their Scottishness, the Frasers aimed to establish their families among the metropolitan bourgeoisie of mid-Victorian London – an aspiration reflected, for example, in *carte de visite* commissioned by Lewis and Sophia Fraser, showing the husband standing next to his seated wife against a background of rich furnishings, from the studio of Camille Silvy, the most celebrated society photographer of the day.[65] The crucial index to the success or otherwise of those aspirations, however, was the history of the marriages contracted by the two couple's offspring, all of whom only reached maturity after their parents had repatriated. Among them, the most socially eminent of the siblings was undoubtedly Adelaide Fraser, the youngest and London-born daughter of James and Ann Fraser who married into the officer corps of the British Army: how she came to meet her husbands (she was married twice) opens potential vistas into the social life of her kin once that they had settled in London – albeit ones which, given the paucity of the surviving documentation, can be explored only superficially.

The family connection with eligible members of the officer corps would appear to have begun with Adelaide's eldest sister, Sophia Cumming Fraser, who had wed an Army officer, Captain Charles Deere James in 1869,[66] some four years before her sibling married Captain Hugh Allen Mackey, Royal Artillery. Yet that still leaves unanswered the question of how the young women concerned came to move in such circles in the first place, given that none of their brothers or male cousins, for instance, appear to have taken commissions. Nor was shared ethnicity in London's 'near diaspora' any clue: Captain James came from a family based in the West of England,[67] and his brother-in-law was likewise of English birth (and buried in the Devon city of Exeter).[68] What is certain, however, that the degree of upward social mobility implied by their marriages – their grandfather, after all, had been a stonemason, however respected that skilled trade would have been in his hometown – was amplified when the widow Adelaide Fraser-Mackey (as she then was), wed for a second time a man whose military career culminated in the rank of Lieutenant-Colonel.

The young widow's first marriage had taken her to the British West Indian island of Jamaica, a feared posting for British soldiers on account of the outbreaks of yellow fever to which it was notoriously prone. It was almost certainly this disease that took her husband at the age of 37,[69] and ironically enough, provided the basis for her remarriage some five years later to a somewhat older widower. Herbert Locock was the London-born, Harrow-educated co-author of an authoritative *Drainage Manual*, and the youngest son of a celebrated medical man, Sir Charles Locock, who had held a position as one of Queen Victoria's obstetricians.[70] His son, an officer in the Royal Engineers, had been posted to Jamaica, more or less contemporaneously with Adelaide Fraser-Mackey and her husband; and it was there, in October 1877, that Locock lost a daughter to yellow fever[71] – and three years later in 1880 also lost his wife, the Canadian-born, Agnes Edith Fanny Coxworthy, whose death left behind four motherless children ranging in ages from 5 to 15.[72] In short, the marriage celebrated in fashionable Christ Church, Lancaster Gate in April 1882 between Fraser-Mackey and Locock was one between two individuals who would have been acquainted for a decade or more, in circumstances that had been calamitous for both.

The newly-weds initially settled in a substantial villa on the outskirts of Croydon, south of London where the Royal Engineers had a base, and where the couple's sole jointly parented child was born in 1883.[73] Subsequently, however, they took up residence in a rather grand terrace in London's South Kensington, a location in which Fraser-Locock presided over a household that included some thirteen servants.[74] The couple continued to live at addresses in this same well-to-do part of London until early in the twentieth century, when they moved to a sizeable country house in Surrey. Advertised as 'two miles from Farnham station and 38 miles from London', Frensham Grove boasted 'ten bedrooms, three reception rooms, a servants hall, a lake ... and stabling for four horses', and was set in among the pine trees on '15 acres of ornamental grounds'.[75] Sadly, they did not enjoy their rural retreat for long. Within less than two years of having moved in, the Colonel died, aged 73, in August 1910, leaving an estate valued at more than £57,000.[76] His widow subsequently relocated to an hotel in central London (the Alexandra, on Hyde Park Corner) before settling into a cottage outside the village of Liphook in Hampshire, some 50 miles south-west of the metropolis and near to where she appears to have had family. It was there that she died, nearly two decades after her husband, in June 1929, at the age of 79.[77]

The elevated social position that Adelaide Fraser-Locock had come to espouse, as the wife of a senior figure in the British military, had distanced her not only from the world of commerce which had characterised her parents' lives in both Singapore and (along with finance) in London but also from the milieu of almost all her siblings. To be sure, her eldest sister's own second marriage had brought her into the Guthrie family – who were among the Lion City's most flourishing and enduring business dynasties. Others of her family were altogether less well-placed. Her middle sister, Margaret Amy, married a businessman whose evident failure as such led to the couple's flight to Italy (where they lived on Capri, lodged in the Villa Discopoli) followed by her husband's death while staying in his London club in 1893, leaving an estate worth a piddling £660.[78] Altogether more dismal was the fate of her youngest brother, Alexander, a Harrow-educated individual whose history was a classic case of 'going down in the world'. Married in Canada, where he may well have gone to try his luck as an entrepreneur, by the mid-1880s he and his Canadian-born wife, Emma, were in London living in a working-class tenement where their neighbours included dressmakers, shoemakers, waiters, footmen, telegraph clerks and the like. It was while still in London in 1897, and described as a 'gentleman' in his probate record, that he died, at the age of 43, in a modest hotel or public house with assets valued at scarcely £100.[79]

The history of Adelaide Fraser-Locock's cousins, the seven offspring of Lewis and Sophia Fraser, was even more mixed: not riches to rags, but nevertheless a cautionary tale. Admittedly, the couple's second eldest daughter, Sophia, had made a notionally exemplary 'dynastic' marriage into the Padday clan of Penang: an extended kin group of Scots origin, they dominated the European business sector of a port that was still of commercial significance in the 1860s. Yet it was in sharp decline thereafter, a mere backwater in comparison to the Lion City and hardly a base from which to rescue her own family's fortunes.[80] Meanwhile, her younger sister, Marjorie, wed a man who was in the silk trade in London and subsequently lived at locations in the south-west of the metropolis that fell somewhat short of the relative affluence to which she had been accustomed in her youth. Long after her husband's death, his presumably impecunious widow emigrated to join family members in Sydney, which is where she died in 1929.[81] Lewis and Sophia Fraser's eldest son, Lewis, Jnr, married a painted glass manufacturer's daughter and, having found employment as 'secretary to a public company', spent most of his married life at a distinctly lower middle-class address (with two teenage servants) in South London, among neighbours who included a watchmaker, a warehouseman, an 'assistant surveyor metropolitan police' and a banker's clerk.[82] Meanwhile, his younger brother, James, self-described rather optimistically as an 'East India Merchant' in the 1881 Census (when was living in a boarding house in central London), subsequently appears to have taken off for Antipodean obscurity.

Meanwhile, three of Fraser-Locock's sisters-in-law (Anna Maria, Emily and Ellen Allan Fraser) did not follow their siblings down the path of matrimony, but instead remained single – as indeed did some 16 per cent of their early twentieth century counterparts (the percentage was even higher in their 'native' Scotland)[83] – and lived out their lives in spinsterly companionship in the English south coast resort of Bexhill-on-Sea. It was there, indeed, that the eldest of them died in 1904 (leaving an estate valued at a little less than £950);[84] while her two siblings, long outliving her, died in the mid-1940s in a retirement home in a rural settling some 30 miles away, with Emily rather pathetically memorialised as the 'last surviving daughter of the late Lewis Fraser, of Singapore'.[85]

Postscript: The Fraser of Fraser's Hill

Following the death of their father, James Fraser, in 1872, Lewis James and George John Fraser continued the family business in London and Singapore. The business itself, however, collapsed ten years later in May 1882, when a notice in the *St James's Gazette* – that graveyard of unsuccessful companies

– informed the public that the two brothers, 'trading as J. & L. Fraser & Co. . . . and also as Maclaine Fraser & Co. of Singapore,' had filed for bankruptcy, with debts estimated at the considerable sum of around £85,000.[86] In fact, the firm had been in severe financial difficulties, and involved in protracted negotiations with its creditors, since the middle of the preceding decade,[87] so that the events of May 1882 were no more than a further act in a long battle with insolvency that dragged on for some years afterwards. The younger of the two siblings appears to have continued in business in the City until 1884, only then disappearing from the public record before dying some three years later at the age of 42, still in London, still living at a relatively 'good' address (Sloane Street, Chelsea), and still described as 'merchant'.[88]

His elder brother long outlived him. He was managing the Singapore end of the business at the time of the bankruptcy and from there literally took to the hills. Variously identified as 'a solitary Scots pioneer', 'a Scottish prospector', 'a Scottish adventurer and Fortune Hunter' or a 'reclusive Scotsman', Lewis James Fraser achieved a degree of posthumous celebrity in latter-day tourist literature. He was purportedly the discoverer of tin – a rather minor lode, as it turned out, and nothing like enough to make his fortune – near the present-day resort of Fraser's Hill (Bukit Fraser) something under 300 miles northwards up the Malay Peninsula from his erstwhile base in Singapore. The locality was to gain a certain notoriety in the mid-twentieth century, as the place where the British High Commissioner, Sir Henry Gurney, was gunned down by communist guerrillas after his Rolls-Royce was ambushed on a mountain road, having proceeded too far in advance of its armed escort.[89]

Almost half a century before that, however, the story of the 'Scots pioneer' had ended in an altogether more mundane fashion many thousands of miles away in a Kentish spa town. Credited with having 'disappeared' from the Malay Peninsula as 'mysteriously' as he had arrived on the scene, what actually happened was that sometime around 1900 he had left 'his' hill and returned to England, where he found lodgings with his very recently widowed, wealthy sister, Sophia Fraser-Guthrie.[90] The association between the Guthrie family and the Fraser clan dated from their days together in the Lion City, where it extended into the civic as well as commercial sphere – in 1848, for instance, Lewis Fraser and James Guthrie had served together on the committee of management of the Singapore Library[91] – and continued thereafter. In April 1871, for example, two young Singapore-born Guthrie women, both in their early twenties, were staying with Lewis Fraser's widow, Sophia Cumming-Fraser, at her York Terrace house.[92] Subsequently, however, it was Adelaide Fraser-Locock's widowed elder sister, Sophia Fraser-James,[93] who had kept up the Guthrie connection by marrying the elderly James Guthrie, himself a widower of very long standing, in London in 1881.[94] The couple subsequently relocated to the spa town of Tunbridge Wells: high and healthy on the Kentish Weald, it was a little over an hour's train ride into central London, and a favourite watering hole and fashionable place of well-heeled retirement for many an ex-colonial. It was there that Guthrie died in 1900, leaving an estate worth nearly £24,000 to his widow (and sole executor), who herself only survived him by less than four years, dying in Tunbridge at the age of 64.[95] Well before that, however, she had been joined by her brother Lewis, fresh from his (failed) mining speculation on the Malay Peninsula.

Thereafter, the latter's fortunes evidently took a turn for the better, and it was most likely in Tunbridge that he met Maria Ellen Cheere, a wealthy spinster some twenty years his junior whose widowed mother had relocated to the town after the death of her Anglican clergyman husband, the gentleman owner of a large Georgian mansion in rural Cambridgeshire.[96] The couple subsequently married in London – and it was Lewis James Fraser's inflated (or perhaps humorous) description of himself on that occasion as heralding from 'Tras Lahang' (a settlement a few kilometres from Fraser's Hill) to which we owe the clue to his whereabouts on the Malay Peninsula in the preceding decade. Fraser himself died in September 1906, in the Austrian city of Salzburg, some five years after his marriage and presumably while on holiday, leaving an estate valued at a little over £2,000. His widow outlived him, however, by more than thirty years, before dying in London in November 1938, when her estate was valued at around ten times that amount.[97]

The central theme of this chapter has been the dynamics of a segment of the diaspora articulated through a variety of networks – familial, mercantile and institutional – which took sojourning members of the 'Forres' Frasers to Singapore (and the Indies) and likewise facilitated their 'homecomings'. Those homecomings, moreover, had a quite specific character. Unlike some of their counterparts (in this case 'returnees'), far from retiring to Scotland and a life of *rentier* ease, settled in London where they continued to be active in financial and mercantile circles for the remainder of their lives. None of their several family histories – ranging from the social success of Adelaide

Fraser through to the posthumous mythical status accorded her sibling – were the stuff from which business dynasties were made, and well before the nineteenth century's end the Fraser 'project' had faded into mercantile obscurity. Several of the Fraser brothers' contemporaries in the Maclaine Watson cohort founded mercantile dynasties that lasted well into the twentieth century, as, indeed, did a few of the Frasers' own contemporaries in the Lion City, notably the Guthries.

The Forres family, however, followed a different trajectory, one illustrative of the variety as well as the coherence of the networks of kinship that supported the global Scots dispersal. Indeed, what gave their search for riches its particular character was the extent of their involvement in business circles in the metropolis itself, where the cycle of boom and bust in which they were caught up in the 1860s largely stymied their ambitions. Successful attempts to insert themselves on a long-term basis into the upper echelons of the mercantile networks of the Scottish diaspora eluded them, and in this dimension their stories were linked to a broader sweep of a diaspora that embraced many social categories – including, of course, the less affluent in addition to the well-to-do who predominated within the Maclaine Watson cohort.

Meanwhile, 'Scotland' in any shape or form seems to have enjoyed a decreasing presence in their lives, at least after the passing of the first generation of diasporans. Most notably, this was reflected in the largely exogamous marriages of James and Lewis Fraser's offspring, both female and male. Instead of being proud instances of some triumphant 'return to Caledonia', the second generation of these particular 'children of the diaspora' were to be found scattered in southern England, in and around London itself, and even as far afield as the Antipodes. Sojourners in Singapore, they became settlers south of the Scottish Border. In this respect, their stories underscore the importance, as well as the ambiguities, of the sojourner phenomenon for a holistic understanding of diaspora in terms not only of leave-taking but also in terms of homecomings and subsequent family histories. But their stories also highlight the complexity of the networks that were as central to the diaspora as they were to the empires in which it was embedded. It is to another of those networks and to a figure who stood out among the Maclaine Watson cohort in terms of his trans-imperial profile, that we can now turn.

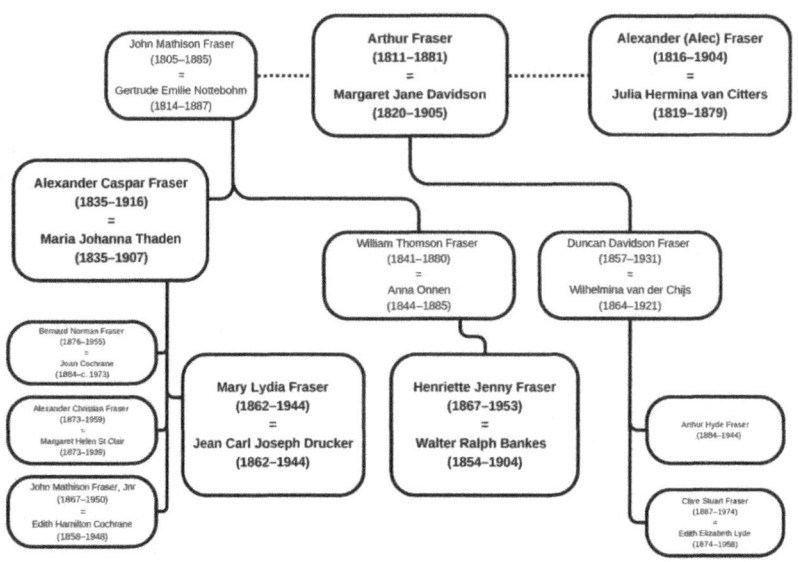
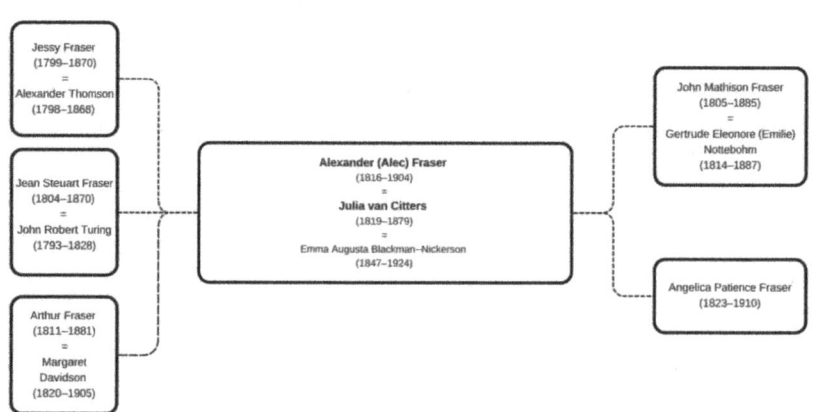

7

Aberdeen, Antwerp and the Indies

> My young friend Arthur Frazer ... is tall and good looking and I fear very susceptible of 'winning smiles from pretty faces' – but who is not at his age, a glorious twenty? He is, however, under my care, and at 33 *I* ought to be a mentor. ... [Moreover, he] is too like his *sister* not to please me if he were even less engaging in his manners ... than he is.[1]

THE SISTER IN QUESTION was Jean Fraser-Turing – the woman whom we first met at the outset of this book as both a wife and a young widow. Gillian Maclaine, co-founder of Maclaine Watson and the writer of this account, which was penned on board ship during his return voyage to Java in the first half of 1832, would have encountered her in the small Scots community in Batavia during the previous decade, together with her husband, John Robert Turing, the fellow colonial merchant whose premature death in 1828 had precipitated Fraser-Turing's flight back to Britain, along with her two young children. Far from severing her family's connection with the Indies, however, her departure proved to be the initial stage of the 'Aberdeen' Frasers' involvement with the Dutch colony that lasted until early in the twentieth century.

Their story is of the evolution of a cosmopolitan kinship network that linked them to the Dutch colonial possessions in maritime Southeast Asia as well as to locations in Scotland itself, London and the 'Home Counties', the Low Countries and their German hinterland. As such, its immediate subjects are two of Fraser-Turing's brothers and the women they married. The elder of the pair spent little more than a decade on Java before returning to Aberdeen and marrying a fellow Scot and enjoying an exceptionally long repatriate afterlife. His younger sibling, on the other hand, a truly trans-imperial businessman of some significance, who had married in the Indies with a colonial-born Dutch woman, enjoyed a lengthy sojourn there, punctuated by a period of 'repatriation', that lasted late into the 1870s. Their respective histories, however, are bound up with those other members of the extended Fraser family whose lives followed very different routes, in Antwerp, Rotterdam, London and elsewhere, and had a distinctly cosmopolitan character. They are histories, moreover, that highlight the role played in – and beyond – the network by its women as well as its men. It is a context in which Jean Fraser-Turing was a far from unique figure.

Fordyce, Fraser and Young: From Aberdeen to The Low Countries.

It was a marriage in Aberdeen late in the eighteenth century between scions of two of the north-east of Scotland's leading mercantile families that had launched the family on its modern trajectory. The groom, Alexander Fraser, Snr, had been born in Inverness, but subsequently moved to the region's major port (and textile manufacturing and shipbuilding centre) of Aberdeen, where he carried on a business as a merchant, corn factor and shipowner, and became the city's provost or civic head. His bride, the 20-year-old Agnes Dingwall Fordyce, came from one of Aberdeen's foremost families, where her father, Arthur Dingwall Fordyce, ended a long legal career in the city as its Commissary or Judge of the probate and divorce court, whilst her mother, Janet Morison, was herself the daughter of another erstwhile city provost.

Although the Fraser-Fordyce couple themselves appear to have remained in Scotland throughout their lives, the same was not true of at least four of their twelve children, who relocated to the Low Countries and developed mercantile careers there – or used Antwerp and Rotterdam as staging posts in a longer 'migration' to the East. The key here was family connections. The fact that the Frasers came to be involved with the Low Countries at all was most likely through the agency of the Aberdeen-born James Young, who was Alexander Fraser, Snr's brother-in-law. Young had departed

Aberdeen for the Dutch port city of Rotterdam in 1814 and remained there carrying on a mercantile business until his death twenty years later.[2] As such, along with other Aberdonian émigrés to the Low Countries, he was known to Gillian Maclaine: indeed, during his travels in Europe in May 1831, Maclaine had reported to his mother that:

> after some curious adventures on the Rhine, [I] reached Rotterdam in safety on the night of the 15th ... [and] I lived with my kind friends Mr and Mrs MacPherson, whose kindness, as well as that of Mr Young and his family, I shall not forget in a hurry.[3]

The Fraser-Fordyce couple's second son, John Mathison Fraser, relocated from Aberdeen very early in the 1830s and set up in business in Antwerp, a promising place for commercial 'start-ups', given the city's status as the major port of the new breakaway state of Belgium, currently in revolt against the Dutch hegemon with which the southern (ex-Austrian/Spanish) part of the Netherlands had been bundled together in the wider post-Napoleonic European settlement a decade and half previously. In 1833, moreover, not long after arriving there, Fraser had made a 'good' – and markedly exogamous – marriage. His bride, Gertrude Eleonore [Emilie] Nottebohm[4] belonged to what has been described as 'the absolute top of the German business world in Antwerp', and whose close kin also had mercantile operations in Rotterdam and Hamburg. As such, the Fraser-Nottebohms became part of the cosmopolitan commercial community that had gravitated to Antwerp following the reopening of the River Scheldt in 1795, after its two-centuries-long closure by the navy of the adjacent Dutch Republic.[5]

Fraser's expanding business in the city appears to have revolved largely around the import of commodities from the New World: cotton from the South Carolina port of Charleston (where his likely commercial contact would have been another Scot, the possibly related John Fraser, head of one of Charleston's leading mercantile houses),[6] tobacco from New Orleans, sugar from the Brazilian port of Bahia, hides from Montevideo and coffee from several destinations in the Caribbean. To judge from the trade advertisements in contemporary newspapers, only a fraction of his business was done with the Dutch East Indies, though this did include occasional consignments of sugar from Batavia and Semarang.[7] For the most part, however, his activities in Antwerp highlighted Scotland's long connection with the Americas and with the forced labour of enslaved Africans that predominated in export production there until well into the second half of the nineteenth century.⁸ Fraser himself would initially appear to have been in business in the Belgian port with members of the Young family, but subsequently operated his own firm of J. M. Fraser & Co. – though sometimes sharing in a consignment with his wife's relatives, the Frères Nottebohm. In the middle months of 1847, however, in the context of a general mercantile crisis, his firm failed – a failure that also engulfed its London and Liverpool correspondents.⁹

Unlike them, Fraser emerged relatively undamaged, possibly thanks to his wife's money and connections; and within a few years of the Antwerp debacle the couple had moved across the North Sea to London and taken up residence at an eminently respectable address by Hyde Park, where their household included their five children, a governess and the rather modest number of four servants.¹⁰ It was in London that Fraser set up in business again, and as J. M. Fraser of 'Craven Hill and Mark Lane' (the latter a City business address) appeared in 1854 as one of the directors of the newly established British and Foreign Life Assurance Society.¹¹ The Fraser-Nottebohm couple subsequently found themselves a country retreat in the

Figure 7.1: Mongewell House, the Thames-side mansion in Berkshire as rebuilt by Alexander Caspar Fraser, c.1893 (Collection of the Author)

Figure 7.2: Boompjes, Rotterdam. Home to Alexander Caspar Fraser and his wife, Maria Thaden during his lengthy sojourn in the Netherlands (Stadsarchief Rotterdam)

shape of a Thames-side mansion, Mongewell Park (Figure 7.1),[12] at Wallingford, on the Oxfordshire-Berkshire border. Mongewell had once been the home of an Anglican bishop, and now became the home of a 'Retired Colonial Broker' and was subsequently to pass into the hands of the couple's eldest son.

The Squire of Mongewell Park:
From the Low Countries to the English 'Home Counties'

At the close of the 1840s, while still an adolescent, Alexander Caspar Fraser, a half-German 'Scot' (his second baptismal name that was presumably a homage to his maternal uncle, Caspar André Nottebohm), had relocated to London with his parents and the rest of the family.[13] Later in the following decade, however, he had moved back to the Low Countries, though to Rotterdam rather than his native Antwerp (Figure 7.2); and it was in the Dutch port that, in 1856, he had married the equally young, locally-born *mejuffrouw* Maria Johanna Thaden. The bride's father, Bernard Antoine Louis Thaden, a partner in the local branch of the Nottebohm businesses, came from the German town of Emden, whereas her mother, Elisabeth Overgaauw, hailed from Rotterdam, where her father was a finance broker.[14]

It was in Rotterdam that Fraser and his family lived for the next quarter century, and where he set up in business, in association with the Nottebohms and his Thaden in-laws.[15] His firm, A. C. Fraser & Co., long outlasted the life of its founder, and at the time of writing was still operating there, primarily in insurance. In Alexander Caspar Fraser's day, however, it was heavily involved in overseas maritime trade, especially with the Indies. The Fraser-Thaden family moved across the North Sea from Rotterdam to London early in the 1880s. Following his father's death in 1884 and that of his mother three years later, however, Fraser and his wife took over Mongewell Park. Not only did he take over the property, he totally rebuilt it in the fashionable William and Mary style,[16] and the much enlarged mansion became the rural seat and main place of residence where the couple set

Figure 7.3: Alexander Caspar Fraser, nephew of Alec Fraser, in his uniform as Deputy Lord-Lieutenant of Berkshire (Stadsarchief Rotterdam)

themselves up as English country gentlefolk.[17] Set in some eighty acres of well-wooded grounds, the mansion boasted a gamekeeper as well as a farm-bailiff (in addition to some fifteen live-in servants, assorted gardeners and the like); and its owner – now styled a 'retired merchant-banker' – became a local Justice of the Peace and as such sat on the Bench of Magistrates further downriver at Henley-on-Thames, and from 1894 onwards held the largely ceremonial but prestigious position of Deputy Lieutenant of the same county. A photograph shows him resplendent in what must surely have been the dress uniform that went with it (Figure 7.3).[18]

In keeping with Alexander Caspar Fraser and his wife's new social standing, they sent their youngest son to Harrow, a sure route to confirming the elevated status of one's descendants. Maria Thaden-Fraser, meanwhile, set up a village school in memory of her late mother, Elisabeth Thaden, and the couple placed a window in the local Anglican parish church as a memorial 'to the late John Mathison Fraser of Mongewell House and Gertrude, his wife, with a brass beneath'. Further emphasising the social distance Fraser had travelled from the Scottish Presbyterian roots of his Aberdonian ancestors, as lord of the manor at Mongewell Park, he was the patron of the local Anglican church, meaning that the clergyman's 'living' at the same church, adjacent to the great house itself, was in Fraser's 'gift' – meaning that he appointed and (largely) paid the incumbent, who in this case was a graduate from the Anglican bastion of Trinity College, Dublin.[19] Maria Thaden-Fraser died in 1907 at Wallingford; her husband followed her to the grave some nine years later, leaving a substantial fortune of over £155,000, and what a contemporary newspaper called 'large bequests to servants', including £3,000 to the two nurses who looked after him in his final years, and £1,000 each to his butler and head gardener – as well as £1,000 to the Morrell Memorial Cottage Hospital. The burial took place in Mongewell churchyard.[20]

The eldest of the 'squire' of Mongewell Park's three male offspring, the Rotterdam-born John Mathison Fraser, Jnr, had embarked on a career in business in his father's footsteps; and, like him, although he kept up commercial ties with the Indies, he never 'went out East' himself. After having spent nearly two decades in the Netherlands, where he took over the management of the family firm early in the new century, he returned to England sometime before the First World War and subsequently set up as a country gentleman in East Sussex, with a town house in London,[21] while maintaining cross-channel business links: among other things, he remained a partner in A. C. Fraser & Co. and its likewise Rotterdam-based associates, E. Suermondt & Zoonen, until 1939.[22] His two brothers, however, never entered 'trade' and – apparently able to support themselves from inherited wealth – opted for the life of country gentlemen. Their father had died in 1885, leaving a personal estate of £69,300,[23] while his very much wealthier widow, who survived him by almost two years, left a far from modest £207,000, the great bulk of it willed in equal shares to her six children.[24]

Moreover, at some considerable remove socially and geographically from the 'dynastic', commercially oriented marital alliances in the Low Countries of their father and grandfather, the wives of all three sons of commerce came from English landed families of some substance. A case in point was the marriage of the Mongewell squire's youngest boy, Bernard Norman Fraser, to a daughter of Blair Onslow Cochrane[25] – a retired captain in the Royal Navy, domiciled near Ryde on the Isle of Wight, where he enjoyed a socially enviable position. Their London wedding had taken place in the neoclassical splendour of St Peters, Eaton Square in March 1909. Described as 'a brilliant social occasion', at which there was a generous sprinkling of titled individuals among the guests, and where pride of place in a collection of lavish wedding gifts was a sapphire brooch from the Queen of Spain (aka Victoria Eugenie of Battenberg, Queen Victoria's youngest granddaughter)[26] 'to whom the bride's family is well known'.[27]

Underlining the extent to which this branch of the Fraser family had forged alliances among the gentry, moreover, was the fact that Bernard Fraser's mother-in-law (Mary Evelyn Cochrane, née Sutton), was the scion of a family of wealthy landowners. Her father, the late Sir Richard Sutton, erstwhile Commodore of the Royal Victoria Yacht Club on the Isle of Wight, had been the proprietor of Benham Park – a grand country house in Berkshire where, at the time of the 1871 Census, he and his wife were installed, together with ten of their children, a governess and twenty domestic servants.[28] To be sure 'Scotland' indeed remained on the agenda for this branch of the extended Fraser family to the extent that one of the three married couples eventually relocated there from the 'near diaspora' south of the Border. Otherwise, however, it took on an essentially mythic form, neatly on display in an enthusiastic newspaper report of the Fraser-Cochrane nuptials: 'whilst the bride's family is of course one of the best known and widely respected in the island,' the groom – actually an individual whose immediate forebears were as much Dutch and German as they were

Scots – hailed from 'one of the oldest Scottish families... and is a descendant of Lord Lovat' (a Jacobite grandee beheaded for high treason in 1747).[29] Nonetheless, for yet other branches of the family of the 'Aberdeen' Frasers, Scotland (and Aberdeen itself) remained central to their lives and repatriate histories. This was strikingly the case with John Mathison Fraser's younger brother – and uncle of the man who became the squire of Mongewell Park.

'Out East': Arthur Fraser's Surabaya Sojourn and Return

Arriving in the Indies in 1832, the youthful Arthur Fraser – the person whose resemblance to his sister had so pleased Gillian Maclaine on their outward voyage from Rotterdam – had soon found himself placed (at Maclaine's behest) in a mercantile house in the East Java port of Surabaya,[30] centre for the rapidly expanding sugar industry of the adjoining Brantas delta and the coastal districts of the island's Eastern Salient (*Oosthoek*). Although only 20 when he arrived there, he evidently flourished in this new setting. Indeed, in 1835, within three years of his arrival and under Maclaine Watson's patronage, he co-founded, with the New Englander William Eaton, the mercantile house of Fraser Eaton as the Batavia firm's agent[31] (and subsequently long-term 'sister house') in a city that was to become the commercial heart of the colony. Fraser himself, meanwhile, made sufficient money to be able to retire from the firm and repatriate to Aberdeen in 1846 after having been a partner in his own business in the port for scarcely eleven years.

Generally speaking this was not a period when 'private' mercantile business was reckoned to flourish in the Indies, not least because the NHM (Nederlandsche Handel-Maatschappij), the state-linked mercantile and banking business established in the Netherlands in 1824, had the lion's share of what were notionally the colony's most profitable commodities (coffee and sugar), and continued to do so until the 1850s.[32] So when Gillian Maclaine informed his mother in 1836 that 'Young Fraser who came out with me has turned out a fine clever fellow and has done well for himself and us in Sourabaya',[33] to what kind of profit-taking was he alluding? Among other things, in Surabaya from 1836 until his departure, 'Young Fraser' was one of the three directors of the local agency of the Java Bank, the colony's state-backed, premier financial institution, along with the NHM's C. A. Granpré Molière and the shady (and very wealthy) East Java businessman

Figure 7.4: Arthur Fraser, partner in Maclaine Watson and husband of Margaret Davidson, whom he married in Edinburgh in 1850 after his return from Java (KITLV/University of Leiden)

Johann Erich Banck. The latter was said to have played fast and loose with the Bank's funds, and was most probably involved in the illicit trade in opium carried on by his associates in the port's leading Sino-Indonesian business community in contravention of the Indies government's monopoly on its importation.[34] Whether 'Young Fraser' himself was similarly involved is uncertain, but what is clear is during the same decade in which he evidently began to prosper, his patron, Gillian Maclaine, had recouped his own faltering fortunes through an extensive engagement in the Country Trade between Bengal, Southeast Asia and what Europeans termed 'the China Coast', and was fully conversant with the 'sleepy commodity' that was one of its staples.[35]

In 1846 Arthur Fraser's story took a radically different turn. Scarcely more than 35 when he repatriated in the middle months of that year,[36] his returnee afterlife was to be a lengthy one. Almost 70 when he died, in the intervening three and a half decades he not only kept up his business interests and established himself as a landed proprietor, but also found time to marry, settle down and start a family. Not that he appears to have been in any hurry in this latter respect. Gillian Maclaine had met and 'reached an understanding' with a young Dutch woman who, together with her patrician family and along with Fraser himself, had also been on the voyage from Rotterdam back in 1832, and to whom he was married within a few weeks of their disembarking in Batavia. Fraser's marriage, on the other hand, was long postponed, and when he finally tied the knot, in Aberdeen in 1850, it was in a thoroughly endogamous fashion, with a woman of solidly Scottish stock from his native turf, where her upper-middle-class family mingled with the local gentry and aristocracy and had a large country mansion, Inchmarlo, as well as a town house in the city itself (Figure 7.4).

Margaret Jane Davidson was around 30 years old at the time of her marriage to Fraser and was the daughter of Duncan Davidson, a retired Aberdonian advocate (or barrister), while her mother, Frances Mary Pirie appears to have come from a manufacturing and mercantile family in Aberdeen.[37] Inchmarlo itself, the Davidson family home, had been extensively remodelled in the 1820s by Duncan Davidson's kinsman, Walter Stevenson Davidson. The latter's career, however, was by no means exclusively confined to the north of Scotland. As a young man, he had migrated to New South Wales and done rather well there as a pastoralist, fostering the 'plague of sheep' that effectively eroded the claims of Australia's aboriginal people to the land of their ancestors,[38] and had subsequently established himself in Macao on the 'China Coast', where he became a significant figure in the opium trade to Canton, further up the Pearl River. Returning to Great Britain, Davidson remained active in the East Asian and Antipodean mercantile fields for virtually the rest of his long life.[39] For good measure, he also secured the marriage of one of his daughters into the Netherlands-based branch of the Turing mercantile 'clan' – the same diasporan Rotterdam family into whom Jean Fraser had married nearly three decades earlier.

Arthur Fraser (her younger sibling) appears to have come to know his wife-to-be through another of his sisters, Jessy Fraser, who was married to the Aberdeen landowner and lawyer Alexander Thomson. Thomson was a public figure of some note, whose country seat was Banchory House, some three miles downstream along the River Dee from Inchmarlo.[40] A lengthy and cautious courtship can be traced through the somewhat cryptic entries in the journal of the bride-to-be's younger sister, Anne Davidson.[41] The first such, in August-September 1849, records the unexplained visit to Inchmarlo of Arthur Fraser's youngest sibling, Angelica Patience Fraser, a woman who, during a long lifetime spent initially in Aberdeen and subsequently in Edinburgh and London, established herself as a noted social reformer:

a tireless proselytiser for the efficacy of prayer, for temperance and for improved hours and conditions for the working poor.[42] Her visit to the Davidson mansion was followed some weeks later by the bald observation that 'Maggie goes to visit at Banchory House',[43] and a sequence of reconnoitres between the parties concerned – interrupted by the death of the Davidson sisters' father in December 1849[44] – concluded in the middle of May 1850, when:

> We had a letter from Mr. Fraser today and Mamma at once answered it. Mr & Mrs Thomson came up to see us most kindly & we all congratulated each other on the prospect of our being more closely united some day. We talked the whole time of Arthur and Maggie for I must bring the mysterious hints that have dropped occasionally from my pen to light now and say at once that we expect God Willing that in due time Maggie will become Mrs Fraser and it gives us all the greatest satisfaction, as he seems so good & so worthy of her. Dear Maggie, we longed to see her, and it is to be regretted that our family bereavement alone prevented our longed-for meeting with our new brother.... [The Thomsons] stayed to our early dinner and I had a walk with Mr Th when he told me much about Arthur. I hope he is as nice as Mr Th himself![45]

The 39-year-old Arthur Fraser, the much-anticipated 'new brother', appeared in person at Inchmarlo for the first time on 18th June:

> At last he came and most favourably impressed us. We had such a cheery evening & went to the garden. I tormented the young people famously! Well, it seems very odd to have him here & it all settled.'

Fraser, joined by other members of his family, stayed for the following fortnight.[46] The marriage ceremony itself took place there some seven weeks later, on 6th August:

> Dear Maggie was so composed & took everything quite cooly.... We bridesmaids entered first, with all the dear little children in our train & posted ourselves near the clergyman & then came Maggie. Arthur stepped up & the ceremony began. I felt so sick. The ceremony was most impressive and all one could wish.... I felt so relieved when Mrs Arthur Fraser was congratulated.... She went up soon to change her dress & Mama and me

only with her. The best man first handed her to the dining room to stick a knife in the cake and then handed her to the carriage. The children strewed the Portico with roses! The nearest gentlemen drained a bottle of Champagne to their happiness and they were off in the midst of deafening cheers & a volley of old shoes [a well-known token of good luck]. We then all marched in to lunch and after peacefully but merrily eating it the toasts began . . .[47]

Following their marriage, the couple settled in Edinburgh, where all but one of their five children were born between 1852 and 1858. Arthur Fraser must have had an interest in civic and public affairs: he was a Justice of the Peace, and was urging his younger brother Alexander (Alec) – who was on the point of himself repatriating from the Indies – to take an active role in national politics by 'becoming a Member of Parliament'.[48] In 1867 it was reported that Fraser (and presumably his family) was abroad,[49] but sometime around the end of the decade they moved south of the Border, into a fine house in London's Hyde Park-Bayswater district.[50] It was but a short walk to the town house of Arthur Fraser's elder brother, John, and his wife, while his younger sibling Alec Fraser bought a mansion some streets away later in the decade. In short, although the Frasers had left Scotland, they had not severed family ties and came together as an extended family of diasporans in a favoured residential part of the metropolis. Arthur Fraser himself, meanwhile, had taken to describing himself as a landowner and as a retired British consular official, thereby neatly circumventing any reference to his years 'in trade' in the Indies, where his diplomatic posting was no more than a prestigious adjunct to his business activities. Maybe it was a designation, conscious or otherwise, that confirmed the diaspora's role in empire, at a time when imperial themes were gaining in importance in the popular imagination.

Subsequently, however, the Fraser-Davidson family was on the move again, relocating to the south-west coast of England, where they established themselves in some opulence with eight servants at a grand villa overlooking the sea at the Devon resort of Torquay. However, one of the servants was a 'sick nurse', and it was there, in May of that year, that her employer died, leaving a modest fortune of some £43,000.[51] After her husband's death, Margaret Davidson-Fraser moved back to London, living in the South Kensington area in the same household as her two unmarried daughters and four female servants.[52] It was not in London, however, but in the French

Provençal city of Cannes, that she died at the age of 85 in 1905. Described in her probate record as domiciled in what was for the émigré British the most celebrated resort on the Côte d'Azur, it seems likely that she had been settled for some years among a British diaspora about 20,000 strong, catered for by some twenty Protestant churches and briefly patronised by Queen Victoria.[53]

Alexander 'Alec' Fraser: A Trans-imperial Businessman

Some twelve months or more prior to Margaret Davidson-Fraser's death in Cannes, her brother-in-law, Alec Fraser, had died in London (Figure 7.5). A moderately wealthy man (his estate was valued for probate at £46,416) he was in his eighty-seventh year. According to the eulogy pronounced by the clergyman at the Presbyterian Church in nearby Marylebone, where Fraser had been a stalwart and generous financial supporter of the congregation for the previous quarter century, 'his physical and mental

Figure 7.5: Alec Fraser, Aberdeen-born partner in Maclaine Watson and subsequently Southeast Asian manager of the NISM (KITLV/University of Leiden)

Figure 7.6: One of the Indonesian artist Raden Saleh's paintings of Javanese antiquities in the collection of Alec Fraser (Smithsonian Institution)

alertness was remarkable right up to the end.'[54] His widow was an American woman (his second wife, herself a widow thirty years his junior whom he had first met in the Indies) and among his possessions in London were four large paintings, commissioned some forty or more years earlier from the eminent Indonesian artist Raden Saleh, depicting both tranquil heavily forested Javanese rural scenes and one of the island's celebrated Hindu antiquities (Figure 7.6).[55] It might be speculated, indeed, that the choice of subjects reflected the Dutch colony as Fraser wished to remember it: an 'orient' whose indigenous glories were located firmly in the past and whose contemporary 'natives', presumably placid tillers of the soil, were largely incidental. What they did not depict, however, were the sugar factories and their mass of commandeered workers from whose output he had initially made his money, nor the inter-island cargo-steamers from whose management in Southeast Asian waters he subsequently drew his salary – nor the major colonial war in which those steamers played an important role in the ferrying of troops and armaments.

It was these dimensions of his lengthy career, nonetheless, that define his role as a trans-imperial figure, one whose life as a businessman was played out in both the Dutch and British empires, and who has some claim to have been the central actor in the Maclaine Watson cohort's many-faceted evolution over the middle decades of the nineteenth century. As such, he had a stake (entrepreneurial, managerial and financial) in ventures in the

Indies and in London, and connections that extended into the Low Countries and possibly further afield. He was a prime example of the way in which, during the 'British Century', the Scottish diaspora spawned a plethora of economic actors (merchants, bankers and business people in general) who operated unconstrained by national or imperial boundaries.

Alec Fraser himself had arrived on Java for the first time in the mid-1840s, probably via Antwerp, where (as we saw) his older brother John Mathison Fraser had relocated from Aberdeen early in the previous decade. On his way to the Indies, the younger man had broken his journey in Calcutta where he had been able to be of assistance to a fellow Scot, Dr Alexander Duff, whose allegiance to the newly founded Free Church had cost him access to the collection of books at the heart of the schools he had established there.[56] Fraser's support presumably reflected the nailing to the mast of his own proclivities in the ongoing disputes among Presbyterians as well as his own practical piety. The mission that brought him to the Indies, however, was a distinctly mercantile one: namely, to join his elder brother, Arthur, in Surabaya in the latter's business – the Fraser Eaton 'sister firm' of the Maclaine Watson concern.

The connection with Fraser Eaton was consolidated as early as August 1845, when Alec Fraser was granted power of attorney to act in the firm's dealings,[57] after which he rapidly became established at the heart of Maclaine Watson's Java operations: indeed, by 1854 a young recent arrival wrote to his father in Scotland that 'Mr Fraser... and Mr [Donald] McLachlan have, I think, the most to say in the management of affairs'.[58] Living in some style in an 'agreeably located' house on the south side of the colonial capital's *Koningsplein*,[59] Fraser was identified by a British visitor as a person 'of high standing in the best society of Batavia',[60] where, among other things, he was to be found, together with two leading figures in the city's Dutch colonial community, on the organising committee for a charity performance to raise funds for the victims of the recent massive earthquake and tsunami in the north-east of the archipelago.[61] Later in the decade, moreover, he was the first to hold the newly created position of British consul at Batavia.[62]

A critical factor in advancing his business career was undoubtedly his marriage in 1850 to an Asian-born Dutch woman and the connections within the colonial establishment that this brought in its train. His bride was Julia Hermina van Citters (Figure 7.7), a widow aged no more than 30, whose her new spouse was scarcely three years her senior. Although she belonged to an extended family of merchants and state functionaries based

Figure 7.7: Julia van Citters, who married Alec Fraser in Batavia in 1850 (Collectie Zeeuws Museum, Middelburg)

in Zeeland in the south-west of the Netherlands, she hailed most immediately from the small, long-established Dutch mercantile communities on the Indian subcontinent. It was there that her father, Jan Willem Frederik van Citters, had been born and spent much of his career before relocating to Batavia in the mid-1820s.[63]

The key figure in this story, however, was his bride's mother, the (by then) widowed Louisa Isabella van Citters, née Bogaardt, the sister-in-law of a man who was successively Colonial Minister in the Hague and subsequently Governor-General (1856–1861). Her younger sibling, Catharina Johanna Wilhelmina Bogaardt, had wed the Dutch-Swiss Charles Ferdinand Pahud, soon after that ambitious and talented young colonial official first arrived in the Indies in the late 1820s.[64] The marriage had ended tragically with the 32-year-old Catherina's death at sea in May 1839 on her way to

Holland, but Pahud himself never remarried, and evidently remained close to his late wife's family, including the widow Bogaardt-Van Citters, and her daughter, Julia. In consequence, as the latter's husband, Alec Fraser, found himself in an enviable position among the Indies' colonial elite. One of the incidental fruits of being wed to Pahud's niece was that the Governor-General shared with him some 'confidential' details relating to Indies government finance, something that (when it accidentally became public knowledge) was subsequently used against Pahud by his political opponents in the Netherlands.[65] From Fraser's point of view, however, an altogether more substantial context concerned a scheme hatched early in the 1860s for building Java's first railway. But mention of Fraser's involvement with railways is to anticipate a later stage in a long career, a stage that began with his 'repatriation' to Britain (a temporary one, as it turned out) at the beginning of the 1860s, after he had been living for more than a decade and a half in the Indies.

An Interlude in the Scottish Borders

In June 1860 Alec Fraser wrote to a friend and former business partner that he and his wife were reckoning to 'say adieu to Java' later in that year and, taking advantage of the 'cold season [when] it is pleasant and easy

Figure 7.8: Fraser in the Scottish Borders, Hartrigge House (Collection of the Author)

travelling' in the subcontinent, to 'carry out a plan I have had for some time of making a trip through the British possessions in India on our way home and visiting the scene of the tragedies of 1857'[66] – meaning the various calamities that had befallen a number of British communities and garrisons during the recent 'Mutiny'. Arriving back in the United Kingdom in the middle months of 1861, Fraser evidently looked around for suitable retreat for a returning nabob – he had come back from Java with a fortune in the region of £67,000 (about £11 million at current prices)[67] – and by the following year had found a very impressive one in the Scottish Borders, where Hartrigge House near Jedburgh had just come up for lease following the death a few months earlier of its proprietor, the eminent Scots lawyer-politician and Lord Chancellor, John, first Baron Campbell of St Andrews (Figure 7.8). According to an advertisement In the Glasgow press, it was:

> ... recently almost entirely rebuilt, and is all newly Papered, Painted, and Furnished. It contains Five Public Rooms, Billiard Room, 23 Family and Servants' Bed Rooms, Dressing Rooms, Bath Rooms, and corresponding Kitchen accommodations. ... Stables and Coach Houses ... the walled Garden contains Hothouses and Fruit Trees in full bearing. The Grounds, to be Let along with the House, are well laid out as a Flower Garden, Shrubbery, Bowling Green, and Lawn. The Game on the Estate affords excellent sport. ... There is good Fishing in the neighbourhood, and the county is regularly hunted by the Duke of Buccleuch's fox-hounds. ... A more beautiful residence is seldom to be met with.[68]

Fraser, together with 'his lady and mother-in-law', took up residence there in July 1862.[69] One early visitor, the young Theodor Adolf von Möller (later a prominent industrialist and politician) left an account of his stay, in evident awe both of a 'Princely Household' and of host's social connections, reflected in a visit in Fraser's company to a Borders grandee of some standing, James Innes-Ker, 6th Duke of Roxburghe, with whom Fraser was evidently on familiar terms. Möller also recalled that breakfast at Hartrigge was preceded by a short religious service, conducted by Fraser himself, that mornings were devoted to riding, shooting, fishing and boating (or whatever other sport the houseful of guests were inclined towards), and that dinner, a formal affair served in the evening, was marked by the observance of the 'strictest English etiquette'.[70]

But another, and altogether more intriguing, visitor appeared at Fraser's country residence toward the end of December 1862. He was an agent for the Confederate side in the American Civil War and, as was widely the case among the British upper classes, was likely to have been assured of a sympathetic reception. We know about him because of a letter addressed from Hartrigge House to another (identified) Confederate agent and mentioning his allegiance to a third.[71] The letter was signed 'Yancey', and though this cannot have been the famed William Lowndes Yancey who, during the latter part of 1861 and the early months of 1862, had been the leading figure in an official Confederate mission to the UK – *that* Yancey's presence at the relevant time in his native Alabama is well documented[72] – it may have been a cousin or possibly a pseudonym, adopted to flummox Union spies, who were also very much present in the country throughout the war. The substance of the letter concerns designs for vessels that might be built, presumably in British shipyards (in potential contravention of Great Britain's declared neutrality), for use either against Union shipping or as blockade runners destined to keep open the trade between Southern ports and Liverpool, the prime destination for cargoes of raw cotton and other 'Confederate' commodities. Could some such project have been the subject of discussion between 'Yancey' and Alec Fraser and other (unknown) guests at his house in those post-Christmas?

Howsoever that may be, it was but one indication that the master of Hartrigge had not simply become a country gentleman whose business career was behind him, even though he had ceased to be a partner in Maclaine Watson itself at the close of 1863.[73] His sojourn in Great Britain coincided with a boom in company promotion in the City of London, largely contingent on a far-reaching easing of the hitherto tight legal provisions surrounding their formation. In this recently deregulated financial environment, new companies mushroomed: the one with which Fraser was most associated from its inception in 1864 (initially as its Deputy Governor) was the London-based Home and Colonial Marine Insurance Co.[74] With offices in the City, an authorised capital of £2,000,000, and a roll call of directors linked to commercial and financial interests in Asia and North America as well as in Great Britain itself, the Home and Colonial proved an enduring concern that survived until the final decade of the century.[75] Nor was it his sole such venture. Fraser was also on the boards of two other newly formed finance companies: the Merchant Banking Company of London,[76] and the (short-lived) British and Netherlands India Bank.[77]

Nor had he cut himself off from his old Indies associates. In conjunction with his erstwhile partners in Maclaine Watson, he was deeply involved in a pioneering railway project designed to link the Central Java port of Semarang with its agriculturally rich hinterland across the mountains to its south. In addition to his role as promoter, it appears that, through his connections in the City, Fraser may also have been responsible for the raising of a large tranche of the necessary capital. Meanwhile, prominent among the Dutch metropolitan supporters and investors in what became the Netherlands Indies Railway Company (Nederlandsch-Indische Spoorweg Mij.), was Fraser's cousin-through-marriage, Charles Pahud, recently returned to Holland after his term as Governor-General had ended in 1861 – and now a 'name' that gave added lustre to the whole venture. As it turned out, that lustre proved important: although the company got the go-ahead in the form of a government concession in 1863, it took ten years before the line was fully operational. Indeed, the company's troubled early financial history – it had to be bailed out by the Dutch home government in 1869 – may have meant that Fraser and his associates burnt their fingers rather than made money. Profits were slow to materialise, and it was only with the completion of the line in 1873 that the company 'began to climb slowly out of the financial morass'.[78]

Back to the Indies: the NISM

It was not railways, however, but steamers, in tandem with the forging of a connection with the ambitious Glasgow- and London-based shipping magnate-in-embryo William Mackinnon, which were to define Alec Fraser's subsequent trans-imperial career. A fellow Scot, albeit a Lowlander, during the 1860s Mackinnon worked to consolidate the core of the international shipping networks that were subsequently to make him famous on the imperial frontier in three continents. In tandem with Fraser, he established a London-based company under the Dutch flag – the Netherlands India Steam Navigation Company (Nederlandsch-Indische Stoomvaart Maatschappij, or NISM) – to take over the government subsidised, inter-island steamer routes in the Netherlands Indies that had evolved over the previous decade.[79] It was his involvement in this venture which took Fraser (together with his wife and mother-in-law) back to the Indies well before the decade was out as the new concern's chief executive. Matters got off to a rocky start: the NISM paid no dividends for the first three years of its operations and there were disputes with the London board over Fraser's remuneration package,[80] but once the new shipping line became fully operational and profitable Fraser settled into his role not only as the key figure in the NISM's operations in Southeast Asia, but also the promoter of potential regular steamer service from the Indies to Britain's Australian colonies to their south. It was not his first venture into the field of Java's Antipodean connections: while still in Great Britain back in the mid-sixties, he had promoted a scheme for an extension of the telegraph through the Indies to Australia.[81] Now, however, he took the opportunity of his position to travel in person to the Antipodean capitals: in Brisbane he was evidently a persuasive enough advocate to get the Queensland parliament to vote a substantial subsidy (some £25,000 annually) should the venture come to fruition, and in Melbourne he appears to have been mistaken for an official emissary of the Governor-General.[82]

The fact that this confusion arose speaks volumes for the nexus that Fraser – and through him the NISM – had established with the Indies government. Foreshadowed by his involvement in the railway consortium during the previous decade, and subsequently reflected in his membership of Batavia's government-appointed Chamber of Commerce and Industry,[83] the nexus ripened during the term of office, from 1872 to 1875, of Governor-General James Loudon. The latter's father, Alexander Loudon, had prospered in Java in the 1830s under the patronage of Governor-General (and subsequently Minister of Colonies) Jean Chrétien Baud, who wrote that the naturalised Scot had 'a Dutch heart'.[84] He had also been a close associate and friend of Maclaine Watson's co-founder. Equally to the point, however, Fraser, together with his deputy manager, Sam van Hulstijn, was on excellent terms with Loudon's influential executive officer, the Chief Secretary H. D. Levyssohn Norman.[85]

A decade later, by which time Levyssohn Norman himself had returned permanently to Holland, he was a prime applicant for the position of NISM representative in The Hague and spoken of by Fraser (who was by then the dominant figure on the NISM's London board) in the most glowing (and revealing) terms. Levyssohn Norman, he reported to his fellow directors, was a man 'intimately connected with the Company's business on Java and a warm and steady friend'. Indeed, wrote Fraser, 'it was he who *with me* [emphasis added] prepared the terms under which the [NISM's] original contract for the mail service was to be renewed for fifteen years'

– something that was only frustrated by the arrival of a new and less sympathetic Colonial Minister in The Hague. It was Levyssohn Norman, moreover, who had also facilitated the awarding to the NISM of a highly lucrative contract – 'a source of much profit to the company' – to carry materials and men to the war zone that had opened in Aceh in the north of Sumatra during 1873.[86] Indeed, it was this colonial war launched by Loudon and Levyssohn Norman and initially disastrous for the Dutch, that did much to cement Fraser's and Van Hulstijn's position in the Indies and metropolitan Holland. Among other things, on account of their 'war service' both men were inducted into the prestigious Order of the Netherlands Lion. Specific mention was made in the citations about their readiness to deploy the NISM's steamers in support of the war effort,[87] while Fraser himself was lauded as 'not only a naturalised Dutchman but also Dutch in sympathy' and as a 'trailblazer'.[88]

It appears, furthermore, that Fraser's business interests in the Indies extended beyond management of the NISM. Among other things, he was evidently on familiar terms with one of the leading figures in Java's large Sino-Indonesian mercantile community. The person in question was Be Biauw Tjoan, the Chinese *Major* (Dutch-appointed community head) in Semarang and, far from coincidentally, the holder of the government concession to retail opium (a major source of government revenue) throughout the port's extensive and densely settled hinterland across the mountains to the south. Whether Fraser himself had a stake in Be's multi-faceted business is no more than speculative. What is well documented, on the other hand, is that when the opium concessionaire came under suspicion for the illicit importation of the commodity – in contravention of the Indies government's monopoly – it was Fraser who (in company with a high-ranking Indies civil servant) successfully pleaded his case with the newly appointed Governor-General Loudon. Subsequently, moreover, *Nonya* Fraser was the woman deputed by a grateful Be to deliver a parcel of jewels to *Mevrouw* Loudon – she was Louise de Stuers, the descendant on both sides of her family of generals who had fought in the Dutch colonial war on Java in the late 1820s – on the occasion of the vice-regal couple's departure from office (a gift that Loudon, in his memoirs, tells us that he felt constrained to return).[89]

Loudon and his wife had left the Indies in 1875, while Fraser himself, now a widower following the death of Julia van Citters in February 1879,[90] had himself repatriated at the end of the decade. He did not return to the

Figure 7.9: 3 Craven Hill, Hyde Park – Paddington. London home of Alec Fraser after his return from Java in the 1870s (Collection of the Author)

Scottish Borders as of old, however, but to a substantial mansion in Craven Hill, a tree-lined street a little to the north of London's Hyde Park, where he spent the final two decades of his life (Figure 7.9). Despite being well into his sixties, moreover, he was evidently not someone who took kindly to 'retirement'. In addition to standing as a Liberal parliamentary candidate for the Northern Irish seat of Downpatrick in the general election of 1880 – despite his strong Presbyterian credentials, he was beaten by the hard men (and, he alleged, unsavoury tactics) of the ultra-Protestant Orange Lodge[91] – Fraser also resumed a number of City directorships, including a position on the board of the Chartered Mercantile Bank of India, London and China, where his colleagues-to-be noted that:

> Mr. Alexander Fraser, formerly of the firm of Messrs. Maclaine, Watson, & Co., of Batavia, . . . would be able to give his whole attention to the affairs of the bank. Their Java business was a large one, and Mr. Fraser's experience of business there would be very valuable to them.[92]

Meanwhile, Fraser got married again, and crossed over to the United States to do so. His new wife, Emma Augusta Blackman-Nickerson, was the New England-born widow of a young American merchant, Pliny

Marshall Nickerson – a scion of a leading Boston ship-owning family, who was U.S. consul at Batavia, as well as being in business there. He died in Batavia at around the same time that Alec Fraser had lost his first wife. Some sixteen months later, in July 1880, his widow married Fraser in Worcester, Massachusetts, close to the New England locality in which her own family was based, and where her father, the late William Moies Blackman, had been a shoe manufacturer.[93]

Back in London, the newly-wed couple took up residence at Craven Hill along with Blackman-Fraser's two Indies-born children (Fraser himself had no children of his own) and five live-in servants. They were soon joined by the widowed Alice Burbank Wheeler (Blackman-Fraser's niece), who appears to have filled the role of lady's companion. She accompanied the couple on a lengthy visit to the Indian subcontinent in 1883 and was frequently recorded as in residence at Craven Hill both before and long after the elderly Alexander Fraser's death in 1904. The story ends posthumously – and quite fittingly perhaps, given the strongly trans-imperial character of his long career – in the United States, a new empire beginning to assert its claims as such outside the immediate confines of the Americas. His widow, having outlived him by two decades, died at Craven Hill in October 1924, leaving an estate valued at £72,700 – most of which went to Alice Wheeler and her North American kin.[94] Among the goods that subsequently accompanied her back to the 'States were Raden Saleh's paintings of Javanese scenes: paintings that were subsequently to find their way into a major American public collection, that of the Smithsonian Foundation.

The Chatelaine of Kingston Lacy

On the British side of the Atlantic, meanwhile, the story of the Fraser network, dating from the 1820s, was far from played out. Back in June 1880, shortly after repatriating, Alec Fraser had written to James Loudon, now living in retirement in the Netherlands, that:

> we have been much afflicted here this week by the sudden death from heart disease of my nephew William Thomson Fraser . . . of Maclaine Watson and formerly British Consul at Batavia. His widow, Anna Onnen, is very inconsolable as you can imagine. She is left with three children – a girl of 13, a boy of 9 and a baby two months old. He was only 38 years old.[95]

We know little about her life, apart from the fact that she had wed Alec Fraser's nephew in Surabaya in 1865, not long after he had arrived in the Indies: we know a good deal more, however, about her eldest child, the 'girl of 13' mentioned in her great-uncle's letter. Born on Java, where she spent much of her childhood before her parents moved to Britain late in the 1870s, Henriette Jenny (or Jane) Fraser became the chatelaine of a grand country house and inheritor of a substantial fortune (Figure 7.10). Left parentless at the age of 17 by the death of her widowed mother, she moved nonetheless in London high society and went on to find (albeit at the relatively late age of 29) a husband of impressive wealth and social standing. Her achievement in this regard helps highlight and illuminate the extent to which diasporan Scots might drift away from their social and cultural as well as purely locational moorings – and, more generally, the extent to which money in late Victorian England could open the route to elevated social status.

Henriette Fraser's family background was solidly in 'trade': notably, though far from exclusively, in that conducted in sugar between Southeast Asia and Europe, which had been the basis for the wealth of her father, uncles and other members of the extended Fraser family from the mid-century onwards. As a businessman, however, her father himself does not appear to have been particularly successful – his 'personal estate' was valued at 'under £3,000' when he died at the end of May 1880[96] – quite possibly because ill-health had forced his premature repatriation from the Indies. Even so, at the time of his death he, his wife and young family were living in a substantial house at the westernmost edge of the eminently respectable residential district that stretched from Bayswater eastward, along the northern flank of the green sward of London's Kensington Gardens and Hyde Park, and they remained so at the time of the widow Anna Onnen-Fraser's own premature death scarcely five years later, leaving an estate valued at some £15,000.[97] The now parentless Henriette Fraser then took up residence nearby in the Bayswater household of her late father's younger brother, the Antwerp-born widower and 'East India Merchant and Bank Director', Arthur Abraham Fraser, together with his two daughters, his widowed mother-in-law and eight live-in domestics.[98] As this suggests, her extended family was a monied one, and doubtless took steps to ensure that three children were not left destitute by the early deaths of both their parents. One sign of expenditure on the orphans was the education at Harrow of the late couple's only son, John Thomson Fraser – a schooling from which he proceeded, by way of the Royal Military College, into a 'smart' cavalry regiment.[99]

This was a milieu that provides a potential clue to his sister Henriette Fraser's 'graduation' from solidly middle-class Bayswater to the 'blue-blood' territory of Belgravia, the acme of aristocratic London, where her husband-to-be had his townhouse.[100] Even so, it still needs more explaining than can be essayed here. She herself maintained, later in life, that she had met her future husband at a country house party somewhere in England,[101] which, though plausible, still leaves open the question – one relating to what has been termed 'the gentrification of the bourgeoisie'[102] – of how she came to be moving in such circles in the first place. It was a context, nevertheless, in which she successfully assumed the role of 'a well-known international beauty' and a much-admired denizen of fashionable watering-places on the Continent as well as in England, and as such appeared on the cover of *Hearth and Home: An Illustrated Weekly Journal for Gentlewomen* (Figure 7.11).[103] Along the way, her late businessman father had become a British 'Consul on Java' rather than a man whose prime occupation had been in the sugar trade, while her mother's family, that of a medical practitioner likewise

Figure 7.10: Henriette Fraser, 1897 (Collection of the Author)

Figure 7.11: Henriette Fraser-Bankes as chatelaine of Kingston Lacy (Hearth & Home, 6 Sept. 1900)

working in the Indies, was putatively aggrandised by the addition of a spurious 'van' to the family name.[104]

Her marriage itself took place, near the end of the London 'season', in mid-July 1897, and the groom was a substantially wealthy West Country landowner who left an estate valued for probate at nearly £240,000 when he died some seven years later.[105] Walter Ralph Bankes was evidently not only well-heeled but also well-connected. Among the guests at the wedding were the Duke and Duchess of Somerset (Wiltshire neighbours of the groom at Maiden Bradley House), a score of earls and countesses – and the Prince and Princess of Pless.[106] The princess was the former Daisy Cornwallis-West, a celebrated late Victorian 'beauty' who had wed (disastrously, as it turned out) at the age of 18, while her husband, Hans Heinrich XV, Prince of Pless, was one of the richest men in Germany, heir to a huge

Figure 7.12: Kingston Lacy, the grand house in the west country of England. Inherited by Henriette Fraser-Bankes – after the death of her husband in 1904 (Collection of the Author)

castle and estate in Silesia and on familiar terms with Kaiser Wilhelm II. The pair were evidently on one of their periodic visits to England, and in the month following the July wedding were in Ireland as guests of the Viceroy (aka 'Lord Lieutenant').[107] In short, the presence of the Pless couple affords one of those tantalising glimpses into the apex of the social circles in which some members of the Fraser family mingled, though it fails to provide any explanation of their dynamics.

Following this grand affair, it was at one of the groom's two country houses, Kingston Lacy near Wimborne Minster in Dorset, a splendid mansion that had been in her husband's family for generations, that the couple took up residence (Figure 7.12). It was an establishment that came to include a sequence of nannies for their three children and nearly a score each of domestic servants and gardeners, not forgetting a couple of stable hands and an estate that had its own 'home farm' and dependent cottages for its resident workforce.[108]

Walter Bankes himself – who is said after his marriage to have become 'an increasingly taciturn husband who preferred solitary country pursuits in Dorset to his social life in London' – died at Kingston Lacy in November 1904.[109] Even so, his partial withdrawal from society evidently had not precluded visits to Kingston Lacy from socially eminent individuals, something that continued after his death when, while staying in the vicinity, both Edward VII and Kaiser Wilhelm II came to pay their respects to the chatelaine – as did the Princess of Wales, the former Mary of Teck.[110] Bankes' widow, who outlived her husband by nearly fifty years, remained at the great house until the early 1920s, and – very much the business-manager of extensive country property – she further developed the estate, building a church, entrance lodges and many more estate cottages.[111] She sent her only son, Ralph Bankes, Jnr, to Eton and subsequently Magdalen College, Oxford.[112] Her two daughters appear to have fared rather less well, monstered by a mother who had absurdly elevated notions of her social status. One of them was disinherited and literally shown the door (her mother's own family history not withstanding) when she married a medical doctor with colonial roots, while the other, who remained single, at some time in her career ran a café on the Dorset coast.[113] Their widowed mother, meanwhile, moved into a town house adjacent to Claridge's, one of London high society's prime watering holes, and it was there that she died in November 1953 at the age of 86, worth around £68,000.[114]

Though several of her cousins entered the sugar business either on Java itself or in Europe, Henriette had found financial support from a quite different direction, through marriage to a substantially wealthy man, whose fortune she inherited (in trust) after his death. It was wealth that came largely from broad acres (60,000 of them) in Dorset and neighbouring counties, along with a graphite mine in Cumberland, in the far north-west of England (although her husband's grandmother, Frances Bankes, née Woodley, was the scion of a family of Caribbean owners of enslaved Africans, only a moiety of their money had come to her Bankes kin).[115] In Henriette's case, in short, the money trail was at some remove from the stereotypical one in which capital earned in (overseas) trade refreshed the diminished resources of an old-established landholding gentry. Instead, left in a potentially precarious financial position by the early death of her businessman father, she had repaired the situation in spectacular fashion through marriage to an exceptionally rich individual from precisely that socio-economic milieu. Moreover, hers was not an exceptional case: the story of one of her cousins exemplifies a similar point, but also highlights several kindred issues: the most important ones relating to women's agency in spheres at some considerable remove from the business world into which they had been born.

The Connoisseur Couple:
Mary Lydia Fraser and Jean Charles Drucker

As amply demonstrated not only by Henriette Fraser but also by her cousin, Mary Lydia Fraser, the agency of *daughters* had a substantial role to play in shifting the extended Fraser family into social and cultural realms that are unlikely to have been imagined by its patriarchs and matriarchs in early nineteenth-century Aberdeen. Significantly, they were not women who employed marriage to consolidate or fortify the Fraser family's mercantile network. Instead, they opted to marry 'out'.

During the mid-1880s, Alexander Caspar Fraser (the future 'squire' of Mongewell Park) and his wife had moved from Rotterdam to the Home Counties of England; and it was around this same time, in July 1886, that their 24-year-old daughter married the Amsterdam-born Jean Carl Joseph Drucker. It was at this point, moreover, that his path likely crossed with that of Henriette Fraser-Bankes: the as yet-unmarried young woman was staying at the same address (the Bayswater house of her uncle Arthur Abraham Fraser) given by Drucker on his marriage certificate as *his* temporary London place of domicile.[116] As we saw earlier, Henriette went on to 'marry into money' in no uncertain fashion, but Mary Fraser-Drucker herself was by no means a poor cousin. Not only was her father a rich man, but her newly acquired husband had recently inherited a fortune from *his* father, Louis Drucker, a leading banker (and financial theorist) in mid-nineteenth-century Amsterdam.[117]

The childless couple appear to have spent much of their time in late Victorian and Edwardian London – and in some style judging from the fact that there were nine live-in servants catering for the two of them – at a decidedly 'good' address in Mayfair.[118] Moreover, from 1890 onwards Drucker himself was a member of the socially exclusive Coaching Club, driving 'four well-made browns' in meets through Hyde Park.[119] Even so, both he and his wife kept up a close connection with the Netherlands, where, starting in the 1890s, they began to assemble an outstanding collection of modern Dutch art[120] – something which culminated in extensive donations to the collection of Amsterdam's Rijksmuseum, the Netherlands' foremost art gallery, and the building there of a dedicated 'Drucker' wing to house them.[121]

Figure 7.13: The Drucker-Frasers. The connoisseur couple, photographed in the late 1930s (Collection of the Author)

Mary Fraser-Drucker was very much an active partner in this enterprise – and possibly an inspiration for it. In reports of their activities as collectors and donors in the Dutch press, they were consistently designated as '*de heer en mevrouw* Drucker-Fraser', at a time when such emphasis on the wife's as well as the husband's family name was far from usual.[122] It was along with her husband that Fraser-Drucker herself evidently kept up a regular correspondence early in the twentieth century with the director of the Rijksmuseum – and it was perhaps an indication of how well they were acquainted that she felt able to complain to him about the amount of socialising involved in her husband's financial dealings on the other side of the North Sea – specifically the 'increasing number of bridge parties' that she was obliged to attend![123] The couple also maintained a close association with the artists from whom they bought paintings: one such transaction in 1898, *Self-Portrait with an Injured Foot* (*Zelfportret met Zieke Voet*) by one of the more celebrated, older members of the so-called Hague School, came together with a charming little note in English:

Dear Mrs Drucker, my sick foot is not quiet till he is in your possession, therefore you will accept this souvenir of ill-days with the pleasure of your recovered servant, Jozef Israëls.[124]

In recognition, moreover, of the 'generous and expert' manner in which Fraser-Drucker ('together with her husband') had contributed to the Dutch public's enjoyment, in 1923 she was awarded a gold medal by a leading Netherlands arts organisation.[125]

Whether the Drucker-Frasers' continuing connection with the Netherlands extended to Jean Drucker's Dutch kin is not known. It would be interesting to know if they had any contact with Drucker's half-sister Wilhelmina Drucker, 'Holland's First Suffragette'.[126] However, the Drucker-Frasers themselves were certainly no strangers to radical ways of thinking, and their anti-war stance after August 1914 cost Drucker – who together with his wife was by this time domiciled in Switzerland – his British passport (he had taken British nationality at the time of his marriage some three decades earlier).[127] Nonetheless, the British connection was subsequently resumed and, having already given paintings to the National Gallery in London prior to the War,[128] it was there, in 1928, that the connoisseur couple were major contributors to the nineteenth-century section of a huge exhibition of Dutch art at the Royal Academy. Among other paintings, there were some fifty Rembrandts on display and the *Illustrated London News* described it as likely 'to become the most important display of Dutch art ever held'.[129]

It was perhaps also the couple's swansong. By the 1930s they appear to have largely retreated to Switzerland. In July 1932, for instance, they were staying in the Alpine resort of St Moritz,[130] but subsequently they moved to Montreux at the eastern end of Lake Geneva, and it was there, at the Palace Hotel, that Jean Drucker and Mary Fraser-Drucker themselves died, within two days of each other, in late August 1944.[131] 'Greatly missed,' according to a death notice posted in a British newspaper around this time, 'by many friends in England, Holland and other countries,' Drucker himself left an estate in England valued for probate three years after his death at £48,452, while his late wife's share of the Drucker-Fraser fortune was said to be a mere £143 6s 3d. Lest this be taken to imply penury, however, it should be pointed out that her executors included an Amsterdam stockbroker with close ties to the Dutch royal family.[132]

Conclusion: Complicating the Diasporan Story

In its broadest dimension, the story of the 'Aberdeen' Frasers – with Alec Fraser, whose trans-imperial career exemplified Scottish entrepreneurship unconstrained by national boundaries, as its centrepiece – concerned members of a mercantile family from the north-east of Scotland, whose modest but astutely managed intermediary role in one of the nineteenth century's major global commodity chains was parlayed by the social actors concerned into something else again. To be sure, part of the story tells of continuing mercantile business in the Low Countries and London – and of a continuing but by no means exclusive connection with 'the East'. Its further ramifications, however, were of a very different order, and both complicate and deepen our understanding of the diaspora under discussion.

One dimension of this complexity is reflected in the stories, rehearsed here, of a woman of mixed Dutch, German and Scottish ancestry and on another whose heritage was similar – and whose formative years had largely been spent in the Dutch mercantile centre of Rotterdam. Both individuals 'married out', to an Englishman with significant cosmopolitan connections and to an Amsterdam-born Dutchman whose background was in that country's long-established Jewish community and its German affiliates. A further and closely related history, meanwhile, tells the story of a half-German, half-Scottish husband and his Dutch-German wife, whose lives were lived first in the Netherlands and latterly in the English home counties.

As well as highlighting issues related to ethnicity and identity, their stories speak, in no uncertain fashion, to the history of the diasporan money trail and, more specifically to the interface between urban mercantile pursuits and gentility. In this context, one outstanding theme that emerges is the degree of social advancement that financial resources brought back from the diaspora made possible – interwoven, in the case of both Henriette Fraser-Bankes and her cousin Mary Fraser-Drucker, with the fact they both married rich men whose wealth came from quite different sources. As such, the two women played a substantial role in shifting the extended Fraser family into largely new social and cultural realms. Their social and marital trajectories, meanwhile, illuminate a dimension of women's agency that is in danger of being submerged in the discussion of their role in diasporan business networks: some women were sufficiently well-placed to opt out of 'dynastic' marriages and to pursue their own rather than familial interests.

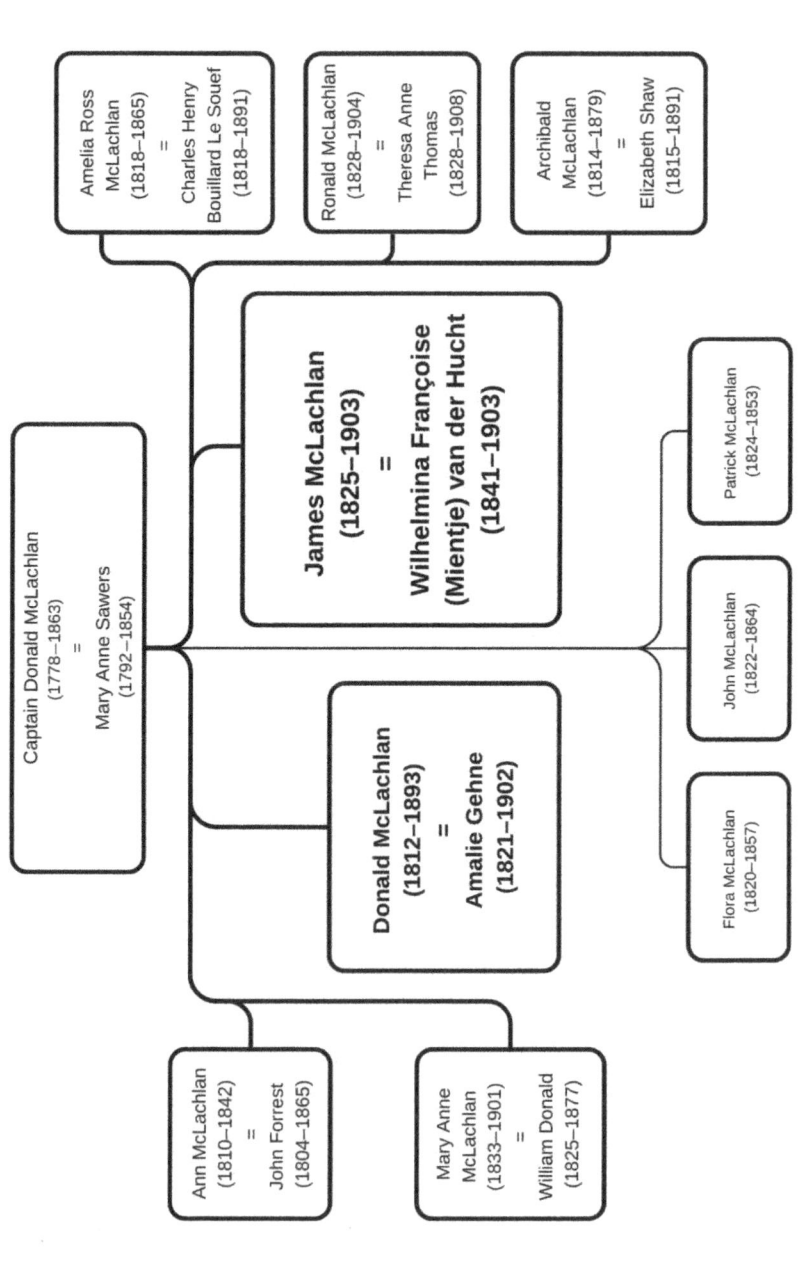

8

Sugar, Sheep and an Empire Family

WHEN THE YOUNG SCOTSMAN Donald McLachlan arrived on Java at the end of May 1839, he did not do so from his native land or anywhere else in Britain. Instead, his point of departure was one of the several British settlements in Australasia – where his family, headed by a retired officer in the British army, had recently arrived. Most immediately, it was from Sydney in New South Wales that he had sailed north-west, towards the Dutch colony.[1] Disembarking in the East Java port of Surabaya, the 27-year-old began working for the firm of Maclaine Watson, founded in the colony more than a decade earlier by a fellow Highland Scot and having among its partners one of McLachlan's distant cousins. He was joined there in 1850 by his much younger brother James, who had spent the previous decade in the Port Phillip district of south-eastern Australia, both in the newly established city of Melbourne and on an extensive farming property in which his father and several other of his siblings had a stake.

Both men grew rich on Java, largely through their participation in the island's rapidly expanding sugar trade, before retirements that took them back to Britain rather than to the Antipodes. Few other major global commodities – apart from cotton and cotton goods – took off so dramatically on the world stage during the nineteenth century. The factories in which cane was converted through a series of steam-driven processes into raw sugar (Figure 8.1), along with the wool sheds in which sheep were shorn by the thousand and their fleeces sorted, compressed and bailed (Figure

8.2), proliferated to feed a commerce that was worldwide, though heavily focused on consumers in Western Europe and North America. Nevertheless, there was a sharp contrast between the very different kinds of colonial appropriation characterising sheep rearing in the Antipodes and sugar manufacture in the Indies: a contrast which was determined less by the presence of settlers or sojourners than by the imperatives of the two commodities. However, they had one key dimension in common: both left the colonies in a form that required further processing in the metropole – sugar refining and weaving wool into cloth. As social actors who traded in them and had a stake in their primary production, the McLachlans were located along commodity chains that had world-wide reach.

Melbourne, the Wimmera and an Ungulate Invasion

The McLachlan family had set out from the Scottish town of Stirling, on the fringe of the Highlands some 36 miles north-west of Edinburgh, in April 1839 and disembarked in the newly established British colonial

Figure 8.1: *A sugar factory in Java, c.1860 (KITLV/University of London)*

Figure 8.2: A wool-shed in Australia, c.1890 (Collection of the Author)

settlement of Melbourne, on Port Phillip Bay (on the south-eastern coast of Australia) some five months later. Part of the initial cost of their venture was presumably defrayed by the sale of his officer's commission when Captain McLachlan retired from the 75th Regiment of Foot in 1838 (after more than a decade of being on half pay), raising perhaps as much as £1,800.[2] Even so, he would likely have deployed some of this on 'cabin class' shipboard accommodation for himself, his wife and their nine offspring, several of whom had adult status (something calculated at between £40 and £70 or more per head). Thereafter, however, the money trail in question goes tepid if not cold.

To be sure, the financial connection between nineteenth-century Highland proprietorship and the profits derived from enslaved African labour in the British Caribbean has been highlighted in a recent study that draws particular attention to the part played by the compensation money paid to slave owners by the British Treasury in the wake of the emancipation in the 1830s.[3] Similar, contemporary links with the Scottish diaspora in the Antipodes, it might be postulated, became a potential source of capital during at least the early phases of the rapidly expanding Australian pastoral industry, in a context in which it was otherwise in short supply. Huge fortunes need not have been involved. As has been aptly remarked, 'Even modest investments in slavery could generate colonial expansion. . . . [S]lavery wealth [might be] just enough to pay off a debt, relocate one's family across the world and obtain a land-grant', and there were indeed people 'embedded in the business of slavery who turned toward the southern hemisphere in the middle decades of the nineteenth century.'[4]

One such was James Monkton Darlot, whose marriage in 1853, almost twenty years after his arrival in the Antipodes, brought him into a family whose 'patriarch', Judge Samuel Firebrace, if not himself a slave owner there, had certainly been a pillar of the slave-holding establishment in Demerara, in what was then British Guiana.[5] But Darlot's association with the McLachlans, to which we shall return shortly, dated from a decade prior to this (putative) access to capital from this source. Meanwhile, one of the Captain's brothers (Ronald) was said to have been 'a planter in the West Indies' (but does not appear among the beneficiaries of compensation money),[6] and the Captain's wife, Mary Anne née Sawers, had undoubted family connections with the Caribbean holding of enslaved Africans: in particular, her uncle, 'John Sawers of Bellfield late of the Island of Jamaica now residing in Stirling' (he died in 1839) had been a recipient of the compensation in question. Yet the sum involved (around £1,100 for fifty-four enslaved individuals) was relatively modest (some contemporary payments to other Scottish recipients ranged from £3,676 through £8,000 to a massive £137,000),[7] and there is no evidence that he bestowed the gains in question on his niece and her husband; his will makes no mention of them.[8]

Evidence for the role in this case of slavery-derived wealth, in short, is far from conclusive, and it remains unclear just how Captain McLachlan was able to successfully re-establish his family on their arrival in Port Phillip in 1839. But re-establish he did. The diarist Georgiana McCrae – a woman who evidently moved in the 'best' circles in newly founded settlement, where the future Lieutenant-Governor and his wife were in her close acquaintance – encountered 'Captain McLachlan and his family' there in March 1841, dined with him, and subsequently had cause to be grateful to 'my kind neighbour, Mrs McLachlan' for her support in the aftermath of the birth of her first Australian-born child in December of the same year.[9]

Meanwhile, the Captain himself had become a founding member of the Pastoral and Agricultural Society of Australia Felix.[10] It was presumably a good foundation – at least in terms of the associates it brought in its train – for his subsequent relocation as a 'gentleman squatter' (substantial stakeholder with as-yet-to-be-confirmed title to the land), in the Wimmera region, about 170 miles to Melbourne's north-west. The venture appears to have begun early in the 1840s, when Captain and Mrs McLachlan's youngest son Ronald, on his recollection no more than a 'lad' at the time (he was about 16), had joined 'the late Mr Darlot . . . in bringing a number of cattle and sheep into the Wimmera', in a venture that brought him first to a property near the (present day) town of Horsham and subsequently some 50 miles to its northeast to what became known as Rich Avon.[11] By the 1850s he and two of his brothers, together with father, had some 15,000 sheep and 2,400 head of cattle grazing its nearly 123,000 acres.[12] It was in the Wimmera, at Rich Avon East sheep station, that the widower Donald McLachlan senior died in October 1863, having survived his wife by the better part of a decade and some twenty years after he had embarked on a 'second' career as a pastoralist or large-scale sheep farmer (permission to graze stock on what was still Crown land had been granted in 1842).[13]

The area was one in which colonial occupation had begun around the same time that the McLachlans had shipped out from Scotland – an occupation signified above all by the arrival of large flocks of sheep, many thousand strong, accompanied by scores of cattle, dogs, bullock-carts, shepherds and would-be wealthy stock owners. Between 1836 and 1840, it was reckoned (albeit perhaps with a touch of hyperbole) that the number of sheep in the districts around Port Phillip Bay increased almost thirty-fold from 26,500 to an estimated 782,000:[14] new arrivals came overland eastwards from New South Wales or were sent by sea northwards from Tasmania. This 'Plague of Sheep', as it has been so aptly designated,[15] undermined the complex and fragile subsistence habitat of the area's Aboriginal First Peoples, along with their way of life.

Primarily hunters and gatherers possessed of sophisticated techniques of land management, they were confronted by an ungulate invasion that inaugurated an era of brutal conflict, the upshot of which was their dispersal and decimation. Violence was endemic along an ever-moving frontier in which 'peacefully inclined [First Nation] camps and blameless settler families frequently became victims of parties bent on indiscriminate revenge'.[16] Indeed, it has been cogently argued in relation to Australia as a whole that:

everyday settler violence, and retributive police expeditions, as opposed to organized warfare, was in the longer term among the worst on British colonial frontiers. . . . There were few other places in the British Empire where the indigenous population was so quickly dehumanized, and so systematically dispossessed and displaced.[17]

The Wimmera itself encompassed many of the ancestral lands of the Dja Dja Wurrung and Jardwadjali peoples and along with adjacent districts was the scene, late in the 1830s and throughout the following decade, of some thirty recorded episodes of violent conflict between settlers on their sheep runs and the local First Nation population. They were conflicts in which the latter invariably came off (far) the worse, as evidenced by the killing in 1839 of nearly forty Dja Dja Wurrung in what may have been a particularly gross 'incident', though not one that ran against the grain of broader settler sentiment: it was a context in which it was said of one particular sheep station owner that he 'was in the habit of shooting every black man, woman and child that he met on his run'.[18] The upshot was that by the close of 1850s the primary 'clearing out' of Aboriginal people in this part of south-eastern Australia was largely complete – something reflected, among other things, in the rapid expansion (to the chagrin of the station-owners) of the numbers of pasture-eating kangaroos, marsupials formerly hunted for food by the now heavily reduced First Nation population.[19]

From the Antipodes to the Indies:
Java Sojourns, Sugar, and Wives

The part played in this course of events by the McLachlans of Rich Avon remains undocumented. What is clear, nonetheless, is that for the brothers Donald and James McLachlan the voyage from the Antipodes to the Indies involved something far more than a mere change of location. Rather, it opens a field of comparisons and contrasts regarding the myriad facets of colonialism. As elsewhere in south-eastern Australia, the construction of a wool shed on the family's Wimmera property signified the replacement by sheep of the area's precolonial inhabitants: ones judged to stand in the way of the expansion of the production of the commodity from which those members of the McLachlan family who opted to remain there reckoned on making their fortunes. Once in the Indies, on the other hand, the brothers found themselves in a very different situation. The ubiquity of the sugar factory in Java's eastern and central lowlands was contingent on the wealth-creating potential present in a densely settled rural Indonesian population, whose land and labour were exploited through a form of 'serf-itude' that utilised (and elaborated and extended) a labour-service regime inherited by the island's Dutch masters from the pre-colonial state. Although enslaved labour in the form of chattel slavery existed on Java until the 1860s, there was no need to employ it in the production of sugar, even had it been feasible to do so: instead, under the aegis of the *Cultuurstelsel*, or System of [State] Cultivations, inaugurated by the colonial government in 1830, the industry drew on the resources of a readily coercible peasantry of small farming households and their dependants.[20]

On this basis, Java's mid-nineteenth-century sugar factories – by around 1850 there were more than 100 of them scattered across the lowlands of Central and East Java – were generally profitable enough to be able to adopt the steam-and-steel technology and scientific know-how that characterised the more advanced sectors of cane-sugar production worldwide. The Maclaine Watson partnership in which both McLachlan brothers participated was instrumental in this process, but for the most part it confined its activities to the financing of third-party manufacturers over whom it held a sometimes monopsonist sway.[21] Astutely managed – and the partners indeed appear to have been singularly adept in this respect – it was a formula that made them rich enough to retire well ahead of their European-based contemporaries.

These sources of wealth and the money trails which they generated were by no means the only contrasts between the colonial Antipodes and the Indies. On arrival in Java, the brothers found themselves surrounded, as had not been the case in Melbourne and its satellite sheep runs, by long-established and extensive quasi-settler colonial communities,[22] which included many individuals of mixed European-Asian heritage. Although skewed, the ratio between men and women was not grossly disproportionate: around the mid-nineteenth century, colonial enumerators counted (along with around 8,000 children) some 6,115 adult male Europeans and 4,577 adult females, a ratio of less than 3-to-2.[23] In short, it was a singular social terrain offering excellent opportunities for a degree of regular domesticity – for marriage and starting a family – that was rare in sojourner European enclaves in 'the tropics', even as it had indeed begun to characterise the

Figure 8.3: Donald McLachlan married Amalie Gehne in Semarang in 1847 – eight years after he left Australia (Collection of the Author)

migrant British and Irish colonial communities that the brothers had left behind in Australia.

The two Indies-bound McLachlan siblings took full advantage of this situation – though in neither case immediately. Indeed, the elder of the two, Donald, had already been working there for Maclaine Watson for more than seven years, when he wed a migrant Dutch schoolteacher's daughter, Amalie Frederika Gehne in Semarang in September 1847 (Figure 8.3).[24] His bride's late father, Carl Friedrich Gehne, had sailed with his family from the Netherlands to the Indies in 1842,[25] only to die there some twelve months later, leaving his widow, Sara Hester Catharina Gehne-Klamberg, to look after – and maybe find husbands for – the three daughters whom the couple had brought out with them. Despite a relatively modest social background, the young women concerned – all well into their teens when their parents had embarked for the Indies – could lay claim to the cultural 'finish' that went with extended residence in the Dutch metropole (it would be expected, for instance, that they were adept at the piano and reasonably fluent in French). Their father's profession, moreover, meant that they had also been exceptionally well educated in a more formal sense.

With qualifications and attributes like these at something of a premium in mid-century Java, it is hardly surprising that their widowed mother achieved such success in the marriage stakes on her daughters' behalf. Before gaining McLachlan as a son-in-law (by this time he was a solidly established businessman who subsequently added British consular postings in Semarang and Surabaya to his commercial portfolio),[26] Gehne-Klamberg had already married another of her offspring, Augusta Carolina to the eligible widower, Coenraad Alexander de Jongh. An eminent figure in legal circles in Semarang, he subsequently relocated to Batavia as Vice-President of the High Court of the Indies. Another of her sons-in-law, meanwhile, held an important position in the business world, as agent in the major Eastern Indonesian port of Makassar for the NHM (Nederlandsche Handel-Maatschappij, Netherlands Trading Society), the colony's leading commercial and financial concern.

Donald McLachlan's younger brother's marital politics, nonetheless, were on an even more elevated plane. James arrived on Java late in 1850.

Figure 8.4: James McLachlan at the time of his marriage to Mientje van der Hucht in Batavia in 1862 (Collection of the Author)

Along with a certain adeptness in the sugar trade, it was marriage that made him. The 37-year-old James McLachlan (Figure 8.4) wed the 21-year-old Wilhelmina Françoise van der Hucht (known familiarly as Mientje, Figure 8.5) in Batavia in 1862, four years after becoming a partner in Maclaine Watson,[27] and by which time he had been domiciled in Java for twelve years or more.[28] The bride's father, Willem van der Hucht, was well known in colonial circles as a pioneering tea-planter in West Java. Subsequently, the capital that he had accumulated there went into helping establish the Netherlands-based Billiton Company to exploit the tin resources of that eponymous Indies outpost, nearly 300 miles due north of Java. The only surviving child of her father's first marriage (her two siblings had died, along with their mother, not long after the family's arrival in the colony in 1844) the young woman, while still a child, had been sent back to the Netherlands to join relatives in Amsterdam – and no doubt received much of her education and social 'finishing' there.[29] Returning to the Indies with her father early in 1861, she appears to have rejected one suitor and to have had McLachlan found for her – 'I believe he is just the man to make Mientje

Figure 8.5: Mientje van der Hucht, wife of James McLachlan, as a girl (Collection of the Author)

Figure 8.6: Donald McLachlan, partner in Maclaine Watson – sometime after he had retired to England in 1850s (KITLV/University of Leiden)

happy' – by a parent who was also concerned about the ill-feeling that evidently existed between his daughter and her stepmother, a woman only ten years her senior. For his part, the bridegroom also appears to have been happy to oblige his future father-in-law by finding a husband for the young woman, notionally an 'adopted daughter', with whom he himself had been cohabiting for some years previously.[30] It proved the prelude to a financially well-upholstered married life, spent first in the Indies and subsequently 'at home' – but neither in McLachlan's native Scotland nor in his wife's adoptive Netherlands. Instead, it was spent in a town which, for all its pastoral location in provincial England, was also a significant node on British imperial circuits and the nurturer of the kind of 'empire family' into which the extended McLachlan kin was being transformed. Most immediately, it became the focus for a veritable 'gathering of the clan'.

Figure 8.7: James and Mientje McLachlan's Holland House in Cheltenham (Collection of the Author)

The McLachlans of Cheltenham: An Empire Family at Home

Not all the 'clan', to be sure. Death had taken its toll on three of the siblings while they were still overseas and unmarried, and James McLachlan's sister-in-law – the Dutch school teacher's daughter who had wed his elder brother Donald (Figure 8.6) – ended her days in a boarding house near Portsmouth on the South Coast of England, where her fellow lodgers, along with an unmarried daughter, included a dressmaker and a hospital nurse.[31] It was a sad decline from glory days spent across the Solent in Karl Marx's 'little paradise' on the Isle of Wight,[32] where the household over which she and her late husband had presided boasted eight live-in servants and a coachman,[33] and reflected a decline in the family fortunes, most likely the result of failed investments in the City of London, that had begun well before the latter's own death in 1893 (when his estate amounted to a modest £8,900).[34]

Nonetheless, the downward trajectory of the McLachlan–Gehne couple was far from typical of the histories of other members of this branch of the 'clan'. For them, sugar in Java and sheep in the Antipodes provided the basis for repatriate afterlives of continuing affluence – carried through, indeed, into the following generation. James and Wilhelmina McLachlan's own story provides the vital cue for a larger family history. Donald McLachlan's younger brother and his wife had visited England from the Indies briefly in 1867; indeed, it was in the Gloucestershire town of Cheltenham, a hundred miles west of London, that their second son was born in July of that year.[35] Back permanently in England three years later, in 1870,[36] they initially established themselves, with a complement of nine servants including a governess and a wet nurse, in London's Hyde Park–Bayswater district, a locale favoured by many of the Maclaine Watson returnees.[37] By the middle of the decade, however, they were back in Cheltenham where McLachlan became the owner of a commanding, three-storeyed, double-fronted, stuccoed mansion newly built on Lansdown Road, one of the expanding town's main boulevards (Figure 8.7). It was there, at Holland House – an appropriate name, given that its construction was financed in part at least by his wife's money (her father had died in the Netherlands in 1874 and she was said to have inherited half of his considerable fortune)[38] – that the couple remained for the rest of their lives, in a household supported by some seven to nine live-in servants, in addition to a coachman and his wife.[39]

Doubtless pre-eminent among the town's attractions for James McLachlan (Figure 8.8) was the presence there of his considerably older brother Archibald McLachlan and his wife, Elizabeth Shaw, who had repatriated in the 1850s together with their four Australian-born daughters.[40] McLachlan – who, like his Java-based siblings, 'married out' – had wed the London-born Shaw, scion of a family of (ex-)Liverpool slave-traders and Caribbean slave-owners, in Melbourne in 1840,[41] while pursuing a business career there, variously as an 'agent' and an 'accountant'. 'Archibald McLachlan, Esq., J.P.' was one of the trustees of the Melbourne Savings Bank, helped set up one short-lived 'gentlemen's club' there, and was a foundational member of its still extant successor. In addition, he bought land in what are now the city's northern suburbs and was also in business with his father-in-law,[42] before embarking, as we have seen, on a more ambitious venture: joining his younger brother, Ronald McLachlan, in the purchase of the Rich Avon sheep station in the Wimmera. His returnee afterlife was

Figure 8.8: James McLachlan in retirement in Cheltenham (KITLV/University of Leiden)

evidently a financially comfortable one: on his death in 1879 he left an estate valued at something 'under £45,000' – not a great fortune, but a respectable one.[43]

Archibald McLachlan and his family, however, were not the only Cheltenham-based relatives. James McLachlan's younger sister, Mary Anne McLachlan, and her husband William Donald were also already settled there: Scottish-born but wed in Australia, they had likewise 'repatriated' and arrived in the town in the mid-1860s. Donald himself was a Wimmera 'pioneer' who lent his name to the eponymous township about seven miles to the north of Rich Avon itself. By the time of the 1871 Census, he and his wife were solidly established (together with their eight children) at Lisle House on Cheltenham's Clarence Square, in a substantial, late Regency building of three storeys and a basement.[44] It was there that William Donald died in 1877, leaving a well-provided-for widow: his estate was valued for probate at something 'under £70,000'.[45] More than a decade earlier, the widow's elder sister, Amelia Ross McLachlan – who had married Charles Henry Bouillard Le Souef in Melbourne some quarter of a century earlier – had also died in Cheltenham, leaving a widower who returned to the Antipodes, where he subsequently remarried.[46]

Meanwhile, the next generation of the extended McLachlan family had gravitated to Cheltenham from the Antipodes and Java, in the person of John Forrest (Figure 8.9), a young man whose father, the military surgeon Dr John Forrest, had married Ann McLachlan, the eldest of Captain Donald and Mrs Mary Anne McLachlan's daughters – in Scotland before the family party had set off for Melbourne in 1839.[47] Dr Forrest and his young wife, however, had disembarked at Cape Town, and it was there that their son was born in February 1842, followed by the death of his mother from tuberculosis some six months later. After having spent his youth mainly in England, John Forrest Jnr had sailed to Java in 1859 to work for the same Maclaine Watson concern in which his two McLachlan uncles were senior partners. He became a partner himself a decade later, in 1870 – and at the same time British vice-consul in Surabaya – but within less than two years he had left the Indies to join other family members in Cheltenham. It was there, in August 1873, that he married Eveline Rodger, the daughter of a wealthy Scot who had been living in the town for some years. Continuing the Cheltenham connection, the couple maintained a residence there for the rest of their lives, although they made their main home a manor house in Buckinghamshire, in the Home Counties, some 40 miles from central London.

Figure 8.9: *John Forrest, partner in Maclaine Watson and early retiree to Cheltenham (KITLV/ University of Leiden)*

But it was not merely happenstance that had brought several branches of the McLachlan family together in one particular locale in the English provinces. Although by the mid-nineteenth century Cheltenham (a place of elegant Regency terraces, crescents and squares)[48] had lost its chic as a place 'to take the waters' in the company of similarly wealthy fashionables, it had undergone a cultural repositioning – and found a new *raison d'être*. It was a repositioning to which, in its broadest sense, the assembled McLachlans both contributed and from which they benefited. James McLachlan himself, for example, was 'closely associated' with the several hospitals and charitable institutions in the town, while his wife was similarly famed for her 'local philanthropy'.[49] Increasingly popular with ex-colonial civilian and military repatriates, well-heeled returnees from British India in particular 'came to Cheltenham on furlough or retirement in large part because they sought to retain contact with the social circles in which they felt most at ease'.[50] Though themselves from a more distant part of the colonial world (and from a different 'Raj'), the family presumably fitted quite well into this milieu: at Holland House among James and Wilhelmina McLachlan's near neighbours were a retired lieutenant-colonel and a Bengal-born 'Retired Indian Merchant'.[51] A specific manifestation of the

Figure 8.10: Cheltenham Ladies' College, where several of the young women of the McLachlan families were educated (Collection of the Author)

role of colonial wealth in shaping British urban cultural and social environments,[52] Cheltenham's case exemplifies how such towns could serve not only as places where returnees might enjoy convivial company, but also as sites that nurtured the growth of empire families who were linked to the (British) imperial project over several generations in both civilian and military capacities.

Much of that nurturing took place in Cheltenham College, one of the leading Public Schools of Victorian England, which had opened in 1841 – and on whose committee of management James McLachlan was a long-serving member[53] – and the equally prestigious Cheltenham Ladies' College (Figure 8.10) which followed twelve years later.[54] As such, the town was not without its attractions for the well-heeled parents of a young family, since their offspring could be (and were) educated in one or other of these establishments. Not for them the long-term separation of children from parents that was often associated with sojourning.[55] In turn, the town's burgeoning reputation as a centre of educational excellence was boosted by (and closely associated with) parallel developments on the religious front, which further burnished Cheltenham's credentials as a hub of empire. A centre of ardent evangelical Christianity, it was remarked (albeit somewhat prior to the McLachlans' arrival) that 'the Sabbath was better observed there than in any town outside Scotland',[56] something which reflected the thirty-year 'reign' in Cheltenham of the Reverend Francis Close:[57] famously, the poet Tennyson called it 'a parson-worshipping place, of which [he] is the Pope'.[58] Although evangelical links to the imperial cause were often ambiguous and varied greatly over time and location,[59] although his numerous publications suggest a prime focus on matters domestic (inter alia, the evils of drink, horse-racing and papists), Close himself was not oblivious to imperial issues and the missionary imperative: viz his 36-page pamphlet of 1858, written in the wake of the great uprising of the previous year, and entitled *An Indian Retrospect, or what has Christian England done for Heathen India?*[60] It was no accident, therefore, that Cheltenham College's curriculum – one in which Close no doubt had a part in devising – 'placed more emphasis on Divinity than on the Classics'.[61]

A Thirst for Empire and
Ongoing Business in the Indies and the Antipodes

Equally importantly, however, the College also taught 'modern' subjects to prepare its graduates for competitive entry into the army and the civil service.[62] As such, it proved an excellent foundation for the substantial military careers of two of James and Wilhelmina McLachlan's sons. It was in British imperial campaigns in Egypt's Nile valley in the nineteenth century's closing decades that the most illustrious of the latter-day 'military' McLachlans, James Douglas McLachlan, their Java-born fourth son, won his spurs as an officer in the Queen's Own Cameron Highlanders, after an education at Cheltenham College had no doubt imbued him with the right spirit to take on such a career – one that echoed that of the founder of the Australian branch of the McLachlan family, who had arrived in the Antipodes as a retiree from the British Army.

Promoted to the rank of lieutenant-colonel, James Douglas McLachlan was stationed, among other places, in the Indian subcontinent (as, indeed, his grandfather had once been), after which he saw combat as a veteran on the Western Front during the First World War, before becoming, in its later stages, the first British military attaché in Washington.[63] In retirement, unlike the majority of his siblings, he opted for London rather than Cheltenham, where he and his wife – the Australian-born Gwendolyn Mabel White lived in the vicinity of Montague Square, in a 'smart' part of the West End. Meanwhile, his elder brother, Donald Maxwell McLachlan had been a captain in the King's Own Royal Lancaster Regiment at the time of his (first) marriage in 1902 and subsequently fought in France as a lieutenant-colonel during the First World War.[64] His cousin, Archibald Sawers McLachlan (English-born elder son of Donald and Amalie McLachlan), also opted for the army – the 1881 Census found him in barracks a few miles south of Edinburgh – as too did the latter's younger brother, Alexander McLachlan, who joined the East Kent Regiment of Foot (aka 'The Buffs').[65]

Nor were the women of the family immune from the attractions of the military sinews of empire. The only one of the McLachlan–van der Hucht daughters to survive into adulthood, Annie Constance McLachlan, had attended Cheltenham Ladies' College and quite possibly followed this up with 'finishing school' in France, as had some of the young women of her Australian sisters-in-law's family.[66] Married in 1909, at the age of thirty-three, with the Irish-born Captain Arthur Colthurst Herbert, an officer in the Royal Warwickshire Regiment, she and her husband, following his return to active service during the War, had settled into Charlton Manor (a substantial early Victorian house) in what was still open countryside a little over two miles from the centre of Cheltenham itself. It was there that her husband died in 1933, worth around £100,000 – not the result of an improbable garnering of an army pension, but reflecting an accumulation of wealth from a quite different source: a post-army career as a company director that underscored the intermeshing of the military dimension of empire with its production of key commodities.[67] As one of the partners in a thriving tea-plantation business in what is now Sri Lanka, Herbert had no doubt benefited from the halcyon days of the 1920s, when the Telbedde Ceylon Estates, of which he was a director, paid dividends as high as 90 per cent to what was most likely only a small, tightly knit group of shareholders (even in 1935, during the subsequent inter-war Depression, the company still managed to pay 17 per cent).[68] In his case, in short, what one recent author has so tellingly diagnosed as 'A Thirst for Empire' – manifest, among other things in the flexing of British military muscle[69] – literally paid handsome dividends. His widow, meanwhile, survived her husband by almost two decades before dying in 1951, leaving an estate valued at some £33,000.[70]

But not all the lives of the second generation of these empire families centred on military muscle and intelligence. Three of James and Wilhelmina McLachlan's four sons kept up the imperial connection in civilian capacities – one of them returning to the Indies, another to the Antipodes, and a third basing himself in London. After being educated, like his brothers, at Cheltenham College, the Batavia-born Alfred Francis McLachlan returned to Java to work for the Maclaine Watson partnership in their Surabaya 'sister firm' – which is where he died of typhoid in February 1901, leaving an Indies-born widow. She was Catharina Maria Hermina Alexandrina Gijselman, amongst whose siblings was a Batavia-based medical practitioner[71] (and several young children).[72] Subsequently, she found her way to England and kept house for a bachelor brother-in-law at Rendcomb Manor in Gloucestershire, some ten miles south of Cheltenham.

That brother-in-law, William John McLachlan, once his college days were over, had been dispatched not to the Indies but to Australia. Although it is not entirely clear what he did there, evidently he was not placed on a sheep station but most likely worked in Melbourne (where, as we shall see, his uncle, Ronald McLachlan, lived), presumably with the capital of £10,000 with which his father had provided him.[73] Could it have been with the great Dalgety firm of wool-brokers (founded in 1841), by whom his father was said to have been employed before relocating from Australia to the Indies?[74] Howsoever that may be, summoned back to Cheltenham by his parents, and having in consequence 'given up his profession in Australia', he was described in his father's will as 'having been for the last nine years of exceptional help to me in the administration of my affairs'.[75] He also took the opportunity back in Cheltenham to join the town's Freemasons.[76]

After his father's death, however, McLachlan showed no apparent inclination to be other than a country gentleman, retiring to his Gloucestershire manor house, where he died some four decades later, in February 1948, leaving a substantial estate of over £171,000.[77] Meanwhile, his younger sibling, the Cheltenham-born Arthur Cecil McLachlan, had spent his active life working as an 'East India Merchant' in the City office of Maclaine Watson. In 1903, shortly after his parent's death, a newspaper report identified him as of '9, Billiter Square', the firm's London address.[78] Evidently a confirmed bachelor, he moved late in life into his London club, St James's in Piccadilly – one of the capital's smaller gentlemen's clubs, founded in 1857. Nonetheless, it was at an address in Cheltenham, the favoured haunt of most of his kin, that he died in 1953 at the age of 80, worth a solid £92,000.[79]

Back to the Antipodes:
Ronald and Theresa McLachlan in Marvellous Melbourne

As these histories suggest, the empire family in question kept up its long-established connections not only with the Indies and its sugar trade but also with the Antipodes. Indeed, this explains why one McLachlan sibling was entirely missing from the 1870s gathering in Cheltenham of repatriates. Unlike his two sojourner brothers, Ronald McLachlan – one of the three partners in the Rich Avon sheep station – had remained in Australia, where he found both a wife and a degree of success as a pastoralist. In 1843, while still 'a lad' of fifteen, he had assisted a prominent Port Phillip squatter in driving sheep (along with cattle and horses) into the Wimmera, where he subsequently had a property near what became the town of Horsham, some

185 or so miles north-west of Melbourne, before shifting yet further north to Rich Avon itself.[80] His wife, the Tasmania-born Theresa Anne Thomas, was the daughter of an early Antipodean pastoralist (one with an ancestry in the Protestant ascendency in Ireland) and had an extensive Australia-based kin network.[81] Perhaps because of this, she and her husband opted to retire to what had been transformed over the decades since the McLachlan family's arrival there into the Marvellous Melbourne of the 1880s: a world city whose half-million population outnumbered that of erstwhile counterparts in the New World – and in much of the Old (European) World as well. As such, it boasted an 'empire' not only of sheep runs and cattle ranches but also of finance that extended across south-eastern Australia to New Zealand and into the islands of the Pacific and drew in massive amounts of investment (as well as migrants) from its British metropole.[82]

It was in Melbourne that Ronald McLachlan – memorialised as 'one of Victoria's oldest settlers ... few men have seen 60 years of the development of what was practically a virgin country'[83] – died in August 1904, followed to the grave four years later by his widow. Long resident in the prime suburb of South Yarra, a place where the city's wealthy elite congregated (and still do), he left, nonetheless, an estate valued for probate at only around £3,500 – perhaps because he had been caught by the 'bust' of the 1890s that followed the boom years of the previous decade. In any event, assuming that a much larger fortune had not been strategically redistributed before his death, he would appear to have been the poor colonial 'cousin' of his repatriated kin in Cheltenham.[84]

Nonetheless, the organic Antipodean connection of this particular empire family, as we have already seen, extended well beyond a single relic of the originally nine-strong group of McLachlan siblings who had disembarked in Port Phillip Bay back in 1839. It also extended to quadrupeds and days at the races. For the 'Cheltenham' McLachlans, the town and its environs offered them excellent opportunities for days of this kind – by the 1870s, regular race meetings had been a fixture for some decades, to the fury of the Evangelicals[85] – and for an equestrian lifestyle such as they would have enjoyed both in Australia and on Java where, during his Indies sojourn, James McLachlan had been the possessor of a number of fine mounts, including ones imported from Sydney,[86] and where several of his closest associates were members of the colonial racing and hunting fraternity. In Australia, meanwhile, equestrian pursuits were a key aspect of life among the rural settler population, and any country town worth the name had a racetrack.

Back in Britain, James McLachlan's only son-in-law, Captain Herbert, evidently shared in these proclivities. A brief obituary in a Gloucestershire newspaper, addressed in particular to 'Hunting folk and Cheltonians', noted that he was a committee member of the nearby Cotswold Hunt and that his son was likewise a 'keen horseman' and amateur steeplechaser.[87] It was, perhaps, more than just a reflection of the continuing nexus between sugar and sheep that two of the sons of James and Wilhelmina McLachlan married into an Australian pastoralist family, the Whites of Havilah in New South Wales – celebrated not only for breeding the ungulates in question but also for the quality of their horses. Indeed, 'the fame as a stud master' of the father-in-law in question, Henry Charles White, 'was eventually both national and international'.[88]

The Sugar Factory, the Woolshed, and an Empire Family

A criss-crossing of the oceans and the imperial divide – moving from Britain to Australia, from Australia to the Indies, and from both the Indies and Australia back to Britain – characterised the lives of the extended McLachlan kin over several generations. At the same time, their colonial careering and repatriate afterlives highlight the extent to which the commodities that drove their stories (raw, unrefined sugar, wool, tallow, and sheep meat) were the outcomes of two very different manifestations of colonialism: one based on the intensive appropriation of the labour of the subject population, the other on its decimation and dispersal. Something of this was reflected, it might tentatively be suggested, in the different settler configurations the McLachlans encountered in the Indies and the Antipodes respectively, and in their responses to them.

Captain McLachlan, the family 'patriarch', together with his wife, died in the Antipodes after more than two decades of residence there. All but one of their surviving offspring, however, returned to Britain (variously from the Indies and Australia) and established themselves as an extended empire family – predominantly in and around the Gloucestershire town of Cheltenham, known for its educational facilities, its evangelical religious fervour, and (however paradoxically) for what it had to offer for devotees of the turf. As such, the McLachlans were sojourners who parlayed their colonial wealth into enhanced social status as returnees, successfully submerging both the violence of the Australian sheep frontier and the mass coercion of the Dutch regime in the Indies in fine houses and (some) philanthropy in a quite singular English provincial town. Their favoured locale clearly demonstrated the intermesh of colony and metropole, and the indivisibility of 'home' and 'away'. While Cheltenham offered a convivial place of (quasi-)retirement for returnees, it also provided the social and cultural foundations for the next generation of a group of kin, that retained its trans-imperial 'civilian' investments in the Indies and the Antipodes while contributing to the military muscle of empire-building. In this context, a focus on the social actors involved underscores the point that (colonial) commodity chains did not exist in isolation from one another – or from the military might that ultimately secured them. Indeed, not the least of the McLachlan family's achievements, in this regard, was that the 'East India merchant', the Australian pastoralist, and the senior British Army officer were quite literally closely related.

FAMILY OF MCLEAN OF BREDA

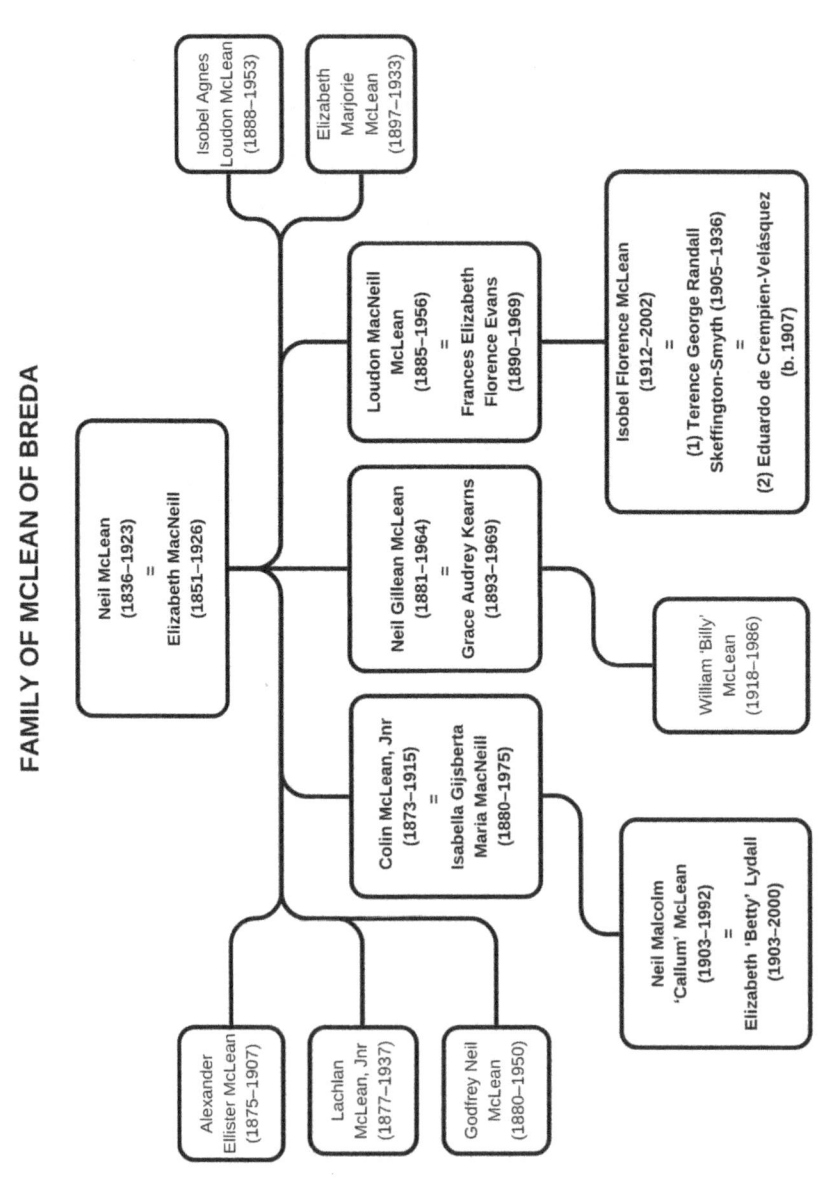

9

Gathering the Clan, Advancing the Empire and the Lure of London

BORN ON ISLAY, Neil McLean, second son of Colin and Margaret McLean née MacNeill, had first 'gone out' to the Indies at the close of the 1850s and finally returned to Scotland some fourteen years later. One of the few public roles he took on during his lengthy repatriate afterlife singled him out from other returnees of the Maclaine Watson cohort, in so far as it reflected an apparently singular espousal of what has been termed the 'clanscaping' of Scotland integral to late Victorian Highlandism. Indeed, not only was he a founding member of the Clan MacLean Association, established in 1892, but also its chairman. As such, his portrait – one showing him seated in mufti *sans* kilt, but with a splendid Scottish deerhound at his side (Figure 9.1) – occupies a prominent place in the *Renaissance of the Clan MacLean*, a pioneering and richly illustrated history dating from 1913, which includes a fifty-page account of 'The Gathering of the Clan' at venerable Duart Castle on the Inner Hebridean island of Mull, in August of the previous year.

Penned by a clansman from Ohio – appropriately enough, since many of the subscribers to the volume were part of the Scottish diaspora domiciled in North America, where the cult of the clan was to take on its most evolved manifestation – the book represented the culmination of years of work in what would today be described as 'consciousness-raising' among Scots in

Scotland itself, in the 'near diaspora' south of the Border, and, very importantly, overseas, where Canada also featured prominently along with the United States.[1] Well before that, however, there are indications that the diaspora acted as a forcing-house for a certain kind of Scottish culture, manifested most obviously in St Andrew's Day celebrations and Burns Nights, which proliferated across the British Empire from the mid-nineteenth century onwards,[2] in tandem with evolving ideas about what it meant to be a 'Scot' – focused on associational identification but by no means confined to it – and which enjoyed a rapid and ongoing adoption among expanding diasporic Scottish communities worldwide.[3]

It was, indeed, among one such community – a very small one located outside the boundaries of the empire – that McLean had spent a formative period of his life, latterly as a married man. It might be surmised that, along with an accentuated sense of their own 'Scottishness', the experience of

Figure 9.1: Neil McLean as president of the newly founded Clan MacLean Association, with Scottish deerhound (J. P. MacLean, 'Renaissance of the Clan MacLean')

living somewhere over which the British flag did not fly may also have contributed to the formation of a British imperial identity that existed in tandem with loyalty to their native land.[4] Accordingly, the pages that follow chart not simply his and his wife's demonstrable interest in at least some of the contemporary manifestations of Highlandism but also an equally demonstrable enthusiasm for empire that transcended any purely Scottish concerns. At the same time, however, the chapter also shows that, counterpoised with the call of 'Ancestral Voices', the 'Lure of London' also came to play a very major part in an evolving story of repatriation and its aftermath.

'The Sooner He Goes Out, the Better': A Younger Brother's Story

Colin McLean, ship's captain turned farmer and family 'patriarch', dispatched his younger son, Neil McLean (Figure 9.2), to the Indies in 1859, utilising connections linking Islay to London and the Netherlands' great Southeast Asian colony that had worked so well for his elder boy earlier in the same decade.[5] A letter (one that wasted few words) from a recently repatriated partner in Maclaine Watson, addressed to his father's brother-in-law, says all that is necessary:

> I have a note from [my Batavia-based brother] . . . in which he says you can send your nephew out and he will find him something to do, so the sooner he goes out the better, I suppose.[6]

Not that this was a path to instant riches. Indeed, there exists a plaintive note from the young man in question to his father, penned a few weeks after his arrival in the Indies, where he had taken up quarters with two other 'juniors' working in Maclaine Watson's Batavia office, and had been visited by his elder brother, Lachlan McLean, who had presumably come over from Surabaya on business. His monthly stipend amounted to 150 guilders (at the time about £12 10s sterling) which, he told his father, was insufficient to meet his modest living expenses. He had raised the matter with the senior partner, Alexander (Alec) Fraser, who informed him that he had arranged for his brother to make up the shortfall at the end of the year if he were overdrawn. A true son of Aberdeen, Fraser had added that:

Figure 9.2: Islay-born Neil McLean, partner in Maclaine Watson in Batavia, where he was British consul in the 1870s (Ancestry.com, public photographs)

this is always what is allowed to young men at first and I can make no exception in your favour. At the end of six months perhaps you may have an increase. I don't say, it all depends on yourself.[7]

In the circumstances, it was probably just as well that before a year was out the younger McLean had been transferred from Batavia to the coastal town of Pasuruan, at the centre of the booming sugar districts of Java's *Oosthoek*.[8] 'My expenses ... are considerably lighter,' he reported, and since the sugar manufacturing season had yet to get into full swing 'my duties here as yet have not been very laborious'. Among other things, along with keeping the books and making out invoices, he oversaw 'the English correspondence', and even though there was not much of it, working through it 'will soon enable me to become thoroughly acquainted with the slang, if I may so call it, of business letters'.[9]

In the middle of the nineteenth century Pasuruan had a European population of fewer than 200, many of them creoles of part-Asian ancestry, living in the town itself or scattered among the score or more sugar factories that operated in its hinterland.[10] Along with Probolinggo, located about 45 kilometres further along the coast, it was the main colonial settlement east of Surabaya itself and:

> of course an extremely dull place in comparison to Batavia, but here its inferiority ceases. As regards climate it is immeasurably superior in my opinion. The mornings and evenings are delightfully cool and if the middle of the day is proportionally hot this is only for a few hours.

Moreover, there was the spectacular scenery to be admired, since:

> within 30 miles of us we have the Arjuna and Sumira, the latter the highest mountain in Java. It is just now in full volcanic play and in the clear evenings we see the smoke rising in columns into the pale blue sky.

Above all, 'what reconciles me, however, most of all to this place is, that the headaches which troubled me a good deal at Batavia have now totally disappeared.'[11] It was perhaps very much apropos that a few months later an old business acquaintance (and fellow Scot) wrote the young man's father that Pasuruan 'is a nice healthy country and I am sure Neil will like it better for his health and morals than Batavia'.[12]

The firm's other employee based in the town was the German-Dutch Gerhard Hermann Miesegaes – 'a nice gentlemanly fellow. I don't doubt but I shall get on very well with him' – who had set up the Pasuruan branch of Fraser Eaton, the Surabaya sister firm of Maclaine Watson, some twelve months earlier (like Neil McLean, Miesegaes was subsequently to become a partner, and his son, very well connected in business circles in the Netherlands, remained with Maclaine Watson until late in the 1930s).[13] Meanwhile, McLean himself would also have found two fellow countrymen already established there, one of them much his senior. 'There is still an old Highlander . . . residing in the town,' one repatriated Scotsman told another in 1860 in respect to Donald McLennan. Born in Kintail in the Western Highlands, he must have arrived on the island around 1820 and later settled in Pasuruan, where he wed the Java-born Johanna Hubner and established himself as a trader and sugar manufacturer: 'He is enormously rich . . . but has become quite blind. He has, I believe, got some coffee-coloured daughters.'[14]

One of those 'coffee-coloured daughters' – Anna Frederika McLennan – had married the only other Scot living in the town, Archibald McGregor, who presumably worked in some capacity or other for his father-in-law. In November 1864, less than a year after McGregor's death, his widow married the expatriate Dutchman Hendricus Spruytenburg and, having outlived both her husbands, died in her native Pasuruan at the splendid old age of 93.[15] Her first husband, meanwhile, had been that rarely documented individual, a satellite of the Maclaine Watson cohort who was evidently of lower social status. He had been born and brought up in the same locality on Scotland's Morvern Peninsula as the firm's co-founder and was, the latter declared, 'The first Ardtornishman I have seen in Java.'[16] Neil McLean had encountered him soon after he himself arrived in Pasuruan in 1860, and reported with some surprise, perhaps, that even after thirty or more years in the colony 'he still remembers his Gaelic', in which, it would seem, McLean was also fluent.[17] He might have been even more surprised to find that McGregor's brother-in-law, Alexander McLennan, eldest son of the 'old Highlander', owned 'a full Highland costume', complete with glengarry (a traditional Scots cap) and claymore (a basket-hilted sword) – which he was forced to put up for sale when his mercantile business in Surabaya failed in 1864.[18]

McGregor's own career in the colony had been an even more troubled one. Soon after his arrival in Batavia early in the 1830s, Gillian Maclaine – who had presumably arranged for him to take ship to the Indies – must have received a warning from his mother, for he replied that 'I hope you are too severe on poor Arch. McGregor', only to find that her animadversions had the ring of truth. Initially, matters went well: McGregor was installed in the office of 'one of the first Houses here' and

> appears very grateful to me . . . and next month commences to pay off his debt to me for passage . . . and board at the lodging house. . . . He dined with me several times and also received much attention from the young gentlemen in my office.[19]

Subsequently, however, after Maclaine had helped set McGregor up in a marine storekeeper's business in Batavia, the relationship soured. By this time (1837) Maclaine's mother was dead, and her son could only lament to his only sibling that:

It is with much pain that I inform you that ... Arch. McGregor has given way entirely to a vile habit of drinking which he must have acquired I suspect in Glasgow. From his not availing even once of invitations I gave him to visit at my house and growing love of low society & his never making a remittance to his parents, though I offered to lend him money if required for that purpose, I formed lately an unfavourable opinion of him but did not like to communicate my suspicions to you. I now however look upon him as a lost man – ruined in health and prospects – an unrecoverable drunkard and disgrace to his countrymen here. . . . Had he remained steady, I held the inclination and likewise the means of being of great use to him, but his beastly conduct has disgusted me & prevents of course my having any communication with him.[20]

From Batavia to Breda: The Call of Ancestral Voices

Neil McLean's time on Java was not punctuated by any such episodes: 'it was not to enjoy myself that I have come so many a long mile from home,' he assured his sister soon after his arrival in the colony.[21] Again, in contrast to McGregor, he was able not only to make it home but to do so with a substantial fortune. At the beginning of the 1870s, after a decade-long absence, he went back to Islay on 'leave' from the sugar business (he was evidently already rich enough to do so) and used his sojourn, as his brother had done before him, to find a marriage partner in the person of his cousin Elizabeth MacNeill – the daughter of an Islay-born returnee member of the Maclaine Watson cohort, whom he wed in Edinburgh in September 1871 before sailing back to the Indies with his bride.

The couple remained there, based in Batavia, for a little over three years before sailing back to Europe, together with the infant Colin McLean, Jnr, their firstborn, in late October 1874.[22] They delayed long enough on their arrival in Marseille or Genoa for the by-now heavily pregnant Elizabeth to give birth, in Nice in mid-January 1875, to their second child.[23] The young family (McLean himself was less than 40 when he repatriated, and his wife was scarcely 25) initially established themselves in the Western Highlands at Barbreck House, in the husband's native Argyll.[24] A grand, three-storey Georgian mansion, it boasted an impressive backdrop of moor and mountain that must have provided excellent cover for Highland pursuits of game. It may also have signified the fact that Neil McLean, on returning to his homeland, had no intention of being overshadowed by his elder sibling's 'princely' establishment on Islay.[25] During the course of 1879, however, the family moved to the east of Scotland and took a long lease on Battleby House in Perthshire, where they remained for a decade or more.[26]

It was a location in which 'Scotland', in the garb of Victorian-era Highlandism, remained firmly on the McLean couple's agenda, reflected, among other things, in their espousal of the increasingly formalised stalking, shooting and fishing milieu inseparable from it. To be sure, recreational outings with a gun would have been on his agenda ever since his youth, as the son of a landowner on Islay, and soon after his arrival in Batavia back in 1859 he was able to gratify his father with a report that similar opportunities had so far been limited 'until tonight, when I managed to bring down a Flying Fox in grand style in the plot of ground before the house'.[27] Prior to departing Java temporarily late in 1869, he had put up for auction much of his household inventory (as was the custom of the country), which included a selection of 'guns of the best English manufacture', among them 'a double-barrel hunting rifle'.[28] Even so, celebration of a 'Glorious Twelfth' that attracted well-heeled (paying) visitors from urban Scotland and the South was something else again: a ritual opening of the grouse shooting season that paid homage to Highland 'traditions' while incorporating them into a re-invented social milieu inhabited both

Figure 9.3: Breda House, Neil McLean's romance with Scottish Baronial (Collection of the Author)

by (newly) genteel Scottish families and by their Sassenach counterparts. 'For years,' one appreciative contemporary visitor recollected, 'I went regularly to the McLeans' on the 12th of August', further recalling a large hall with a wood fire burning in it, a 'gothic staircase built in stone', a 'splendid drawing room', the whole house 'exquisitely furnished', and dinner served at eight to the family and assorted guests.[29] It is not known how extensive the shoot was at Battleby during Neil and Elizabeth McLean's time there, but when they moved further north into Aberdeenshire, the estate which they purchased was advertised as promising 'almost 200 brace of Grouse . . . per season',[30] and a report on the opening day of the season in 1893 credited 'Mr Neil McLean of Breda, 4 guns, 46½ brace of grouse'.[31]

Although set in the country's north-eastern Lowlands (near the rural town of Alford, less than 30 miles west of Aberdeen), rather than in the Highlands, the Breda mansion (Figure 9.3) nonetheless conformed to the Highland mode that characterised the kilted gentry of late nineteenth-century Scotland. Advertised as a 'residential and sporting estate', it had been bought in 1892 for around £27,000. Set on 2,000 acres near the rural town of Alford, some 25 miles west of Aberdeen – north-east Scotland's largest city and major port – in addition to three reception rooms, seven bedrooms, and the usual domestic offices, it was furnished with 'a gun-room and a game-larder' to service the requirements of the 'always plentiful' supply of game (grouse and other birds complemented a stock of roe deer, hares and rabbits) from that half of the property not given over to the arable farming of the estate tenants.[32]

Breda represented more than a simple relocation, however, for the couple's occupancy saw the rapid transformation of their new house along lines that reflected their evolving identities. Built form was eloquent on this score, and the espousal of Gothic Revival or Scots Baronial was as integral to Highlandism as was Sir Edwin Landseer's stag painting *The Monarch of the Glen*. It was scarcely an accident, therefore, when their choice for architect fell on an eminent Aberdonian, Alexander Marshall Mackenzie, who was currently working on the extensive reconstruction of Aberdeen's Marischal College – 'one of the . . . most ambitious secular Gothic Revival projects in Britain.'[33]

Breda was an altogether more modest affair, but under Marshall Mackenzie's direction it re-emerged as a skilful exercise in the style for which he was famous. With a turreted and crenellated tower-house addition

Figure 9.4: Neil and Elizabeth McLean in their later years (Ancestry.com, public photographs)

at its western end, the reconstructed Breda presented a unified whole, whose interior now boasted 'a very handsome staircase with turned balusters and elaborate finials' running up the three floors of the tallest part of the house, glazed with heraldic devices and complemented by a sculpted panel displaying the newly minted McLean coat of arms situated over the front door.[34] Even so, perhaps Breda's most striking feature was that it was clad in pink granite, thereby giving the lie to any notion that this stone, famously and widely quarried in Aberdeenshire, was a uniform grey.[35]

Neil and Elizabeth McLean's enthusiasm for 'the Highlands' in all its manifestations did not preclude escaping to enjoy the generally milder weather south of the Border. In April 1891, for example, part of the family was staying in the South Coast resort of Bournemouth, while the beginning of the following decade found them in Hove. Indicative that this was no mere short vacation, their recorded household had nine servants, including a governess, a nurse, cook, kitchen maids, housemaids, a butler and a page.[36] In 1911, the couple, this time without their now grown-up children, were staying at the recently built Empire Hotel – lauded at its opening as a 'palace of luxury' and 'the most modern and up to date hotel in the city' – in the English spa town of Bath.[37] It was at Breda, nonetheless, that the couple remained for the rest of their long lives (and where their descendants continued in residence into the present century): Neil died there aged 87 in 1923, followed by his 79-year-old widow some three years later (Figure 9.4).

Advancing the Empire: The Consul and the Colonel

Following in his brother's footsteps, Neil McLean was appointed British consul in Batavia in 1871.[38] Though the position – 'hereditary' among the Maclaine Watson partners prior to the appointment of a full-time career diplomat shortly before the outbreak of the First World War – was no more than an adjunct to the business of trading in sugar, it nonetheless carried with it a useful connection to the Dutch official world on Java, including rich opportunities for networking, as well as social cachet in colonial society more generally. Above all, it reinforced in its holder his sense of the British Empire and of his position as its representative: it was not incidental that, as consul, McLean presided over regular meetings of the 'British residents of Batavia'.[39] In short, though McLean's enthusiasm for 'Scotland' had been intensified during his sojourn overseas, there were also other dynamics at play. Much the same must have held true for his wife.

Indeed, alongside her personal contribution to the 'birthscapes of empire'[40] (she was the mother of eight children),[41] Elizabeth McLean developed her own political agenda. Broadly congruent with that of her husband, it was focused less on 'Scotland' itself than on the imperial enterprise with which it enjoyed a symbiotic relationship. As such, in the mid-1880s, while still living at Battleby, she became local branch secretary of the recently established Primrose League. Alongside its encouragement of women's participation (women comprised around 50 per cent of the League's total membership by the early twentieth century), it was the 'the role of Empire that was pivotal to the League's creation'. Consequently, its followers took very seriously indeed that part of their Pledge that committed them to the maintenance of 'the estates of the realm and of the Imperial ascendency', and, accordingly, the League was strongly opposed to Home Rule for Ireland and very much in favour of a forward movement in southern Africa and of the British advance up the Nile.[42]

The McLean couple (as reported in the press) were frequent attendees at Primrose League functions in their part of Aberdeenshire, as indeed had earlier been the case in Perthshire.[43] It was in the latter county, for example, that in 1888 they had attended:

> a garden party given by Captain and Mrs Black of Balgowan Park [where] ... the company, which numbered fully 300, a considerable portion being ladies, were entertained to a sumptuous tea by the generous host and hostess in a handsome marquee ... where temperance refreshments were liberally distributed to all and sundry'.

They were also entertained, moreover, by speakers extolling country, religion, and the Queen, and alluding darkly to 'attacks ... by persons of eminent positions, attacks, they might say, on the stability of the Empire itself'.[44]

Although much of the prevailing 'discourse' in this regard centred most immediately on the future status of Ireland, there is no doubt that what was felt to be at stake was the 'supremacy of the British Empire' worldwide, as alluded to, for example, by a speaker at a meeting (at which the McLeans were present) of the Central Aberdeen Habitation (or Branch) of the Primrose League in August 1897 in the grounds of Castle Forbes – a few miles south of Breda and home of one of the north-east's most socially prominent families.[45]

In short, Elizabeth McLean and her husband, after their return to Scotland, became keen promoters of what has been described as a 'cult of the hero, patriotism and militarism'.[46] Given this family background, it was surely no accident that three of their six sons took up the cause of Empire in a practical fashion by joining the British Army – and that a fourth devoted his life to imperial civil administration. Of those who made military careers, the most distinguished was undoubtedly Lieutenant-Colonel Colin McLean, the couple's first-born, who, going on from Harrow to the Royal Military College, Sandhurst, saw service as an officer in India and in South Africa both before and during the Boer War. No more than was the case with his parents, however, had imperial enthusiasms estranged their eldest son from his native Scotland, and on retirement from the army, after a career that culminated in the position of Commanding Officer of the Sixth Battalion Gordon Highlanders, he and his wife, the half-Dutch Isabella Gijsberta Maria MacNeill, and their two young children, settled at Auchintoul, a short distance south of Breda itself. On the outbreak of the First World War, having previously re-enlisted, he went with his regiment to northern France where, in the wake of the informal 'Christmas

Truce' of 1914, he confessed in a letter to his wife that 'it rather makes one feel what rot it is having this war . . .' Less than three months later, in March 1915, he was dead, killed by a German sniper while about to join his men in the trenches.[47]

The Lure of London and High Society

Two of the late Colonel's brothers lived quietly in retirement in London: one of them, Major Godfrey Neil McLean, as a bachelor 'gentleman of private means' in modest accommodation in the West End, where he died, leaving an estate valued at almost £13,000.[48] The other, Lachlan McLean, an ex-colonial administrator, was likewise a single man; he shared a house with his younger sister, Isobel Agnes Loudon McLean (Figure 9.5), and died leaving an estate valued at more than £25,000, after having been for many years 'one of the mainstays of the Hampstead Chess Club' in North London.[49] Two other of the male siblings, however, charted a very different course, one that took them – very much in the wake of their respective wives – in spectacular fashion through the capital's high society.

Neil Gillean McLean and his younger brother, Loudon MacNeill McLean, had both sailed to the Indies while still in their early twenties, and subsequently became partners in one branch or another of the Maclaine Watson concern before repatriating as substantially rich men. Both had undoubtedly benefited from the massive but short-term hike in world sugar prices in the aftermath of the First World War, and both appear to have taken at least some of their capital out of the firm before the more subdued sugar market of the 1920s caused it to dwindle. The younger of the two siblings had made an exogamous marriage while still overseas, wedding Frances Elizabeth Florence Evans (known, apparently, as Flossie)[50] in Semarang in 1911.[51] His bride was the Java-born, half-Dutch daughter of a Welshman (Lloyd Evans) who had shipped out to Java as an adventurous 16-year-old around 1880 and (like his future son-in-law) had subsequently found a wife there, Anna de Beus. She came from among the elite of that city's Dutch colonial community, and her late father, the Amsterdam-born Carel Gijsbert de Beus,[52] had been one of its leading lawyers.[53] Nonetheless, it remains uncertain to what extent this family connection may have helped her husband on his way up a ladder of achievement in business, which culminated in a position on the governing body of Surabaya's Chamber of Commerce and Industry.[54]

Evans himself had 'repatriated' around 1917 and spent much of his retirement in Belgium, before being forced back across the Channel by the advance of the German army in 1940.[55] His daughter and son-in-law, however, when they left the Indies in 1924,[56] evidently had very different aspirations. While still in Batavia, the couple had lived in some style: a notice for one of their regular 'at home' receptions advised 'Costume: White' and they drove around in a large and resplendent American motorcar – a Hudson Super Six.[57] Settled in London, they launched themselves onto metropolitan high society, taking up residence on Eaton Square, one of the most fashionable and expensive addresses in London's West End, in a grand house previously occupied by the British prime minister, Stanley Baldwin[58] (they subsequently moved to Mayfair). Something of their success can be gauged from the fact that, in 1932, 'the well-known society hostess Mrs Loudon McLean' –

Figure 9.5: London High Society. 'Presented at court', 1932 (Collection of the Author)

*Figure 9.6: The 'party-going' Isobel McLean, early 1930s
(Yevonde Portrait Archive)*

a woman 'who will be well remembered in Java', according to the gushing account in the social pages of the *Java Gazette*, the monthly magazine for Indies expats and repatriates – accompanied her daughter, Isobel Florence McLean, when the latter was 'presented at Court' as a debutante during the London summer season. A photograph in the same issue shows both women suitably and splendidly attired for the occasion (Figure 9.5).[59]

Meanwhile, the younger of the two women, 'one of the most popular members of the dance-going set, and always beautifully turned out,' sat for a portrait by Madame Yevonde, the celebrated society photographer whose 'baroque approach to the treatment of her subjects combined with her interest in the issue of female identity and gender roles' was said to have 'created a new contemporary audience of her work'.[60] The *Gazette* columnist reported on 'Mrs Loudon McLean's famous cocktail parties',[61] and the party-going Isobel McLean herself was spotted at one such event, strikingly dressed *en Cosaque* (Figure 9.6) – a fashion already popular in Paris, readers were assured, and becoming so in London.[62]

Figure 9.7: Isobel and Terence Skeffington-Smyth at the Salzburg Festival, 1935 (Collection of the Author)

The family's rise to eminence reached its apogee in December 1934, with the spectacular society wedding (there were twelve bridesmaids decked out in gold costumes) at the ultra-fashionable St Margaret's, Westminster, followed by a reception for 700 guests at Curzon House in Mayfair, of Isobel McLean and Terence George Randall Skeffington-Smyth,[63] a man about town and the nephew of an Anglo-Irish viscount. However, the Scottish connection was not lost, for the brief report of the wedding in the Aberdeen daily paper reminded readers that the bride was 'the granddaughter of the late Mr and Mrs Neil McLean of Breda', while also noting that she was cousin of the present laird and 'often spends holidays in Aberdeenshire'.[64] Meanwhile, the groom himself was described in one contemporary newspaper report as having 'an unusual personality.... Many of his hundreds of acquaintances regarded him as a young man difficult to make out'.[65] As such, he existed on the fringe of the Bright Young People (well past their 1920s heyday) satirised by Evelyn Waugh in *Vile Bodies* (1930): as described by their latter-day chronicler, they formed an extensive coterie of 'louche, irregularly employed . . . indefinably glamorous, and well-connected', obsessively partying scions of wealthy families, among whom Skeffington-Smyth's chief claim to fame was his close friendship with a fellow socialite whose trial and acquittal in 1932 for the murder of her lover had attracted a good deal of notoriety.[66]

The newly-weds were subsequently 'seen' at the opera at Covent Garden and at the Salzburg Festival (Figure 9.7),[67] before embarking on a world cruise in 1936.[68] Among other places, it took them to Shanghai and it was there, early in March of that year, that Skeffington-Smyth died – probably of an overdose after visiting the city's opium dens: the inquest found that he and the bartender from a nightclub had visited several such establishments before he returned to his luxurious hotel, the newly completed Broadway Mansions, built in the Art Deco style and 'pre-War Shanghai's closest approach to an American skyscraper'.[69] Apparently unfazed by this turn of events, his 23-year-old widow continued to Japan and on to San Francisco, staying there with the Gump family, proprietors of the eponymous city retailer, famous for its stock of Orientalia. She also got married again. A wealthy 29-year-old South American friend of her late husband's, Eduardo de Crempien,[70] had evidently accompanied her on the voyage from Yokohama to the west coast of the United States, and the pair wed while in Los Angeles in May 1936. After that, she sailed back to England with her new husband, disembarking in Liverpool in June 1937, and returned to the same 'smart' London address from which she and Skeffington-Smyth had departed less than eighteen months earlier.[71] It was sometime prior to their arrival that a newly taken photograph of the bride appeared in a report in the *Aberdeen Press and Journal* ('Married Husband's Friend'), where she was identified as '*Signora* Eduardo de Crempien-Velásquez, granddaughter of Mr and Mrs Neil McLean of Breda'.[72]

De Crempien himself was no stranger to the British Isles, having been a student at Oxford around the beginning of the 1930s, though his whereabouts after his marriage remain a matter of speculation. He appears to have been caught up in a major homosexual scandal in Buenos Aires early in the 1940s, and the last trace of him is his arrival (travelling solo) by air in New York in 1962, on a journey that had probably started in Switzerland.[73] His wife, meanwhile, had made an appearance some eight years earlier when, travelling alone but still as Isobel de Crempien, she embarked in Liverpool for Nassau in the Bahamas in January 1954, giving as her address her mother's residence in the Home Counties.[74]

By this time, the erstwhile society hostess Flossie Evans herself had long been divorced,[75] and her former husband, Loudon McLean, the wealthy Indies repatriate, had remarried. He and his new wife moved to a mansion in a rural town about 35 miles west of central London,[76] before relocating to Switzerland and staying in Montreux at the Lake Geneva resort's premier hotel, The Palace. But it was in the Sussex town of Brighton that Loudon died in 1956, at the Norfolk Hotel, a majestic Victorian pile on the seafront. Even then, after decades of high living and what must have been an expensive divorce, he still left an estate valued at the substantial sum of £55,000.[77] His first wife survived him by well over a decade before herself dying (at a 'good' address in the Home Counties) in 1969. Their daughter, meanwhile, made what may have been her final appearance in the public record in *Vogue* in 1972, when Isobel de Crempien was included among a several other globetrotters in a feature article entitled 'Insiders' Tips: How People Really Travel'. Her own contribution appeared under the heading 'A survival kit'.[78] Since she herself survived for another thirty years,[79] it was evidently a subject on which she could claim a degree of expertise.

Meanwhile, her young cousin, the Eton-educated William 'Billy' McLean, had launched on a very different trajectory – as a politician and a much-celebrated British Army intelligence officer during the Second World War – that nonetheless reflected the high-society circles in which *his* parents likewise moved after they came back from Java.[80] His father, Neil Gillean McLean, had married the British Guiana-born Grace Audrey Kearns[81] in England in 1918, before returning to Batavia and the sugar business after several years of war service in the British Army. According to her son, however, his mother did not much care for the Indies, which may account for her husband's decision, early in the 1920s, to leave an active role in the Maclaine Watson partnership and to repatriate.[82] Once returned, they appear to have divided their time between a country house in Northamptonshire and a grand apartment in an equally grand town house in central London's St James's district, within close proximity to both Green Park and the Palace.[83]

From this base, the young Billy McLean's mother played out her part as a society hostess: according to one of her son's close friends, writing half a century later, she was 'an extravagant flapper' whose 'every whim was indulged' by her older husband, though 'for both of them sport and society took precedence over intellectual activity or artistic endeavour', and even though the couple were 'sticklers for convention ... she herself affected an exotic mien which bordered on the ostentatious ...'.[84] The couple appear to have maintained a townhouse in Edinburgh in addition to their London establishment, but it was not until 1937 that the Scottish connection was renewed in any substantial fashion, when they purchased a 20,000-acre hunting and fishing estate ('one of the best stretches of salmon fishing in the North of Scotland') known as Glen Calvie Lodge. Near the village of Ardgay, some 40 miles north of Inverness, it cost them something in the region of £20,000,[85] and was no doubt bought for its place in a metropolitan social calendar in which 'Scotland' was somewhere to which one took oneself in time for the Glorious Twelfth or for a spot of deerstalking and trout tickling – whenever the London 'season' went into recess. Even so, it may have offered a handy retreat during the Blitz, which impacted even on the well-to-do of London's West End from August 1940 onwards.[86]

Unlike that of his older brother Loudon, Neil Gillean McLean's fortune seems to have been largely dissipated by the end of his life – or else it had been well-advisedly salted away from the inquisitorial gaze of the Inland Revenue, one indication of which was that, sometime after the War, he and his wife had relocated to the tax haven of Jersey. It was, indeed, in a Jersey nursing home that he died in 1964, leaving (in England at least) an estate valued at a paltry £357.[87] Their son's biographer asserts the 'unimaginably reduced [financial] circumstances' in which the couple found themselves in the mid-1960s at the time of Neil Gillean McLean's death, and reports that their Jersey house was sold for £26,000 to cover their debts, leaving enough to place the widowed Audrey in an hotel for the remainder of her life.[88] Nonetheless, destitution is a relative matter, and she survived him by some five years before dying in London in 1969, credited with more than £29,000 worth of assets.[89]

Gathering the Clan, Advancing the Empire, and the Lure of the South

The import of the story of the Laird of Breda and his family, for the diasporan themes discussed in this book, relates first and foremost to sojourner repatriation and what it may have signified both for Scotland and for the social actors concerned. Perhaps most striking was the enthusiasm with which Neil and Elizabeth McLean embraced 'Highlandism' in the shape of built form and communal bonding. The mansion house and landed estate west of Aberdeen, which became their ultimate resting place, were reconstructed in the Scots Baronial mode by one of its most approved practitioners, while their owner took on an important role in the revival of 'ancient' Scottish clanship.

Nor was there any necessary disconnect between 'clanscaping' and the imperial concerns that evidently also played a big part in the couple's evolving ideology. Indeed, quite the contrary, inasmuch as 'clan' often found its most fervent apologists in overseas Scottish communities within (as well as outside) the empire. It was Elizabeth MacNeill-McLean's activism as an imperialist, embodied in the Primrose League, that gave her own career as a repatriate its singular character. Given the paucity of documentation directly reflecting her (and her husband's) 'inner life', it can at least be posited that the couple's experience in a part of the world over which the British flag did *not* fly not only intensified their Scottish identity but also honed their loyalty to the empire to whose core they had subsequently returned. As has been argued, it was the degree of her attachment to the late nineteenth-century British imperial 'project' that most likely influenced the career paths of the four of her six sons who took up the 'burden of empire' in military or civilian capacities.

Even so, serving the imperial cause in either fashion did not keep the money flowing, and it looks as if the couple's two remaining sons were 'designated' to continue in the sugar business in the Indies, in which their father (and uncle) had been a partner, and in which their grandfather had been a close associate of co-founder Gillian Maclaine back in the 1820s. It proved highly profitable, and they both returned from 'the East' as substantially wealthy men. At the same time, nonetheless, the very extent of their financial success turned out to be the basis on which these scions of an indubitably Scottish family became firmly domesticated in England rather than on their native turf. Both men, unlike the males of earlier generations of their family, had 'married out' to overseas-born women with no Scottish connection and, post-repatriation – and still in their early forties – they and their wives used the sugar money from Java to set themselves up in London high society. The Call of the South also resounded, moreover, in the ears of their other surviving siblings, and the lairdship of Breda itself, together with the 'curatorship' of the family's Scottish heritage, fell to the lot of

Neil and Elizabeth McLean's grandson, the sole male offspring of their first-born, a British army officer killed in the First World War. We shall return to his history in a later chapter.

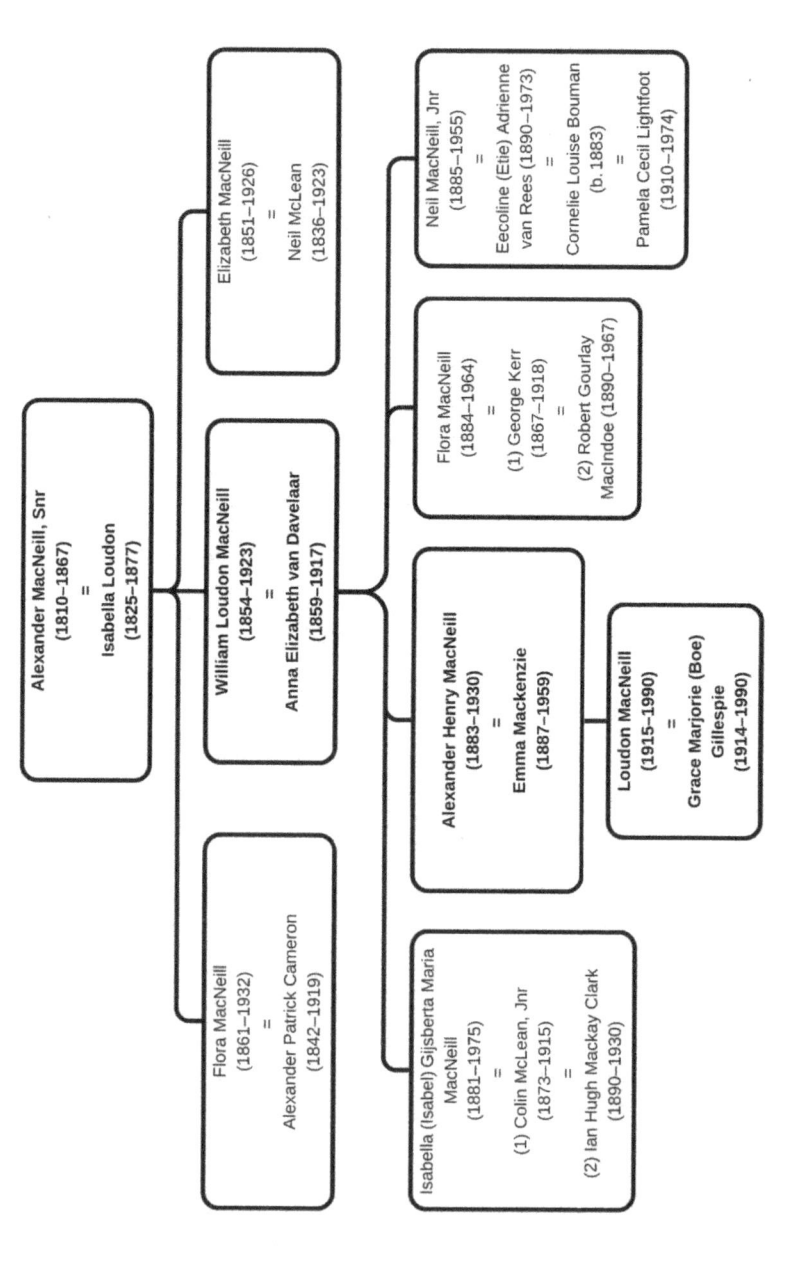

10

A House Built from Sugar

SHENNANTON STANDS AMID what was originally a 900-acre estate in Wigtownshire in Scotland's far south-west, in undulating country on the fringe of the high hills that today form the part of the Galloway Forest Park (Figure 10.1). Built by a wealthy sugar trader, William Loudon MacNeill (Figure 10.2), it was not the first such house to be so financed in this part of Scotland: less than eight miles away, in Wigtown itself, the proceeds from sugar manufacture and trade had already been expended on a house called 'Barbados' dating from the mid-1830s (Figure 10.3). An imposing, seven-bedroom villa, it was built for John McGuffie, scion of a family that had sugar-trading interests in Liverpool – as well as in the Caribbean, where McGuffie himself had been active in his younger days as a general merchant and partner in a plantation worked by well over a hundred enslaved Africans. In part at least, Barbados was paid for by the financial 'compensation' paid in the 1830s by the British government to the owners of emancipated slaves.[1]

The sugar from which Shennanton was built originated in very different conditions. On Java, chattel slavery on the New World model was unknown and unnecessary in the production of sugar: instead, during the middle decades of the nineteenth century its colonial rulers had instituted a kind of serfitude under which the densely settled peasantry of the island's central and eastern lowlands provided the requisite land and labour. To be sure, by the time that William Loudon MacNeill became a partner in the Maclaine

Figure 10.1: The house built from sugar. William Loudon MacNeill's Shennanton in Wigtownshire (Collection of the Author)

Figure 10.2: William Loudon MacNeill, partner in Maclaine Watson and wealthy retiree in London and Scotland (KITLV/University of Leiden)

Watson sugar trading concern (in the 1880s), some aspects of the primaeval coercion that had characterised the heyday of the Dutch colonial government's Cultivation System had given way to something more complex, spawned among other things by the increasing landlessness of a rapidly growing rural population. Nonetheless, the broad parameters under which rural resources were made 'available' to the sugar industry continued to be characterised by constraint orchestrated by colonial sugar companies in a sometimes-uneasy alliance with the relevant agencies of the colonial state.

None of these differences in the manner of their funding meant, however, that there were not substantial similarities between the Barbados and Shennanton mansions. Both played a role in promoting and sustaining the social aspirations of their owners. However, unlike McGuffie, who demonstrated the aspiration of a local boy made good, although the MacNeills likewise successfully enhanced their social status in the aftermath of repatriation, they had no prior connection to the Wigtown area in which they eventually settled after repatriation: it was at least a hundred miles to the south of their native turf in the Inner Hebrides.

There were also contrasts in the way of life which the two houses were intended to facilitate. To be sure, back in the 1830s, McGuffie might have supposed that his mansion in Wigtown would receive his kin and acquaintances from further afield, not least from among his Liverpool mercantile connection. It seems hardly likely, nonetheless, that either he or his mixed-race, Caribbean-born daughter Margaret McGuffie, who also lived there and

Figure 10.3: Barbados in Wigtown. John McGuffie's villa built in the mid 1830s (Collection of the Author)

inherited the house from him,[2] would have anticipated the late Victorian and Edwardian transformation of large swathes of Scotland's uplands into deer-forests and grouse-moors catering for the seasonal leisure pursuits of the newly rich. Theirs was a pre-eminently urban rather than rural existence and, in his daughter's case, an apparently increasingly reclusive one in the three-decade-long interval between her father's death and her own in 1896.[3] In short, to equate the repatriate McGuffie's setting up in a (relatively) grand manner in Wigtown in the 1830s with the social and economic milieu surrounding the Shennanton MacNeills early in the following century risks conflating a sequence of discrete historical developments, distinguished by markedly different impulses and occasions.[4]

MacNeill's Shennanton (completed a few years before the outbreak of the First World War) differed from both the classic, chaste Palladian of 'Barbados' and the exuberant varieties of Scots Baronial on display in the scores of mansions and hunting lodges erected across the Highlands and Borders during the preceding half-century or more. Instead, it was built to designs by the celebrated Glasgow architect Henry Edward Clifford, in what has been described as the English Tudor style.[5] As such, complete with decorative stonework and red tile roofs and with ample fenestration and well-lit interiors, the house was something of a rarity in the Scotland of its day. Socially, however, Shennanton's allegiance to the prevailing Highlandist ethos was inescapable: its sixteen bedrooms, spacious reception rooms, grand billiard room with a hammer-beam roof (and, of course, a dedicated gun room) represented a show of wealth clearly meant to accommodate and impress the parties of guests who would arrive to enjoy the sporting opportunities of the surrounding estate – and the excellent salmon fishing (then) to be had in the River Bladnoch.

Reflecting something of this opulence, one of the main themes of the story that follows concerns the considerable social elevation, paid for by sugar money from Java, enjoyed by the builder of Shennanton and his immediate descendants, while also charting what happened when the money ran out. In so doing, moreover, it highlights the theme – by no means an invariable one in this book – of repatriate afterlives spent for the most part north of the Border. The story begins, however, not in Scotland but in the Indies – and with the fabric of a colonial society marked, amongst other things, with a familial domesticity that left a novel degree public 'space' for its womenfolk.

Making Good in the Indies: Matrimony and More

Shennanton's builder was the second son of one of the foundational couples of the Maclaine Watson cohort of families, Alexander MacNeill and his wife Isabella Loudon-MacNeill. His father had grown rich in the Dutch colony, where he had joined his elder brother, the businessman John MacNeill, in the north coast port of Semarang sometime in the 1830s, before repatriating towards the end of the following decade, after having spent some ten years in the partnership. He was not so rich, however, that his male heirs could afford to adopt the same gentlemanly mode (town house in Edinburgh and country property in the Scottish Borders immediately to its south) that had characterised their father's repatriate existence. Admittedly, one of the couple's sons had indeed opted out of 'trade' and embarked instead upon a career as an officer in the British Army, though it was one terminated prematurely by his death in combat on the imperial frontier in Egypt at the age of 23. His three surviving brothers, however, all spent time in the Indies, while two of their five female sisters were likewise enmeshed in what was indeed the 'family firm', as the wives of individuals who were also partners in Maclaine Watson.

William Loudon MacNeill himself – the second of the siblings to 'go out East' – had arrived on Java in February 1876 by the Dutch steamer *Prins van Oranje*,[6] presumably having just spent some time in the Netherlands learning his trade and the Dutch language. Once settled in the Indies, he made his career in Surabaya, the colony's major port and the business centre of its ever-expanding sugar industry, as well as being the base of Maclaine Watson's East Java sister firm of Fraser Eaton in which he eventually became senior partner. Well before that, however, back in 1880 when he had scarcely been four years in the colony, he had married an Indies-born Dutch woman, Anna Elizabeth van Davelaar. Her parents were a high-ranking government official, recently retired as Vice-President of the High Court of the Netherlands Indies, and his wife, a scion of a solidly middle-class Dutch family resident in The Hague, where her father had been a noted medical practitioner. Like their newly acquired Scottish son-in-law, the couple were decidedly sojourners, who repatriated in the same year that MacNeill married their daughter.[7] Even so, MacNeill had also gained an influential Java-based brother-in-law, Jacobus van Davelaar, an up-and-coming young Netherlands-educated lawyer whose career in government culminated in a position on the *Raad van Nederlandsch-Indië* (Council of the Indies), the Governor-General's advisory body and the pinnacle of the colonial bureaucracy.[8]

In short, for the young MacNeill, exogamy ('marrying out') not only secured him a home life that would have been envied by at least some of his sojourner contemporaries elsewhere in Asia, but also an entrée into Java's Dutch colonial elite (Figure 10.4). The extent to which he had 'arrived' was implicit, for instance, in his presence in 1896 on the committee formed to organise the celebrations marking the Resident of Surabaya's hugely prestigious promotion to membership of the Council.[9] It was, however, Neil MacNeill, 'Jnr', William Loudon MacNeill's Java-born second son, whose infiltration of the Dutch colonial establishment in the Indies put his father's achievements in this regard into the shade. In 1911, before even becoming a partner in the business, he married a 21-year-old Dutch woman who could scarcely have been better connected. Eecoline (Etie) Adrienne van Rees was the granddaughter of a Governor-General (Otto van Rees) and only daughter of the Vice-President of the Council.[10] Indies-born and subsequently educated during her teens in the Netherlands, followed by finishing school in Lausanne, on her mother's side Van Rees was the granddaughter of a Governor of Aceh, the war-torn region of north Sumatra where the Dutch had been attempting to exert control since the

Figure 10.4: Business and Leisure. William Loudon MacNeill and fellow golfers in Surabaya, 1890s (Collection Ann Crickhowell, London)

early 1870s. No matter that Van Rees divorced MacNeill some five years and four children later, and then launched herself on a career that made her a painter and famed ceramicist in the mid-century Netherlands:[11] the marriage still signalled the remarkable extent of the Maclaine Watson partners' entrenchment in the Indies.

Anyone for Tennis?

Leisure – as well as business and matrimony – demonstrated the extent to which, over several generations, the key families of the Maclaine Watson cohort had successfully inserted themselves into the fabric of the extensive Dutch colonial communities in the Indies. By the 1890s (the culminating decade of William Loudon MacNeill and Anna Davelaar-MacNeill's sojourn in the Indies), it was lawn tennis that was at the forefront in this regard. Before that, the game scarcely merited a mention in the colonial newspapers, but subsequently a plethora of advertisements offering for sale tennis balls, suitable clothing and other requisites began to appear. As, too, did remarks that the game was now 'much in vogue',[12] together with grumbles that young people were neglecting their education by spending too much time playing it.[13] It was fully characteristic when, late in the same decade, William Loudon MacNeill and his wife sold up in Surabaya prior to their departure for Europe, the lengthy inventory of their goods included something described by the auctioneer as a *'Compleet Lawntennisspel'*,[14] the wherewithal for a game that they may have played predominantly in the large garden of their mansion in the elite Kayun district, since the Surabaya Lawn Tennis Club appears only to have been formed a few years after they repatriated.[15]

In Batavia, however, such a club had already been established late in the 1880s and – underscoring remarks in the press that the game was 'exceptionally well-suited to women'[16] – its president, as identified in a contemporary handbill, was a '*Mrs* C. H. E. Robertson'.[17] Born into a Dutch family in what became South Africa, Henriette Anna Philippine Robertson-Van Dolder had been employed in her youth as a governess in the English county of Gloucestershire,[18] but had subsequently relocated to the Indies and married a broker who later 'repatriated' (he had been born in Penang) to Britain – where his widow, outliving him by some fifteen years, died at the age of 82 in the English South Coast resort of Hove.[19] Back in Batavia well over half a century earlier, in 1888 – when its president was a very

Figure 10.5: Everyone for tennis. Java, c.1890s (KITLV/University of Leiden)

recently married young woman of 25 – four of the Lawn Tennis Club's seven committee members were female, all of them of Dutch descent, while the remaining three males were British (Figure 10.5). Even so, they were not the only men formally involved with the club, among whom was William Loudon MacNeill's elder brother, Neil, who acted as 'referee' at a tournament held in Batavia in November of that year.[20]

A Repatriate Afterlife: New Men and New Money

It was in the neighbouring residence of the Surabaya agent of the Chartered Bank of India Australia and China[21] that the MacNeill-van Davelaar couple bid a formal farewell to their Dutch as well as English friends and acquaintances in mid-April 1897, shortly after auctioning off their household goods (as was the custom on departing the Indies), including – as befitted a high-ranking business executive and his 'lady' – antique inlaid and walnut pieces and a 'grand piano from the major German firm of Zeitter and Winkelmann', though since the latter was billed as 'good as new', it may have served an ornamental rather than musical function.[22] Once repatriated, they and their family initially lived in London, in Frognal, on the lower reaches of the steep road that runs up to the western rim of Hampstead Heath.[23] There were six live-in servants, three of whom were Scots – but that simple enumeration conceals the extent to which, in relocating to London from Surabaya, hierarchy of race had given way to one of class. 'It seemed strange that ... the servants were white,' it was remarked of a near-contemporary situation. 'I had never seen white ladies in that role before.'[24] To be sure, the British-born MacNeill would himself have been familiar with this from his childhood and youth in Scotland, but it would have seemed strange indeed to his wife who had been born in the Indies and most likely spent much of her formative years there, prior to almost two decades of running a household in Surabaya with a bevy of domestics who were, by definition, invariably people of colour.

Just when it was that the William Loudon MacNeill and his wife moved their household from London to Wigtownshire in the far south-west of Scotland is not clear from the public record, but their great house at Shennanton must have reached a sufficient stage of completion for them to have moved in prior to the wedding there in January 1911 of their eldest son. At the same time, they maintained an apartment in Queen Anne's Mansions, Westminster, said to be 'a stupendous pile which, for solidity, comfort and general convenience, sets all rivals at defiance'. Its public rooms were the epitome of late-Victorian splendour and it boasted not only London's first hydraulic lift but also, in Edwardian times, the presence of Sir Edward Elgar, who apparently composed his Violin Concerto while staying there.[25] Nevertheless, it was evidently no more than a pied-à-terre, convenient for the couple's visits to London – but with only enough additional accommodation for a solitary servant, a lady's maid.[26]

MacNeill and his family's establishment in rural Wigtownshire looks to have been a case of new men with new money supplanting their financially embarrassed predecessors from an older 'Scotland'. Quite what had brought them to a part of the country so far removed from MacNeill's ancestral location in the Inner Hebrides is altogether more speculative, however: the connection may well have been forged by the marriage in April 1906 of

Flora MacNeill, the younger of the MacNeill-van Davelaar couple's two daughters, to George Kerr, the solicitor son of a prominent banker and solicitor at Newton Stewart, the nearest town in Wigtownshire to Shennanton. The marriage itself took place, however, in Hampstead parish church, while the bride was still living with her family in the Frognal house into which they had moved late in the previous decade.[27]

The real estate transactions possibly brokered by George Kerr himself (he subsequently became estate factor there) that made the successful ex-Java sugar trader the 'laird' of Shennanton would appear to have been set in motion in 1907. It was then that south-west Scotland's premier aristocrat, the cash-strapped Randolph Henry Stewart, 11th Earl of Galloway, put up for sale not only his hereditary seat, Galloway House, a few miles south of Wigtown, but also the 23,500 acre estate attached to it.[28] Their (main) purchaser was Sir Malcolm Donald McEacharn, a ship-owner, businessman and politician recently returned to Britain from the Antipodes – a 'shrewd open-minded capitalist ... the typical colonial financier of Scottish birth' according to the eminent British socialists Sidney and Beatrice Webb who had encountered him in the First Class accommodation of the liner bringing them back from Australia a decade earlier[29] – who bought the great house itself, a massive Georgian-Victorian pile that boasted around thirty-six bedrooms, along with an extensive acreage of moorland, forest and farmland. Since MacNeill evidently acquired the Shennanton sector of the Galloway estate around this same time, the presumption might be that he was either a co-bidder with McEacharn or subsequently purchased it from him in a deal perhaps brokered by his son-in-law. The 11th Earl of Galloway himself, meanwhile, retreated to a secondary residence in the district, Cumloden near Newton Stewart, a former hunting lodge,[30] which was inherited on his death a decade later by the 12th Earl (whom we shall meet again shortly).

Sugar and Social Standing

Unlike his parent, and presumably because the latter was wealthy enough not to have to send his first-born back into trade, Alexander Henry MacNeill instead made a considerable career in the British Army as an officer in the King's Own Scottish Borderers (KOSB), thereby enabling him, to complete a social transformation begun by his father. At the age of 25, in 1908, he had joined the Fifth Battalion at a period when, as one commentator has remarked, 'a career in the army had been a leisurely avocation – plenty of sport, especially riding and hunting: truly an occupation for a gentleman.'[31] Then came the horrors of the First World War in which MacNeill himself saw action in the Gallipoli Campaign, Egypt and Palestine, and subsequently fought on the Western Front, where his bravery gained him the *Croix de Guerre*, an award bestowed by the French on both their own and allied soldiers. When peace came, he stayed with the Army and, now as Colonel MacNeill, commanded the Fifth Battalion of the KOSB, based at Dumfries, some 40 miles east of the family home.[32] On his father's death in 1923, he was the main legatee, the recipient of some three-quarters of the estate which the widower William Loudon MacNeill (his wife had died at Shennanton some six years earlier, quite possibly of TB) bequeathed to his offspring[33] – a more than substantial enough sum, one presumes, for him to manage the upkeep of Shennanton and the social expectations associated with his high military rank and position in the county.

Just how elevated that position had become was revealed some seven years later when, in November 1930, MacNeill died in an Edinburgh nursing home, at the age of 46, leaving a widow and one child.[34] As was reported in the several obituary notices in Scottish newspapers, the late Colonel had taken a great interest in the British Legion and in work for ex-servicemen generally, and he was evidently well regarded by the lower ranks, who turned out in large numbers for his funeral at a country church just outside Newton Stewart. What was particularly impressive about the funeral, however, was the 'exceptionally large concourse of mourners representative of the principal county families and societies' of Scotland's south-west, reflecting no doubt the fact that MacNeill belonged to highest 'social and military circles in the South of Scotland.' Those in attendance included the Lord Lieutenant of the County, Sir Herbert Maxwell, the Scottish novelist, essayist, artist, antiquarian, horticulturalist and Conservative politician whose deputy MacNeill had been,[35] as well as two Earls (of Galloway and Stair respectively), several high-ranking military officers, one of them a General, and an Admiral of the Fleet.[36]

For a man whose grandfather, Alexander MacNeill, 'Snr', had been the 'son of a small Argyllshire Laird' (to borrow Gillian Maclaine's description of the latter's elder brother, John MacNeill),[37] the transformation was remarkable. Separated from trade by a generation, by broad acres of good sporting country, by a public-school education and by the officer corps of the British Army, the late Colonel MacNeill had circulated among the gentry and aristocrats who comprised the social elite of Wigtownshire and neighbouring Kirkcudbrightshire. To be sure, it was not a simple rags-to-riches story. The colonel's great-grandfather, Neil MacNeill 'the first', was one of a rural elite of tacksmen (tenants-in-chief), and had kin both on Islay and further north at Ardnacross on Mull, the largest of the Southern Hebrides.[38] These were not poor crofters who 'made good' in the colonies. Rather, MacNeill's ancestors were people of some substance, leaseholders of a kind who sublet a portion of the lands they held to lesser farmers.[39] But Islay during the first half of the nineteenth century was an impoverished place, where the economic distinction between 'smaller lairds' and tenant farmers was a rather fine one, and where only one family – the Campbells of Islay House (near Bowmore) – could be classified as large landholding proprietors. In that sense, their time spent in the diaspora and the fortune that it brought them enabled the MacNeills not only to consolidate a social rank that they already possessed but also greatly to enhance it. Even so, in retrospect the Colonel had stood at the apogee of that achievement.

Widowhood at Shennanton: Emma Mackenzie-MacNeill's Story

It is no exaggeration to say that among the MacNeill kin, following the head of the family's premature death in 1930, the menfolk tended to recede into the background, underscoring the part played by the women of the Maclaine Watson cohort in shaping its overall history. Two of the women were the late Colonel MacNeill's sisters, Isabella (Isabel) Gijsberta Maria MacNeill and her younger sibling, Flora. The latter was twice-married, and after the death of her first husband in September 1918 (a brief and discreet report appeared in the *Dumfries and Galloway Standard* noting simply that George Kerr had died as 'the result of a gunshot wound' and that the 51-year-old 'had been in poor health recently')[40] subsequently returned to the Indies (she had been born on Java) and evidently took on the role of bringing new talent into the firm.

Robert Gourlay MacIndoe, seven years her junior and an accountant who was already working for Maclaine Watson[41] when Flora MacNeill-Kerr married him in Semarang in April 1921, went on to become a key partner in the firm while still on Java – and after repatriation late in the 1930s continued to shepherd Maclaine Watson's fortunes at the London end of the business. How she passed her time in the rural fastness in which they had installed themselves near Guildford is something at which we can only guess, although the public record does tell us that she was on the committee of the local branch of the Women's Institute and became involved in wartime fundraising.[42] Her husband, meanwhile, in addition to running an amateur cricket team,[43] took a seat on the board of the Shanghai and Hong Kong Banking Corporation – along with the firm of Butterfield and Swire, one of the two great bastions of the fading British Empire in East Asia – and became chairman of the (London) board of the Scottish Union and National Insurance Company. As such, MacIndoe was a significant enough figure in the City to merit a short obituary in *The Times*.[44]

Neither of the sister's stories, however, quite matches that of their cousin, the Colonel's widow. Alexander Henry MacNeill had wed a fellow Scot, Emma Mackenzie, in Edinburgh in 1911. Like him, his bride was both overseas-born and a youthful returnee from the diaspora. Her father, Gilbert Proby Mackenzie, a graduate of medical school in Edinburgh, had gone to the subcontinent to work as a surgeon for the Indian Army's Bengal Medical Service sometime in the 1870s, and had died at sea while on a return voyage to Britain, leaving a widow and five young children. His wife, Jane Scott-Mackenzie, had subsequently settled in Musselburgh, just outside Edinburgh, where her father had been a medical practitioner,[45] and where she herself had been born and wed.[46] The family lived there (on 'private means') looking out across the Musselburgh racecourse in the solidly middle-class surroundings of Albert Terrace, and in the genteel but somewhat straightened circumstances suggested by the fact that although the family could afford two live-in servants, the latter were both still in their teens.[47] The diaspora had not only taken their family to 'the East', however, but also to South America. Indeed, Emma Mackenzie's paternal grandfather had been a slave–owning planter in Demerara, in part of what is now Guyana.[48] Her own story, however, was firmly rooted in the Scottish border counties.

Following her husband's death in 1930, his widow remained at Shennanton – and did so until her death almost three decades later. As such, she was the dominant figure in her immediate family's subsequent history.[49] Her only child, Loudon MacNeill, may well have been the 'young laird of Shennanton', as a contemporary newspaper described him on his coming of age there in 1935, shortly after he had returned to Scotland from agricultural college south of the Border;[50] but it was his mother, the diminutive and formidable widow, who made the running. To be sure, her son's marriage in 1939 to Grace Marjorie (Boe) Gillespie (Figure 10.6)

Figure 10.6: The marriage of William Loudon MacNeill's grandson to Grace Gillespie, 1939 (Collection of the Author)

signalled a further step in the MacNeill family's social positioning. She was the daughter of an 'establishment' solicitor in nearby Castle Douglas, while her mother, Helen Marjorie Todd, hailed from a prominent Edinburgh legal dynasty. Moreover, the wedding itself was followed by a reception in the imposing location of nearby Argrennan House ('kindly lent by Mrs Aikman Smith'), a late Georgian mansion,[51] fully suited to the many 'representatives of the county families' who attended.[52]

Yet as may also have been the case with fortunes of other of the 'county families' represented at the wedding, the situation was potentially fraught. William Loudon MacNeill, the builder of Shennanton, had died a substantially wealthy man, and had bequeathed over £390,000 (on which duties of around £90,000 were paid) comprising the Shennanton property itself, valued for probate at almost £168,000, and a balance of some £225,000 in his 'Personal Estate'. Apart from a modest tranche, amounting around £21,000, invested in ventures back in the Indies, its composition was heavily weighted towards railway stock and government bonds in a multiplicity of locations worldwide, ranging from the Argentine and Canada to India and the Philippines.[53] What may have looked solid at the beginning of the 1920s, however, had taken on a very different appearance a decade later. The Colonel's demise in 1930 meant that death duties were again levied on the estate after an interval of less than seven years. Worse, the Wall Street Crash of 1929 and its aftermath in the inter-war Depression would have diminished the value of the shareholdings that comprised the bulk of the MacNeill portfolio. In short, by the end of the 1930s the financial underpinning of the Shennanton 'project' initiated by his grandfather had been considerably weakened.

To all appearances, his grandson devoted his energies largely to shooting and stalking and, above all, to fishing. Indeed, it was fishing (in Aberdeenshire) that featured prominently, along with a visit to the Isle of Skye, in plans for the newly-weds' honeymoon.[54] According to his descendants, his passion for fishing was indeed such that he would take himself off to Ireland when the prospects for angling were dim on his home territory.[55] Unlike her son, Mackenzie-MacNeill was an activist, immersed in the local politics of Wigtownshire and neighbouring Kirkcudbrightshire. Her late husband had himself been prominent in Galloway's Conservative Unionist organisation,[56] and by the late 1930s she herself was sufficiently well-regarded in Unionist (Tory) circles in south-west Scotland to be elected as one of the Galloway constituency's four representatives on the Central Council of the Scottish Unionist Association along, among others, with Randolph Algernon Ronald Stewart, 12th Earl of Galloway.[57] Evidently Emma Mackenzie-MacNeill mixed with people of considerable regional clout and consequence.

As such, she subsequently became involved, prior to the British general election of July 1945, in moves to rid the party of the sitting member for Galloway, John Hamilton McKie, whose sympathy throughout the 1930s for the Nazi cause in Europe was well publicised. The Earl of Galloway – the chair of the constituency party who clearly supported what was afoot and may even have initiated it – was a long-term associate of McKie's: they were both Old Harrovians, were both landowners in the district, and had both been members, prior to September 1939, of the Right Club, founded by another Scot from an aristocratic family, Captain Archibald Maule Ramsay Unionist MP for Peebles (whose suspectedly treasonous manoeuvrings had led to his imprisonment for much of the Second World War).[58] What had caused the falling-out between the Earl and McKie is not clear, but the upshot was a motion to deselect him, proposed by Emma Mackenzie-MacNeill, not with any overt reference (which would have been awkward) to his stance in the 1930s but with a more general complaint that:

she was aware of the increasing loss of confidence in Mr McKie as Parliamentary representative of Galloway ... [a] feeling that was not confined to one section of the community.

Her son was also at the meeting and offered loyal support to his mother in the form of the assertion that criticism of the sitting member was to be 'heard in the markets, public houses and in the streets,' though he avowed that he knew of 'nothing more definite'.[59] Notwithstanding that the motion to deselect was passed by a solid majority, McKie lost the battle but won the war: standing as an 'Independent Unionist' he retained the seat – and was readmitted to the party three years later. Even so, it might be imagined that such harmony as had existed among the 'county families' of Wigtownshire and Kirkcudbrightshire prior to the War was unlikely to have been restored and that Emma Mackenzie-MacNeill would have been remembered as the Earl of Galloway's ally in an intra-elite spat, the precise origins of which appear likely to remain obscure. The essential point, however, about her involvement in the McKie affair is that it underscores the extent to which the MacNeills had been accepted into the web of county families who formed the top social stratum of the part of Scotland's south-west in which Shennanton was located.

Aftermath: Liability and Privilege

Following his mother's death at the age of 72 in July 1959, Loudon MacNeill and his wife eventually took up residence in the great house itself, and it was at Shennanton that both husband and wife died in the same year (1990). They were the last of their family to live there: faced with the massive costs of the upkeep of such a large property, their descendants, while remaining in the district, took up residence in other, smaller and altogether more practical locations. Shennanton itself, and a by-then much reduced surrounding estate, was sold by the MacNeill family.

The property had assisted them in achieving a social standing in 'the county' and, more specifically, of accommodating the shooting parties and the like that were a central feature of country-house life in the Scottish Borders and Highlands. But Shennanton's future was clouded with financial uncertainty. Unlike some of their counterparts in the Maclaine Watson cohort, this branch of MacNeill family opted for rural gentility and had neither gone into business in the metropole after repatriation nor developed careers as entrepreneurs in fields outside the immediate sphere in which they had initially made their money. Yet the wealth underpinning this gentility was not self-perpetuating, and the upshot was that the Colonel's heirs at Shennanton (his widow and his only son) inherited an ultimately unsustainable financial position. Its builder's eldest son and heir opted for a successful career in the British Army, which, although it evidently brought him social prominence in the Borders, contributed little to the family fortune. Moreover, the one individual of his generation who might have replenished the coffers, his younger brother, the thrice-married Neil MacNeill, as a partner in Maclaine Watson during the so-called 'Dance of the Millions' around 1920, when world sugar prices temporarily skyrocketed, would have made very good money. But he had little to do with Shennanton. Instead, on repatriation he settled in London or thereabouts, and subsequently had a Scottish establishment of his own some 15 miles south-west of Edinburgh which is where he died in 1955.[60]

Meanwhile, the prospects of recourse to the Indies (by then the Republic of Indonesia) to replenish the family fortunes were rapidly dwindling. A takeover of foreign assets had begun in 1959, including Maclaine Watson two years later. To be sure, William Loudon MacNeill's great-grandson, Michael Loudon Lorne MacNeill, worked in London for the old 'family firm' for some time during the 1960s. As he recollected, it was still very much a going concern (trading in tin, rubber and tea) doing well out of commission business, and linked to the Singapore office, which had taken over the Southeast Asian end of Maclaine Watson after the sequestration of the firm's Indonesian operations.[61] Even so, this was not the road to making the kind of fortune that his forebears had once enjoyed, and he subsequently successfully took up farming in Galloway on part of Shennanton's erstwhile estate. One of his sons, meanwhile, set up an innovative saw-milling business close by. The MacNeills of Shennanton were not the only cohort family caught in a financial ebb tide: so too was the last of their cousins in the McLean family to enter the Maclaine Watson partnership. Before turning to that story, however, we shall explore the history of the 'other' main branch of the MacNeill family, likewise descendants of 'patriarch' Alexander MacNeill, whose colonial careering ended in the 'alternative metropole' across the North Sea from Scotland.

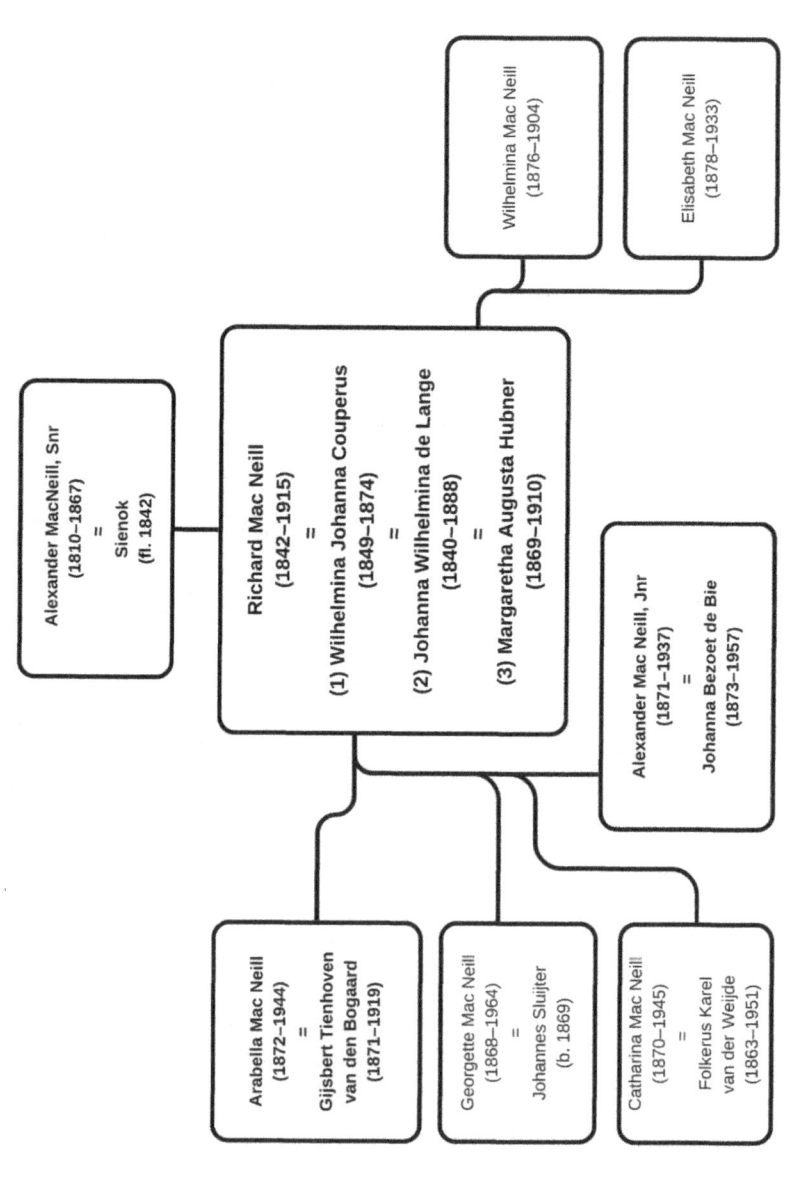

11

Upper Deck and *Indisch*

On 1st February 1890 the Dutch steamer *Burgemeester den Tex*[1] sailed from Batavia, carrying fourteen or more First Class adult passengers and assorted children (Figure 11.1). Among them was a wealthy businessman who had been born on Java and was making what must have been his third journey to Western Europe. The proud bearer of a Scots name, twice a widower with six Java-born offspring (four of whom, all daughters, were travelling with him on this occasion), he was the stepbrother of two Scotsmen with equally long careers in the Indies: William Loudon MacNeill and Neil MacNeill, Snr. Like them, he was a man grown rich through the trade in Java's sugar. Unlike his stepbrothers, however, Richard Mac Neill was of mixed, Javanese-Scottish ethnicity, and when he finally left Java, he relocated 'back' to the Netherlands – where he and his kin went under the appellation of 'Mac Neill', following standard Dutch usage – rather than to the British Isles.

His and his family's history, *Indisch* (in the sense 'of the Indies'), is illustrative of the centrality of the 'unsettling of boundaries' to an understanding of diaspora[2] – boundaries which in this case were ethnic as well as imperial. The great majority of the men, women and children who made up the long-established Dutch quasi-settler communities were of creole European-Asian descent, something which was no bar to the assumption of Dutch social and legal identity both in its Asian colony and in the Netherlands itself. The social acceptance of Eurasians of either

Figure 11.1: SS Burgemeester den Tex, which brought Richard Mac Neill and his family to Europe in 1890 (Collection of the Author)

gender as part of 'polite' colonial society had once been common enough in the Dutch colony's British counterparts in the Indian subcontinent as well as in Singapore and the Malay Peninsula. From the second half of the nineteenth century onwards, however, this became decreasingly the case and a marked trend towards ethnic or 'racial' exclusivity pushed individuals of identifiably mixed ethnicity to the margins of colonial society or denied them a place there altogether. In British Malaya, for example, 'mere suspicion of Eurasian blood was enough to set the ceiling of a man's promotion or blight a woman's marriage prospects' and 'although individuals were occasionally absorbed into the European group, Europeans disapproved very strongly when Eurasians tried to construct themselves as Europeans'.[3] Indeed, at the beginning of the twentieth century, two of the authors of the Report of the *Census of India* might loftily observe that 'Eurasians are prone to describe themselves as Europeans' and congratulate their enumerators on their increased 'success in distinguishing between pure Europeans and persons of mixed descent'.[4]

Their statistician counterparts in the Indies harboured no such ambitions. Instead, they contented themselves with establishing how many of their European population were of Netherlands-birth (very much the minority) and how many were born locally. Admittedly, there evolved a late colonial discourse relating to the 'dangers of miscegenation' generated by (and reflected in) imaginative literature, polemical journalism and popular manuals aimed at socially acclimatising newcomers to the colony. This discourse was a significant one, not least because of its productive capacity in encouraging the disparagement of people of mixed ethnicity, neatly encapsulated in the formula that 'You must have inherited this trait from your Eurasian mother'.[5] Nonetheless, in terms of everyday social reality, the horse had long bolted through a wide-open stable door. Both marriage and less formal relationships across the racial 'divide' continued strongly to characterise late colonial society in the Indies: in the 1920s, for example, some one in four marriages contracted by Europeans in the Indies took place across ethnic lines.[6] The contrast between imperial conventions in this regard was not something that escaped the jaundiced eye of one early twentieth-century Maclaine Watson partner, who caustically observed that whereas:

> the line of demarcation is very strongly drawn in the British colonies between full-blood Europeans and half-castes . . . it is not so in the Dutch East Indies. This is a mistake for which the Dutch will probably suffer one day.[7]

It is within this broader context that the story that follows serves both to complicate conventional Scottish diasporan narratives of sojourner 'returns to Caledonia' and to illuminate a comparison between the two empires in question (Britain and the Netherlands) in terms of the social acceptance of individuals of mixed European and Asian ethnicity.

The Genesis of an *Indisch* Family

Richard Mac Neill's father, Alexander MacNeill, Snr, had been born in Scotland, the son of a Highland laird from the island of Islay and arrived in the Indies in the mid-1830s to join his considerably older brother in a mercantile business, MacNeill & Co, that the latter had established in Semarang, on the north coast of Central Java. It was as a newly wealthy man that he subsequently returned to his native Scotland and married a Scottish woman with whom he had nine children, two of whom on reaching maturity also became major figures in the same mercantile concern in which their father had been involved.[8] So, too, did Richard Mac Neill – but *his* background was rather different.

Before he left the Indies, Alexander MacNeill had fathered a girl and a boy with a Javanese woman, Sienok, with whom he had lived for some years in Semarang. No other information has survived about Sienok – a woman whose recorded 'name' may have been a Javanese term of endearment akin to 'the little one'[9] – but it appears both that the couple's daughter died while her father was still in Semarang, and that her mother may also have done so. The son, however, born in 1842, was a different matter. Officially recognised by his father, who thereby conferred European status on the boy in accordance with standard Dutch practice in the Indies, the juvenile Richard Mac Neill accompanied his father back to Europe. We may speculate that his schooling took place in the Netherlands, where his father would have had business contacts, rather than in his father's native Scotland. What is not speculative, however, is that Richard Mac Neill was not mentioned in his father's will made shortly after the latter's Edinburgh marriage in July 1850 (an indication, perhaps, that Alexander MacNeill kept his Java and

Figure 11.2: Wilhelmina Johanna Couperus, beloved first wife of Richard Mac Neill (Collection Elisabeth del Court König-Van Essen, The Hague)

post-Java lives strictly compartmentalised)[10] and that, towards the end of that decade, he returned to his Indies birthplace of Semarang.

Once there, he worked initially for the MacNeill & Co.'s extensive sugar business, and it was doubtless the same commodity that took him, sometime in the mid-1860s, eastwards to the colony's prime sugar-producing districts in the narrow coastal plain of Java's *Oosthoek* and to employment with Fraser Eaton, the Surabaya 'sister house' (like its Semarang counterpart) of the Batavia-based Maclaine Watson. Sent to work in Probolinggo, some 100 kilometres east of Surabaya, young Mac Neill, now in his mid-twenties, was in the proximity of a handful of factories in which Fraser Eaton most likely had an interest.

It was also where he found a wife. Wilhelmina Johanna Couperus (Figure 11.2) was the daughter of the highest-ranking Dutch official in the area, the Indies-born *resident* Petrus Theodorus Couperus, and had been born at one of her father's earlier postings, on the west coast of the island of Sumatra, where Couperus had cohabited with 'the Indonesian woman Sarinah'. As such, she was one of the couple's several 'recognised' Eurasian children who had accompanied him back to Java.[11] The wedding, which took place in Probolinggo in 1867, provided Mac Neill not only with a spouse but also with an entrée into the elite circles of the powerful Dutch colonial bureaucracy – no mean advantage for a man who was to make his fortune trading in a commodity that was produced primarily by factories still heavily dependent on colonial officialdom for access to peasant land and labour.[12] While living there – and subsequently in Pasuruan, another 'sugar town' 50 or so kilometres along the coast to the west – the young couple had four children: three girls and one boy. Wilhelmina Mac Neill-Couperus, however, died there in 1874, aged no more than 25; but the family connection would have remained potent. As indeed did the memory of the young woman herself: sometime in the 1890s a contemporary portrait of her was lovingly refurbished, presumably at Richard Mac Neill's behest.

In May 1875, sixteen months or more after his young wife's death, and no doubt faced with the exigencies of a nest of motherless offspring, Mac Neill had married again. This time, however, his choice fell on a colonial-born woman past the first flush of youth and, to all appearances, less well connected than her predecessor. Even so, Johanna Wilhelmina de Lange was a scion of a locally based, Indies-Dutch family (one of typically European and Asian ancestry) that had been settled in the *Oosthoek* for a generation or more. The couple subsequently had two children, both girls, while continuing to be based in East Java, primarily in Surabaya itself, where De Lange died, aged 48, in January 1888. Prior to that, however, in 1882,[13] she had accompanied her husband and all six of their joint children on a European visit that had ended, somewhat abruptly, two years later, when pressing business affairs in Java called Mac Neill back to the Indies.

Departing Amsterdam in mid-April 1884 and disembarking in Batavia a little over a month later,[14] Mac Neill went on to play a key role in salvaging Maclaine Watson's fortunes, at a time when many similarly placed enterprises went under, in the wake of a crisis affecting sugar manufacturers and traders worldwide, as a result of the sudden collapse of the global price for the commodity.[15] He then remained in the Indies for another six years, during which time he became a partner in the firm (a position he continued until 1906) and took part in the establishment of sugar-industry research stations designed, among other things, to improve the quality of cane varieties available in the colony. Most immediately, however, they were called into existence to combat the effects of a serious cane disease that was rife throughout the island.[16] Mac Neill also went on the board of De Volharding, one of Surabaya's pioneering engineering works, geared primarily to servicing the increasingly heavily mechanised sugar industry of the surrounding districts.[17] In short, by the time he left the Indies again, early in 1890, he had unquestionably entered the circles of Java's leading 'sugar men', well versed not only in the sugar trade itself but also in many crucial aspects of the commodity's production. Though this proved to be his definitive return to a country that he had first come to know as a child the better part of half a century earlier, it was not the termination of his family's connection with the Indies and with the East Java town of Probolinggo in particular.

At Home among the *Haagse* Bourgeoisie

Imaginative literature such as that of the celebrated Dutch novelist Louis Couperus fills some of the gaps left, in the case of this family, by the absence, apart from valuable photographs, of private letters, memoirs and the like: not least, because the author was distantly related to the Mac Neills and may have encountered them in their adopted city. One of his best-known works was set there, and deals, although only in passing, with a wealthy ex-Indies family, the Ruyvenaers, who may have some resemblance to his distant cousins. The wife, who had brought with her into the marriage the sugar factory that kept her family rich (her elder boy was typically 'in the sugar' himself but presently on leave in The Hague), was unmistakeably *Indisch* in appearance and manners, as were her daughters. Her sister-in-law, at whose house the novelist has the Ruyvenaers attending a soiree, had herself been born in the Indies and her husband's career had kept him there for most of his life: but she and her immediate kin:

> were ultra-Dutch and always laughed a little at the Ruyvenaers, while cheerfully resigning themselves to the Indies strain, which shocked them a bit . . . [and] made them a trifle uncomfortable in the presence of their purely Dutch friends and acquaintances.

Nonetheless, the significance of the ties that linked such bourgeois Indies families to their Dutch counterparts was not lost on her (nor on the novelist himself), and she:

> carried her family pride to the point of maintaining that all that formed part of the family was good . . . [and] always looked severe when her children . . . laughed at Aunt Ruyvenaer and the nieces, who were good children, always cheerful, always amiable, bright and pleasant.[18]

For such young people (as well as, in the case of the Mac Neills, their surviving parent) The Hague had a great deal that was familiar, even allowing for the disparity of its winter climate. The Dutch seat of government was a magnet for ex-colonials. Around 1920 more than 7,500 Indies-born individuals were living there, and three decades earlier several thousand were already similarly domiciled, mostly in the better-heeled quarters of the city, along with many others who had been born in the Netherlands but who had repatriated after an often-lengthy sojourn in the colony.[19] Moreover, in addition to the permanently relocated, at any given time there were also staying there scores of individuals and families, *verlofgangers* or 'people on furlough' from government jobs or positions in business in the Indies.[20] Above all they were attracted by the ambience of a city that prided itself on the primacy of its Indies links and boasted cafés, clubs, restaurants and shops that catered for them, underpinned by the presence of a substantial (though statistically largely invisible) pool of Indonesian servants, brought over from the Indies by their erstwhile Dutch employers or discharged from boats serving the colony.[21]

Richard Mac Neill had sailed to Europe in February 1890 in the company of four of his five daughters. A fifth daughter was already in Europe, having apparently been left there when her family had last visited some six years earlier. Meanwhile, his only son, Alexander, Jnr, was also already there, enrolled in the Senior High School in Arnhem. Aged 19, he graduated in November of the same year that his immediate family arrived in the Netherlands[22] – and was soon sent back to work 'in the sugar' (as the Dutch saying went) in the Indies. Richard's daughters, however, all five of them now reunited, evidently remained in The Hague, where their father took a recently built and rather grand house on the Koninginnegracht ('Queen's Canal'), where he remained for the rest of his life (Figure 11.3).

Photographs from the turn of the century report his choice as an elegant quasi-boulevard, flanked on one side by mansions, running westward along a broad canal from the older parts of The Hague towards the fishing port and seaside resort of Scheveningen, with its fin-de-siècle casino, pier and promenade. It was a most desirable part of the city, where the Mac Neills' neighbours included several fine specimens of the *Haagse* bourgeoisie. At its rear was the Archipelbuurt, 'the archipelago neighbourhood', whose streets were for the most part named after locations in the Indies, and a little further off was the Willemspark. Both were favoured destinations for wealthy ex-colonials. Even so, there may have been limits to what Richard

Figure 11.3: Koninginnegracht, The Hague, where Richard Mac Neill had his mansion, c.1900 (Collection of the Author)

Mac Neill was able to achieve socially after he settled in The Hague. It was the case, for example, that he never obtained membership of De Witte, the city's most exclusive gentlemen's club.[23] Nor, rather more surprisingly, since his father had been a lifelong member of the brotherhood, did he belong to either of The Hague's masonic lodges.[24] Even so, an address on the Koninginnegracht constituted an impressive base from which to establish the Mac Neills in polite Dutch society and begin the work incumbent on a newly arrived widower with six unwed offspring.

Louis Couperus had nothing to say about the subsequent marital history of the 'always amiable, bright and pleasant' young women of the Ruyvenaer family. That of their Mac Neill counterparts, however, can be detailed with some certainty, along with the extent of their incorporation into the upper levels of Dutch metropolitan society. There exists among the treasured possessions of Richard Mac Neill's descendants a remarkable studio photograph, taken in The Hague very early in the twentieth century,[25] one showing Mac Neill himself, very much the benevolent patriarch, seated in the midst of his extended family: three sons-in-law are there with their wives, flanked in turn by two unmarried daughters, his only son and daughter-in-law and some six grandchildren (Figure 11.4). As such, it provides in graphic form the basis for a story of four weddings – and a funeral.

Figure 11.4: Richard Mac Neill amidst his extended family, The Hague, c.1903 (Collection Elisabeth del Court König-Van Essen, The Hague)

It is a story that begins in the Indies, but which continues in the Netherlands, where the patriarch's ongoing business career as a successful company promoter and director, and as a sugar-industry lobbyist, plainly had a bearing on the marital history of his progeny. His presence on Dutch company boards meant that he had dealings with key figures in what has been designated as 'the Indies Business Community' (*het Indische Bedrijfsleven*) operating in the metropole.[26] Among them was Samuel Pieter van Eeghen, the celebrated '*Mijnheer* S.P.' who, supported by his aristocratic brother-in-law, Jhr Willem Hendrik van Loon, was to become the uncrowned king of the Amsterdam financial and business world,[27] while in Rotterdam Mac Neill was similarly associated with members of the Suermondt family, prominent in that city's banking and mercantile circles.[28]

Other contacts placed him firmly among the *Indischgasten* ('Old Indies Hands') settled in the Netherlands: indeed, the one individual who stood out in terms of the ubiquity of his presence over the years at the weddings of the Mac Neil offspring (at which he several times acted as a witness) was Jacob Carel Laurens Cambier. Indies-born, but a scion of an old-established Dutch patrician family whose roots went back to the seventeenth-century, he was the son of a Dutch *resident* and his probably Eurasian wife.[29] Settled back in the Indies after an education in the Netherlands, Cambier established himself as a coffee planter in the *Oosthoek*, where he married (as had Richard Mac Neill himself) into the De Lange clan. Their families were evidently close. Indeed, after Cambier and his wife (Louise Cornelia de Lange) relocated to the Netherlands early in the 1880s and settled in Arnhem, they most likely lodged Richard Mac Neill's only son, when Alexander Mac Neill, Jnr was sent from Java to continue his education in the Netherlands. That only son (as we shall see), in turn, found a wife among similarly *Indischgasten* circles. As 'Indies' backgrounds morphed into something altogether broader, however, his sisters made marriages that located them firmly in a metropolitan setting in the Netherlands itself.

Above all, it was the marriage of Arabella Mac Neill, Richard Mac Neill and Wilhelmina Johanna Couperus's youngest child, to the 29-year-old civil engineer, Gijsbert van Tienhoven van den Bogaard[30] that underscored the extent to which the family had pivoted from its Indies origins (Figure 11.5). The groom's father (*Burgemeester* of Werkendam and eventually member of the North Brabant provincial assembly) had made his money as a major government contractor engaged, among other things, on the huge Waterlinie project – an aquatic Dutch version of France's subsequent Maginot line

Figure 11.5: Arabella Mac Neill and Gijsbert van Tienhoven, who wed in The Hague at the beginning of the twentieth century (Collection Elisabeth del Court König-Van Essen, The Hague)

designed, with a series of forts and sluices, to inundate vast stretches of the central Netherlands in the event of an enemy attack. He had envisaged his son following in his footsteps, and the youth was enrolled in the Polytechnic School of Delft, subsequently the Delft Institute of Technology, under which name it achieved worldwide fame. A member of the Polytechnic's Student Corps – and hence assured of a place among the educated elite of his generation – Gijsbert van Tienhoven van den Bogaard graduated in 1898, a year after his father's sudden death.

He found work in the rapidly expanding Dutch glass industry and subsequently became general manager of a large glass-blowing enterprise at Vlaardingen, located along the River Maas to the west of Rotterdam. Unlike her sisters' spouses, Arabella Mac Neill's husband's career thus took him nowhere near the Indies and had nothing to do with sugar. Indeed, the couple lived out their married life exclusively in the Netherlands (where their two children were born): and it was there, in The Hague in 1919, scarcely 48 years old, in the great house on the Koninginnegracht which had previously been owned by Richard Mac Neill, that Van Tienhoven van den Bogaard died, only four years after his father-in-law.[31]

From the standpoint of the Mac Neill family's 'arrival' among the Dutch bourgeoisie, however, the point was not simply that Arabella wed a locally based company executive and never returned to the country of her birth. Rather, its greater significance related to the family connections that flowed from the marriage. In this regard, the star presence at his nephew's wedding more than four decades earlier had been his uncle, Gijsbert van Tienhoven, who had a formidable profile as politician and civic administrator, and whose greatest single claim to fame was to have been *Burgemeester* of Amsterdam during a period in the late nineteenth century when a number of major civic projects – the Concertgebouw and the Rijksmuseum among them – had been initiated or completed, thereby restoring Amsterdam's reputation as a world city. To have such a man at the wedding of his youngest daughter was a social achievement of a high order for a 'Scot' born to a Javanese mother back in Semarang well over a half a century earlier.

Arabella van Tienhoven-MacNeill outlived her husband by some two and half decades, and died in Arnhem, at her son-in-law Dr J. L. F. van Essen's house, in the late summer of 1944, when the city was still under German occupation during the later stages of the Second World War. Indeed, it may well have been the War that had brought about her move from the Hague, since the occupiers' determination to frustrate any Allied seaborne invasion on this part of North Sea coast led them to drive a massive anti-tank ditch through some of the city's choicest residential districts, resulting in the destruction of many houses. Further indicative of the times – and with an irony that would hardly have been lost on a woman long familiar with other prime commodities of the Indies – on the same front page of the newspaper in which the notice of her death appeared, there featured an advertisement for *SMALSKO*, a coffee substitute, with the claim that 'of course, you will not have forgotten what real coffee is like, but the taste and aroma of this is so good that you will be happy with it'.[32]

The family patriarch himself, Richard Mac Neill, had died almost 30 years earlier in October 1915, at the age of 73, having outlived by five years his considerably younger third wife (Margaretha Augusta Hubner), whom he married in The Hague in 1906, and who may have been his housekeeper and who certainly enjoyed little of the social standing of the other family connections that he had forged in the Netherlands since his arrival in 1890 (Figure 11.6). The notice of Mac Neill's death, which appeared in The Hague's main daily paper, indicated that the burial would take place at the

Figure 11.6: Hubner and the Mac Neills, 1909 (Collection Elisabeth del Court König-Van Essen, The Hague)

General Cemetery – a peaceful location on the dunes between the city and its seaside satellite of Scheveningen. It looks as if many were expected to follow the coffin, since the death notice also mentioned that the procession from the deceased's house would begin at 11am 'on Wednesday next'.[33]

'In the Sugar': the *Tuan* and *Nyonya Besar* of Oemboel

Prominent among the mourners were the deceased's only son and his wife, who had returned from a lengthy stay in the Indies some four years previously. Johanna Elisabeth Bezoet de Bie, had wed Alexander Mac Neill, Jnr in The Hague in mid-February 1897 (Figures 11.7 and 8),[34] only a few months after the groom himself had arrived there on leave from his job in the Indies. Shortly afterwards, he sailed back to the colony with his bride to resume work in time for the commencement of the next campaign or manufacturing season. It was the prelude to the couple's long history in the colony and metropole – and their association with sugar.

Neither was a stranger to Java, since both had been born there and it was the *Oosthoek* town of Probolinggo, the husband's birthplace, that was their destination. What was novel for her, however, was her situation as the wife of the newly appointed general manager of a sugar factory on the

Figure 11.7: Johanna Bezoet de Bie and Alexander Mac Neill. Studio portrait taken at the time of their wedding in the Hague, 1897 (Collection Richard MacNeill, Melbourne)

Figure 11.8: Johanna Mac Neill-Bezoet de Bie and her first child, c.1900 (Collection Richard MacNeill, Melbourne)

Figure 11.9: The tuan besar, the nyonya besar and their children, c.1905. Portrait taken at the Kurkdjian Studio, Surabaya (Collection Richard MacNeill, Melbourne)

outskirts of Probolinggo. As the *tuan besar* ('big man') and the *nyonya besar* (Indies equivalent of the *memsahib* of British India) of Oemboel, the couple belonged to a group of Indies-born individuals who were heavily represented among the managerial and technical personnel of the industry (Figure 11.9). By the time of his marriage, Mac Neill himself had been 'in the sugar' for seven years, following in the footsteps of his maternal uncle, John Couperus, who appears to have spent most of his adult life at factories in the *Oosthoek*.[35] Latterly, Mac Neill himself had been a plantation overseer,[36] a position that gave him responsibility for supervising, through a team of Indonesian *mandur* (foremen) the hundreds of Indonesian labourers of both sexes, by then casually employed on day wages and of varying degrees of skill, who comprised the great bulk of the industry's field workforce.[37]

Supervisory positions of this kind usually went to locally born individuals, pre-eminently Eurasian, rather than to 'raw' expatriate Dutchmen who had little familiarity with the rural Javanese environment and less still with its language: young Mac Neill, brought up in the locality and no doubt speaking at least some rudimentary 'kitchen Javanese' learnt from the servants of his parents' household, would have been well-suited to the job. Local knowledge was critical. For example, a similarly placed man working at an adjacent factory was said to be particularly adept at managing the labourers under his control because of his 'outstanding command of Madurese', the native tongue of many of the seasonal workers who streamed across the strait from their home island during the sugar campaign. For the most part, such supervisors had only modest formal qualifications (this man had basic primary education and a diploma of sorts from one of the 'sugar schools' that the industry ran in East and Central Java), and quickly reached the limits of their promotability.[38] Alexander, however, was able to cross the boundary into the industry's managerial elite by virtue of his European education and his father's wealth and position in industry circles. Broadly speaking, only the *resident* and his deputy stood above the *tuan besar* of a sugar factory in the colonial hierarchy of provincial Java (Figure 11.10).

The *nyonya besar*'s own background was somewhat different. Johanna's father was a scion of a mercantile family established in Rotterdam, who had been taken to the Indies by his parents as a youth early in the 1860s.[39] Reaching adulthood in Surabaya and following the premature death there of his father in 1865, Hermann Bezoet de Bie set up in business in the city in the wholesale import-export trade: indeed, he evidently made enough of a success of it to marry an Indies-born woman, Sara Sijthoff, the daughter of a high-ranking government official. Bezoet de Bie's daughter spent her first sixteen years on Java, mostly in Surabaya, before accompanying her mother, siblings and repatriating father to Europe at the end of the 1880s.

Figure 11.10: Oemboel Sugar Factory, Probolinggo, East Java, c.1904, where Alexander Mac Neill was administrateur or general manager (KITLV/University of Leiden)

Despite this markedly 'Indies' background, she nonetheless apparently laid claim to totally Dutch parentage: indeed, late in life she reportedly spoke disparagingly of those among her cousins who were both Indies-born and indubitably of mixed ethnicity.[40] If this was indeed the case, then the sole account of her during her heyday at Oemboel to appear in print, highly sympathetic as it was, might well have vexed her considerably.

A Hill-Station and an English Governess

In September 1907, the Dutch writer Cornelia Margaretha Vissering, during a holiday spent largely with Indies-based family members, visited the hill station of Sukapura, high up in East Java's Tengger Mountains. While there, she paid a social call on a woman who was staying, together with her children and their governess, in a villa near the one in which she herself was lodged. A brief account appeared in her subsequently published narrative of *A Journey through East Java* (1912) from which it is possible to identify the woman concerned as the *njonja besar* of Oemboel.[41] The sugar manufacturing season had not yet ended, so that while his family had been able to retreat to the cool of the hills, Alexander would have had to remain at his post down on the plain. Her host that evening in Sukapura, Vissering told her readers, was a creole – that is to say, colonial-born – woman, and since (as she remarked) women of this ilk were often disparaged in the Netherlands, she was at pains to set the record straight:

> surrounded by her children, [she] received us with that certain easy friendliness which is characteristic of the refined class . . . her personality found expression in the particular beauty of her countenance, her stateliness of posture, the elegance of her dress and her good manners.

But she also hinted at her host's mixed ethnicity and in describing the family's 'blonde governess' drew an explicit contrast between her and the 'darker' complexion of her employer and 'the dark eyes and almost jet-black hair' of her offspring.[42]

The presence of that governess was an indication that, despite their location in a 'remote' segment of the diaspora and couple's diverse ethnic background, the feeling remained strong that their offspring should retain something, at least, of the heritage implied by the Mac Neill family name.

Figure 11.11: Eugenie Jackson (the family's governess, pictured left) in the swimming pool at Oemboel (Collection Richard MacNeill, Melbourne)

To be sure, the woman in question was not a Scot, but neither was she Dutch or *Indisch*. Instead, the 37-year-old Eugenie Jackson (Figure 11.11) was the daughter of a prosperous shopkeeper from Maidenhead, in south-east England. Prior to joining the Mac Neill-Bezoet de Bie family, she had been employed as a children's nurse in the well-to-do household of the Town Clerk of Croydon, in the Surrey suburbs south of London.[43] It is not clear how she subsequently came to be employed by the Mac Neill family, but she accompanied them to the Indies when they sailed back to Java in March 1904 (after an eight-month sojourn in The Hague)[44] – and stayed in their service for the next seven years, remaining on Java after her employers and their children left for the Netherlands again in 1911 (she appears to have still been in the Indies at the close of the 1920s, at which point she disappears from the public record).[45] The social position of the governess in many metropolitan as well as colonial households was often ambiguous.[46] At Oemboel, however, there appears no doubt – on the evidence of surviving photographs – that she was 'one of the family'.

Family was indeed of the essence – and one of the most telling images in the archive is of children's bath-time at the manager's residence at Oemboel, soon after the turn of the century. It depicts three infants and their mothers, among whom is the *nyonya besar* in company with the two of her sisters who had likewise married 'into the sugar' and were settled in East Java (Figure 11.12). Meanwhile, a third sister had married the owner-manager of a steam-driven rice-mill on the not-so-distant island of Lombok, and another had wed a junior army officer who subsequently took his bride with him to the Indies.⁴⁷ Nor was this a final count. At the nearby Wonolangan sugar factory the *administrateur* (Netherlands-born Johannes Sluijter) was also very much 'family', since his wife was Alexander Mac Neill's elder sister Georgette. Another of his siblings (Catharina Rica Mac Neill) had wed an Indies-born Dutch naval officer, Folkerus Karel van der Weijde, who, after several tours of duty there, had taken up a job in one of his father-in-law's factories.⁴⁸

The centre of this extended family life, along with its somewhat grander counterpart at Wonolangan, would have been the *administrateur's* residence at Oemboel itself: a contemporary photograph reports potted palms, solid furniture, gasoliers (a type of chandelier) and a piano, all strongly reminiscent of a bourgeois drawing room in The Hague (Figures 11.13 to 15). Unlike its metropolitan counterparts, however, what Oemboel also boasted was a swimming pool. As identified by a contemporary commemorative plaque, it had been paid for by a 'Miss A. Grant' – most likely a descendant of the wife of the British 'pioneer' who had established the sugar factory there well over half a century before Richard Mac Neill took it over in the 1890s.⁴⁹ It was evidently a magnet for the European factory personnel of the surrounding district – and remained such for decades.⁵⁰ In the mid-1930s,

Figure 11.12: Children's bath-time at Oemboel, c.1904 (Collection Richard MacNeill, Melbourne)

Figure 11.13: Interior of MacNeill and Bezoet de Bie's house at Oemboel, c.1900 – note the piano and music stand in the background (Collection Richard MacNeill, Melbourne)

Figure 11.14: Party scene at Oemboel, c.1900. Pictured front left, Bezoet de Bie in rocking chair (Collection Richard MacNeill, Melbourne)

Figure 11.15: Bezoet de Bie in kabaya and sarong at Oemboel (Collection Richard MacNeill, Melbourne)

for example, long after the Mac Neill-Bezoet de Bie couple had left, an item in a colonial newspaper recorded the setting up of a 'club' to keep the pool open after the factory itself had closed following the collapse of Java's overseas sugar markets during the inter-war Depression. In the past, it was noted, Oemboel's personnel and their guests had made full and much appreciated use of the facility. Indeed, another such report (two years earlier), told of the attendees at a staff party – one held to celebrate the opening of the campaign at the still-open neighbouring Wonolangan factory – driving over to the pool at Oemboel for afternoon tea and a swim.[51]

These were among the simple pleasures of a colonial community that had come into existence in Probolinggo and the surrounding areas, largely in response to the opportunities offered not only by sugar but also by other world commodities, notably coffee. That community, in turn, was characterised both by people whom the Dutch described as *trekkers* (transients) and *blijvers* (who had come and stayed). Clues to the anatomy of the early twentieth-century colonial social and economic elite of Probolinggo and surrounding districts, among whom the extended Mac Neill-Bezoet de Bie family circulated, are provided by what we know of the membership of the town's Veritas Masonic Lodge, into which Alexander Mac Neill (following in the footsteps of his grandfather who had been a leading member of the Lodge in Semarang in the 1840s) was initiated soon after his arrival at Oemboel late in the 1890s. Most were people for whom the Indies was, predominantly, a place of permanent domicile.[52] Among them were members of the Larsen family, proprietors of the oldest established European mercantile concern in the town. Danish in origin, the family patriarch Rasmus Samuel Thal Larsen, together with his Amsterdam-born wife, Johanna Bernardina Levert, had arrived in the *Oosthoek* while still in their twenties and died there in their eighties. The couple's children, however, mostly relocating to the Netherlands, married and settled there.[53]

Others of their contemporaries, however, followed different trajectories, among them the leading coffee planters at Loemadjang in Probolinggo's mountainous hinterland, the stepbrothers Jean Guillaume and Gerrit Christiaan Renardel de Lavalette. Alexander Mac Neill and his wife are likely to have known them well, as Mac Neill's aunt was married to the estate's *administrateur*.[54] Very much in the fashion of 'the Old Indies World', the elder of the two Lavalette brothers had married a locally-born woman, Sie Poddie (she was presumably of Sino-Indonesian origin) and their only child, Margaretha Johanna Cornelia Renardel de Lavalette, had herself married locally to an expatriate Dutchman and, like him, spent the rest of her life in the colony.[55] Others had even more pronounced settler credentials. The sugar factory *administrateur* Robert Erland Nicolai Soesman, for example, was a long-term *blijver* whose forebears had first arrived in the colony in the 1820s.[56]

Transitions: 'Home' and 'Away', 1911–1957

The Mac Neill-Bezoet de Bie couple themselves, however, were not among such *blijvers*, despite their lengthy second sojourn on Java (the same held good for Alexander Mac Neill's two sisters and their husbands, who ended their days in Belgium and Switzerland respectively). 'These people led interstitial lives,' one recent student of the Indies colonial elite has remarked, and 'were always in some kind of transition.'[57] Their lives entered a new phase late in 1911 when Mac Neill retired from his position at Oemboel, and the couple left Java for the Netherlands. They sailed in company with several other sugar factory *administrateurs* who were evidently taking advantage of the end of the sugar campaign to go on a vacation.[58] For the Mac Neills, however, this was no vacation but an ostensibly permanent relocation in 'patria' that saw them settled by January of the following year in a relatively new, upper-class district of The Hague, within walking distance of the patriarch Richard

Mac Neill's mansion. The family was to remain in The Hague, at various addresses, until late in the 1920s: for the first time in both their lives, they became solidly established 'back' in the metropole – albeit one in which they had neither been born nor spent more than a few years during their teens.

Among other things – and at some remove from the preoccupations conventionally associated with the retired *administrateur* of a sugar factory and his *nyonya besar* – the Mac Neill-Bezoet de Bie couple gravitated towards the city's renowned circle of artists of the Second Hague School. Mac Neill himself had some aspirations as a painter, and the couple evidently became associated with Floris Arntzenius, the dominant figure among artists based in the city. He did portraits of both husband and wife. Evidently, these were no mere 'outsider's' commissions, since in 1930 the couple's nephew, Willem van der Weijde, married one of Arntzenius's daughters, suggesting that the extended Mac Neill family and Arntzenius moved, to some extent at least, in similar social circles in The Hague.[59] To be sure, none of this meant a complete break with the Indies, for Arntzenius was also of Indies birth, and counted many similarly Indies-born individuals among his artistic associates in the Netherlands.[60] Moreover, simply living in The Hague in the opening decades of the twentieth century meant being immersed in a society at all levels of which the Indies was a pervasive presence.

It can be assumed that one motive for leaving Oemboel had been the couple's desire to reunite with their sons, who had been left there to continue their education at the end of the couple's previous visit to the Netherlands some two years earlier, and with their own ageing parents. Hermann Bezoet de Bie, the wife's father, died in the same year (1915) as her father-in-law; but his widow, Sarah Bezoet de Bie-Sijthoff, survived her husband by almost two decades, and lived in The Hague only a few streets away from her daughter, as did other members of the extensive Bezoet de Bie family. The couple's offspring, meanwhile, assimilated into their adopted country by marrying into Dutch middle-class families who were devoid of any direct Indies connections. Their two sons subsequently had successful careers in the eminently bourgeois fields of banking and finance, while their daughter's husband was in insurance.[61] Nonetheless, despite the extent of the Mac Neills' domestication in the Netherlands, the Indies proved reluctant to let go of its own. Hence when Richard 'Dick' Mac Neill, the football-playing, internationally renowned young sportsman of the family, proved particularly valiant in defence of his metropolitan team's goal, he was hailed in the colonial press as 'an *Indischman* by the name of Mac Neil'.[62]

For his parents, the colony proved quite literally inescapable. Alexander Mac Neill had evidently parlayed his lengthy experience in the sugar industry into a job that took him back, however temporarily, to the Indies on several occasions during the 1920s as a salesman for a British firm that specialised in steam ploughs – intended in this case for use in the Java sugar fields.[63] Then, once all three of their children were married and 'off their hands', he again returned to the Indies, this time together with his wife. Instead of going back to their old location in the *Oosthoek*, however, the couple settled on the edge of the mountains of Central Java, at Bandungan, in the neighbourhood of the town and military cantonment of Ambarawa, some 40 kilometres south of Semarang where Alexander Mac Neill's Scots grandfather (also Alexander) had started out in business almost a century earlier. Literally and metaphorically, they were at some considerable distance from their former life at Probolinggo, more than 400 kilometres away to the east, and set about forging a new and different colonial identity, one in which Johanna Mac Neill-Bezoet de Bie was much to the fore (Figure 11.16).

Her previous colonial persona as the *nyonya besar* of a sugar factory's general manager would not have left her idle: quite the contrary, since her likely position as the family's chief letter writer – her husband being largely consumed by the business of the factory – would have placed her at the centre of the communications network that linked the Indies colonial elite to its metropolitan counterpart, while at the same time maintaining ties between 'family' in the colony itself.[64] Her new role, however, as the marital partner of an ailing retiree was no longer a 'behind the scenes' one. Instead, she became the driving force in a small venture that produced strawberries and other cool climate crops for sale to the resort hotels in Ambarawa as well as in Semarang itself.

After her husband's death, the widowed Johanna Mac Neill-Bezoet de Bie did not remain long in the Indies. Indeed, in May 1937 she sailed back to the Netherlands[65] (where she remained until her death at the age of 83 some two decades later) and was reunited there with both sides of her family. Shortly afterwards, a street photographer in The Hague shot a picture of an elegantly dressed older woman and three boys in their early teens (her grandsons) in joyful, even exuberant mood (Figure 11.17). The Second World War, the German invasion of the Netherlands and the subsequent 'loss' of the Indies, all of which would further reshape the Mac Neill family's trajectory, were only a very few years away, but in this photograph, at least, that corner had yet to be turned.

Figure 11.16: 1930s – Johanna Bezoet de Bie and friends in her market garden at Bandungan, Central Java (Collection Richard MacNeill, Melbourne)

Figure 11.17: Back in the Hague, c.1938 – Bezoet de Bie and grandchildren (Collection Richard MacNeill, Melbourne)

GEALLIEERDE ✚ ROODE KRUIS

CONCERT EN BALLET

LILY KRAUS & DODA CONRAD
NANNAN NASH & HAAR LEERLINGEN

ZATERDAG 12 OCTOBER 1940

7.30 n.m. precies

in het

„OPENLUCHT THEATER"

KAJOON 72/74

(ten huize van den Heer N.M. McLean)

NA AFLOOP : SOUPER,

CABARET.

DANSEN

SIMPANG CLUB ORKEST
„THE HUNGARIAN SWINGERS"

ENTRéE; F. 2.00

Ten bate van:

Het Nederlandsche, Fransche en Poolsche Roode Kruis in Engeland en het Britsche Roode Kruis.

Iedereen is welkom!

U zult waar voor Uw geld krijgen!

VóóRVERKOOP TOEGANGSKAARTEN BIJ:

Whiteaway Laidlaw, Toendjoengan 1
G. Mager, Juweliers, Toendjoengan 15
G. Kolff & Co.. Toendjoengan 73
Secr. Simpangsche Societeit
Fraser Eaton & Co, Soerabaia (ook schriftelijk).

3418

Figure 12.1: Red Cross fundraiser concert, starring Lili Kraus at Callum McLean's Surabaya mansion, October 1940 (Collection of the Author)

12

Expatriates and Survivors

EARLY IN OCTOBER 1940, the internationally renowned pianist Lili Kraus gave a concert in the East Java port of Surabaya, the Indies' pre-eminent commercial hub, playing music by Schumann and Haydn (Figure 12.1). Relayed through loudspeakers to a large crowd estimated at around two thousand, her performance was followed by a cabaret and dancing that reportedly went on until dawn. The event, held at the house and extensive grounds of the leading Surabaya businessman, Neil Malcolm 'Callum' McLean, was primarily a fundraiser for the Allied Red Cross.[1] The time was opportune: hostilities in Europe that had begun in September 1939 had recommenced on a massive scale in May 1940: of most immediate concern for McLean and his colleagues, London and elsewhere in the south-east of England had suffered from heavy and repeated bombing in the previous weeks, and the Battle of Britain was still raging in the air over the Channel. In stark contrast, the Second World War and Japanese invasion that was to destroy the European colonial order there had not yet reached Southeast Asia, and although the Netherlands itself had fallen to the German invader some six months earlier, the Indies remained the free 'outpost' of an empire whose metropole was now under foreign occupation and whose government had fled to London. There had been a short undeclared military confrontation between Japan and Vichy France in northern French Indochina (Vietnam) in September 1940, but it was not until July 1941 that a full-scale Japanese

Figure 12.2: A concert artist in her prime: pianist Lili Kraus, c.1939 (Collection of the Author)

invasion took place there, and not until the early months of 1942 that the Indies themselves became a theatre of conflict.

Both Lili Kraus and her host in Surabaya that evening in October 1940 were well-established in their respective professions: the Hungarian-born Kraus, as a sought-after performer of the Austro-German classics (Figure 12.2), and the Scots-born McLean, as a prominent member of the city's European mercantile community. While Kraus was Jewish, McLean identified with another diaspora that saw sojourner and settler Scots located on every continent in numbers quite disproportionate to the scant population of their homeland. Kraus had shipped out from Rotterdam in April 1940 only a few weeks before the German *blitzkrieg* put the port out of action for the duration of the War and presaged the swift overrunning of the Netherlands by the Wehrmacht.

Unlike McLean's, Kraus's was a transient presence in the Indies, contingent on the exigencies of war in Europe and the cultivated tastes of a colonial elite to which she did not belong – but to which McLean and his ilk most certainly did, albeit while retaining their claim to an identity separate from the Dutch who comprised the great bulk of its members. Kraus's life story, that of a flamboyant character as well as an exceptional pianist, has already been told in some detail.[2] Not so that of McLean. It is one that reflects the radically changed circumstances in which the diasporan Scots families found themselves during the inter-war decades of the twentieth century. Among other things, they were caught up in a vortex of trans-imperial rivalries and antagonisms which were entering a new, redefining phase. During the same decades, moreover, issues surrounding 'expatriality' and identity came to the fore to a far greater extent than had been the case with previous generations of the Maclaine Watson cohort. It is a story whose location shifts between the British Isles and the Indies and, more especially, between a country mansion in the north-east of Scotland and the European residential and business districts of Surabaya, the East Java metropolis.

For Callum McLean, there can be little doubt that 'Scotland' was epitomised by Breda, his grandfather Neil McLean's country house (which his grandson inherited) and by his own parental home at Auchintoul, a short distance to its south. Although only some 28 miles west of the city of Aberdeen, and at some remove from the Highlands proper, Breda and neighbouring Auchintoul belonged firmly there in the figurative sense of their location in a late Victorian and Edwardian social scene dominated, in terms of diversions, by the stalking of deer, the shooting of grouse and fly-fishing for salmon, centred on life in newly fashioned Scots-Baronial mansions and adorned with the paraphernalia of 'the clan'. As such, it was a mode of life anchored at Breda in the wealth of the Indies brought back from Java (and subsequently reinvested) by the immediate descendants of the family patriarch, Colin McLean, Snr – a rough ship's captain from the Inner Hebridean island of Islay who had befriended the young Gillian Maclaine during the latter's early days in the Dutch colony.

Neil McLean himself, the younger of the patriarch's two sons, died at Breda in 1923 in his eighty-seventh year, after enjoying a repatriate afterlife of almost half a century. His grandson Callum McLean was one of the pallbearers, as was the latter's uncle, Neil Gillean McLean[3] – by that date a very wealthy semi-retiree who had returned from the Indies a few years earlier, after having been a partner in Maclaine Watson between 1913 and 1921, during part of which time he did war service on the Western Front. No doubt, it was under his patronage that his nephew was subsequently 'sent out' to join the firm. Before that, however, the young man attended Dartmouth College (the British naval academy in the south-west of England), possibly because his late father, Colin McLean, Jnr, had intended his only son for a life in the armed forces that would have paralleled his own distinguished career in the British Army, where service in India and South Africa had culminated in the position of Commanding Officer of the Sixth Battalion Gordon Highlanders. Re-enlisting after retirement when the First World War broke out in August 1914, however, McLean *père* was killed fighting on the Western Front in March of the following year.

His widow, the half-Dutch Isabella Gijsberta Maria née MacNeill, subsequently married another army officer, Ian Hugh Mackay Clark, who almost certainly had been a friend of her late husband's: the two men both hailed from the Alford district, some 24 miles west of Aberdeen, and both were officers in the Sixth Gordon Highlanders. Immediately prior to the War, Clark (who had originally worked in a local bank, as had his father) had begun a new career as a tea planter in Ceylon, where several members of his extended family were already established in the industry, and after he was demobilised in 1919 returned there with his wife. In consequence, Isabel MacNeill-Clark intermittently spent much of the 1920s in 'the East', before returning permanently to Scotland after her second husband's premature death (he was only 40) on his plantation early in 1930. Clark had been very badly wounded on the Western Front in 1916 (so much so that he had been unable to return to active service), and it seems likely that the long-term effect of his injuries had taken a fatal toll on his health.[4]

His widow, outliving him by more than three decades, spent the rest of an exceptionally active life (she died there in her ninety-fifth year) in the proximity of Alford where, in her 'retirement', she was heavily involved with the Scottish Women's Rural Institutes, both as Federation Treasurer and as President of the local branch. Indeed, as early as 1923, when on 'furlough' with her husband, 'a great treat was provided by Mrs Ian Clark ... who gave a racy and humorous description of a hunting trip in Ceylon' at a meeting of the Alford branch of the Rural Institute,[5] and there were many subsequent appearances there as a speaker. Meanwhile, she was also active in the Red Cross.[6]

Her only son, possibly urged on by his late father's younger brother, Lachlan McLean, Jnr (who held a position in the British colonial service in British Malaya and South Africa before retirement in London),[7] applied in April 1921 for a place at Cambridge's Corpus Christi College. Admitted the following October, he never finished his degree, evidently opting instead to go straight into the 'family' business.[8] By this date, the business had cemented itself into its Dutch colonial milieu in no uncertain fashion, something that reached its public apogee in 1927, when Neil MacNeill,

'Jnr', by then the firm's most senior Indies-based partner, was made an officer in the *Orde van Oranje-Nassau* (the highest honour which the Dutch state could bestow) in connection with Maclaine Watson's centenary celebrations. An occasion for spectacularly flower-bedecked festivities at both the Hôtel des Indes (the colonial capital's foremost watering hole) and the firm's office in downtown Batavia. Amply lubricated by a champagne fountain reportedly capable of delivering the equivalent of a thousand bottles per hour, the latter gathering was attended not only by the city's business elite and virtually the whole of the diplomatic corps, but also by several senior bureaucrats. Even the Governor-General sent his adjutant.[9]

The firm's newest recruit might well have also been in attendance. After having spent some time in Maclaine Watson's London office to familiarise himself with matters mercantile, Callum McLean had sailed to the Indies around the middle of the decade. Subsequently, however, it was not in Batavia but in Surabaya that he was found a job in the Maclaine Watson 'sister firm' of Fraser Eaton. He became a partner in the firm in 1932, some six years after he had first arrived in the colony, and, seven years later took over as its chief executive – and as such was also the city's British vice-consul.

Surabaya, although largely unsung in Anglophone discussions of imperialism, was substantially comparable with other great port cities. Long established at the mouths of the River Brantas in East Java, the city had rapidly increased in commercial importance during the nineteenth century, spurred by the huge expansion of the production of agricultural commodities that took place in the colony under Dutch auspices from around 1830 onwards. Indeed, by the 1920s, aptly dubbed by its leading Western historian as the 'city of work', Surabaya had become a major trans-imperial focus for mercantile business and banking, replete not only with the Indies head offices of almost all the big metropolitan Dutch firms but also with those of British, Japanese and American enterprises that had established themselves in the colony. Moreover, the completion during the course of the same decade of an elaborate system of modern docks meant that by the mid-1920s Surabaya was 'unquestionably the best equipped and most effective port in the whole of Southeast Asia'.[10] Its complex of warehouses, together with engineering factories, iron foundries and the workshops of hundreds of skilled artisans, serviced Indonesia's largest industrial conglomerate: one composed of upwards of ninety sugar factories located in its dual hinterlands of the upper and lower Brantas river valley and the adjoining coastal plain of Java's Eastern Salient (*Oosthoek*).[11]

In short, McLean had relocated from rural Scotland to one of Asia's key commercial and industrial hubs and colonial Indonesia's premier city (even though the seat of government itself remained in Batavia). Among other things, this eminence was reflected in the cosmopolitan character of the communities among which he found himself.[12] The great bulk of Surabaya's population was made up of people (more than a quarter of a million) who would have identified as belonging to one of the scores of ethnic groups living within the archipelago, the majority of whom were Javanese. Lording it over them were some 20,000 Dutch settlers and sojourners, the majority of whom were individuals of mixed European and Asian heritage, and around 1,000 'other Westerners' – among them the city's roughly 400-strong British contingent (87 families and 217 adult males)[13] – who by this date largely thought of themselves as 'expats' even if the term itself was not yet in wide currency. Catering for them, as well as for the city's embryonic Indonesian middle class, were such modern amenities as cinemas, electric trams and new suburbs built in a quasi-European style,[14] in tandem with the encroachment of the motor car and asphalt on 'traditional' street life,[15] and shops full of Western and Japanese imports, most notably the British-Indian-based Whiteaway Laidlaw emporium (founded in Calcutta in 1882, by the 1920s the firm also had stores in Shanghai and Singapore) in the city's downtown.[16]

Expatriates in a Tropical Netherlands

To call someone like McLean, an 'expatriate' has connotations highly pertinent to the evolution of this segment of the Scottish diaspora. Along with being 'birds of passage' and the strength of their identification with 'home', was the extent of their divorce from their overseas surroundings, from which they were insulated by a life that was privileged and luxurious in comparison to that of the mass of the population amongst whom they were temporarily located. Social 'enclavement' of this kind took place, moreover, along largely racial lines, formalised in the shape of an 'expatriate community' often with its own distinctive community organisations.

However, the contention of one contemporary chronicler that 'the British' (including the Scots) kept to themselves and 'seldom mingled with the members' of the city's other national communities is wide of the mark.[17] For example, there was a continuing interface between the Scots and their likewise predominantly Calvinist Dutch colonial 'hosts'. The 'Congregation of British Protestants in East Java', noteworthy for its strongly Scots element (in the 1930s both its chairman, the Maclaine Watson partner George Cruden, and its treasurer, Robert Gourlay MacIndoe, came from solidly Scottish backgrounds), enjoyed a close association with its Dutch co-religionists. Indeed, when in September 1930 the Reverend Charles Theodore Cribb (son of an Anglican evangelical missionary who had worked in China before taking a parish in London's East End and himself British chaplain for Java from 1925 to 1932) officiated at the laying of the foundation stone for an 'English church', the newspaper report alluded not only to great enthusiasm on the part of the *'Engelsche kolonie'*, but also on the matching enthusiasm of their Dutch counterparts.[18] The church's dedication the following year was even more revealing: it was attended, among other prominent people, by the Governor of East Java, the *Resident* of Surabaya and the city's *Burgemeester*, and in the speeches after the ceremony special thanks were extended to 'the members of the Dutch Reformed Church at Surabaya'.[19]

Although it is not at all clear that the British in the city (Callum McLean among them) consciously saw themselves as 'expats', the vital conditions for expatriality in its modern sense were solidly in place by the inter-war decades. Among other things, the concept of 'home leave' achieved an unprecedented currency,[20] facilitated not only by ongoing refinements to sea travel in terms of frequency, speed and comfort but also, and critically, by the advent of civil air transport – by 1940 Surabaya had a modern airport.[21] But this new degree of connectedness to 'home' was not just a matter of physical presence: regular air services also heralded the arrival of the airmail, which meant that the notional turnaround time for correspondence (both commercial and family) was reduced to around a fortnight or even less.[22] Then there was the radio. In May 1937, members of Surabaya's British community were able to hear a live broadcast, transmitted by the BBC Empire Service (established five years earlier), of George VI's coronation in London's Westminster Abbey – and held a grand reception at the Simpang Club, the city's prime colonial watering hole.[23]

The sense of being an expatriate was strongly reinforced for the British contingent in the Indies by the emergence in the inter-war decades of organisations, together with a newsletter, that underscored the ties binding the British sojourner to the 'mother country'. The prime mover here was the London-based British Chamber of Commerce for the Netherlands

Indies, founded in 1919,[24] and its attendant organ, the *Java Gazette,* dating from 1932 but superseding the *Netherlands Indies Review* that had been launched twelve years earlier. 'A monthly magazine devoted to travel and trade,' along with a plethora of miscellaneous information regarding the comings and goings, promotions and repatriations of the British contingent in the Indies, and a regular column of social 'Jottings from London', the *Gazette* also carried extensive coverage of the Chamber's annual general meetings in the metropolis.[25] The coming into existence of both journals exemplified the qualitative change in ties to the home country that was an essential ingredient in the evolution of Callum McLean and his British contemporaries in the Indies from old-style sojourners into modern-day expatriates.

Key aspects of this evolving expatriality were demonstrated by what we know of the lives lived in the 1920s and 1930s by the family of the Lowland Scot who was McLean's immediate predecessor as senior partner in Fraser Eaton and one of the key newcomers into the twentieth-century Maclaine Watson cohort. George James David Ramsay Cruden first arrived on Java around 1909 as a tea-planter before subsequently joining the Maclaine Watson concern, and married Daisy Ruth née Morgan in her native West Country while on home leave from the British Army, in which he had enlisted soon after the outbreak of the Great War in 1914. Unlike Callum McLean's father, he survived the War and subsequently shipped back to Java with his wife; and during the decade that followed, the couple (eventually with three young children) travelled at least twice back and forth between the Indies and the British Isles, where they maintained a house in the English provincial city of Bath in addition to their domicile on Java. In April 1930, however, his wife and their children (now aged between 8 and 11) returned to England without Cruden, most likely so that the children's perceived educational needs could be 'properly' taken care of (they had earlier employed an English tutor in Surabaya). It was a separation common enough among the 'empire families' of the British Raj in the Indian subcontinent, and no doubt was a strategy adopted widely by wealthy sojourners elsewhere in Asia.[26] In the specific case of the Indies, one contemporary remarked that, 'As is known, British parents prefer to send their children home at 6 to 8 years.'[27]

The Cruden couple (now *sans* children) were evidently reunited on Java in February 1934 and then returned to England together the following year for a period of 'home leave'. Later that same year, however, they were back on Java, and by April 1936 had relocated from Batavia to Surabaya, where Cruden took over at Fraser Eaton as senior partner. Along with the demands of running a mercantile business, his recreational portfolio was extensive to say the least: in his Batavia days, in addition to being chair of the British Club, he often trod the boards at performances by the Batavia Players,[28] and had at one time been a keen devotee of polo as well as of horse racing.[29] In Surabaya, he was the chair of the city's golf club, and it was on the links where his Indies career came near to being abruptly terminated, when he and his golfing partner narrowly missed being struck by the lightning that killed their Javanese caddy on Surabaya's Gunung Sari course in late February 1939.[30]

Prior to that lucky escape, he and his wife were joined in the Indies by their eldest child and only daughter, Penelope Ann: the 20-year-old, together with her partner in mixed doubles, won second prize in a competition at the Surabaya Cricket and Tennis Club in January 1938. Only a few months later, however, mother and daughter were on board a liner heading for Southampton and what may have been a family crisis 'back home'. Howsoever that maybe, almost exactly three months after her arrival in Great Britain, Daisy Cruden herself (this time travelling alone) was on her way back to the Indies, where she rejoined her husband in Surabaya. Even so, she then only enjoyed around six months there before the well-travelled pair finally repatriated in April 1939, looking forward, it was reported, to a happy reunion with their children after a brief stop-over in South Africa (made feasible by the fact that by the 1930s some of the Dutch liners on the heavily used route between Europe and the Indies opted to sail round the Cape rather than through Suez).[31] All told, the Crudens' was a two-decade-long schedule of international travel quite unthinkable for the couple's nineteenth-century predecessors, but apparently quite feasible for well-heeled, inter-war 'expatriates' like themselves.

In short, there was nothing out of the ordinary about the fact that for McLean himself, his sojourn on Java, unlike those of previous generations of his family, was punctuated, in true 'expatriate' style, by rather frequent home leave to the Scottish home that complemented his establishment on Java. In all, he returned to Scotland some five or six times in the decade prior to the outbreak of the Second World War, mostly by ship but once by air,[32] and it was during one such period of leave, moreover, that he got married.

A Marriage for Scotland: Callum McLean and Betty Lydall

One facet of the increased ease of travel between Western Europe and 'the East' experienced during the inter-war decades was that relatives might now holiday with their sojourning kin: in McLean's case, this meant that his mother was able to 'go out' to the Indies to visit him for a few weeks in the middle months of 1933, before returning home to Scotland via Ceylon (where she no doubt visited her late husband's family and friends).[33] The widow Isabel Clark, as she now was, had been accompanied to Surabaya by a young woman whom, as she happily explained to a family connection on Java, 'she had deliberately brought... out with the intention of marrying her to Callum, as she thought she was just the right person for Breda'. Not least, because she was deeply concerned that he might marry (as, indeed, had two of his uncles) a woman whose chief aspiration was a socialite's life in the metropolis. Evidently, matters did not go entirely smoothly, since the intended groom had apparently got it into his head that the young woman's interests lay elsewhere, in another 'expat' whom she had met after arriving on the island, and consequently was reluctant to push his suit. Nothing deterred – though having to admit that she 'had had a most trying time lately, because Callum would simply not come up to scratch' – Clark, in alliance with her Java-based sister Flora MacIndoe, 'did practically everything short of actually doing the proposing'. Not surprisingly, the as-yet-single 'expat' to whom we owe this account went on to remark that 'I think [Isabel] ... and Flora are the most extraordinary people. I hope to goodness they don't get it into their heads to marry me off to someone.'[34]

The young woman concerned was the Buenos Aires-born Elizabeth (Betty) Hawthorne Lydall – whose people came from Sussex but who had been living for some time with her aunt and uncle, Emily and William Theodore Haughton, about ten miles from Breda and from McLean's mother's home at Auchintoul. Prior to that, she attended 'finishing school' somewhere on the Continent.[35] Her family was a remarkable one. Her father, Charles Hawthorne Lydall, was an electrical engineer with an international reputation and a career that had taken him virtually all around the world;[36] and one uncle was an artist and landscape designer of some distinction, who had been educated at Rugby and Cambridge, before taking himself off to art school in Paris. Nonetheless, the key figure in Betty Lydall's early life was clearly her aunt Emily, a dynamic individual who had

Figure 12.3: The wedding of Callum McLean and Betty Lydall. Aberdeenshire, December 1935 (Collection of the Author)

played a big role in her niece's upbringing and who, during the 1930s and 1940s, filled the Haughton mansion at Williamstown first with Jewish refugees from Nazi Germany, then with Canadian airmen, and then, when the War was over, with students from the Commonwealth and abroad 'without distinction', it was said, 'of creed or colour.' In short, the Haughton household to which Lydall belonged was anything but parochial in its tastes and connections – and their 'Scotland' was one that complicates any stereotypical picture of gentry life devoted to the leisured country pursuits.[37]

Callum McLean, who had flown back from Java only a few days before the ceremony, married Betty Lydall in the large Episcopal church in the small isolated hamlet of Folla Rule, some 25 miles north-west of Aberdeen, in December 1935 (Figure 12.3).[38] Despite coming from the south of England, his bride was evidently accepted as 'our Betty' by the local gentry among whom she had settled. Indeed, as reported in the press, Lydall was 'one of the foremost members of the [Aberdeen] hunt', and at the reception at the Haughton's residence that followed the ceremony, she was spoken of with obvious affection as somebody who, 'although she has not been many years in the county, [has] endeared herself to everyone'.[39] The assembled company, in turn, neatly reflected the social circle among whom the McLeans of Breda moved by the early twentieth century, at the pinnacle of which stood the foremost guest of honour, the recently widowed Lady Gwendolen Emily Mary, Countess of Sempill. Evidently a friend and neighbour, her family's ancestral seat, Craigievar Castle – a tower-house completed early in the seventeenth century for 'Danzig Willie' Forbes, a Scottish merchant who, like the McLeans two centuries later, had got rich in the diaspora – lay some seven miles south of Breda.[40]

Marriage cemented not only the young laird's relationship with the elite of Scotland's north-east but also that with the local community around Breda itself. When McLean had returned there from Java on his first leave, back at the end of the twenties, he had thrown a Christmas party at the great house for tenants and employees, remarking in a little speech that although he was soon returning again to 'the Far East', he had just 'spent a delightful holiday among the old scenes and old friends.'[41] The nexus was further strengthened on his and Betty's wedding day: the couple's honeymoon was spent at Breda, and on the bridal party's arrival there by car from the church, ropes were attached to it and it was pulled along to the house by the estate tenants and employees who were lining the sides of the drive awaiting the laird's return. The festivities continued with the lighting of a large bonfire and a short round of toasts and speeches.[42] For the tenants and employees, however, the main event had already taken place during the previous week, when the laird had hosted a dinner to celebrate the forthcoming nuptials – and the local clergyman had spoken of the laird's 'exile' in Java and expressed the wish that he would soon return to 'take his rightful place' at the helm of the estate.[43] In fact, that 'exile' was eventually to take McLean even further from his native Scotland than Surabaya or the Indies in general.

Back in Surabaya:
Trans-Imperial Tensions and Oil Troubling the Waters

The port-city of Surabaya to which McLean, together with his bride, returned very early in 1936, was one which, since the beginning of the decade, had been experiencing the effects of the 'Great Dislocation' that impacted so mightily on its global counterparts during the inter-war Depression that had begun with the Wall Street Crash of 1929, but which had deeper roots in unresolved issues stemming from the Great War.[44] In the case of the Indies and its prime commercial hub, the 'Dislocation' was associated, above all, with the collapse of the sugar trade that had lain at the heart of its prosperity for the previous half-century or more, but which now fell precipitately in value and volume. Surabaya and its hinterland had been particularly hard-hit – together, of course, with the fortunes of the Fraser Eaton mercantile business in which McLean was now a partner. Although the firm was able to an extent to diversify, and thereby saved itself from closure, profits were meagre and any expectations that he may have had of emulating the financial success in the Indies of his grandfather and two of his uncles were sadly disappointed.

Meanwhile, and ultimately altogether more threatening to McLean and his kind than the immediate impact of the Depression itself, was a profound transformation of the parameters of the trans-imperial location of the Netherlands' great Asian colony which the Maclaine Watson cohort had exploited so profitably for the past century or more. Prior to the First World War, that nexus had revolved around 'border-crossings' between the British and Dutch empires that certainly had their uneasy side. Indeed, one analysis of the Anglo-Dutch political and diplomatic interface alludes to 'a very unpleasant relationship',[45] reflecting among other things the fact that, at the very beginning of the twentieth century:

> the South African War [had] inflamed anti-British sentiment among the Dutch in the East Indies to new heights, because the war seemed yet another example of international British heavy-handedness – in this case against a [colonial] population descended from the Dutch.[46]

Moreover, during the First World War, the vexed issue of Dutch neutrality had stirred up ill feeling in respect to British attempts to thwart German plans to subvert their imperial power both in the Indian subcontinent and in Southeast Asia itself. Almost from the very start of hostilities in Europe, London's justified suspicions that, however unwittingly and unwillingly, the Dutch authorities had allowed the Indies to become a base for enemy operations, added fuel to a fire that had never entirely gone out.[47]

How these tensions between empires played out in the commercial sphere is another matter. In Surabaya itself, the *Handelsblad* (the port city's main newspaper) was solidly anti-German in its sympathies throughout the hostilities.⁴⁸ Even so, prior to the War, in 1913, the British Foreign Office had found it expedient to install career consuls (that is to say, professional diplomats trained in intelligence work) in the main Indies ports, breaking with an arrangement that had held good since the mid-nineteenth century, whereby Maclaine Watson had supplied consular services in Surabaya and Semarang as well as in the colonial capital itself. Whatever had been the stance of his predecessors, the first of the new breed, Consul-General W. R. D. Beckett, was sufficiently hostile to the Dutch interest as to propose to London that the Indies (Java apart) be split up between the British and the Japanese who were, at that time, Britain's allies in Asia.⁴⁹

During the following two decades, nonetheless, there were significant countervailing forces at work, not least being the massaging of the transimperial relationship by the British Chamber of Commerce for the Netherlands Indies and by its counterpart, the London-Java Association, which brought together a mixture of business people, old Indies hands and members of London's Dutch diplomatic community. In July 1933, for instance, the Chamber had engineered something of a coup by giving a private luncheon in London's Mayfair Hotel for the visiting Dutch Prime Minister, Hendrik Colijn. An ex-director of the great BPM oil company, a formidable figure in Dutch political circles and a former (and future) Colonial Minister in The Hague, Colijn was joined by some 42 guests drawn from the top echelons of the Anglo-Dutch business world – among them representatives of Maclaine Watson.⁵⁰

As for the Association, the guests of honour at its annual dinner in 1937 were the newly-appointed Dutch ambassador J. P. Graaf van Limburg Stirum, a former Governor-General of the Indies, and his wife, Countess Catharina Maria Rolina van Sminia, scion of an old aristocratic family from the province of Friesland in the north-west of the Netherlands.⁵¹ Nor was the ethos of the gathering unique: at a dinner given by the Association two years earlier, for example, its president reminded his listeners that 'the British community in Java enjoyed the experience of living in a foreign colony – an experience which does not come to many' – and added that 'our Dutch friends did all in their power to make ... [the British] feel that although foreign, they were not strangers'.⁵²

Other foreigners making their appearance in the Indies during the inter-war decades, on the other hand, were indeed strangers. Above all, there were 'the Japanese' who formed a small but growing contingent in Surabaya where their numbers (businessmen included) increased significantly during the 1930s, from a little over 700 at the beginning of the decade to over 1,300 by its end.[53] It was no coincidence, indeed, that from 1933 onwards, Surabaya boasted a Japanese-owned department store, Cijoda (Chiyoda), employing scores of Indonesian and Sino-Indonesian as well as Japanese staff.[54] Meanwhile, the Japanese commercial presence in the Indies burgeoned, reflected by the 1930s in the establishment in Surabaya of three Japanese banks (Mitsui, Yokohama Specie Bank, the Bank of Taiwan), seven import-export houses, twenty-one wholesale import houses and numerous small businesses of one kind or another.[55] In short, the port's history as a trans-imperial mercantile locale was entering a new phase, contingent on the Indies being drawn into the orbit of a newly-expanding *Asian* empire.

That empire's commercial and strategic interest in the Indies was several-fold, not least as a vent for its cotton goods and other manufactures, but also for the commodities that the Dutch produced. Initially, raw sugar for Japan's refineries had been high on the list, but by the 1930s the output of Japan's own sugar colony on Formosa (Taiwan) relegated Java to very much a secondary position for the Japanese and Sino-Indonesian businesses concerned. What took its place was oil. Unlike the sugar on which Callum McLean's firm had built its fortunes, oil was a relatively new but very important commodity on the colonial Indonesian scene: indeed, production from wells in the so-called Outer Islands of Sumatra and Kalimantan (Borneo) had increased exponentially since the beginning of the twentieth century, so that by 1940 the Indies ranked among the world's top five producers of the commodity.[56] This brought handsome profits to the multinational companies (Dutch-British-American) involved, but also dangers for the Netherlands Indies, the vast colony of a minor European power.

Most obviously, the danger came from Japan, for whom the Indies and its expanding oil industry were of interest to a major industrialising power – and one which from 1937 onwards was engaged in a bitterly contested struggle for hegemony two thousand or more kilometres to the north, where the conflict between its forces and those of the Nationalist regime which raged in China made the question of secure access to colonial Indonesia's oil (and other war materials) an increasingly urgent one. A further complicating factor, moreover, was the apparent determination of the United States, the other emergent imperial power in the Asia-Pacific region, to qualify or deny that access. In short, trans-imperial relationships in which McLean and his partners were enmeshed were becoming altogether more complex in consequence of the appearance on the scene of Japan and the United States as imperial contenders. Exactly what all this might presage for the Maclaine Watson cohort's future was something presumably unforeseen – not least because their attention, understandably enough, was focused elsewhere.

War in Europe and the Netherlands Indies

Towards the close of 1938, Callum and Betty McLean paid a return visit to Scotland, and from there, in mid-December, the couple shipped to New York – and it was in the United States that Lydall-McLean was to remain until 1946, initially looking after her ailing father, who had taken up residence there. Her husband subsequently made his way alone back to the Indies via Rotterdam, arriving there around the end of January 1939.[57] Seven months later, war again broke out in Europe, a little over two decades after the end of the previous conflagration. This time, however, the hostilities were to take on a truly global dimension: indeed, the outbreak of the Second World War might best be dated from the Japanese invasion of Nationalist China some two years earlier rather than from the German invasion of Poland in September 1939. Nevertheless, it was from around the latter date that McLean's public persona in Surabaya appears largely to have been shaped by concerns to foster what Surabaya's leading newspaper, the *Handelsblad*, characterised as the 'spirit of friendship and solidarity' between the British and Dutch sectors of the colonial community. In line with this, at a succession of charity events, McLean and those associated with him were involved in raising funds for the Red Cross, for the Spitfire Fund and the Dutch *Prins Bernhard Fonds*, all of them geared to support of the Allied war effort in the West.[58] That effort, of course, became ever more pressing after May 1940 when the German army overran the Netherlands and the Dutch government fled to London – where they were joined by Queen Wilhelmina, who had been hastily embarked off the coast of Zeeland in the south-west of the country on a British warship.

Meanwhile, back in the Indies, now cut off from its European metropole, McLean was involved in what might be supposed to have been an effort to bolster the commitment of the Indies Dutch to the ongoing struggle against the Axis powers. The speed and effectiveness of the German onslaught in May 1940 had engendered a degree of 'defeatism' among the

Dutch political leaders who had fled to London in its wake.[59] There is, on the other hand, no apparent evidence that the Indies government ever contemplated a deal with the Japanese akin to that of their French counterparts in Indochina,[60] where the Vichy-backed regime in the colony, in return for allowing in Japanese military units (together with access to Indochina's coal and rubber), had secured a deal that was to keep them safe from sequestration or worse until the very last months of the War.

McLean was by this time British vice-consul in Surabaya – a non-diplomatic, largely commercial posting that he had inherited from his erstwhile colleague George Cruden when the latter repatriated in 1939,[61] and as such would have acted in close association with the port's British consul, Ernest William Frederick Meiklereid. A professional diplomat and a fellow Scot who came from a shipping family in Glasgow, Meiklereid had served in Bangkok and Batavia prior to his promotion to Surabaya in October 1938, and remained there until May 1941, when he was transferred to Saigon.[62] His wife, the Paris-born Katherine née Pérouse de Montclos, scion of a bourgeois family that originated in the French province of Dauphiné,[63] was clearly a vital fixture at the fundraisers organised by the port's British community: 'it is no secret,' Surabaya's leading daily reported, that *Mevrouw* Meiklereid was one of the driving forces behind this charity work. At the same time, she was President of the Ladies Committee that was busy with the knitting of apparel for the troops of the Allied armies. As for McLean, one of *his* last reported initiatives in Surabaya (at the end of August 1941) was an appeal, in his role as chairman of the now united Spitfire and *Prins*

Figure 12.4: Kayun Surabaya, c.1940. Location of Callum McLean's mansion (KITLV/University of Leiden)

Bernhard Fonds, for donations to replace the Dutch destroyer *Jan van Galen*, which had gone down off Rotterdam fighting the Germans in May 1940.[64]

Among McLean's earlier initiatives was the large and very well attended party held in his house and grounds in the Kayun district of Surabaya in October 1940 (Figure 12.4). In addition to Lili Kraus' piano recital, speeches stressing the theme of the joint war effort were given by the Governor of East Java, by the consul and by McLean, who also accepted a large cheque made out to the British Spitfire Fund[65] – enough for the purchase of one new addition to the fleet of such aircraft currently defending Britain against the Luftwaffe. The heavy symbolism of the fact that during its course two paintings by a local artist were auctioned, titled respectively *Windsor Castle* and *An Indies Landscape*, could hardly have escaped the assembled company.

For Kraus, the Indies was to have been the first leg of a tour that was planned to keep her on Java for four months of concerts, after which she was scheduled to go to the Antipodes and then on to California, where she was to make her American debut with the San Francisco Symphony, under the baton of the distinguished French conductor Pierre Monteux.[66] In fact, events fell out rather differently. Having arrived at Batavia in the middle of May 1940, she embarked on a round of concert giving (Figure 12.5) – one which lasted until the close of the following year – throughout the main colonial centres of Java and Sumatra, initially often together with the celebrated violinist Szymon Goldberg, whom the Nazis had forced out of

Figure 12.5: Enjoying the Concert, Surabaya, October 1940 (Collection of the Author)

the position of concertmaster of the Berlin Philharmonic Orchestra some six years earlier, and the Polish bass, Doda Conrad – an individual likewise of Jewish heritage, who would appear to have made a timely departure from his base in Paris at about the same time as Kraus left the Netherlands.[67] Having escaped war in Europe, war was again soon to interrupt the plans of all three artists, yet when the pianist performed *chez* McLean in October 1940, Java was a haven of peace.

The Second World War Arrives in Southeast Asia

Thereafter, however, the situation in which the 'orphaned' Dutch colony found itself grew increasingly fraught. The geopolitical context was, broadly speaking, one of attempts to deflect Japanese ambitions away from the region's militarily precariously weak Dutch and British colonies and to avoid doing anything that would provoke an aggressive Japanese response. By the middle of 1941, however, these attempts had largely exhausted their potential, and the idea (and reality) of imposing sanctions on the Japanese (embargoing the export of oil and other commodities that might be used to further their war aims in China) gained traction in both London and Washington, hand-in-hand with a serious under-estimation of Japan's capacity and willingness to retaliate. Pearl Harbour, and its Southeast Asian aftermath in the fall of the British 'fortress' of Singapore, was only months away – as was the collapse into chaos of the British, Dutch and American colonial regimes in Southeast Asia.[68]

How far the British contingent in the Dutch colony grasped the enormity of what might happen in the wake of Pearl Harbour is questionable. As late as the beginning of February 1942 the British Consul-General in Batavia, the Irish-born Henry Francis Chester Walsh, was continuing to hold 'at-homes' in his house on the city's Nassau Boulevard – among other things, showing short films of wartime Britain.[69] Wartime Asia, meanwhile, was about to erupt into the city. Indeed, some 700 kilometres to the east, Japanese bombs had already fallen on Surabaya on 3rd February – and a little over a month later, the Japanese army had taken over there.[70]

At this point, Callum McLean and Lili Kraus's lives diverged markedly. Kraus had lingered in the Indies after her appearances in Surabaya and elsewhere in Java; while her colleague Goldberg formed a String Quartet, along with fellow Jewish 'exiles' Eugenia Wellerson, Robert Pikler and Louis

Mojzer, which gave its initial performance in Batavia in October 1940.[71] He and his fellow string-players appear to have escaped from Java before the Japanese invasion, but Kraus herself did not. Unlike many of the members of her pre-war audience, and possibly because she was thought to be an Axis rather than Allied citizen, she appears to have remained at liberty until June 1943, some fifteen months after the invasion; and it was only at this point that she was interned, undergoing many privations, in a series of camps specifically for women on the outskirts of Batavia/Jakarta.

She had been there for almost a year when she was released into a form of house arrest somewhere in the city – possibly as the result of the successful intercession of the Japanese orchestral conductor Nobuo Iida, who had been posted to Java in 1942.[72] The war over, in the closing months of 1945 she and her family left the Indies for Australia, where she resumed her international career – and where she remained, giving concerts and broadcast recitals for more than six months.[73]

For McLean, the situation was grimmer. Some few of Surabaya's European business elite contrived to escape from the city before the Japanese army arrived there – among them the oil company executive, Barend Nicolaas Oudraad, Surabaya manager of the Bataafsche Petroleum Maatschappij (BPM), the colony's largest oil producer and key constituent of the Royal Dutch-Shell combine. Together with his wife and their three teenage children, he took passage on the Java-China-Japan shipping line's freighter *Tjinegara* and fled (together with eight other Europeans) first to the Antipodes and then on to the United States. The *Tjinegara* reached New Orleans in late April 1942, where the family disembarked en route to join relatives in California.[74]

McLean was altogether less fortunate. The son of a professional soldier, it would appear that (while still in Surabaya) sometime in 1941 he had signed up as a Reservist (with the rank of Lieutenant) in the British Army. As such, in mid-December of that year, he accompanied Dutch military units to the island of Ambon in the north-east of the archipelago – a strategically important location that the Dutch, joined by Australian forces, planned to reinforce against any Japanese attack. The outcome was disastrous. At the very beginning of February 1942, the Allied defenders were overwhelmed by superior Japanese forces in a matter of days; around 300 Allied prisoners of war were massacred in situ later the same month, and the remainder shipped off to uncertain fates. Initially listed as missing in action, McLean himself seems to have escaped, along with other members of his unit, into the considerable jungles of Ambon, and to have evaded capture until late in March. Subsequently he was sent first to Java and then on to Singapore.[75]

One of the fates awaiting the captive males in Java's European population was to be shipped by their Japanese captors to Thailand, where they were used as forced labour on the Burma railway, along with many thousands of equally hapless Indonesian workers. Many did not survive – or even get to their destinations.[76] McLean himself may have been relatively lucky in being sent to Japan, where he was held in one or more prison camps. According to a contemporary account of one such camp, the enlisted men were sent to work down a coal mine, while officers were employed, among other things, in administrative tasks. The exact nature of McLean's own experience is unknown. What is clear from the official record, however, is that he was liberated at the beginning of September 1945, after some three and a half years as a prisoner of war. A year later, he was in Quebec, on his way from London to the United States. Once there, he was reunited with his wife, who then accompanied him back to Britain on board the *Queen Elizabeth* early in December 1946.[77] The couple no doubt returned to Breda, the great house in Aberdeenshire, although McLean himself remained connected to Maclaine Watson. Indeed, billed as one of the company's London-based directors, he was in Surabaya in April 1951, among other things for presentations to long-serving company staff. Less than a month later, however, he boarded a Qantas-BOAC plane for Singapore, on his way back to Scotland.[78]

It was there, as the Laird of Breda, that McLean spent the rest of his long life, and it was there that he died at the age of 87 in 1992. His wife and widow, Betty Lydall-McLean, outlived him by some eight years, as did his sister Anna Elizabeth McLean, his only sibling. Public documentation for those many years is scanty: one newspaper report from the early 1970s, however, suggesting a degree of involvement in local affairs, had McLean throwing open his grounds, for the first time it would seem, for a fundraiser for Guide Dogs for the Blind: 'Breda is ideal for a fete,' he was quoted as saying. 'We have a three and half acre lawn in front of the house.'[79] It was, of course, some thirty years earlier, in Surabaya, that a similar 'throwing open of the grounds' for charity had taken place under McLean's patronage and sponsorship. This time round at least, it did not prove to be a prelude to war.

'Expats' and Survivors: A Postlude

Instead, it was a postlude of sorts. What McLean would over time have become familiar with, was the fact that, post-1945, the pre-War, pre-Depression order, on which the Maclaine Watson cohort had relied to make its money, was not going to be restored. As such, McLean's personal history was bound up with that of his segment of the Scottish diaspora, and with that of the colony's British contingent in general, in developments that culminated in late 1949 with the transfer of power by the Dutch to the Indonesian Republic, under the presidency of Sukarno. To be sure, during the Indies' transformation into Indonesia in the wake of the Japanese defeat and its aftermath of national revolution, the full impact of the emergence of independent Indonesia on British business people was not immediately apparent. The terms of the transfer of power to the Republic had guaranteed the position of foreign assets in the new state, and while it was hardly 'business as before', there remained (in Surabaya as elsewhere) a substantial Dutch mercantile presence. British firms, Maclaine Watson prominent amongst them, continued to operate. Even golf continued to be played, though as before the Scots did not necessarily dominate the fairways: indeed, in an inaugural game played to celebrate Saint Andrew's Day in 1951 in Medan, the main commercial centre of western Indonesia, the 'Scots' were forced to concede to a team sported by 'the rest'.[80]

The close of the 1950s, however, brought major disruption, not only to Maclaine Watson's vestigial operations and British interests in general, but also to the substantial remnants of the ex-colonial Dutch communities in Indonesia with whom they had so long been associated. Tensions between Sukarno's administration and The Hague over the future of Western New Guinea – the only territory of the former Dutch East Indies not handed over to the Republic in 1949 – culminated in the nationalisation of the remaining, and very substantial Dutch assets in Indonesia, and the expulsion of thousands of Dutch nationals. A similar fate awaited the British early in the following decade when Sukarno took issue with London over the establishment of the new state of Malaysia on Indonesia's northern boundaries. In these circumstances, Maclaine Watson remained something of an anomaly: not exactly British (since its headquarters remained, nominally at least, in Jakarta) and certainly not Dutch (though some of its post-war personnel may well have been). Possibly in consequence of this, it was not formally taken over by the Indonesian authorities until 1964, only a little over twelve months before an incremental coup brought down Sukarno – and saw his replacement by Suharto, an army general who, in the evolving Cold War, was viewed as 'a friend of the West' and, as such, sympathetic to Western business interests (though his real sympathies probably lay with the Sino-Indonesian mercantile and financial interests with whom he was closely associated).[81]

Even so, the chain of events that had begun in the late 1950s saw the definitive closure of the Indonesian end of the mercantile business that Callum McLean had joined more than three decades earlier. It also saw the definitive termination of a diasporan history that had begun well over a hundred years earlier in the 1820s, and that of the cohort of Scottish families that had drawn their wealth in a trans-imperial context predominantly from the trade in colonial commodities, above all from their key role in the export of Java's sugar to destinations worldwide. That strategy – effective for the better part of a century – began to come seriously adrift late in the 1920s as the commodity in question lost its footing in an increasingly fragmented international sugar economy. It was then further imperilled when the Indies became enmeshed in trans-imperial rivalries, centred on access to its huge reserves of oil, a relatively new global commodity that appears never to have come within the purview of the Maclaine Watson partners. It was the outcome of those rivalries, in the collapse of the island's colonial regime, that was to shatter any remaining hope that Java sugar might somehow recover its pre-Depression role as the financial underpinning for successive generations of sojourning diasporan Scots. In this sense, it is not overly dramatic to describe Callum McLean not only as a survivor but also the last as well as the first of the expatriates.

Conclusion

Scotland's Diaspora Refracted Through the Lens of the Indies

FIRSTLY, THE BASIS of the mercantile success of the people of this small and notionally remote segment of the diaspora further unsettles any vestiges of a heroic narrative of 'what we Scots achieved'. That deconstruction has focused to date largely on the gross exploitation of enslaved Africans in the Atlantic Zone and, to a substantially lesser extent, on the infamous trade in opium to East Asia. As this book suggests, however, it is important to focus on the whole range of commodity chains and gains which made diasporan Scots (and putatively Scotland) rich: in this case those surrounding the production of sugar in part of maritime Southeast Asia. Manufactured in exponentially increasing quantities on the island of Java from the middle decades of the nineteenth century onwards, it was central to the profitability of Maclaine Watson for the better part of a century and the prime source of its partners' fortunes. To be sure, the size of those fortunes was determined by price fluctuations on what had become a world market for the commodity in question, as well as by an element of well-honed commercial acumen. Even so, they were ultimately contingent on cheap access to Java's rural resources 'privileged' by the coercive power of the colonial state exercised under the aegis of the Cultivation System. Devised in the 1830s by the Dutch government of the Indies as a scheme for expanding exportable commodity production through the commandeering of peasant land and labour, although formally abandoned some fifty years later, it left an enduring aftermath of compulsion in its wake.

Secondly, the cohort's stories contribute not only to a better understanding of the 'Scots Abroad' but also support a holistic approach to the diaspora that takes account of repatriation as well as of departures and overseas sojourns or settlement. More specifically, it raises the issue of what 'Scotland' meant for returnees at a time when Victorian and Edwardian notions of a North Britain rooted in Highlandism and Clanscaping was gaining ground both literally and metaphorically, albeit as the minority pursuit of a landed elite that was heavily infiltrated by wealthy elements from South of the border. Moreover, although a few of the cohort's members indeed responded wholeheartedly to the call of what they perceived to be Scottish ancestral voices, for the majority of Maclaine Watson repatriates and their immediate descendants Scotland was a place to visit rather than a place to live. Nor was it a place to invest the capital that they had accumulated in the Indies, the bulk of which was placed overseas either directly or through the intermediary of metropolitan banks and finance companies: very little found its way into investment in the land of their birth. The picture of repatriate afterlives is further complicated, moreover, by questions about the persistence of self-conscious Scottish identity in a social context that was otherwise strongly English. An Anglicised repatriate country gentleman might go to his grave in a tartan-draped coffin; a pageboy at a society wedding in London might be dressed in a full 'Highland' rig; and public allusion might be made to (distant) noble Scottish ancestors. Yet mundane social reality indicated a significant 'shedding of Scottishness'.

Thirdly, as this suggests, the cohort's group biography engages with the vexed issue of identity that is central to the concept of diaspora. In the Indies, the celebrated tokens of 'Scottishness' were indeed present – including St Andrews Day Dinners, still going strong a century after they were inaugurated, and the ceremonial wearing of the kilt, remarked upon (by a Dutchman) as being the quintessential indicator of what it was to be a Scot. Yet the parameters of identity extended (it scarcely needs saying) far beyond such outward show and, as such, were something that the histories of the Maclaine Watson partners and their families illuminate in a quite distinctive way.

Most immediately, what was distinctive was their trans-imperial location in the Asian heart of the empire of another European power. As we have seen, they appear to have ridden the *political* tensions inherent in this situation with a remarkable degree of success. Their firm's centenary celebrations in 1927, attended not only by a who's who of the colonial business community in Batavia but also by high-ranking Dutch officials and an emissary of the Governor-General, was in a sense the culmination (lubricated on this occasion by a champagne fountain) of a nexus that had begun almost a hundred years earlier with the marriage in Batavia between Maclaine Watson's co-founder and an exceptionally well-connected young Dutch woman. Further contributing to the smoothing out of any difficulties that the cohort's commercial activities might otherwise have encountered, by the middle of the nineteenth century the firm had forged what proved to be an enduring connection with one of Amsterdam's leading mercantile houses and took good care to admit a small number of Dutchmen into the partnership. But there was more to the dynamics of the Scottish presence in the Indies than political and mercantile acuity alone.

As has been argued throughout this book, the Dutch colony was a singular location in so far as its long-established colonial communities were culturally familiar to Scottish sojourners, above all in the important matter of a common religion (the Kirk and the Dutch Reformed Church both adhered to the Calvinist variant of Christianity) and, albeit to a lesser extent, by a shared interest in Freemasonry (itself often considered a hallmark of a the diaspora in question), which in the Indies had preceded the arrival of the first 'Maclaine Watson' sojourners by several decades. In short, key factors often posited globally as differentiating the Scots from their 'host' communities in this instance served, instead, to promote a degree of congruity.

Even so, significant difference *was* evident in another important respect. As the nineteenth century progressed, the ethnic and racial assumptions that characterised the Dutch communities in the Indies – and on Java in particular – increasingly set them apart from their counterparts in main bastions of the *British* empire in Asia, while informing a social milieu conducive to a degree of marital domesticity usually only associated with designated 'white settler colonies' such as the Scots would have encountered in North America, Australasia and southern Africa. In the Indies, men and women of part-Asian heritage participated (and had European legal status) at all levels of colonial society: what came to be termed (pejoratively) 'miscegenation' was no bar to a career or to marriage. Among the cohort, this was reflected, most notably, in the presence among the partners in the 1880s and 1890s of a man who was of Scots-Javanese ethnicity and whose wives (he was a widower twice over) were likewise Eurasian. He subsequently repatriated, together with his five daughters, not to Britain but to the Netherlands – where his mixed-race children and grandchildren carved out successful careers and marriages for themselves in their 'alternative' metropole. Nevertheless, identification with Scotland remained potent: most obviously, they continued to carry a Scottish family name, consequent on their formal 'recognition' by their male parent – and for its bearers their lineage as Scots remained an indelible part of their persona.

Admittedly, his was a rare instance among the Maclaine Watson cohort of regular family formation beyond the confines of the (minority) 'white creole' and expatriate circles of polite colonial society. Nonetheless, the cohort's males found wives and established families within those circles to an extent that both confounds any supposition that endogamy was an important element of the reputed cohesion of the 'Scots Abroad' and belies the notion that for sojourners regular marriage (as distinct from cohabitation) was something postponed until repatriation or at most only achieved during a spell of home leave. To be sure, some members of the Maclaine Watson cohort did precisely that: the co-founder noted in the late 1830s (not perhaps without a touch of amusement) that a colleague was going back on leave to Scotland to find 'a wee wifie' in his hometown, and a century later a man on his way to becoming senior partner flew to Britain to marry in a church near Aberdeen (though he had been introduced to the English woman concerned while still on Java). Most of the cohort's mid- and late-nineteenth century partners, however, including some very senior figures indeed, found marital partners locally during their Indies' sojourns.

Yet (as we have documented in some detail) these same people – unless death intervened – almost invariably opted for repatriation rather than for remaining in the Indies. Why they did so can best be explained, paradoxically enough, by the very fact that they became rich, married and started families in the colony. First and foremost, they had gained a financial 'independency' – a term much used by Maclaine Watson's co-founder – way beyond anything that they had previously enjoyed and, in that sense, had achieved what they had set out to do. Settlement rather than sojourning had never been part of their plans, the more so since they appear to have been determined that their offspring should have the British identity conferred on them by a British education, a desideratum common to sojourner histories of the British Empire from at least the mid-nineteenth century onwards. Even so, the consequent returnee afterlives of the individuals and families concerned were themselves far from straightforward or one-dimensional, not least because Highland Homecomings were only part of the story – and (as we have seen) the lesser part at that.

Meanwhile, the history of the enmeshment of the Maclaine Watson cohort in the strongly matrimony-and-family-oriented social formation of the Dutch colonial communities in the Indies highlights the inadequacy of thinking about sojourning in terms predominantly or exclusively of men – a point that carries over, quite emphatically, into discussion of repatriate afterlives. To be sure, as was remarked at the outset of the book, the account given here inevitably relies heavily on the insertion of women into an existing narrative, and on their placement in relation to the functioning of the family-and-business networks in which they played a critical role. Any analysis of *how* critical must needs begin with the co-founder's remark that his wife's contacts in Java's colonial elite meant that 'my interest ... at court is just as great as a merchant requires.' It continues, almost a century later, with the marriage of one of the young women of the cohort to an (English) outsider who, brought into the family in this way, proved to be a key element in keeping Maclaine Watson operating on Java in the 1930s and subsequently in London.

What the book also outlines, however, are several trajectories 'owned' by individual women themselves, as was the case of the chatelaine of Kingston Lacy and of one of her cousins whose *partnership* with her husband in connoisseurship lasted for more than half a century. The chatelaine, herself a woman of Scots-Dutch ancestry, had 'married out' in no uncertain fashion by finding a husband who came from the upper reaches of the English landed gentry and had no connection with trade. Her cousin, the only daughter who survived into adulthood of a very wealthy couple who identified as Scottish but settled in the Home Counties of England and whose ancestry was predominantly Dutch and German, made a similarly 'exogamous' marriage to the wealthy son of a Dutch banker of Jewish-German descent who never saw the inside of a counting house or any latter-day equivalent.

Even so, women continued to play *multifaceted* roles in the diasporic family networks that were as central to sojourner dispersal and repatriation, as to the migrant exodus with which they are more commonly associated. As such, their stories underpin the argument, central to this book, for the need to refresh our understanding of the diaspora and of its imperial context, by bringing to bear what we know of the lived experiences of individuals and families. Although they might initially appear marginal to the diaspora's key narratives, in fact they serve both to enhance and productively complicate them. Yet, equally obviously, those stories also fold into a larger history. The 'Scottish Experience' in the Indies differed in several respects from that of their sojourner counterparts elsewhere in Asia – not least because of its trans-imperial dimension and, paradoxically enough at first glance, the cultural affinities with their hosts that distinguished this beyond-the-Empire location from (for example) those on the China Coast. At the same time, nonetheless, that 'Experience', and specifically the history of Scottish men and women who made up the Maclaine Watson cohort, belongs unequivocally to pan-diasporan narrative and re-enforces an on-going revisionist critique of the provenance of diasporan wealth while breaking new ground regarding the analysis of repatriate afterlives. As such, *Kin, Kilts and Kolonie* locates the cohort's history – a substantially trans-imperial one, as we have seen – in the context of the broader themes articulating discussion of the Scottish 'dispersal'.

Endnotes

Introduction

[1] Marriage: Turing–Fraser (22 Jan. 1822, in St Michael's, Cornhill, London), in England, Select Marriages, 1538–1973; 'Farmer-Hastings-Kerr-Laidlaw Family Tree', wc.rootsweb.com, accessed 6 Jan. 2023; 'Henry Turing 7th Bt (1791–1860)', wikitree.com, accessed 31 Jan. 2021; *Bataviasche Courant* [hereinafter *BC*], 7 Sept. 1822, 6 Mar. 1824, 21 Sept. 1825, 25 Nov. 1826, 10 Mar. 1827, 18 Dec. 1827, 31 Jan. 1828, and 9 Sept. 1828; and [Proceedings of the] Gouverneur-Generaal in Rade, 21 Nov. 1828/24, Nationaal Archief [hereinafter NA], The Hague, Archief Ministerie van Kolonien, 2819; Wilfred Hicks Daukes, *The 'P. & T.' Lands: An Agricultural Romance of Anglo-Dutch Enterprise*, [London], [E. Fisher], 1943: 7–14; 1841 Census; 1851 Census; 1861 Census; England and Wales, Civil Registration Death Index, 1837–1913. Unless otherwise stated, genealogical and related information (e.g. Census data, Probate records, Church of England Marriages, UK Electoral Register, Australia Marriage Index) has been accessed via the [paywall] Ancestry.com and Findmypast.com websites and via the [free access] Dutch websites WieWasWie and Open Archieven.

[2] Andrew Hodges, *Alan Turing: The Enigma*, London, Penguin Random House, 2014, orig. pub. London, Burnett Books, 1983: 3–11.

[3] T. M. Devine, *To the Ends of the Earth: Scotland's Global Diaspora, 1750–2010*, London, Allen Lane, 2011.

[4] Marjory Harper, *Adventurers and Exiles: The Great Scottish Exodus*, London, Profile Books, 2003: 1.

[5] Angela McCarthy and John M. MacKenzie (eds), *Global Migrations: The Scottish Diaspora since 1600*, Edinburgh, Edinburgh University Press, 2016; Tanja Bueltmann, Andrew Hinson and Graeme Morton, *The Scottish Diaspora*, Edinburgh, Edinburgh University Press, 2013; Donald MacRaild, Tanja Bueltmann and J. C. D. Clark (eds), *British and Irish Diasporas: Societies, Cultures and Ideologies*, Manchester, Manchester University Press, 2019.

[6] Georgina Tsolidis, 'Introduction: Does Diaspora Matter When Living Cultural Difference?', in Tsolidis (ed.), *Migration, Diaspora and Identity: Cross-National Experiences*, Dordrecht, Springer, 2014: 1–15, at 3–4 (quoting 'monogamy of place' from Ulrich Beck, *Cosmopolitan Vision*, trans. Ciaran Cronin, London, Polity, 2006: 43).

[7] Eric Richards, 'Afterword', in McCarthy and MacKenzie, *Global Migrations*: 272–280, at 273.

[8] Donald Harman Akenson, 'Ever more "Diaspora": Advances and Alarums', *Journal of Irish and Scottish Studies*, 4/1 (2010): 1–15, at 6.

[9] Paul Basu, 'Roots Tourism as a Return Movement: Semantics and the Scottish Diaspora', in Marjory Harper (ed.), *Emigrant Homecomings: The Return Movement of Emigrants, 1600–2000*, Manchester, Manchester University Press, 2005: 131–150, at 139.

[10] Siobhan Talbott, 'Diasporic or Distinct? Scots in Early Modern Europe', in MacRaild, Bueltmann and Clark, *British and Irish Diasporas*: 100–135, at 105.

[11] Talbott, 'Diasporic or Distinct?': 113 [emphasis added].

[12] A. James Hammerton, 'The Late Twentieth-Century "British" Diaspora: Last Gasp or Robust Revival?', in Philip Payton (ed.), *Emigrants and Historians: Essays in Honour of Eric Richards*, Adelaide, Wakefield Press, 2016: 39–57, at 40–45.

[13] Tanja Bueltmann, *Clubbing Together: Ethnicity, Civility and Formal Sociability in the Scottish Diaspora to 1930*, Liverpool, Liverpool University Press, 2014: 12.

[14] Bueltmann and Graeme Morton, 'Partners in Empire: The Scottish Diaspora since 1707', in MacRaild, Bueltmann and Clark, *British and Irish Diasporas*: 209–243, at 214.

[15] Andrew Mackillop, 'Locality, Nation and Empire: Scots and the Empire in Asia, c.1695–c. 1813', in John M. MacKenzie and T. M. Devine (eds), *Scotland and the British Empire*, Oxford, Oxford University Press, 2011: 54–83, at 56–58.

[16] Talbott, 'Diasporic or Distinct?': 120.

[17] Erika Rappaport, *A Thirst for Empire: How Tea Shaped the Modern World*, Princeton, NJ, Princeton University Press, 2017: 13; Steven C. Topik and Allen Wells, 'Commodity Chains in a Global Economy', in Emily S. Rosenberg (ed.), *A World Connecting: 1870–1945*, Cambridge, MA, The Belknap Press of the Harvard University Press, 2012: 593–812.

[18] T. M. Devine (ed.), *Recovering Scotland's Slavery Past: The Caribbean Connection*, Edinburgh, Edinburgh University Press, 2015; David Alston, *Slaves and Highlanders: Silenced Histories of Scotland and the Caribbean*, Edinburgh, Edinburgh University Press, 2021; Alan L. Karras, *Sojourners in the Sun: Scottish Migrants in Jamaica and the Chesapeake, 1740–1800*, Ithaca, NY, Cornell University Press, 1992: 46–80 ('The Caribbean Connection: Scots in Jamaica').

[19] Margot C. Finn, 'Material Turns in British History: IV: Empire in India, Cancel Cultures and the Country House, *Transactions of the Royal Historical Society*, 31 (2021): 1–21, at 8; Andrew Mackillop, 'Scotland, Scots and the Boundaries of the Indian Ocean World', *Journal of Indian Ocean World Studies*, 5/2 (2021): 150–157.

[20] Margot C. Finn, 'Material Turns in British History: I: Loot', *Transactions of the Royal Historical Society*, 28 (2018): 5–32.

[21] e.g. James Hunter, review of *Opium and Empire: The Lives and Careers of William Jardine and James Matheson* by Richard J. Grace, in *Northern Scotland*, 8/1 (2017): 109–110; and Jim [James] Hunter, 'Opium, Hong Kong and Long Memories', *Aberdeen Press and Journal*, 1 Apr. 2021.

[22] R. K. Newman, 'Opium Smoking in Late Imperial China: A Reconsideration', *Modern Asian Studies*, 29/4 (1995): 765–794.

[23] Marjory Harper (ed.), *Emigrant Homecomings: The Return Movement of Emigrants, 1600–2000*, Manchester, Manchester University Press, 2005; Mario Varricchio (ed.), *Back to Caledonia: Scottish Homecomings from the Seventeenth Century to the Present*, Edinburgh, John Donald, 2012.

[24] Andrew Mackillop, 'Europeans, Britons, and Scots: Scottish Sojourning Networks and Identities in Asia, c.1700–1815', in Angela McCarthy (ed.), *A Global Clan: Scottish Migrant Networks and Identities since the Eighteenth Century*, London, I. B. Tauris, 2007: 19–47, at 19.

[25] Claude Markovits, *The Global World of Indian Merchants, 1750–1947: Traders of Sind from Bukhara to Panama*, Cambridge, Cambridge University Press, 2000: 4–5.

[26] Marjory Harper, 'Introduction', in Harper, *Emigrant Homecomings*: 1–14, at 2.

[27] Mackillop, 'Europeans, Britons, and Scots': 19.

[28] Andrew Mackillop, *Human Capital and Empire: Scotland, Ireland and Wales and British Imperialism in Asia, c.1690–c. 1820*, Manchester, Manchester University Press, 2021: 1–29, 192–214, 254–267.

[29] Mackillop, *Human Capital*: 13, quoting Felicity A. Nussbaum, 'Introduction', in Nussbaum (ed.), *The Global Eighteenth Century*, Baltimore, MD, Johns Hopkins University Press, 2003: 1–18, at 10.

[30] Elizabeth Buettner, *Europe after Empire: Decolonisation, Society and Culture*, Cambridge, Cambridge University Press, 2016: 6–7.

[31] Daniel Hedinger and Nadin Heé, 'Transimperial History—Connectivity, Cooperation and Competition', *Journal of Modern European History*, 16/4 (2018): 429–452; Jonathan Curry-Machado, 'Global Histories, Imperial Commodities, Local Interactions: An Introduction', in Curry-Machado (ed.), *Global Histories, Imperial Commodities, Local Interactions*, Basingstoke, Palgrave Macmillan, 2013: 1–14; Bernhard C. Schär, 'Introduction: The Dutch East Indies and Europe, ca. 1800–1930: An Empire of Demands and Opportunities', *BMGN – Low Countries Historical Review*, 134/3 (2019): 4–20.

[32] David Rock, 'The British in Argentina', and Robert Bickers, 'Shanghailanders and Others: The British Communities in China, 1843–1957', in Bickers (ed.), *Settlers and Expatriates: Britons over the Seas*, Oxford, Oxford University Press, 2010: 117–145 and 269–301.

[33] Deborah Cohen, 'Love and Money in the Informal Empire: The British in Argentina, 1830–1930', *Past & Present*, 245 (2019): 79–115, at 79.

[34] John Darwin, *Unlocking the World: Port Cities and Globalization in the Age of Steam, 1830–1930*, London, Allen Lane, 2020.

[35] Gary B. Magee and Andrew S. Thompson, *Empire and Globalisation: Networks of People, Goods and Capital in the British World, c.1850–1914*, Cambridge, Cambridge University Press, 2010: 45–63, 134.

[36] Margot Finn, 'Anglo-Indian Lives in the Later Eighteenth and Early Nineteenth Centuries', *Journal for Eighteenth-Century Studies*, 33/1 (2010): 49–65.

[37] e.g. Julia Clancy-Smith and Frances Gouda (eds), *Domesticating the Empire: Race, Gender and Family Life in French and Dutch Colonialism*, Charlottesville, VA, University of Virginia Press, 1998: 1–20; Elsbeth Locher-Scholten, *Women and the Colonial State: Essays on Gender and Modernity in the Netherlands Indies 1900–1942*, Amsterdam, Amsterdam University Press, 2000; Ann Laura Stoler, 'Sexual Affronts and Racial Frontiers: European Identities and the Cultural Politics of Exclusion in Colonial Southeast Asia', in Frederick Cooper and Stoler (eds), *Tensions of Empire: Colonial Cultures in a Bourgeois World*, Berkeley, CA, University of California Press, 1997: 198–237; G. Roger Knight, 'A Sugar Factory and its Swimming Pool: Incorporation and Differentiation in Colonial Java', *Ethnic and Racial Studies*, 24/3 (2001): 451–471.

[38] Ipshita Nath, *Memsahibs: British Women in Colonial India*, London, Hurst Publishers, 2022; Margaret MacMillan, *Women of the Raj: The Mothers, Wives, and Daughters of the British Empire in India*, new edn, London, Thames & Hudson, 2018, orig. pub. 1988: 7–29; cf. Eugenie Fraser, *A Home by the Hooghly: A Jute Wallah's Wife*, London, Corgi Books, 1991: 108–111; Bueltmann, *Clubbing Together*: 167.

[39] Hilde Greefs, 'The Role of Women in the Business Networks of Men: The Business Elite in Antwerp during the First Half of the Nineteenth Century', *XIV International Economic History Congress, Session 54*, Helsinki, 2006: 1–16; Leonore Davidoff and Catherine Hall, *Family Fortunes: Men and Women of the English Middle Class, 1780–1850*, rev. edn, London, Routledge, 2002, orig. pub. Chicago, University of Chicago Press, 1987: 279–289.

[40] Margot Finn, 'The Female World of Love & Empire: Women, Family & East India Company Politics at the End of the Eighteenth Century', *Gender & History*, 31/1 (2019): 7–24, at 11 and 20–21.

[41] Bueltmann, *Clubbing Together*: 167.

[42] T. M. Devine and Angela McCarthy (eds), *The Scottish Experience in Asia, c.1700 to the Present*, Basingstoke, Palgrave Macmillan, 2016.

[43] Emma Rothschild, *The Inner Life of Empires: An Eighteenth-Century History*, Princeton, NJ, Princeton University Press, 2011: 1–10.

[44] Tessa Hadley, 'The Italianness of it all: Iris Origo', *London Review of Books*, 10 May 2018: 19.

1. From the 'Land o' Cakes'

[1] *Javasche Courant* [hereafter *JC*], 9 Dec. 1838.

[2] Elizabeth Buettner, 'Haggis in the Raj: Private and Public Celebrations of Scottishness in Late Imperial India', *Scottish Historical Review*, 81/2 (2002): 212–239, at 221.

[3] R. G. de Neve and D. van Duijn, 'De Vrijmetselarij in Oost-Indië: De Oprichters van de Loge "De Ster in het Oosten" te Batavia', *Indische Navorscher* (new series), 7/3 (1994): 194–220, at 199; JC, 30 Oct. 1841, 25 Dec. 1841, 17 Nov. 1841.

[4] John M. MacKenzie, 'Foreword', in Andrew Mackillop and Steve Murdoch (eds), *Military Governors and Imperial Frontiers c.1600–1800: A Study of Scotland and Empires*, Leiden, Brill, 2003: xiii–xxi, at xix; David Stevenson, 'Four Hundred Years of Freemasonry in Scotland', *Scottish Historical Review*, 90/2 (2011): 280–295, at 282–285.

[5] Th. Stevens, *Vrijmetselarij en samenleving in Nederlands-Indië en Indonesië 1764–1962*, Hilversum, Verloren, 1994: 51–106.

[6] Roy Jordaan and Peter Carey, 'Thomas Stamford Raffles' Masonic Career in Java: A New Perspective on the British Interregnum (1811–1816)', *Journal of the Malaysian Branch of the Royal Asiatic Society*, 90/2 (2017): 1–34.

[7] Andréa Angela Kroon, 'Masonic Networks, Material Culture and International Trade: The Participation of Dutch Freemasons in the Commercial and Cultural Exchange in Southeast Asia (1735–1853)', PhD thesis, Leiden University, 2015: 266.

[8] Angelie Sens, *De kolonieman. Johannes van den Bosch (1780–1844), volksverheffer in naam van de koning*, Amsterdam, Balans, 2019: 62–64.

[9] Gillian Maclaine [hereinafter GM] to Angus Maclaine, 29 Dec. 1837. Greenfield Papers (in private possession, UK, National Records of Scotland, NRAS1285), the source, unless otherwise stated, of Gillian Maclaine's correspondence quoted subsequently.

[10] Donald Maclaine to Murdoch Maclaine 6 Oct. 1839, as quoted in Eric Richards, 'The Highland Passage to Colonial Australia', *Scotlands*, 2 (1995): 28–44, at 39.

[11] *Sumatra Post*, 2 Dec. 1935.

[12] GM to Hector Maclaine, 8 Feb. 1837; GM to Angus Maclaine, 29 Dec. 1837.

[13] 'Uit de Regeerings Almanak van 1824. Engelsche en Armenische namen', *De Indische Navorscher*, 1/4 and 1/5 (1934); 'Toelatingsbesluiten van de goverveur-generaal in Rade 1819–1875' [aka 'Residency Permits'], transcription from data in the Nationaal Archief [hereinafter NA], The Hague, Archief Ministerie van Koloniën, kindly supplied to the author by R. S. (Ralph) Ravestijn, Indische Genealogische Vereniging, The Hague.

[14] Nicholas Maclean-Bristol, 'Lieutenant Hector Maclean 14th Regt. of Foot: A Cadet of Coll?', *Scottish Genealogist*, 18/1 (1971): 11–12; Peter Carey, *The British in Java, 1811–1816: A Javanese Account*, Oxford, published for The British Academy by Oxford University Press, 1992: 16.

[15] Carey, *The British in Java*: 2–13, 90, 137; G. Roger Knight, *Trade and Empire in Early Nineteenth-Century Southeast Asia: Gillian Maclaine and his Business Network*, Woodbridge, The Boydell Press, 2015: 137–198, 149–150; Shohei Okubo, 'An Armenian Opium Revenue Farmer in Java: His Business Partnerships with British and Chinese Entrepreneurs under the Dutch Colonial Regime ca. 1820–1835', *Acta Asiatica: Bulletin of the Institute of Eastern Culture*, 123 (2022): 67–85, at 73–77.

[16] Knight, *Trade and Empire*: 25–56.

[17] *Bataviasche Courant* [hereinafter BC], 1 Feb. 1826; *JC*, 7 Sept. 1833, 5 June 1839.

[18] GM to Marjorie Maclaine, 7 Aug. 1820; GM to John Gregorson, 30 Sept. 1820.

[19] GM to Marjorie Maclaine, 4 Jan. 1821.

[20] GM to Marjorie Maclaine, 4 Jan. 1821.

[21] GM to Marjorie Maclaine, 20 Oct. 1820.

[22] Knight, *Trade and Empire*: 57–118.

[23] GM to Marjorie Maclaine, 1 May 1833.

[24] '[GM] [memorandum written on board] Ship *Anthony* – off the Cape of Good Hope, 30 April 1832', attached to GM to Angus Maclaine, 16 June 1832.

[25] GM, 'Journal of a Voyage from Rotterdam to Batavia in 1832', entry for 24 Apr. 1832. Greenfield MSS.

[26] GM to Marjorie Maclaine, 28 Dec. 1834.

[27] GM to Marjorie Maclaine, 21 Nov. 1831; GM to Marjorie Maclaine, 6 Jan. 1832; GM to Angus Maclaine, 19 Sept. 1834.

[28] 'Being (or fancying myself) in love with Miss Katherine van Beusechem...', enclosed in GM to Angus Maclaine, Batavia, 16 June 1832 (emphasis as in original).

[29] Catherine Maclaine to Marjorie Maclaine, Batavia 13 June 1833.

[30] GM to Marjorie Maclaine, 25 Sept. 1832.

[31] GM to Marjorie Maclaine, Balie Dono [Central Java], 25 Sept. 1832. NB there is a splendid print, Johan Conrad Greive, 1869 'Gezicht op een waterval en landweg in Preanger op Java' in Collectie Rijksmuseum.

[32] Gelders Archive, Arnhem (Netherlands) www.geldersarchief.nl, Civil registration marriages, Burgerlijke stand Gelderland ... Culemborg, 207/5906, 31-03-1813, Culemborg/6.

[33] Volkstelling Gouda 1830, copy in the Gemeente Archief, Gouda, The Netherlands.

[34] Peter Christiaans, 'Van Beusechem', *Indische Navorscher*, 16 (2003): 1–7.

[35] GM to Angus Maclaine, 16 June 1832.

[36] GM to Marjorie Maclaine, 12 July 1832.

[37] GM to Marjorie Maclaine, 25 Sept. 1832.

[38] GM to Marjorie Maclaine, 1 May 1833.

[39] GM to Marjorie Maclaine, 25 Sept. 1832.

[40] Henk Boets, Janny de Jong and C. A. Tamse (eds), *Eer en fortuin. Leven in Nederland en Indië 1824–1900. Autobiografie van gouverneur-generaal James Loudon*, Amsterdam, De Bataafsche Leeuw, 2003: 21–36; 'Loudon', in *Nederland's Patriciaat: Genealogieën van Bekende Geslachten*, The Hague, Centraal Bureau voor Genealogie, 1910–, vols 21 (1933–4): 240–249, and 53 (1967): 158–167; F. de Haan, 'Personalia der Periode van het Engelsch Bestuur over Java 1811–1816', *Bijdragen van het Koninklijk Instituut voor Taal-, Land- en Volkenkunde*, 92 (1935): 477–681, at 597–598.

[41] GM to Angus Maclaine, 30 Jan. 1837.

[42] GM to Marjorie Maclaine, 25 Sept. 1832.

[43] GM to Marjorie Maclaine, 31 Dec. 1822.

[44] 'Gregorson' index entries in Jo Currie, *Mull: The Island and its People*, Edinburgh, Birlinn, 2000; Philip Gaskell, *Morvern Transformed: A Highland Parish in the Nineteenth Century*, Cambridge, Cambridge University Press, 1996, orig. pub. 1968: 23, 28–29.

[45] GM to Marjorie Maclaine, 20 Oct. 1820.

[46] GM to Marjorie Maclaine, 6 Oct. 1826.

[47] GM to John Gregorson, Semarang, 30 Sept. 1820.

[48] Peter Carey, *The Power of Prophecy: Prince Dipanagara and the End of an Old Order in Java, 1785–1855*, Leiden, Brill, 2008: 93, 436, 630.

[49] Knight, *Trade and Empire*: 105–119.

[50] GM to Marjorie Maclaine, 13 June 1824.

[51] GM to Marjorie Maclaine, 25 Sept. 1832 (emphases as in original).

2. *Tempo Doeloe* and Highland Homecomings

[1] G. Roger Knight, *Trade and Empire in Early Nineteenth-Century Southeast Asia: Gillian Maclaine and his Business Network*, Woodbridge, The Boydell Press, 2015: 150, 155–156; Angus Maclaine to William Osborne Maclaine, 26 July 1846. Osborne-Maclaine MSS, Gloucester Records, Gloucester, UK.

[2] Angus Maclaine to Hector Maclaine, 2 July 1846 / 26 July 1846 (emphasis as in original).

[3] Angus Maclaine to Hector Maclaine, *Achilles* Steamer off Tunis, 30 May 1846.

[4] Angus Maclaine to Hector Maclaine, Batavia, 23 July 1846.

[5] *Java Gazette*, Mar. 1933: 10–11; 'A Short History', All Saints Jakarta, www.allsaintsjakarta.org/short-history, accessed 2 Oct. 2022.

[6] Joost Coté, 'Romancing the Indies: The Literary Construction of *Tempo Doeloe*, 1880–1930', in Joost Coté and Loes Westerbeek (eds), *Recalling the Indies: Colonial Culture and Postcolonial Identities*, Amsterdam, Aksant, 2005: 133–172.

[7] Gillian Maclaine [hereinafter GM] to Hector Maclaine, 8 Feb. 1837. Greenfield MSS (in private possession, UK, National Records of Scotland, NRAS1285), the source, unless otherwise stated, of Gillian Maclaine's correspondence quoted subsequently.

[8] Angus Maclaine to Hector Maclaine, Batavia, 23 July 1846.

[9] E. M. Beekman, 'Preface' and 'Introduction' to Rob Nieuwenhuys, *Mirror of the Indies: A History of Dutch Colonial Literature*, trans. Frans van Rosevelt, ed. E. M. Beekman, Amherst, MA, University of Massachusetts Press, 1982: i–xxiv.

[10] Marga C. Kerkhoven (ed.), *Eduard Julius Kerkhoven. 20 Indische brieven 1860–1863 verzameld uit de Hunderensche Courant*, Renkum, Theefamilie Archief, 2010: 53.

[11] Rob Nieuwenhuys, *Komen en blijven. Tempo doeloe—een verzonken wereld*, Amsterdam, Querido, 1982: 20; Scott Merrillees, *Batavia in Nineteenth Century Photographs*, Richmond, Surrey, Curzon, 2000: 258–260.

[12] Cora Vreede-de Stuers, 'Adriana: Een Kroniek van haar Indische Jaren, 1809–1840', *Bijdragen tot de Taal-, Land- en Volkenkunde*, 152 (1996): 74–108, at 77.

[13] 'Verslag van het Beheer en den Staat der Koloniën over 1855', *Bijblad van de Nederlandsche Staatscourant*, 1857–8 [hereinafter Verslag Koloniën 1855], vol. 2: 424.

[14] Anthony Reid, '"Slavery so Gentle": A Fluid Spectrum of Southeast Asian Conditions of Bondage', in Noel Lenski and Judith Cameron (eds), *What is a Slave Society? The Practice of Slavery in Global Perspective*, Cambridge, Cambridge University Press, 2018: 410–428, at 412.

[15] Nancy Fraser, *Cannibal Capitalism: How Our System Is Devouring Democracy, Care, and the Planet—and What We Can Do About It*, London, Verso, 2023, reviewed by Alison Caddick in 'Where Does Value Lie?', *Arena Quarterly* (Melbourne), 16 (2023): 87.

[16] Robin Blackburn, *The Reckoning: From the Second Slavery to Abolition, 1776–1888*, London, Verso, 2024: 2–23.

[17] G. Roger Knight, *Sugar, Steam and Steel: The Industrial Project in Colonial Java, 1830–1885*, Adelaide, University of Adelaide Press, 2014: 95–132.

[18] J. W. B. Money, *Java, or, How to Manage a Colony: Showing a Practical Solution of the Questions Now Affecting British India*, 2 vols, London, Hurst and Blackett, 1861, vol. 1: 37–39, and vol. 2: 220–221; C. Fasseur, 'Gemengd onthaal. De weerklank op Money's "Java" in Nederland', *Bijdragen en Mededelingen betreffende de Geschiedenis der Nederlanden*, 105/3 (1990): 368–378, at 369.

[19] Gouda, Frances, *Dutch Culture Overseas: Colonial Practice in the Netherlands Indies, 1900–1942*, Amsterdam, Amsterdam University Press, 1995, reprint, Sheffield, Equinox, 2008: 28; Verslag Koloniën 1855: vol. 2: 424.

[20] e.g. Esther Mijers, 'Scotland, the Dutch Republic and the Union: Commerce and Cosmopolitanism', in Allan I. Macinnes and Douglas J. Hamilton (eds), *Jacobitism, Enlightenment and Empire, 1680–1820*, London, Pickering & Chatto, 2014: 93–109; P. W. Klein, '"Little London": British Merchants in Rotterdam during the Seventeenth and Eighteenth Centuries', in D. C. Coleman and Peter Matthias (eds), *Enterprise and History: Essays in Honour of Charles Wilson*, Cambridge, Cambridge University Press, 1984: 116–134, at 128–133.

[21] Catherine Hall, *Civilising Subjects: Metropole and Colony in the English Imagination, 1830–1867*, Cambridge, Polity Press, 2002: 72.

[22] Verslag Koloniën 1855: vol. 2: 424.

[23] Tanja Bueltmann, *Clubbing Together: Ethnicity, Civility and Formal Sociability in the Scottish Diaspora to 1930*, Liverpool, Liverpool University Press, 2014: 167.

[24] *Javasche Courant*, 13 Oct. 1847; *Daily News*, 20 Oct. 1849; 1901 Census; Probate, 1867, Bonhote, John Lewis; Probate, 1904, Bonhote, Margaret Still.

[25] Walter Kinloch, *De Zieke Reiziger; or, Rambles in Java and the Straits in 1852 by 'Bengal Civilian'*, London, Simpkin, Marshall & Co., 1853, reprint, Singapore, Oxford University Press, 1987: 59.

[26] Donald McLachlan to Alexander MacNeill, 18 Feb. 1853. Macpherson Papers (in private possession, UK).

[27] Norbert van den Berg and Steven Wachlin, *Het album voor Mientje. Een fotoalbum uit 1862 in Nederlandsch-Indië*, Bussum, Thoth, 2005: 43.

[28] *Java-Bode*, 2 Nov. 1853.

[29] Jean Gelman Taylor, *The Social World of Batavia: European and Eurasian in Dutch Asia*, Madison, WI, University of Wisconsin Press, 1983: 52–77; Cees Fasseur, *Indischgasten. Indische levensgeschiedenissen*, Amsterdam, Bert Bakker, 1997; Ulbe Bosma, *Indiëgangers. Verhalen van Nederlanders die naar Indië trokken*, Amsterdam, Bert Bakker, 2010: 7–39; Egbert Fortuin, *Indische adel. De koloniale lotgevallen van de Indische familie Van Braam*, Zutphen, Walburg Pers, 2024: 157–182.

[30] Nieuwenhuys, *Komen en blijven*: 35; 'Van Motman', *Nederland's Patriciaat: Genealogieën van Bekende Geslachten*, The Hague, Centraal Bureau voor Genealogie, 1910–, vol. 40 (1954): 314–324; Van den Berg and Wachlin, *Album*: 29, 44; P. C. Bloys van Treslong Prins, 'Genealogie Van Motman', *Indische Navorscher*, 5/11 (1939): 114–117, and 6/1 (1940): 1–3.

[31] Van den Berg and Wachlin, *Album*: 29.

[32] Maclaine Watson to Van Eeghen, 20 Apr. 1863, Stadsarchief, Amsterdam, 447/1091, Archief Handelshuis Van Eeghen, Inkomende Brieven 1863.

[33] Tom van den Berge, *Karel Frederik Holle. Theeplanter in Indië 1829–1896*, Amsterdam, Bert Bakker, 1998: 192–201; Van den Berg and Wachlin, *Album*: 10–96; Nieuwenhuys, *Komen en blijven*: 9–23.

[34] Kerkhoven, *Eduard Julius Kerkhoven*: 57.

[35] Ulbe Bosma and Remco Raben, *Being 'Dutch' in the Indies: A History of Creolisation and Empire, 1500–1920*, trans. Wendie Shaffer, Singapore, NUS Press, 2008, originally published in Dutch as *De oude Indische wereld* [The Old Indies World] *1500–1920*, Amsterdam, Bert Bakker, 2003.

[36] Homi K. Bhabha, 'Of Mimicry and Man: The Ambivalence of Colonial Discourse', *Discipleship: A Special Issue on Psychoanalysis*, 28 (1984): 125–133, at 130.

[37] Frances Gouda, '*Nyonyas* on the Colonial Divide: White Women in the Dutch East Indies, 1900–1942', *Gender & History*, 5/3 (1993): 335.

[38] Henk Boets, Janny de Jong and C. A. Tamse (eds), *Eer en fortuin. Leven in Nederland en Indië 1824–1900. Autobiografie van gouverneur-generaal James Loudon*, Amsterdam, De Bataafsche Leeuw, 2003: 23.

[39] G. W. Earl, *The Eastern Seas* (with an introduction by C. M. Turnbull), Singapore, Oxford University Press, 1971, orig. pub. London, W. H. Allen & Co., 1837: 54–55.

[40] *Bataviaasch Handelsblad* [hereinafter *BH*], 15 Feb. 1862, 6 July 1862.

[41] Robert Menzies (c.1795–1859). 1841, 1851, 1871, and 1881 Censuses. London Church of England Deaths, 1813–2003; Probate, 1859, Menzies, Robert.

[42] Edward Watson, '[Narrative] of the Events of My Life [c. 1856]', typescript of an original MSS in private possession, London, and copy kindly supplied to the author by Watson's descendant, Mr Jeremy Carter, by email 30 Mar. 2017.

[43] 'Sankey Family History', Airgale Family History Pages, www.airgale.com.au/sankey/d6.htm, accessed 21 July 2024.

[44] *BH*, 15 Feb. 1862.

[45] 'John Alexander Maclennan', Van der Grond Genealogical Database, ewww.vandergrond.eu/getperson.php?personID=&=tree1, accessed 18 Jan. 2019; *De Oostpost*, 12 May 1863.

[46] Elizabeth Buettner, *Empire Families: Britons and Late Imperial India*, Oxford, Oxford University Press, 2004: 1–21.

[47] Archibald Geikie, *Life of Murchison*, 2 vols, London, John Murray, 1875, vol. 2: 225–226.

[48] Mario Varricchio (ed.), *Back to Caledonia: Scottish Homecomings from the Seventeenth Century to the Present*, Edinburgh, John Donald, 2012; Marjory Harper (ed.), *Emigrant Homecomings: The Return Movement of Emigrants, 1600–2000*, Manchester, Manchester University Press, 2005.

[49] Ian McCrorie, *Steamers of the Highlands and Islands: An Illustrated History*, Greenock, Orr, Pollock & Co., 1987: 6–19.

[50] e.g. W. Hamish Fraser, 'Urban Society. 5. Urbanization, 1800 onwards', in Michael Lynch (ed.), *The Oxford Companion to Scottish History*, Oxford: Oxford University Press, 2001: 628–629.

[51] Charles McKean, 'Edinburgh: 3. 1750 onwards', in *Oxford Companion*: 220–224.

[52] Onni Gust, 'Remembering and Forgetting the Scottish Highlands: Sir James Mackintosh and the Forging of a British Imperial Identity', *Journal of British Studies*, 52/3 (2013): 615–637, at 624; Charles Withers, 'The Historical Creation of the Scottish Highlands', in Ian L. Donnachie and Christopher Whatley (eds), *The Manufacture of Scottish History*, Edinburgh, Polygon, 1992: 143–156; John Morrison, *Painting the Nation: Identity and Nationalism in Scottish Painting, 1800–1920*, Edinburgh, Edinburgh University Press, 2003; Paul Basu, *Highland Homecoming: Genealogy and Heritage Tourism in the Scottish Diaspora*, London, Routledge, 2007; Mary Miers, *Highland Retreats: The Architecture and Interiors of Scotland's Romantic North*, New York, Rizzoli, 2017: 45–67, 77–93, 126–147.

[53] Iain MacKinnon and Andrew Mackillop, 'Plantation Slavery and Landownership in the West Highlands and Islands: Legacies and Lessons. A Discussion Paper', Glasgow, University of Glasgow, 2023, https://eprints.gla.ac.uk/321913, accessed 1 July 2025.

[54] Margot C. Finn, 'Material Turns in British History: IV: Empire in India, Cancel Cultures and the Country House', *Transactions of the Royal Historical Society*, 31 (2021): 1–21, at 12–14.

[55] Andrew Mackillop, 'The Political Culture of the Scottish Highlands from Culloden to Waterloo', *Historical Journal*, 46/3 (2003): 511–532; Katie Louise McCullough, 'Building the Highland Empire: The Highland society of London and the Formation of Charitable Networks in Great Britain and Canada, 1778–1857', PhD thesis, University of Guelph, 2014.

[56] e.g. Tanja Bueltmann, Andrew Hinson and Graeme Morton, *The Scottish Diaspora*, Edinburgh: Edinburgh University Press, 2013: 1, 8, 153–170.

[57] Graeme Morton, 'Caledonian societies', in *Oxford Companion*: 60; Stana Nenadic, 'Introduction', in Nenadic (ed.), *Scots in London in the Eighteenth Century*, Lewisburg, PA, Bucknell University Press, 2010: 13–45.

[58] *The Standard*, 24 June 1854.

[59] Knight, *Trade and Empire*: 36.

[60] T. F. T. Baker, Diane K. Bolton and Patricia E. C. Croot, 'Paddington: Tyburnia' and 'Paddington: Bayswater', in *A History of the County of Middlesex*, vol. 9: *Hampstead, Paddington*, ed. C. R. Elrington, London, Victoria County History, 1989, *British History Online*, www.british-history.ac.uk/vch/middx/vol9/pp90-198 and /pp204-212, accessed 18 Jan. 2021 and 20 June 2021.

[61] GM to Marjorie Maclaine [1818—undated]. Osborne-Maclaine MSS.

[62] Keith M. Brown and Allan Kennedy, 'Land of Opportunity? The Assimilation of Scottish Migrants in England, 1603–ca. 1762', *Journal of British Studies*, 57/4 (2018): 709–735; Brown and Kennedy, '"Their Maxim is *Vestigia Nulla Restrorsum*": Scottish Return Migration and Capital Repatriation from England, 1603–c. 1760', *Journal of Social History*, 52/1 (2018): 1–25; Brown and Kennedy, 'Becoming English: The Monro Family and Scottish Assimilation in Early-Modern England', *Cultural and Social History*, 16/2 (2019): 125–144.

3. The Kilted Dancer and an Antipodean 'Ardtornish'

[1] Gillian Maclaine [hereinafter GM] to Hector Maclaine, Batavia, 8 Feb. 1837; GM to Angus Maclaine, 29 Dec. 1837. Greenfield Papers.
[2] GM to Marjorie Maclaine, 16 Dec. 1836.
[3] GM to Angus Maclaine, 30 Jan. 1837.
[4] GM to Angus Maclaine, Batavia, 18 Aug. 1838.
[5] *Javasche Courant* [hereafter *JC*], 26 Oct. 1844.
[6] Lorne Maclaine of Lochbuie (ed.), *Siol Eachainn: The Race of Hector*, Sydney, Amazon, 2019: 94.
[7] F. de Haan, 'Personalia der periode van het Engelsch bestuur over Java 1811–1816', *Bijdragen van het Koninklijk Instituut voor Taal-, Land- en Volkenkunde*, 92 (1935): 477–681, at 659.
[8] Ton de Graaf, *Voor handel en maatschappij. Geschiedenis van de Nederlandsche Handel-Maatschappij, 1824–1964*, Amsterdam, Boom, 2012; W. M. F. Mansvelt, *Geschiedenis van de Nederlandsche Handel-Maatschappij*, 2 vols, Haarlem, De Erven F. Bohn, 1924–1926.
[9] P. Kal, 'Genealogie van het geslacht Du Puy in de Oriënt', *De Indische Navorscher* [hereinafter *INN*] (new series), 9 (1996): 49–56, 108; P. A. Christiaans, 'De belangrijkste ambtenaren te Batavia anno 1837, alsmede een aantal geïnteresseerde officieren', *INN*, 6 (1993): 122–136, 175–180, at 124–125; *Stukken betreffende het onderzoek der (bij besluit van den Gouverneur-Generaal van Nederlandsch Indië van 8 December 1853, no. 10) benoemde commissie voor de opname der verschillende suikerfabrieken op Java*, Batavia [n.p.], 1857, accessed via Delpher/Google Boeken, 11 Nov. 2020.
[10] Ulbe Bosma, 'Sailing through Suez from the South: The Emergence of an Indies-Dutch Migration Circuit, 1815–1940', *International Migration Review*, 41/2 (2007): 511–536.
[11] 'Lijst van Nederlandsch schepen . . . tot St Helena aangekomen', *JC*, 25 Oct. 1834; Christiaans, 'De belangrijkste ambtenaren': 125.
[12] *JC*, 6 Mar. 1841.
[13] Jhr. Mr W. A. Baud, *De semi-officiële en particuliere briefwisseling tussen J. C. Baud en J. J. Rochussen, 1845–1851*, 3 vols, Assen, Van Gorkom, 1983, vol. 1: 16.
[14] *JC*, 6 Jan. 1844.
[15] *JC*, 6 Mar. 1841.
[16] 'Pahud de Mortanges', in *Nederland's Patriciaat: Genealogieën van Bekende Geslachten*, The Hague, Centraal Bureau voor Genealogie, 1910–, vols 2 (1911): 388–389, and 39 (1953): 222–227, at 222–224.
[17] *Java-Bode* [hereinafter *JB*], 2 Sept. 1856; Wilfred Hicks Daukes, *The 'P. & T.' Lands: An Agricultural Romance of Anglo-Dutch Enterprise*, [London], [E. Fisher], [1943]: 7–32.
[18] Baud, *Briefwisseling*, vol. 1: 16.
[19] *JB*, 28 Nov. 1857.
[20] *JB*, 26 July 1854, 19 July 1854.
[21] Femme Gaastra, 'The Experience of Travelling to the Dutch East Indies by the Overland Route, 1844–1869', in Gordon Jackson and David M. Williams (eds), *Shipping, Technology, and Imperialism: Papers Presented to the Third British-Dutch Maritime History Conference*, Brookfield, VT, Ashgate, 1996: 120–137.
[22] Angus Maclaine to Hector Maclaine, Batavia, 23 Jul. 1846. Osborne-Maclaine MSS.

23 *JC*, 14 Mar. 1855; *Algemeen Handelsblad*, 12 Sept. 1855.

24 [James Robertson], *The Mull Diaries: The Diary of James Robertson, Sheriff Substitute of Tobermory, 1842–1846*, transcribed and edited by Joseph Buist Loudon, Lochgilphead, Argyll and Bute Library Service, 2001: 108. I am grateful to Mr Iain Thornber, the authority on Morvern and surrounding areas, for drawing my attention to this source.

25 Maclaine, *Siol Eachainn*: 89–92; [Robertson], *Mull Diaries*: 108, 112, 127; Jo Currie, *Mull: The Island and its People*, Edinburgh, Berlinn, 2000: 370–373.

26 *The Scotsman*, 22 Aug. 1855; *Glasgow Constitutional*, 6 Sept. 1855.

27 *Glasgow Herald*, 2 Nov. 1855.

28 T. M. Devine, *The Scottish Clearances: A History of the Dispossessed*, London, Penguin/Random House, 2019: 132.

29 *Glasgow Herald*, 2 Nov. 1855.

30 *Elgin Courant*, 12 Aug. 1859.

31 Maclaine, Donald (Wills and testaments Reference SC51/32/13, Dunoon Sheriff Court), 1863: 66–87, ScotlandsPeople, www.scotlandspeople.gov.uk, accessed 21 Apr. 2021.

32 Currie, *Mull*: 243.

33 *JB*, 1 Oct. 1856, 31 Jan. 1857.

34 *JB*, 23 Aug. 1856.

35 *JB*, 24 Feb. 1858.

36 *JB*, 24 Feb.1858, 14 Apr.1858.

37 *Caledonian Mercury*, 24 July 1858.

38 As cited in *Home News from India, China and the Colonies*, 2 Oct. 1858.

39 *The Scotsman*, 6 Feb. 1861; *Morning Post*, 11 Feb. 1861; *JB*, 23 Mar. 1861; *Bataviaasch Handelsblad*, 27 Mar. 1861.

40 1861 Census.

41 [Robertson], *Mull Diaries*: 107, 123; 'Toelatingsbesluiten [aka 'Residency Permits'] van Gouverneur-Generaal in Rade 1819–1875', transcription, from data in the Nationaal Archief [hereinafter NA], The Hague, Archief Ministerie van Koloniën, kindly supplied to the author by R. S. (Ralph) Ravestijn, Indische Genealogische Vereniging, The Hague (entry for 1846 Alexander Campbell Maclaine).

42 A. James Hammerton, *Migrants of the British Diaspora since the 1960s: Stories from Modern Nomads*, Manchester, Manchester University Press, 2017.

43 David S. Macmillan, *Scotland and Australia, 1788–1850: Emigration, Commerce and Investment*, Oxford, Clarendon Press, 1967; Eric Richards, 'Scottish Voices and Networks in Colonial Australia', in Angela McCarthy (ed.), *A Global Clan: Scottish Migrant Networks and Identities since the Eighteenth Century*, London, I. B. Tauris, 2007: 150–182; Don Watson, *Caledonia Australis: Scottish Highlanders on the Australian Frontier*, Sydney, Collins, 1984; Malcolm Prentis, *Scots in Australia: A Study of New South Wales, Victoria and Queensland, 1788–1900*, Sydney, UNSW Press, 2008; Fred Cahir, Alison Inglis and Anne Beggs Sunter (eds), *Scots under the Southern Cross* [Ballarat, Victoria], Ballarat Heritage Services, 2015; Benjamin Wilkie, *The Scots in Australia, 1788–1938*, Woodbridge, Boydell & Brewer, 2017.

44 Eric Richards, 'The Highland Scots of South Australia', *Journal of the South Australian Historical Society*, 4 (1978): 33–64.

45 GM to Angus Maclaine, Batavia, 18 Aug. 1838.

46 Richards, 'Scottish Voices': 155.

47 Currie, *Mull*: 224–225, 288; G. Roger Knight, *Trade and Empire in Early Nineteenth-Century Southeast Asia: Gillian Maclaine and his Business Network*, Woodbridge, The Boydell Press, 2015: 26.

48 Lesley Abell and G. Roger Knight, '"So Like Home": Angus Maclaine (1799–1877), Sheep Farmer and Sojourner in South Australia', *Journal of the Historical Society of South Australia*, 33 (2005): 40–55.

49 Angus Maclaine [to Donald Maclaine], 19 Jan. 1847. Scottish Record Office, GDI74/2340/2, as quoted in Richards, 'Highland Scots': 37–38.

50 'St. Andrew's Day', *South Australian Register*, 4 Dec. 1841.

51 Angus Maclaine to Murdoch Maclaine [John Maclaine's father], 23 Jan. 1843, as quoted in Currie, *Mull*: 390.

52 [Robertson], *Mull Diaries*: 108. Entry for 28 Aug. 1844.

53 For the voyage of the *Mazeppa*, see 'Overseas Arrivals to South Australia – 1846', LocalWiki, https://localwiki.org/adelaide-hills/Overseas_Arrivals_to_South_Australia_-_1846, accessed 24 Jan. 2022.

54 'Power of Attorney to George Morphett *re* arrangement with John Campbell Maclaine', 18 Jun. 1847, State Records of South Australia.

55 'Toelatingsbesluiten van Gouverneur-Generaal in Rade 1819–1875', 1852 John Maclaine.

56 Maclaine, Donald (Wills and testaments Reference SC51/32/13, Dunoon Sheriff Court), 1863, 66–87. ScotlandsPeople, www.scotlandspeople.gov.uk, accessed 21 Apr. 2021.

57 Australia, Death Index, 1787–1985; Probate, 1885, Maclaine, John Campbell.

58 *Victoria Government Gazette*, 25 July 1856: 1206; 'Find a Grave', Allan Maclaine d. 22 Feb. 1875.

59 Alexander Campbell Maclaine. *City of Benares*. Victoria Outward Passenger Lists 1852–1915.

60 Alexander Fraser to Alexander MacNeill, 6 Jun. 1860. Macpherson Papers (in private possession, UK).

61 Maclaine, 1863 (NRS, SC51/32/13).

62 'World Book of Maclaines' [accessed via Ancestry.com]; Australian Marriage Register 1786–1950; Scotland Select Birth and Baptisms; Massachusetts Birth Records 1840–1915: Quebec, Canada, Vital and Church Records (Drouin Collection), 1621–1968; Australia Birth Index 1788–1922.

63 *JC*, 1 Oct. 1853; *Inverness Advertiser*, 15 Nov. 1853.

64 Franz Wilhelm Junghuhn, *Java, zijne gedaante, zijn plantentooi en inwendige bouw*, 4 vols, The Hague, Mieling, 1853–4, vol. 2, pt. 1: 253–7, accessed via Delpher, 1 Jan. 2022; D. Schoute, *De geneeskunde in Nederlandsch-Indië gedurende de negentiende eeuw*, The Hague, Kolff, 1935: 181–182.

65 Currie, *Mull*: 391.

66 1871 Census.

67 Anthony Vincent Maclaine to Van Eeghen, 15 August 1868, 447/57; Maclaine to Van Eeghen, 2 July 1870, 447/63; Finlay & Co. to Van Eeghen, 29 June 1869, 447/59, in Archief van Handelshuis Van Eeghen en Co., Stadsarchief, Amsterdam; *London Gazette*, 18 Oct. 1870.

68 1881 Census; Probate 1882 Maclaine Emilie Guillaumine.

69 For an extended and referenced discussion what follows, see G. Roger Knight and William Woods, 'Ancestral Voices, Highland Homecomings and High Society: The Lochbuie Family of Mull, ca. 1855–1920', *Journal of Scottish Historical Studies*, 42/2 (2022): 217–242.

70 *Clifton Society* (Bristol), 6 May 1909.

4. Islay and the Wealth of the Indies

[1] Donald McLachlan to [his cousin] Alexander MacNeill, 18 Feb. 1853. Macpherson Papers (in private possession, UK).

[2] Alexander MacNeill to Colin McLean, 18 Apr. 1853. Macpherson Papers.

[3] Peter Carey, *The British in Java 1811–1816: A Javanese Account*, Oxford, Published for The British Academy by Oxford University Press, 1992: 2–13, 90, 137; G. Roger Knight, *Trade and Empire in Early Nineteenth-Century Southeast Asia: Gillian Maclaine and his Business Network*, Woodbridge, The Boydell Press, 2015: 137–198, 149–150; F. de Haan, 'Personalia der Periode van het Engelsch Bestuur over Java 1811–1816', *Bijdragen van het Koninklijk Instituut voor Taal-, Land- en Volkenkunde*, 92 (1935): 477–681, at 534–535; Shohei Okubo, 'An Armenian Opium Revenue Farmer in Java: His Business Partnerships with British and Chinese Entrepreneurs under the Dutch Colonial Regime ca. 1820–1835', *Acta Asiatica: Bulletin of the Institute of Eastern Culture*, 123 (2022): 67–85, at 73–77; *Parliamentary Papers GB*, 'Select Committee of the House of Lords on the East India Company 1830', vol. 6, 'Evidence of John Deans': 233–235; Anthony Webster, *The Richest East India Merchant: The Life and Business of John Palmer of Calcutta, 1767–1836*, The Boydell Press, 2007.

[4] F. J. A. Broeze, 'The Merchant Fleet of Java (1820–1850). A Preliminary Survey', *Archipel*, 18 (1979): 251–269, at 269; Michael Greenberg, *British Trade and the Opening of China 1800–42*, Cambridge, Cambridge University Press, 1969, orig. pub. 1951: 95, 97, 118, 120.

[5] Knight, *Trade and Empire*: 27–29; Philip Gaskell, *Morvern Transformed: A Highland Parish in the Nineteenth Century*, Cambridge, Cambridge University Press, 1996 orig. pub. 1968: 152–153; 'McLachlan, Glensanda', unpublished MSS, courtesy of Mr Iain Thornber, Knock House, Lochaline, Morvern.

[6] Gillian Maclaine [hereinafter GM] to Marjorie Maclaine, 31 Dec. 1822.

[7] Stephen Foster, *A Private Empire*, Millers Point, Sydney, Pier Nine, 2010: 188.

[8] Freda Ramsay, *John Ramsay of Kildalton J.P., M.P., D.L.: Being an Account of His Life in Islay and including the Diary of His Trip to Canada in 1870*, Toronto, Peter Martin, 1969: 29.

[9] 1861 Census.

[10] GM to Marjorie Maclaine, undated, c. Jan. 1828.

[11] Margaret Storrie, *Islay: The Biography of an Island*, Islay, OA Press, 2nd edn, 1997: 163–174.

[12] 1861 Census.

[13] John Crawfurd to Colin McLean, 24 Aug. 1854. Macpherson Papers.

[14] 'Campbell, Walter Frederick (1798–1855), of Islay House, Argyll and Woodhall, Lanark', *History of Parliament: The House of Commons, 1820–1832*, ed. D. R. Fisher, Cambridge, Cambridge University Press, 2009, online edn, www.historyofparliamentonline.org/volume/1820-1832/member/campbell-walter-1798-1855, accessed 21 June 2022.

[15] John Crawfurd to Colin McLean, 24 Aug. 1854. Macpherson Papers.

[16] 'Campbell, Walter Frederick (1798–1855), of Islay House, Argyll and Woodhall, Lanark', *History of Parliament: the House of Commons 1820–1832*, ed. D. R. Fisher, Cambridge, Cambridge University Press, 2009, online edn, https://www.historyofparliamentonline.org/volume/1820-1832/member/campbell-walter-1798-1855, accessed 21 June 2022.

[17] Storrie, *Islay*: 149–169; Ramsay, *John Ramsay*: 27–28.

[18] McLean, Colin [Inventory] (Wills and testaments Reference SC51/32/12, Dunoon Sheriff Court), 1862: 83–84, National Records of Scotland [NRS], https://www.nrscotland.gov.uk, accessed 25 Apr. 2021.

[19] John Francis Campbell to Colin McLean, 1 Dec. 1852. Macpherson Papers.

[20] John Francis Campbell to Colin McLean, 8 Feb. 1855. Macpherson Papers.

[21] Colin McLean to John Francis Campbell, 9 Dec. 1852. Macpherson Papers.

[22] Storrie, *Islay:* 141–149.

[23] McLean [Inventory], 1862 (NRS, SC51/32/12).

[24] *De Oostpost*, 21 Mar. 1864.

[25] 'Kilchoman Free Church', 31 Oct. 2008, Welcome to Islay Blog, www.islay.blog/article.php/kilchoman-free-church, accessed 27 June 2022.

[26] See Index to Islay Civil Registration for Marriages 1855–1875, 1881 and 1891, http://homepages.com/~steve/islay/civil/f0330185.htm#kilchoman.

[27] For Cameron, see Chapter 5: 'Death in Bournemouth and a Surrogate Scotland.'

[28] Elizabeth McLean to Anna Ballingal (née McLean), Batavia 15 Aug. 1867. Macpherson Papers.

[29] J. H. Schmiedell, *Gedenkblätter zum 50-jährigen Bestehen der Firma Erdmann & Sielcken in Java, 1875–1924*, np. nd. [1924]: 31; Vincent J. H. Houben, *Kraton and Kumpeni: Surakarta and Yogyakarta, 1830–1870*, Leiden, KITLV Press, 1994: 287.

[30] Jaarverslag Batavia Factorij Nederlandsche Handel-Maatschappij 1884 (59): 7; Nationaal Archief, The Hague, Archief Nederlandsche Handel-Maatschappij [old numbering] 4552.

[31] G. Roger Knight, *Sugar, Steam and Steel: The Industrial Project in Colonial Java, 1830–1885*, Adelaide, University of Adelaide Press, 2014: 30.

[32] Arsip Bank Indonesia, Jakarta: De Java Bank. Notatie DJB 40, no. 114 (29 Apr. 1872). [A record of interview between officials of the Bank with Gerhard Hermann Miesegaes, at that date a senior partner in Maclaine Watson, kindly supplied to the author by Alexander Claver, The Hague, whose *Dutch Commerce and Chinese Merchants in Java: Colonial Relationships in Trade and Finance, 1800–1942*, Leiden, Brill, 2014, is based on a unique exploration of the DJB Archive.

[33] Lachlan McLean to Neil McLean, Islay House, 31 May 1875. Macpherson Papers.

[34] MacLean, Lachlan (Wills and testaments Reference SC51/32/27, Dunoon Sheriff Court), 1880: 129–146. ScotlandsPeople www.scotlandspeople.gov.uk, accessed 16 Apr. 2021.

[35] e.g. Andrew Mackillop, 'The Highlands and the Returning Nabob: Sir Hector Munro of Novar, 1760–1807', in Marjory Harper (ed.), *Emigrant Homecomings: The Return Movement of Emigrants, 1600–2000*, Manchester, Manchester University Press, 2005: 233–261; Alistair Mutch, 'Agriculture and Empire: General Patrick "Tiger" Duff and the Shaping of North-East Scotland', *Review of Scottish Culture*, 22 (2010): 85–98.

[36] T. M. Devine and John M. Mackenzie, 'Scots in the Imperial Economy', in Mackenzie and Devine (eds), *Scotland and the British Empire*, Oxford History of the British Empire, Oxford, Oxford University Press, 2011: 227–254; John Darwin, *The Empire Project: The Rise and Fall of the British World-System, 1830–1970*, Cambridge, Cambridge University Press, 2009: 116–119.

[37] Stuart Muirhead, *Crisis Banking in the East*, Aldershot, Scholar Press, 1996: 44–124 and 124–129; 'Chartered Bank of India, Australia and China', Wikipedia, https://en.wikipedia.org/wiki/Chartered_Bank_of_India,_Australia_and_China, accessed 23 May 2022.

[38] *Greenock Telegraph and Clyde Shipping Gazette*, 21 July 1870.

[39] J. Rogge, *Het Handelshuis Van Eeghen. Proeve eener geschiedenis van een Amsterdamsch handelshuis*, Amsterdam, Van Ditmar, 1949: 248–249.
[40] *Java-Bode*, 17 Mar. 1868.
[41] Elizabeth McLean to Anna Ballingal, Batavia, 15 Aug. 1867. Macpherson Papers.
[42] Lachlan McLean to Neil McLean, Cannes, 14 Mar. 1880. Macpherson Papers.
[43] 1871 Census.
[44] McLean [Inventory], 1862 (NRS, SC51/32/12).
[45] 1871 Census.
[46] *The Standard*, 5 Apr. 1877; *Pall Mall Gazette*, 5 Apr. 1877.
[47] Notice dated Calcutta, 31 Dec. 1851, *London Gazette*, 7 Jan. 1853, 1861; Census; 1871 Census; Probate, 1878, Hunter, Robert Holmes.
[48] Andrew Mackillop, *Human Capital and Empire: Scotland, Ireland and Wales and British Imperialism in Asia, c. 1690–c. 1820*, Manchester, Manchester University Press, 2021: 234–235.
[49] William MacDonald and John Murdoch, *Descriptive and Historical Sketches of Islay*, Glasgow, 1850, reprinted with an introduction by John Newton, Bowmore, Celtic House, 1997: 29.
[50] Caroline Dakers, *A Genius for Money: Business, Art and the Morrisons*, New Haven, CT, Yale University Press, 2011: 198–200.
[51] *The Field*, 26 Sept. 1891.
[52] *Glasgow Herald*, 5 Sept. 1870: 'Islay Regatta . . . a complete success', as quoted in Islay History, http://islayhistory.blogspot.com, accessed 20 Oct. 2019.
[53] Lachlan McLean to Neil McLean, Cannes, 14 Mar. 1880. Macpherson Papers.
[54] 1871 Census.
[55] 1871 Census.
[56] Storrie, *Islay*: 165–180.
[57] David Cressy, *Shipwrecks and the Bounties of the Sea*, Oxford, Oxford University Press, 2022.
[58] *Inverness Courier*, 26 May 1859.
[59] *The Scotsman*, 7 Mar. 1849.
[60] Lachlan McLean to Neil McLean, Islay House, 9 Oct. 1871. Macpherson Papers.
[61] Probate, 1880, McLean, Lachlan.
[62] MacLean, Lachlan, 1880 (SC51/32/27, Dunoon Sheriff Court, ScotlandsPeople).
[63] 'Fatal Railway Accident Near Clonmel', *Waterford Standard*, 29 Apr. 1899; *Norwich Mercury*, 6 May 1899; *Diss Express*, 5 May 1899.
[64] 1881 Census; England, Oxford Men and Their Colleges; 'Blackheath Proprietary School', Wikipedia, https://en.wikipedia.org/wiki/_Proprietary_ and 'Blackheath High School', accessed 2 May 2022.
[65] T. F. T. Baker, Diane K. Bolton and Patricia E. C. Croot, 'Hampstead: Frognal and the Central Demesne', in *A History of the County of Middlesex*, vol. 9: *Hampstead, Paddington*, ed. C. R. Elrington, London, Victoria County History, 1989, *British History Online*, www.british-history.ac.uk/vch/middx/vol9/pp33-42, accessed 24 May 2022.
[66] McLean-Rivers Thompson 18 June 1891 at St Jude's Church, Kensington in Marriage Certificates; 'Rivers Thompson', Wikipedia, https://en.wikipedia.org/wiki/Rivers_Thompson, accessed 7 May 2022.
[67] Census 1901.
[68] Church of England Banns and Marriages 1854–1938.

[69] Alwyn Ladell, 'Branksome Tower Hotel, Branksome Park, Poole Dorset', www.flickr.com/photos/alwyn_//72157624313791681.

[70] British Army World War Index Cards ... Harold Whitman Woodall; Probate, 1959, Woodhall, Elizabeth Nora of 1 Waterston Manor.

[71] Church of England Banns and Marriages 1854–1938, for Alexander McLean/Francine Henriette Gill, '*widow*, daughter of Hendrik Adriaanus Moll', at Hampstead 1900.

[72] Electoral Registers, 1922; Civil Registration Deaths, 1929; Probate, 1857, McLean, Francina Henriette of 83 Cadogan Gardens, SW3.

[73] Probate, 1937, McLean, Alexander Colin of Culcabock House, Inverness; Probate, 1963, 'Thompson or McLean, [Dora] Georgina of Croc-na-boull, Muir of Ord, Ross-shire'.

[74] 1911 Census; 'The Landmark London', Wikipedia, https://en.wikipedia.org/wiki/The_Landmark_London, accessed 21 June 2022.

[75] 1921 Census; England and Wales Civil Registration Death Index.

[76] Probate, 1953, 'McLean, Lucy Campbell of Flat 8, 231 Sussex Gardens, Hyde Park W2'.

5. Death in Bournemouth and a Surrogate Scotland

[1] Death notice in *The Sun*, 20 Apr. 1867; England & Wales Electoral Register 1939.

[2] Andrew O'Hagan, 'Bournemouth', *London Review of Books*, 42/10 (21 May 2020): 7 – citing and quoting Walter Besant and James Rice, *The Seamy Side: A Story*, London, Chatto & Windus, 1880: 224, and Charles Henry Mate, *Bournemouth: 1810–1910, the History of a Modern Health and Pleasure Resort*, London, W. Mate, 1910: 77; 'Royal National Sanatorium, Bournemouth', The National Archives (Discovery), https://discovery.nationalarchives.gov.uk/details/r/d9b43bbc-e60b-4572-8d51-81ce16776493, accessed 6 July 2021.

[3] Information courtesy of Jac. Piepenbrock, Cultureel Maçonniek Centrum 'Prins Frederik', The Hague (and thanks also to Tom van den Berge).

[4] Neil Cameron, 'The MacNeills of Ardnacross and Islay', *Scottish Genealogist*, 27/3 (1980): 115–117.

[5] 1851 Census.

[6] 1841 Census; *Daily News*, 29 Sept. 1849.

[7] 'Loudon', in *Nederland's Patriciaat: Genealogieën van Bekende Geslachten*, The Hague, Centraal Bureau voor Genealogie, 1910–, vol. 21 (1933–4): 240–249.

[8] *Edinburgh Evening Courant*, 7 June 1851.

[9] *North British Agriculturalist*, 19 Jan. 1859; Kenneth C. Jack, 'The 6th Duke of Atholl', *Square Magazine*, online, 10 (Oct. 2021), www.thesquaremagazine.com/mag/article/202110the-6th-duke-of-atholl/, accessed 2 Feb. 2023.

[10] *Edinburgh Evening Courant*, 7 June 1851.

[11] *The Field*, 13 Apr. 1878.

[12] Alexander MacNeill, Bordlands Cottage, to Colin McLean, 11 July 1853; Colin McLean, Laggan, Islay, to John Francis Campbell, 23 July 1853; John Francis Campbell, Pont Street, London, to Colin McLean, Laggan, 1 Aug. 1853. Macpherson Papers (in private possession, UK).

[13] 1861 Census.

[14] Andrew Mackillop, 'The Highlands and the Returning Nabob: Sir Hector Munro of Novar, 1760–1807', in Marjory Harper (ed.), *Emigrant Homecomings: The Return Movement of Emigrants, 1600–2000*, Manchester, Manchester University Press, 2005: 233–261; Alistair Mutch, *Tiger Duff: India, Madeira and Empire in Eighteenth-Century Scotland*, University of Aberdeen Press, 2017; Alistair Mutch, 'Agriculture and Empire: General Patrick "Tiger" Duff and the Shaping of North-East Scotland', *Review of Scottish Culture*, 22 (2010): 85–98; Charles Baillie, *The Call of Empire: From the Highlands to Hindostan*, Montreal, McGill-Queen's University Press, 2017; Stephen Foster, *A Private Empire*, Millers Point, Sydney, Pier Nine, 2010; George McGilvery, 'Return of the Scottish Nabob, 1725–1833', in Mario Varricchio (ed.) *Back to Caledonia: Scottish Homecomings from the Seventeenth Century to the Present*, Edinburgh, John Donald, 2012: 90–108.

[15] *Edinburgh Evening Courant*, 7 June 1851.

[16] 'Inventory of the personal estate of John MacNeill Esq.', in MacNeill, John (Wills and Testaments Reference SC51/32/9. Dunoon Sheriff Court, 1858: 255–257, www.scotlandspeople.gov.uk, accessed 8 June 2021.

[17] 'Inventory of the personal estate of Alexander MacNeill Esq. of Bordlands, Peebles 12th October 1867', in MacNeill, Alexander (Wills and testaments Reference SC42/20/8, Peebles Sheriff Court), 1867: 34–70, ScotlandsPeople, www.scotlandspeople.gov.uk, accessed 21 Sept. 2024.

[18] T. M. Devine and John M. MacKenzie, 'Scots in the Imperial Economy', in MacKenzie and Devine (eds) *Scotland and the British Empire*, Oxford: Oxford University Press, 2011: 227–254, at 242–254; Christopher Schmitz, 'The Nature and Dimensions of Scottish Foreign Investment, 1860–1914', *Business History*, 39/2 (1997), 42–68.

[19] Probate, 1877, Loudon or MacNeill, Isabella Maria.

[20] See Chapter 8: 'Gathering the Clan, Advancing the Empire and The Lure of London: The Laird of Breda, his Wife and Family.'

[21] 1891 Census.

[22] *Soerabaijasch Handelsblad*, 14 Apr. 1897.

[23] Probate, 1892, MacNeill, Isabella Gillis, and MacNeill, Agnes Webster; B. Walter Foster and J. Tatham, 'On the Influenza Epidemic of 1892 in London', *British Medical Journal*, 2/1650 (13 Aug. 1892): 353–356, at 353.

[24] *The Gentlewoman*, 6 Feb. 1892; 'The Gentlewoman', Wikipedia, https://en.wikipedia.org/wiki/The_Gentlewoman, accessed 16 June 2021.

[25] *Java-Bode*, 31 May 1873; *Bataviaasch Nieuwsblad*, 25 Apr.1891.

[26] 1911 Census.

[27] 'Sandringham House', Wikipedia, https://en.wikipedia.org/wiki/Sandringham_House, accessed 4 June 2021.

[28] Harry Hopkins, *The Long Affray: The Poaching Wars, 1760–1914*, London, Secker & Warburg, 1985: 246–270; 'Oliver Robinson, 2nd Marquess of Ripon', Wikipedia, https://en.wikipedia.org/wiki/Oliver_Robinson,_2nd_Marquess_of_Ripon, accessed 4 June 2021.

[29] *Norfolk News*, 3 July 1901.

[30] *Yarmouth Independent*, 3 Aug. 1935; *Lynn Advertiser*, 25 Oct. 1935.

[31] Gillian Maclaine to Marjorie Gregorson, 16 Dec. 1836. Greenfield MSS.

[32] *Handboek voor cultuur- en handelsondernemingen in Nederlandsch-Indië*, Amsterdam, J. H. de Bussy, 1888–1940, vol. 22 (1910): 174, 681.

[33] Information courtesy of the late Peter Christiaans, CBG Centrum voor Familiegeschiedenis, The Hague, 2016.
[34] Civil registration marriages, Wedde (The Netherlands), 17 July 1920, Huwelijksregister, 1920, record number 26.
[35] *Diss Express*, 22 Aug. 1947.
[36] UK Passenger Lists 1 Apr. 1932, *Naidera*, Alexander MacNeill.
[37] Probate, 1956, MacNeill, Eila.
[38] Jane Robinson, *A Force to Be Reckoned With: A History of the Women's Institute*, London, Virago, 2011: 1–2.
[39] *Lynn Advertiser*, 6 Apr. 1956.
[40] Church of England Marriages, etc. Cameron-McNeil 1891.
[41] 1901 Census; 1911 Census; Probate, 1919, Cameron, Alexander Patrick.
[42] See Chapter 4: 'Islay and The Wealth of The Indies: Local Networks, Global Reach and Returnee Afterlives.'
[43] *The Scotsman*, 8 Apr. 1905; 6 Feb. 1906; 29 Mar. 1906.
[44] 'Ardsheal House', Canmore, https://canmore.org.uk/site/277516/ardsheal-house, accessed 9 June 2023; *Inverness Courier*, 6 July 1906.
[45] See tombstone transcription at Duror Burial Ground, Ballachulish, Scotland, in UK and Ireland, Find a Grave Index, 1300s–Current.

6. Good Steady Scotsmen

[1] Copy of on-voyage diary kept by Angus Maclaine between [Marseille?] and Batavia, 1846, in Angus Maclaine to William Osborn Maclaine, 26 July 1846. Osborne-Maclaine MSS, Gloucestershire Archives UK; David Dobson, *Scots in Latin America*, Baltimore, MD, Clearfield, 2003: 30 (under 'Alexander G. Cumming, MD, born 1817, son of John Cumming a Banker in Morayshire ... died in Rio de Janeiro, 19.3.1845').
[2] Charles Burton Buckley, *An Anecdotal History of the Old Times in Singapore*, 2 vols, Singapore, Fraser & Neave, 1902, vol. 1: 216, and vol. 2: 568; *Singapore Free Press and Mercantile Advertiser*, 14 Oct. 1853.
[3] Andrew Mackillop, 'Locality, Nation and Empire: Scots and the Empire in Asia, c.1695–c.1813', in John M. MacKenzie and T. M. Devine (eds), *Scotland and the British Empire*, Oxford, Oxford University Press, 2011: 54–83, at 61; 'Brodie, Alexander,' in R. Thorne (ed.), *The History of Parliament: The House of Commons, 1790–1820*, 1986, online edn, www.historyofparliamentonline.org/volume/1790-1820/member/brodie-alexander-1748-1818, accessed 9 June 2022.
[4] Andrew Mackillop, *Human Capital and Empire: Scotland, Ireland and Wales and British Imperialism in Asia, c. 1690–c. 1820*, Manchester, Manchester University Press, 2021: 245.
[5] D. T. Moore, 'Falconer, Hugh (1808–1865)', *Oxford Dictionary of National Biography*, Oxford, Oxford University Press, 2004, online edn, www.oxforddnb.com/view/article/9110, accessed 26 May 2022.
[6] Gillian Maclaine [hereinafter GM] to Marjorie Maclaine, 10 Sept. 1823. Greenfield Papers.
[7] G. Roger Knight, *Trade and Empire in Early Nineteenth-Century Southeast Asia: Gillian Maclaine and his Business Network*, Woodbridge, The Boydell Press, 2015: 25–56.

8 GM to Angus Maclaine, Canton, 17 Dec. 1824. Greenfield MSS.
9 C. M. Turnbull, *The Straits Settlements, 1819–1867: Indian Presidency to Crown Colony*, London, Athlone Press, 1972: 31–36.
10 Turnbull, *Straits Settlements*: 22–23, 53.
11 Buckley, *Anecdotal History*, vol. 1: 216, 377.
12 Turnbull, *Straits Settlements*: 24.
13 *Singapore Free Press and Mercantile Advertiser*, 21 Feb. 1839.
14 Tanja Bueltmann, *Clubbing Together: Ethnicity, Civility and Formal Sociability in the Scottish Diaspora to 1930*, Liverpool, Liverpool University Press, 2014: 12.
15 Buckley, *Anecdotal History*, vol. 1: 320.
16 Buckley, *Anecdotal History*, vol. 2: 439.
17 Buckley, *Anecdotal History*, vol. 1: 387, and vol. 2: 419, 531.
18 Sven Beckert, *Empire of Cotton: A Global History*, New York, Alfred A. Knopf, 2015.
19 Straits Settlements Records, as quoted in Turnbull, *Straits Settlements*: 179.
20 Buckley, *Anecdotal History*, vol. 2: 696.
21 Carl A. Trocki, *Opium and Empire: Chinese Society in Colonial Singapore, 1800–1910*, Ithaca, NY, Cornell University Press, 1990: 50.
22 Richard J. Grace, *Opium and Empire: The Lives and Careers of William Jardine and James Matheson*, Montreal, McGill-Queen's University Press, 2014.
23 Eric Tagliacozzo, *Secret Trades, Porous Borders: Smuggling and States along a Southeast Asian Frontier, 1865–1915*, New Haven, CT, Yale University Press, 2005: 186–196; Anthony Webster, 'The Development of British Commercial and Political Networks in the Straits Settlements 1800 to 1868: The Rise of a Colonial and Regional Economic Identity?', *Modern Asian Studies*, 45/4 (2011): 899–929; Carl A. Trocki, 'The Rise of Singapore's Great Opium Syndicate, 1840–1886', *Journal of Southeast Asian Studies*, 18/2 (1987): 58–80.
24 Atsushi Kobayashi, 'The Role of Singapore in the Growth of Intra-Southeast Asian Trade, c.1820s–1852', *Southeast Asian Studies* (Kyoto), 2/3 (2013): 443–474.
25 Knight, *Trade and Empire*: 146–147; James R. Rush, *Opium to Java: Revenue Farming and Chinese Enterprise in Colonial Indonesia, 1860–1910*, Ithaca, NY, Cornell University Press, 1990.
26 Peter A. Coclanis, 'Southeast Asia's Incorporation into the World Rice Market: A Revisionist View', *Journal of Southeast Asian Studies*, 24/2 (1993): 251–267, at 265.
27 Toshiyuki Miyata, 'Tan Kim Ching and Siam "Garden Rice": The Rice Trade between Siam and Singapore in the Late Nineteenth Century', in A. J. H, Latham and Heita Kawakatsu (eds), *Intra-Asian Trade and the World Market*, London, Routledge, 2006: 114–132.
28 Court of Chancery Clerks of Records and Writs Office, Pleadings 1861–1875. Cumming v. Cumming, [C 16/921/C117] National Archives, Kew UK. Plaintiffs: Elizabeth Chambers Cumming, widow. Defendants: James Bannerman Cumming and William Anastasius Barff.
29 Coclanis, 'Southeast Asia's Incorporation': 254.
30 GM to Marjorie Maclaine, 16 Dec. 1836.
31 1871 Census.
32 Will with codicil of James Fraser, proved 4 April 1872, England & Wales Government Probate Service, https://probatesearch.service.gov.uk, accessed 16 February 2022.
33 Scotland Marriages 1561–1910.
34 *The Lands and People of Moray, Part 29 – The Burgh and Parish of Forres from 1800 to 1850*, 'Year 1818'.

[35] *The Lands and People of Moray, Part 29 – The Burgh and Parish of Forres from 1800 to 1850*, 'Year 1833'; *Blackwood's Magazine*, 6 Oct. 1819: 112.

[36] *Forres Gazette*, 5 Nov. 1845.

[37] Buckley, *Anecdotal History*, vol. 1: 233.

[38] *Singapore Free Press and Mercantile Advertiser*, 7 Sept. 1849; *Elgin Courier*, 6 July 1849.

[39] I am grateful to Mr. Brian Kerr, Secretary of the Lodge St Lawrence in Forres, for information collected from various contemporary sources.

[40] Buckley, *Anecdotal History*, vol. 2: 437, 497.

[41] Buckley, *Anecdotal History*, vol. 1: 173, quoting *Singapore Free Press and Mercantile Advertiser*, 28 Jan. 1853.

[42] *Morayshire O S Name Books 1868–1871: Forres*. National Records of Scotland, series OS1/12/14: 15.

[43] *Isle of Wight Observer*, 18 Aug. 1860.

[44] Knight, *Trade and Empire*: 36; GM to Marjorie Maclaine, 8 Jan. 1818.

[45] *City Press*, 2 Dec. 1865; Bueltmann, *Clubbing Together*: 40–48; Thomas Hamilton, 'Macleod, Norman (1812–1872)', rev. H. C. G. Matthew, *Oxford Dictionary of National Biography*, Oxford, Oxford University Press, 2004, online edn, Jan. 2007, www.oxforddnb.com/view/article/17679, accessed 5 May 2022.

[46] e.g. *Public Ledger and Daily Advertiser*, 18 Sept. 1862, 12 Feb. 1869, and 17 Apr. 1871.

[47] Will with Codicil of James Fraser, 4 Apr. 1872, England & Wales Government Probate Service, https://probatesearch.service.uk, accessed 16 Feb. 2022.

[48] Charles A. Jones, *International Business in the Nineteenth Century: The Rise and Fall of a Cosmopolitan Bourgeoisie*, Brighton, Wheatsheaf Books, 1987: 160.

[49] Stanley Chapman, *The Rise of Merchant Banking*, London, Routledge, 1984: 39–69; P. L. Cottrell, *Investment Banking in England 1856–1881: A Case Study of the International Financial Society*, vol. 1, London, Routledge, 2012.

[50] Buckley, *Anecdotal History*, vol. 2: 673; *The Standard*, 1 May 1862; *Morning Advertiser*, 11 June 1866; *Money Market Review*, 19 Apr. 1873, as quoted in *Java-Bode*, 19 June 1873.

[51] e.g. *Morning Advertiser*, 3 Nov. 1863; *Daily News*, 8 Jan. 1867; *The Standard*, 3 Oct. 1864.

[52] e.g. *The Standard*, 27 Sept. 1862; *Northern Whig*, 22 May 1862; *Public Ledger and Daily Advertiser*, 5 Nov. 1863, and *The Standard*, 19 Jan. 1864; *Buckingham Advertiser and Free Press*, 7 July 1866.

[53] Michael Stenton, *Who's Who of British Members of Parliament*, vol. 1: 1832–1885, Hassocks, Harvester Press, 1976: 285; Sandip Hazareesingh, 'Interconnected Synchronicities: The Production of Bombay and Glasgow as Modern Global Ports c.1850–1880', *Journal of Global History*, 4/1 (2009): 7–31, at 18.

[54] *Report from the Select Committee on Sugar Duties*, London, House of Commons, 1862: 236–242, 386–387.

[55] Pamela Ffolliott and E. L. H. Croft, *One Titan at a Time: The Story of John Paterson of Port Elizabeth, South Africa, and His Times*, Cape Town, H. Timmins, 1960; *Daily News*, 3 Oct. 1863; 'Standard Bank (historic)', Wikipedia, https://en.wikipedia.org/wiki/Standard_Bank_(historic), accessed 28 Mar. 2022.

[56] e.g. *The Standard*, 3 Oct. 1864.

[57] 1861 Census; Probate, 1902, Borradaile, John.

[58] Jones, *International Business*: 169; *Morning Advertiser*, 24 Jan. 1848; 1861 and 1871 Censuses; Probate, 1877, Hackblock, John.

[59] Derek Matthews, Malcolm Anderson and John Richard Edwards, *The Priesthood of Industry: The Rise of the Professional Accountant in British Industry*, Oxford, Oxford University Press, 1998: 32.

[60] See: Michel W. Pharand (ed.), *Benjamin Disraeli Letters*, vol. 10: 1868, Toronto, University of Toronto Press, 2014: 277; 1861 and 1871 Censuses; *Liverpool Mercury*, 24 Apr. 1862; 'Archibald Paull: Profile & Legacies Summary', Centre for the Study of the Legacies of British Slavery, www.ucl. ac.uk/lbs/person/view/10808, accessed 5 May 2022; Bonnie Martin, 'Slavery's Invisible Engine: Mortgaging Human Property', *Journal of Southern History*, 76/4 (2010): 817–866.

[61] 'Michel Emmanuel Rodocanachi', Wikipedia, https://en.wikipedia.org/wiki/Michel_Emmanuel_Rodocanachi, accessed 27 May 2020.

[62] David Kynaston, *The City of London*, vol. 1: *A World of its Own, 1815–1890*, London, Pimlico (Random House), 1995: 238–240, quoting *The Times*, 12 May 1866; John D. Turner, *Banking in Crisis: The Rise and Fall of British Banking Stability, 1880 to the Present*, Cambridge, Cambridge University Press, 2014: 80–84.

[63] Probate Records; 27 Feb. 1868, he died at 6 Montague Square, aged 56 (see *The Standard*, 28 Feb. 1868).

[64] 1871 Census.

[65] 'Lewis and Sophia Fraser', The Library of Nineteenth-Century Photography, www.19thcen- turyphotos.com/Lewis-and-Sophia-Fraser-125699.htm, accessed 5 May 2022.

[66] England Marriages, 1869: James Fraser.

[67] Newman McHaffie Family Tree on Ancestry. com, accessed 21 Aug. 2024.

[68] UK, Officer Service Records, 1764–1932; UK and Ireland, Find a Grave Index, 1300s–Current.

[69] Probate, 1878, Mackey, Hugh Allen; 1881 Census.

[70] G. T. Bettany, 'Locock, Sir Charles, first baronet (1799–1875)', rev. Anne Digby, *Oxford Dictionary of National Biography*, Oxford, Oxford University Press, 2004, online edn, www.oxforddnb.com/view/article/16915, accessed 26 May 2022.

[71] *Kingston Gleaner* (Jamaica), 1 Nov. 1877.

[72] Joseph Mack Family Tree on AC, accessed 4 Jan. 2021; 1871 Wales Census.

[73] *Portsmouth Evening News*, 16 July 1883.

[74] 1891 Census.

[75] *Morning Post*, 25 June 1908.

[76] Probate, 1910, Locock, Herbert.

[77] 1911 Census; Probate 1929, Locock, Adelaide.

[78] 1881 Census; Probate, 1893, Fraser, Edward Seymour.

[79] 1871 Census; England and Wales Electoral Rolls, 1832–1932; 1891 Census; Probate, 1897, Fraser, Alexander.

[80] *Morning Post*, 28 Jan. 1867; Anthony Reid, *An Indonesian Frontier: Acehnese and Other Histories of Sumatra*, Singapore, National University of Singapore Press, 2004: 270–272.

[81] *Pall Mall Gazette*, 3 Feb. 1881; 1881 Census; 1891 Census; UK Outbound Passengers, 20 Apr. 1928, Marjorie Read Coleman; Australia Death Index, 1929, Marjorie Read Coleman.

[82] *Morning Post*, 23 Apr. 1890; 1891 Census.

[83] F. L. M. Thompson, *The Rise of Respectable Society: A Social History of Victorian Britain, 1830–1900*, London, Fontana Press, 1988: 53–54, 91–92.

[84] Probate 1903 Fraser, Anna Maria.
[85] Probate 1942 Fraser, Helen; Probate 1945 Fraser, Emily; *The Times*, 28 July 1945.
[86] *St James's Gazette*, 18 May 1882.
[87] e.g. *London Gazette*, 25 Aug. 1875.
[88] *Morning Post*, 14 May 1887; Electoral Registers 1832–1932; Great Western Railway Shareholders, 1835–1932.
[89] 'Henry Gurney', Wikipedia, https://en.wikipedia.org/wiki/Henry_Gurney, accessed 30 Dec. 2023.
[90] 1901 Census.
[91] *Singapore Free Press and Mercantile Advertiser*, 3 Feb. 1848.
[92] 1871 Census.
[93] Probate 1878 James, Charles Deere.
[94] *Pall Mall Gazette*, 14 Nov. 1881.
[95] *Illustrated London News*, 17 Nov. 1900; Guthrie, James, Probate, 1900; Probate, 1904, Guthrie, Sophia Cumming.
[96] *Sussex Agricultural Express*, 12 July 1901; 'Papworth Everard: Manors and other estates', in *A History of the County of Cambridge and the Isle of Ely*: vol. 9, *Chesterton, Northstowe, and Papworth Hundreds*, ed. A. P. M. Wright and C. P. Lewis, London, Victoria County History, 1989: 359–361, www.british-history.ac.uk/vch/cambs/vol9/pp359-361, accessed 26 May 2022; *Sevenoaks Chronicle and Kentish Advertiser*, 11 Nov. 1938.
[97] Probate, 1906, Fraser, Lewis James; Probate, 1938, Fraser, Maria Ellen.

7. Aberdeen, Antwerp and the Indies

[1] Gillian Maclaine, 'weekly journal' kept on board the *Anthony*, entry for Sat. 3 Mar. 1832, Lat. 42° N, Long. 13°12' W [emphasis in original]. Greenfield MSS (in Private Possession, UK).
[2] A. J. [Alexander Johnston], *A Short Memoir of James Young, etc.*, Aberdeen, J. Craighead & Co., 1860, https://archive.org/details/ashortmemoirjam00youngoog, accessed 23 Sept. 2022.
[3] Gillian Maclaine [hereinafter GM] to Marjorie Gregorson, Paris, Jun. 1831. Greenfield MSS.
[4] Gertrude Eleonore (Emilie) Nottebohm, later Mrs John Mathison Fraser (b. 1814), as a young girl', after Ary Scheffer (Dordrecht 1795 – Argenteuil 1858), filed in THIS Folder, www.nationaltrustcollections.org.uk/object/1252018, accessed 10 Oct. 2022.
[5] Hilde Greefs, 'The Role of Women in the Business Networks of Men: The Business Elite in Antwerp during the First Half of the Nineteenth Century', *XIV International History Congress*, Helsinki, 2006: 1–16, at 7–9; S. T. Bindoff, *The Scheldt Question to 1839*, London, Allen & Unwin, 1945: 138–230.
[6] Stanley Chapman, *Merchant Enterprise in Britain: From the Industrial Revolution to World War I*, Cambridge, Cambridge University Press, 1992: 96–97.
[7] *Algemeen Handelsblad*, 8 Apr. 1833, 23 Apr. 1835; *De Avondbode*, 27 Nov. 1837 16 Aug. 1838, 21 Sept. 1838, 26 June 1839; *Algemeen Handelsblad*, 19 June 1839, 30 Mar. 1840, 19 May 1843, 28 Nov. 1846, 15 June 1846.
[8] See Introduction: 'A Cohort of Scottish Families and The Dutch East Indies'.
[9] *Nieuwe Rotterdamsche Courant*, 27 Aug.1847; *The Standard*, 19 Oct.1847; *Morning Advertiser*, 25 Aug. 1847; *Shipping and Mercantile Gazette*, 25 Aug. 1847.

[10] 1851 Census.
[11] *Morning Advertiser*, 13 Apr. 1855; *Illustrated London News*, 9 Dec. 1854; *Morning Advertiser*, 7 Feb. 1856.
[12] 'Mongewell', Wikipedia, https://en.wikipedia.org/wiki/Mongewell, accessed 4 July 2024.
[13] 1851 Census.
[14] *Rotterdamsche Courant*, 17th Jan. 1815.
[15] Rotterdam Address Boeken, c.1858–c.1883, Stadsarchief Rotterdam.
[16] 'Mongewell', Wikipedia, https://en.wikipedia.org/wiki/Mongewell, accessed 5 Mar. 2024.
[17] *Kelly's Directory for Oxfordshire*, London, Kelly & Co., 1901 and 1911, under 'Alexander C. Fraser'; 1911 Census; *Oxford Weekly News*, 27 June 1894; *Reading Mercury*, 14 Apr. 1894.
[18] In Stadsarchief Rotterdam.
[19] *Kelly's Directory*, 1911, for Alexander Caspar Fraser, Esq., JP, DL.
[20] *Reading Mercury*, 6 Jan. 1917.
[21] Electoral Registers, 1832–1932, for 1910, 1919, 1930; *Sussex Agricultural Express*, 7 June 1935; Electoral Register, 1939; 'Buckham Hill House', Historic England, https://historicengland.org.uk/images-books/photos/item/IOE01/13901/27#.
[22] *Handboek voor cultuur- en handelsondernemingen in Nederlandsch-Indië* [hereinafter HCHO], Amsterdam, J. H. de Bussy, 1888–1940, vol. 29 [i.e. 30] (1918): 626, 642, 670; *HCHO*, vol. 18 (1906): 693; *Algemeen Handelsblad*, 14 Nov. 1950.
[23] Probate Records.
[24] See information re the Will of 'Mrs Emilie Fraser . . . late of Palace Houses, Bayswater', in *Boston Spa News*, 10 June 1887.
[25] 'Blair Cochrane', Wikipedia, https://en.wikipedia.org/wiki/Blair_Cochrane, accessed 26 May 2024.
[26] 'Victoria Eugenie of Battenberg', Wikipedia, https://en.wikipedia.org/wiki/Victoria_Eugenie_of_Battenberg, accessed 14 Sept. 2024.
[27] *Bedfordshire Mercury*, 19 Mar. 1909; *Berks and Oxon Advertiser*, 12 Mar. 1909.
[28] 1871 Census; *Aberdeen Weekly Journal and General Advertiser*, 5 Oct. 1878. Probate 1878 Sutton, Sir Richard Bart.
[29] *Isle of Wight Observer*, 6 Mar. 1909.
[30] GM to Marjorie Maclaine, 30 Oct. 1833, Greenfield MSS.
[31] *Javasche Courant* [hereinafter *JC*], 13 May 1835; GM to Marjorie Maclaine, 24 Aug. 1835. William Eaton retired from the firm at the close of 1843; see *JC*, 20 Jan.1844.
[32] G. Roger Knight, 'Rescued from the Myths of Time: Toward a Reappraisal of European Mercantile Houses in Mid-Nineteenth Century Java, c. 1830–1870', *Bijdragen tot de Taal-, Land- en Volkenkunde*, 170 (2014): 313–341; Knight, 'Neglected Orphans and Absent Parents: The European Mercantile Houses of Mid-Nineteenth-Century Java', in Ulbe Bosma and Anthony Webster (eds), *Commodities, Ports and Asian Maritime Trade since 1750*, Basingstoke, Palgrave Macmillan, 2015: 127–143.
[33] GM to Marjorie Maclaine, 16 Dec. 1836.
[34] *JC*, 20 Apr. 1836; J. J. Rochussen to J. C. Baud, 26 June 1847, and Rochussen to Baud, 29 Oct. 1847, in Jhr. Mr. W. A. Baud, *De semi-officiële en particuliere briefwisseling tussen J. C. Baud en J. J. Rochussen, 1845–1851*, 3 vols, Assen, Van Gorkom, 1983, vol. 2: 262, 304, n. 3, vol. 3: 155, n. 4; Geert, Banck, *Van de Javaanse suikercultuur naar de Nederlandse elitecultuur. Twee generaties in de 19e eeuw. Johann Erich Banck en John Eric Banck*, Diemen [Amsterdam], AMB Uitgeverij, 2016:

23–36; Eric Tagliacozzo, *Secret Trades, Porous Borders: Smuggling and States Along a Southeast Asian Frontier, 1865–1915*, New Haven, CT, Yale University Press, 2005: 186–208.

[35] Knight, *Trade and Empire:* 143–150.

[36] *JC* 9 May 1846.

[37] Scotland Select Marriages; McLeod-Schindler-Hohler-Hood family tree.

[38] See Chapter 7: 'Sugar and Sheep: A Global Clan and Trans-Imperial Careering across Three Continents.'

[39] D. R. Hainsworth, *The Sydney Traders: Simeon Lord and his Contemporaries, 1788–1821*, Melbourne, Cassell Australia, 1971: 67–69; Michael Greenberg, *British Trade and the Opening of China 1800–42*, Cambridge, Cambridge University Press, 1969, orig. pub. 1951: 29–30, 70–71; Janette Holcomb, *Early Merchant Families of Sydney: Speculation and Risk Management on the Fringes of Empire*, Melbourne, Australian Scholarly, 2013: 59–70.

[40] George Smeaton, *Memoir of Alexander Thomson of Banchory*, Edinburgh, Edmonston & Douglas, 1869: 37–38, 404–405.

[41] A transcription of the journal covering the years 1844–1851 is available at 'The Journal of Miss Anne Davidson [hereinafter ADJ] & The Memoirs of Mrs Gertrude Robertson', https://freepages.rootsweb.com/~missannedavidson/history/, accessed 24 Sept. 2022.

[42] Serena Kelly, 'Fraser, Angelica Patience (1823–1910)', *Oxford Dictionary of National Biography*, online edn, https://doi.org/10.1093/ref:odnb/59507, accessed 1 May 2024; W. D. Askew, *Angelica Patience Fraser: The Story of Her Life with Pages from Her Diary*, London, The John Williamson Company, 1923: 49, 56–57, 110–115, 125, 149-59.

[43] *ADJ*, 1849, 13 Aug. and 11 Sept.

[44] *ADJ*, 1850, 11 and 13 Feb. and 4 Mar.

[45] *ADJ*, 1850, 16 May.

[46] *ADJ*, 1850, 18 Jun. and 2 Jul.

[47] *ADJ*, 1850, 6 Aug.

[48] Alexander Fraser to Alexander MacNeill, Batavia, 6 June 1860. Macpherson Papers.

[49] McNeill, Alexander (Wills and testaments Reference SC42/20/8, Peebles Sheriff Court), 1867: 34–70, ScotlandsPeople, www.scotlandspeople.gov.uk, accessed 21 Sept. 2024.

[50] Census 1871.

[51] 1881 Census; Probate Records, 1881.

[52] 1891 Census.

[53] Gilles Teulié, 'Monarchy, Spirituality & Britishness: The Anglican Diaspora in Grasse 1880–1950', in Claire Davidson *et al.* (eds), *Provence and the British Imagination*, Milan, Ledizioni, 2013: 145–156.

[54] *Daily News*, 13 Jul. 1904; Probate, 1904, Fraser, Alexander.

[55] The paintings, including Raden Saleh, *Forest and Native House* (1860), are now in the Smithsonian American Art Museum. I am grateful to Professor Marieke Bloembergen of the University of Leiden and to the Indonesian art historian and curator Amir Sidharta for drawing my attention these paintings, their provenance and present location.

[56] Smeaton, *Memoir*: 306–307; 'Alexander Duff (missionary)', Wikipedia, https://en.wikipedia.org/wiki/Alexander_Duff_(missionary), accessed 6 Mar. 2021.

[57] *JC*, 9 Aug. 1845.

[58] Lachlan McLean to Colin McLean, 18 Jul. 1854, Macpherson Papers.

[59] *Bataviaasch Handelsblad*, 4 Oct. 1869.

60 W. T. Money, *Java, or, How to Manage a Colony: Showing a Practical Solution of the Questions Now Affecting British India*, 2 vols, London, Hurst and Blackett, 1861, vol. 1: 53.

61 *Java-Bode*, 16 Feb. 1853; '1852 Banda Sea earthquake', Wikipedia, https://en.wikipedia.org/wiki/1852_Banda_Sea_earthquake, accessed 2 Mar. 2024.

62 National Archives, UK, Foreign Office . . . General Correspondence before 1906 . . . Holland . . . Consuls at Batavia, FO 37/396.

63 P. H. van der Kemp and D. A. Overbeek, 'De jaren 1817–1825. Der Nederlandsche factorijen aan Hindostans Oostkust. Naar onuitgegeven stukken', *Bijdragen tot de Taal-, Land- en Volkenkunde van Nederlandsch-Indië*, 74, no. 1–2 (1918): 1–13; Engelbertus de Waal, https://edewaal.me/bogaardt-parenteel-2/, accessed 4 May 2016; 'Netherlands, GenealogieOnline Trees Index, 1000–2015', accessed 4 May 2016.

64 'Pahud de Mortanges', in *Nederland's Patriciaat: Genealogieën van Bekende Geslachten*, The Hague, Centraal Bureau voor Genealogie, 1910–, vols 2 (1911): 388–389, and 39 (1953): 222–227, at 222–224.

65 C. Fasseur, 'Gemengd onthaal. De weerklank op Money's "Java" in Nederland', *Bijdragen en Mededelingen betreffende de Geschiedenis der Nederlanden—Low Countries Historical Review*, 105/3 (1990): 368–378, at 369–371, 375–376.

66 Alexander Fraser to Alexander MacNeill, Batavia, 6 June 1860. Macpherson Papers.

67 Archief Bank Indonesia, Jakarta: De Java Bank. Notatie DJB 40, no. 114 (29 Apr. 1872), volgnummer 10–12. (A record of interview between officials of the Bank with Gerhard Hermann Miesegaes, at that date a senior partner in Maclaine Watson, kindly supplied to the author by Alexander Claver, The Hague, whose *Dutch Commerce and Chinese Merchants in Java: Colonial Relationships in Trade and Finance, 1800–1942*, Leiden, Brill, 2014, is based on a unique exploration of the DJB Archive.)

68 *Glasgow Herald*, 6 Aug. 1861.

69 *Kelso Chronicle*, 18 Jul. 1862.

70 Heidrun Walther (ed.), *Aus dem Leben von Theodor Adolf von Möller. Nach unvollendet hinterlassenen Aufzeichnungen über die Jahre 1840–1890*, Neustadt an der Aisch, Verlag Degener, 1958: 27–28. My thanks for this reference to Herr Wolfgang Schindler by email, 3 May 2018. [The capitalisation in the quotation is as in the original.]

71 'Yancey' to North, Hartrigge House, Jedburgh (G.B.), 29 December 1862, in *Official Records of the Union and Confederate Navies in the War of the Rebellion*, ser. 2, vol. 3, Washington, DC, Government Printing Office, 1896; repr., Rockville, MD, Wildside Press LLC, 2012: 325.

72 Eric H. Walther, *William Lowndes Yancey and the Coming of the Civil War*, Chapel Hill, NC, University of North Carolina Press, 2006: 283.

73 *Java Bode*, 15 Feb. 1865.

74 See Chapter 6: '"Good Steady Scotsmen": Forres, The Lion City and London.'

75 *Daily News*, 18 Apr. 1864.

76 *The Standard*, 19 Jan. 1864; *The Globe*, 4 Nov. 1863.

77 *Morning Advertiser*, 27 Jul. 1864.

78 *Nederlandsche Staatscourant*, 1 Oct. 1863; S. A. Reitsma, *Korte geschiedenis der Nederlandsch-Indische spoor- en tramwegen*, Batavia, G. Kolff, 1928: 10–22; G. Veenendaal, 'De locomotief van de moderniteit. Aanleg van het net van spoor- en tramwegen', in Wim Ravesteijn and Jan Kop (eds), *Bouwen in de Archipel. Burgerlijke openbare werken in Nederlands-Indië en Indonesië 1800–2000*, Zutphen, Walburg Pers, 2004: 63–91, at 67.

[79] J. N. F. M. à Campo, *Koninklijke Paketvaart Maatschappij. Stoomvaart en staatsvorming in de Indonesische archipel, 1888–1914*, Hilversum, Verloren, 1992: 39–73; J. Forbes Munro, *Maritime Enterprise and Empire: Sir William Mackinnon and his Business Network, 1823–1893*, Woodbridge, The Boydell Press, 2003: 75–76, 130–132, 138–139, 377.

[80] Fraser's (reduced) salary stood at 1,500 guilders (about £125 sterling) per month in 1868. NISM's first dividend (of 5 per cent) was paid in 1869 and the company's best years (dividends ranged between 10 and 20 per cent) were between 1873 and 1883. S. van Hulstijn to Alexander Fraser, 5 June 1868, SOAS McKinnon Papers, box 95, file 7; 'Statement of capital and dividend 1866–1890', Mackinnon Papers Box 6, file 23.

[81] *Evening Mail*, 17 Sept. 1866.

[82] Verbaal Kolonien [openbaar] 24.11.1871/13-1621, 20.8.1872/ 1041/14. ANMK.

[83] Besluit GG 21.7.1875/ 22. ANMK.

[84] J. C. Baud to J. van den Bosch, 8 Nov. 1831, in J. J. Westendorp Boerma (ed.), *Briefwisseling tussen J. van den Bosch en J. C. Baud, 1829–1832 en 1834–1836*, 2 vols, Utrecht, Kemink en Zoon, 1956, vol. 1: 76.

[85] Cees Fasseur, *Indischgasten. Indische levensgeschiedenissen*, Amsterdam, Bert Bakker, 1997: 140–141.

[86] 'Levyssohn Norman' in 'List of applicants for the post of Resident Director [of the NISM] at The Hague prepared by Mr. A. Fraser', Mackinnon Papers, Box 6, File 21.

[87] Verbaal 9.6.1873/O15 Kabinet ANMK.

[88] Verbaal 8.5.1874/B14 Kabinet Geheim ANMK; *De Oostpost*, 10 Sept. 1857; Alexander Fraser granted 'brieven van naturalisatie'. I am also grateful for information concerning Fraser's membership of the *Orde* kindly supplied from the resources of the late Peter Christiaans, formerly of the CBG, The Hague.

[89] Henk Boets, Jenny de Jong and C. A. Tamse (eds), *Eer en fortuin. Leven in Nederland en Indië 1824–1900. Autobiografie van gouverneur-generaal James Loudon*, Amsterdam, De Bataafsche Leeuw, 2003: 308–309. For Be Biauw Tjoan, see James R. Rush, *Opium to Java: Revenue Farming and Chinese Enterprise in Colonial Indonesia, 1860–1910*, Ithaca, NY, Cornell University Press, 1990: 77–78, 93–96.

[90] *Pall Mall Gazette*, 19 Feb. 1879; *Bat. Handelsblad*, 8 March 1879.

[91] Alexander Fraser to James Loudon, 3 Apr. 1880, 10 Apr. 1880, in Nationaal Archief, The Hague, Archief James Loudon 2.21.183.50/30; *Belfast Telegraph*, 1 Apr. 1880.

[92] *Daily News*, 21 Apr. 1880.

[93] 1850 United States Federal Census.

[94] Probate, 1924, Blackman-Fraser, Emma.

[95] Alexander Fraser to James Loudon, 3 June 1880, NA, Archief James Loudon, 2.21.183.50/30 (underlining as in original).

[96] Probate, 1880, Fraser, William Thomson.

[97] 1881 Census; Probate, 1886, Fraser, Anna Hermina Sophia Cornelia.

[98] 1891 Census.

[99] John Thomson Fraser, in 'Middlesex, Harrow School Photographs of Pupils & Masters 1869–1925'; *London Gazette*, 22 Oct. 1889.

[100] Walter Ralph Bankes in Electoral Register, 1900.

[101] Viola Bankes, *A Kingston Lacy Childhood: Reminiscences of Viola Bankes Collected by Pamela Watkin*, Wimborne Minster, Dorset, Dovecote Press, 2017, orig. pub. 1986: 13.

[102] F. L. M. Thompson, *The Rise of Respectable Society: A Social History of Victorian Britain, 1830–1900*, London, Fontana Press, 1988: 161–165.
[103] Bankes, *Kingston Lacy Childhood*: 12; *Hearth and Home*, 6 Sept. 1900.
[104] Bankes, *Kingston Lacy Childhood*: 12.
[105] Probate, 1904, Bankes, Walter Ralph.
[106] *Morning Post*, 22 July 1897.
[107] Mary Theresa Olivia Pless, *Daisy Princess Daisy of Pless, by Herself*, ed. Desmond Chapman-Huston, New York, Dutton, 1928: 69, https://archive.org/stream/daisyprincessofp017081mbp/daisyprincessofp017081mbp_.txt, accessed 21 Aug. 2022.
[108] 1901 Census; Anthony Fletcher and Ruth M. Larsen, *Mistress: A History of Women and their Country Houses*, New Haven, CT, Yale University Press, 2025: 175-181, 226–227, 235–236, 248–249.
[109] 'Bankes of Kingston Lacy', Landed families of Britain and Ireland, https://landedfamilies.blogspot.com/2018/12/356-bankes-of-kingston-lacy.html, as quoted in 'Ralph Bankes (landowner)', Wikipedia, https://en.wikipedia./wiki/Ralph_Bankes_(landowner), accessed 2 Sept. 2022; *Western Gazette*, 25 Nov. 1904.
[110] Bankes, *Kingston Lacy Childhood*: 86–91.
[111] 'Bankes of Kingston Lacy', Landed families.
[112] 'Ralph Bankes (landowner)', Wikipedia.
[113] Bankes, *Kingston Lacy Childhood*: 9–13.
[114] Electoral Register, 1932; Probate, 1954, Bankes, Henrietta Jane, otherwise Henriette Jenny.
[115] 'William John Bankes. Unsuccessful Claimant St Kitts 705', in UCL Legacies of British Slavery, www.ucl.ac.uk/lbs/person/view/2146645443; Anne Sebba, *The Exiled Collector: William Bankes and the Making of an English Country House*, Wimborne Minster, Dorset, Dovecote Press, 2009, orig. pub. London, John Murray, 2004: 14–19, 37; History of Parliament Online, 'Bankes, Henry (1756–1834)', https://www.historyofparliamentonline.org/1790-1820/member/bankes-henry-1756-1834; and 'Bankes, William John (1786–1855)', https://www.historyofparliamentonline.org/1790-1820/member/bankes-william-john-1786-1855; 'Cumberland Mine Owner's Will', *Lancashire Evening Post*, 7 Dec. 1904.
[116] Church of England Marriages and Banns, 1886.
[117] Marianne Braun, 'De ware beginselen van het staatskrediet. Louis Drucker, een leven lang in de oppositie', *De Moderne Tijd* [Amsterdam], 7/1 (2023): 78–102.
[118] London City Directories 1890, 1895, 1900 and 1905; 1911 Census.
[119] e.g. *Sporting Gazette*, 24 May 1890; *The Standard*, 4 June 1898.
[120] J. F. Heijbroek and E. L. Wouthuysen, *Portret van een kunsthandel. De firma Van Wisselingh en zijn compagnons 1838–heden*, Zwolle, Waanders, and Amsterdam Rijksmuseum, 1999: 258–259.
[121] E. P. Engel, 'Het ontstaan van de verzameling Drucker-Fraser in het Rijksmuseum', *Bulletin van het Rijksmuseum*, 13/2 (1965): 45–66; Wiepke Loos, Marijn Schapelhouman and R. J. A. te Rijdt, *Aquarellen van de Haagse School. De collectie Drucker-Fraser*, Amsterdam, Rijksmuseum; Zwolle, Waanders, 2002: 6–133.
[122] e.g. *Provinciale Overijsselsche en Zwolsche Courant*, 16 Aug. 1910; *Zutphensche Courant*, 16 Jan. 1919; *De Standaard*, 25 Sept. 1929.
[123] Mary Fraser-Drucker to Van Riemsdijk, 18 Oct. 1908, as quoted in Engel, 'Verzameling Drucker-Fraser': 65.
[124] Engel, 'Verzameling Drucker-Fraser': 47.

[125] *Maandbulletin van het Nationaal Bureau voor Vrouwenarbeid* [Monthly Bulletin of the National Office for Women's Labour], 4 (1923): 192.

[126] 'Lensing, Wilhelmina Elisabeth (1847-1925)' [aka Drucker], Digitaal Vrouwenlexicon van Nederland, Huygens Instituut voor Nederlandse Geschiedenis, https://resources.huygens.knaw.nl/vrouwenlexicon/lemmata/data/Lensing, accessed 6 Apr. 2024; *Daily Mirror*, 8 Dec. 1925.

[127] J. C. J. Drucker, *Some correspondence concerning a British passport confiscated by H.B.M.'s minister in the land of Guillaume Tell*, Montreux, Société de l'Imprimerie et Lithographie, n.d. [1919?].

[128] *Evening Mail*, 25 May 1910.

[129] *Illustrated London News*, 29 Dec. 1928.

[130] *Algemeen Handelsblad*, 22 July 1932.

[131] Probate, 1949, Drucker, Jean Carel Joseph; *Daily Telegraph*, 20 Nov. 1944; *Bayswater Chronicle and West London News*, 24 Nov. 1944; *Algemeen Handelsblad*, 16 Jan. 1946 (a notice posted by Th. L. Lauer-Drucker, dated Dec. 1945 [N.B.] from the Palace Hotel, Lugano).

[132] Probate, 1949, Drucker, Mary Lydia ('Probate granted to Rudolph Drucker, engineer and [Jhr.] Arnoud Jan de Beaufort, stock-broker').

8. Sugar, Sheep and an Empire Family

[1] *Javasche Courant* [hereinafter *JC*], 20 May 1839; 'Bardaster (1833 ship)', Wikipedia, https://en.wikipedia.org/wiki/Bardaster_(1833_ship), accessed 30 Nov. 2019.

[2] 'Purchase of commissions in the British Army', Wikipedia, https://en.wikipedia.org/wiki/Purchase_of_commissions_in_the_British_Army [c.1833], accessed 29 June 2025.

[3] Iain MacKinnon and Andrew Mackillop, 'Plantation Slavery and Landownership in the West Highlands and Islands: Legacies and Lessons. A Discussion Paper', Glasgow, University of Glasgow, 2023, https://eprints.gla.ac.uk/321913, accessed 1 July 2025.

[4] Zoë Laidlaw, 'National Biographies and Transnational Lives: Tracing Connections between Slavery and Settler Colonialism', *Australian Journal of Biography and History*, 6 (2022): 143–170, at 147, 162.

[5] James Monckton Darlot (1811–1903), obituary, *The Argus* (Melbourne), 27 January 1903, *Obituaries Australia*, Australian National University, https://oa.anu.edu.au/obituary/darlot-james-monckton-16565, accessed 8 July 2021; William Piggott Firebrace (1832–1908), obituary, *The Argus* (Melbourne), 29 June 1908, *Obituaries Australia*, Australian National University, https://oa.anu.edu.au/obituary/firebrace-william-piggott-16579, accessed 8 July 2021.

[6] 'McLachlans of Salachan', *Notes and Queries*, 171/11 (12 Sept. 1936): 192; UCL Legacies of British Slave-ownership Database, www.ucl.ac.uk/lbs.

[7] MacKinnon and Mackillop, 'Plantation Slavery and Landownership': 6, 15.

[8] 'John Sawers the Younger', UCL Legacies of British Slave-ownership Database, www.ucl.ac.uk/lbs/person/view/17915.

[9] Hugh McCrae (ed.), *Georgiana's Journal: Melbourne 1841–1865*, Sydney, William Brooks, 1978: 55, 80.

[10] Paul de Serville, *Port Phillip Gentlemen: And Good Society in Melbourne before the Gold Rushes*, Melbourne, Oxford University Press, 1980: 212.

[11] 'Memo' R.M. McLachlan, Iona [Melbourne] 21 Sept. 1903, in the possession of Mr. Giles Forrest (a direct descendant of Ronald McLachlan's sister, Ann McLachlan) who kindly sent the author a copy by email 7th July 2025.

[12] Thomas Young, *Pioneer Station Owners of the Wimmera* [n.p., n.d., c. 1930]: 11, copy in State Library of Victoria, Melbourne; 'Rich Avon', Donald Historical Society, http://donaldhistory.org.au/ welcome/rich-avon-3, accessed 19 July 2025.

[13] 'Depasturing Licence Issue', *Geelong Advertiser*, 3 Oct. 1842.

[14] Frederick Harwood Noble and Robert Morgan, *Speed the Plough: A History of the Royal Agricultural Society of Victoria*, [Melbourne], Royal Agricultural Society of Victoria, 1981: 1.

[15] Elinor G. K. Melville, *A Plague of Sheep: Environmental Consequences of the Conquest of Mexico*, Cambridge, Cambridge University Press, 1994. For Australia specifically, see e.g. Marie C. Hedrick, 'Australia's Colonial Wool Industry: A Sheep-Walk for the Benefit of British Imperialism, 1788–1851', MA thesis, University of Hawai'i at Manoa, 1998; Leigh Dale, 'Empire's Proxy: Sheep and the Colonial Environment', in Helen Tiffin (ed.), *Five Emus to the King of Siam: Environment and Empire*, Leiden, Brill, 2007: 1–14.

[16] Henry Reynolds, *Forgotten War*, Sydney, NewSouth, 2013: 88.

[17] William Beinart and Lotte Hughes, *Environment and Empire*, Oxford, Oxford University Press, 2007: 94–110, quotation from 95 ('Sheep, Pastures and Demography in Australia'); Melville, Plague: 60–77 ('The Australian Experience'); Bill Gammage, *The Biggest Estate on Earth: How Aborigines Made Australia*, Crows Nest, NSW, Allen & Unwin, 2011; Don Watson, *Caledonia Australis: Scottish Highlanders on the Australian Frontier*, Sydney, Collins, 1984; Benjamin Wilkie, *The Scots in Australia, 1788–1938*, Woodbridge, The Boydell Press, 2017: 61–73 ('Scottish Migrants and Indigenous Australians'); James Belich, *Replenishing the Earth: The Settler Revolution and the Rise of the Anglo-World, 1783–1939*, Oxford, Oxford University Press, 2009: 272–275; Stephen Foster, *A Private Empire*, Millers Point, Sydney, Pier Nine, 2010: 234–251 ('War with the Blacks').

[18] Ian D. Clark, *Scars on the Landscape: A Register of Massacre Sites in Western Victoria, 1803–1859*, Canberra, Aboriginal Studies Press, 1995: 85–101, 141–168.

[19] e.g. Margaret Kiddle, *Men of Yesterday: A Social History of the Western District of Victoria, 1834–1890*, Melbourne, Melbourne University Press, 1961: 304–305.

[20] G. Roger Knight, *Sugar, Steam and Steel: The Industrial Project in Colonial Java, 1830–1885*, Adelaide, University of Adelaide Press, 2014, and the extensive references therein.

[21] Alexander Claver and G. Roger Knight, 'A European Role in Intra-Asian Commercial Development: The Maclaine Watson Network and the Java Sugar Trade c.1840–1942', *Business History*, 60 (2018): 202–230.

[22] e.g. Ulbe Bosma and Remco Raben, *Being 'Dutch' in the Indies: A History of Creolisation and Empire, 1500–1920*, trans. Wendie Shaffer, Singapore, NUS Press, 2008, originally published in Dutch as *De oude Indische wereld* [The Old Indies World] *1500–1920*, Amsterdam, Bert Bakker, 2003; Jean Gelman Taylor, *The Social World of Batavia: European and Eurasian in Dutch Asia*, Madison, WI, University of Wisconsin Press, 1983; Cees Fasseur, *Indischgasten. Indische levensgeschiedenissen*, Bert Bakker, 1997: 7–39; G. Roger Knight, 'A Case of Mistaken Identity? *Suikerlords* and Ladies, *Tempo Doeloe* and the Dutch Colonial Communities in Nineteenth Century Java', *Social Identities*, 7/3 (2001): 379–391.

[23] 'Verslag van het Beheer en den Staat der Koloniën over 1855', *Bijblad van de Nederlandsche Staatscourant*, 1857–8, vol. 2: 424.

[24] *The Argus* (Melbourne), 14 Jan. 1848; *JC*, 9 Oct. 1847.

[25] Genealogie Online, entries for 'Carl Friedrich Gehne (c. 1792–1843)', www.genealogieonline.nl/indische-bikken/I192041249581.php, and 'Sara Hester Catherina Klamberg (c. 1790–1858)', www.genealogieonline.nl/stamboom-willems-hoogeloon-best/.php, accessed 24 Jan. 2022; CBG Familie Archieven, https://cbg.nl, under Gehne.

[26] Norbert van den Berg and Steven Wachlin, *Het album voor Mientje. Een fotoalbum uit 1862 in Nederlandsch-Indië*, Bussum, Thoth, 2005: 88; *JC*, 4 Jul. 1840, and *Java-Bode* [hereinafter *JB*], 10 Feb. 1858.

[27] *JB*, 13 Feb. 1858.

[28] For the information *re* James McLachlan and Willem van der Hucht in this and the following paragraphs, see Van den Berg, and Wachlin, *Album*: 10–96; Rob Nieuwenhuys, *Komen en blijven. Tempo doeloe—een verzonken wereld*, Amsterdam, Querido, 1982: 9–23; 'Toelatingsbesluiten van Gouverneur-Generaal in Rade 1819–1875', 1819–1875, under Mac Lachlan.

[29] Van den Berg and Wachlin, *Album*: 44.

[30] Van den Berg and Wachlin, *Album*: 88–90.

[31] 1901 Census. Unless otherwise stated, genealogical data in this chapter has been sourced via Ancestry.com, Findmypast and the (Dutch) websites WieWasWie and Open Archieven.

[32] A. E. Laurence, 'Karl Marx on the Isle of Wight', *Society* (New Brunswick), 23 (1985): 54–60, at 54.

[33] 1861 Census.

[34] Probate, 1893, McLachlan, Donald.

[35] 1871 Census.

[36] *De Locomotief*, 19 Mar. 1870, 11 May 1870.

[37] 1871 Census.

[38] Van den Berg and Wachlin, *Album*: 115.

[39] 1881, 1891 and 1901 Censuses.

[40] Giles Forrest's 'Descendants of Donald McLachlan' on Ancestry.com, accessed 11 July 2021.

[41] Victoria, Australia, Marriage Index, 1837–1950; David Pope, 'The Wealth and Social Aspirations of Liverpool's Slave Merchants in the Second Half of the Eighteenth Century', Appendices 1 and 2, in David Richardson, Suzanne Schwarz and Anthony Tibbles (eds), *Liverpool and Transatlantic Slavery*, Liverpool, Liverpool University Press, 2007: 194–208, 288; 'John Wybergh Shaw', UCL Legacies of British Slavery Database, www.ucl.ac.uk/lbs/person/view/2146646255, accessed 28 June 2025; 1823, Former British Colonial Dependencies, Slave Registers, 1813–1834, 'National Archives, Kew, B 3/4616 ('In the matter of John Wybergh Shaw and Adam Wallace Elmslie of Fenchurch Buildings, London, merchants, bankrupts... 1823 December 27').

[42] De Serville, *Port Phillip Gentlemen*: 192 (Appendix 2: 'Gentlemen in Society. Gentlemen by profession, commission and upbringing, prominent in society and noted by contemporaries'); *Kerr's Melbourne Almanac and Port Phillip Directory for 1842: A Compendium of Useful and Accurate Information Connected with Port Phillip*, Melbourne, Kerr and Thompson, 1842; *The Port Phillip Almanac and Directory, for 1847*, Melbourne, [n.p.], 1847.

[43] Probate, 1879, McLachlan, Archibald.

[44] 1871 Census.

[45] Probate, 1877, Donald, William.

46 Gloucestershire, England, Burials, 1813–1988; Australia, Marriage Index, 1788–1950, 1871, under Le Souef.

47 Information kindly supplied by Mr Giles Forrest (see above); 'Toelatingsbesluiten van de Governeur-Generaal in Rade 1819–1875', under Forrest, European Migration and Settlement in the Dutch East Indies database, International Institute of Social History, http://www.iisg.nl/migration/europese-immigratie.php ; JB, 15 Feb.1860, 9 Sept. 1869; *The First One Hundred Years, 1827–1927, of Maclaine Watson & Co., McNeill & Co. and Fraser Eaton & Co.* [n.p., n.d., Batavia, 1927]: 5; *De Locomotief*, 24 May 1870; Church of England Marriages: Forrest/Rodger Cheltenham, 14 Aug. 1873.

48 Gwen Hart, *A History of Cheltenham*, Leicester, Leicester University Press, 1965: 173–241, 355–366.

49 *Cheltenham Chronicle*, 25 Apr. 1903 (Obituary, James McLachlan); 'Funeral of Mrs McLachlan', *Cheltenham Chronicle*, 11 Apr. 1903.

50 Elizabeth Buettner, *Empire Families: Britons and Late Imperial India*, Oxford, Oxford University Press, 2004: 219–222.

51 1891 Census.

52 For an exposition of kindred themes in a broader frame, see Margot C. Finn, 'Material Turns in British History: IV: Empire in India, Cancel Cultures and the Country House', *Transactions of the Royal Historical Society*, 31 (2021): 1–21, at 1–13; Margot Finn and Kate Smith (eds), *The East India Company at Home, 1757–1857*, London, UCL Press, 2018.

53 Obituary: James McLachlan, *Cheltenham Chronicle*, 25 Apr. 1903.

54 Buettner, *Empire Families*: 165–166, 225–226; Deborah Gorham, *The Victorian Girl and the Feminine Ideal*, London, Routledge, 2012: 25, 97, 165.

55 Buettner, *Empire Families*: 110–145.

56 Phyllis Hembry, *British Spas from 1815 to the Present: A Social History* (edited and completed by Leonard W. Cowie and Evelyn E. Cowie), London, Athlone Press, 1997: 48; see also 'Cheltenham History: The Victorian Town 1840–1900', The Wilson, www.cheltenhammuseum.org.uk/collection/cheltenham-history-4-the-victorian-town-1840-1900, accessed 13 July 2021.

57 'Francis Close', Wikipedia, https://en.wikipedia.org/wiki/Francis_Close, accessed 12 Nov. 2022; A. F. Munden, 'Close, Francis (1797–1882), dean of Carlisle', in *Oxford Dictionary of National Biography*, online edn, Oxford: Oxford University Press, 2004, https://doi.org/10.1093/ref:odnb/5703, accessed 26 Feb. 2023.

58 As quoted in Hart, *Cheltenham*: 211.

59 Andrew Porter, 'Religion and Empire: British Expansion in the Long Nineteenth Century, 1780–1914', *Journal of Imperial and Commonwealth History*, 20/3 (1992), 370–390; Norman Etherington, 'Introduction', in Etherington (ed.) *Missions and Empire*, Oxford, Oxford University Press, 2005: 1–18.

60 London, Hatchard, 1858.

61 Hembry, *British Spas*: 49.

62 Hembry, *British Spas*: 49.

63 'James Douglas McLachlan', Wikipedia, https://en.wikipedia.org/wiki/James_Douglas_McLachlan, accessed 4 July 2021.

64 1881 Census; England and Wales Civil Divorce Records 1858–1918 (1906); Obituary: Col. D. M. McLachlan, *Gloucestershire Echo*, 1 Feb. 1940.

[65] 1891 Census.

[66] Daisy White, *Daisy in Exile: The Diary of an Australian Schoolgirl in France (1887–1889)*, introduced and annotated by Marc Serve Rivière, Canberra, National Library of Australia, 2003.

[67] 1891 and 1911 Censuses; UK Officer Service Records; Probate, 1933, Herbert, Arthur Colthurst.

[68] *Yorkshire Evening Post*, 24 Jan. 1934; 'Telbedde', History of Ceylon Tea, www.historyofceylontea.com/tea-estates/estates-registry/telbedde--2164.html, accessed 10 July 2021; *Dundee Courier*, 21 Apr. 1925; *Aberdeen Press and Journal*, 9 Oct. 1926; *Western Mail*, 13 Apr. 1936.

[69] Erika Rappaport, *A Thirst for Empire: How Tea Shaped the Modern World*, Princeton, NJ, Princeton University Press, 2017: 94–104.

[70] Probate, 1951, Herbert, Annie Constance.

[71] e.g. *Het Nieuws van den Dag voor Nederlandsch-Indië*, 3 June 1907.

[72] *Gloucestershire Echo*, 6 Feb.1901; *Bataviaasch Nieuwsblad*, 8 Feb.1901.

[73] Probate, 18 May 1903, McLachlan, James.

[74] Obituary: James McLachlan, *Cheltenham Chronicle*, 25 Apr. 1903.

[75] Will of James McLachlan, *Cheltenham Chronicle*, 23 May 1903.

[76] England, United Grand Lodge of England Freemason Membership Registers, 1751–1921, via Ancestry.com (for William John McLachlan, 1897).

[77] 1911 Census; Probate, 27 Feb. 1948, 'McLachlan, William James, of Rendcombe Manor, Nr Cirencester'.

[78] *Cheltenham Chronicle*, 23 May 1903.

[79] 1911 Census; England and Wales Electoral Register 1920–1932 (1925); Probate, 1 June 1958, 'McLachlan, Arthur Cecil, of 6 Spa Buildings, Cheltenham'.

[80] Ronald McLachlan, MSS note, Iona (Melbourne), dated 21 Sept. 1903 ('In case of my death . . . I may not live much longer'), copy in the possession of Mr Giles Forrest (by email, 7 July 2025).

[81] Australia, Marriage Index, 1788–1950; Hunter Family Tree (on Ancestry.com); 'Thomas Family', The Companion to Tasmanian History, www.utas.edu.au/library/companion_to_tasmanian_history/T/Thomas%20family.htm.

[82] e.g. Belich, *Replenishing the Earth*: 356–364.

[83] *The Argus* (Melbourne), 13 Aug. 1904.

[84] Probate, 1904, McLachlan, Ronald.

[85] Hart, *Cheltenham*: 227–229; Peter Gill, *Cheltenham Races*, Stroud (Glos.), Sutton Publishing, 1997: 9–20.

[86] Van den Berg and Wachlin, *Album*: 95; *De Locomotief*, 25 Mar. 1870.

[87] Obituary: Captain Arthur Colthurst Herbert, *Gloucestershire Echo*, 30 Oct. 1933.

[88] White, *Daisy in Exile*: 7–29, 188–189; 'Havilah Station (c.1850–)', Unlocking Regional Memory, University of New England Heritage Centre, Armidale, NSW, https://www.nswera.net.au/biogs/UNE0204b.htm, accessed 8 July 2021; *Sydney Morning Herald*, 27 Feb. 1905 (Obituary, Henry Charles White), as reproduced at https://oa.anu.edu.au/obituary/white-henry-charles- 14584, accessed 8 July 2021.

9. Gathering the Clan, Advancing the Empire and the Lure of London

[1] John Patterson MacLean, *Renaissance of the Clan MacLean: Comprising also a History of Dubhaird Caisteal, and the Great Gathering on August 24, 1912: Together with an appendix containing letters of Gen'l Allan MacLean, etc.*, Columbus, OH, F. J. Heer Printing Company, 1913.

[2] Jonathan Hyslop, 'Making Scotland in South Africa: Charles Murray, the Transvaal's Aberdeenshire Poet', in David Lambert and Alan Lester (eds), *Colonial Lives Across the British Empire: Imperial Careering in the Long Nineteenth Century*, Cambridge, Cambridge University Press, 2004: 309–334; Elizabeth Buettner, 'Haggis in the Raj: Private and Public Celebrations of Scottishness in Late Imperial India', *Scottish Historical Review*, 81/2 (2002): 212–239.

[3] Tanja Bueltmann, 'Ethnic Associational Culture in the Scottish Diaspora: Definitions, Approaches and Perspectives', in Bueltmann, *Clubbing Together: Ethnicity, Civility and Formal Sociability in the Scottish Diaspora to 1930*, Liverpool, Liverpool University Press, 2014: 1–26.

[4] cf. Onni Gust, 'Remembering and Forgetting the Scottish Highlands: Sir James Mackintosh and the Forging of a British Imperial Identity', *Journal of British Studies*, 52/3 (2013): 615–637.

[5] See Chapter 4, 'Islay and the Wealth of the Indies.'

[6] Thomas Bonhote to [Alexander] MacNeill, 18 Mar. 1859. Macpherson Papers (in private possession, UK). I am grateful to Mrs Janet and the late Mr Neil Macpherson for access to these papers and for their kind hospitality in Inverness in October 2016.

[7] Neil McLean to Colin McLean, 22 Nov. 1859. Macpherson Papers.

[8] R. E. Elson, *Javanese Peasants and the Colonial Sugar Industry: Impact and Change in an East Java Residency, 1830–1940*, Singapore, Oxford University Press, 1984.

[9] Neil McLean to Colin McLean, Pasuruan, 1 July 1860; Lachlan McLean to Neil McLean, 24 May 1860. Macpherson Papers.

[10] *Almanak van Nederlandsch-Indië voor het jaar 1849*, Batavia, Lands Drukkerij, 1849: 300–302.

[11] Neil McLean to Colin McLean, Pasuruan, 1 July 1860. Macpherson Papers.

[12] Alexander MacNeill to Colin McLean, 13 Aug. 1860. Macpherson Papers.

[13] Obituary: G. H. Miesegaes, *Straits Times*, 30 Apr. 1913; J. de Vries (ed.), *Herinneringen en Dagboek van Ernst Heldring (1871–1954)*, 3 vols, Utrecht, Nederlands Historisch Genootschap, 1970, vol. 2: 1299 (re August Friederich Miesegaes, 1863–1938); Arjen Taselaar, *De Nederlandse koloniale lobby. Ondernemers en de Indische politiek, 1914–1940*, Leiden, Research School CNWS, School of Asian, African, and Amerindian Studies [CNWS Publications, 62], 1998: 61.

[14] Alexander McNeill to Colin McLean, 13 Aug. 1860. Macpherson Papers; P. C. Bloys van Treslong Prins, *Genealogische en Heraldische Gedenkwaardigheden betreffende Europeanen op Java* [hereinafter *GHG*], 4 vols, Batavia, Albrechts/Koninklijke Drukkerij De Unie, 1934–9, vol. 1: 312–313.

[15] *Regerings-almanak voor Nederlandsch-Indië*, Batavia, Lands-Drukkerij, 1846: 305; 1864: 104; 1866: 15; *GHG*, vol. 1: 303.

[16] Gillian Maclaine [hereinafter GM] to Marjorie Maclaine, 14 Jan. 1834. Greenfield MSS.

[17] Neil McLean to Colin McLean, Pasuruan, 1 July 1860. Macpherson Papers.

[18] *De Oostpost*, 4 June 1864.

[19] GM to Marjorie Maclaine, 14 Jan. 1834 Greenfield MSS.

[20] GM to Angus Maclaine, 30 Jan. 1837 Greenfield MSS.

[21] Neil McLean to Anna McLean, 4 June 1860. Macpherson Papers.

[22] *Java-Bode*, 26 Oct. 1874.
[23] 'CarolineM Family Tree', Ancestry.com, accessed 17 Aug. 2021; 1891 Census.
[24] Probate, 1877, McLean, Margaret.
[25] See Chapter 4 : 'Islay and the Wealth of the Indies'.
[26] Probate, 1880, Mclean, Lachlan; *De Locomotief*, 3 Jan. 1880.
[27] Neil McLean to Colin McLean, Batavia, 22 Nov. 1859. Macpherson Papers.
[28] *De Locomotief*, 7 Dec. 1869.
[29] 'Genealogical notes of Roland J. MacNeill (1861–1934)', typescript fragment (undated) in the possession of Mevrouw Elisabeth del Court König-Van Essen in The Hague. I am grateful to Mevrouw del Court König for access to this document.
[30] *Aberdeen Journal*, 16 Apr. 1892.
[31] 'The Moors', *Aberdeen Journal*, 15 Aug. 1893.
[32] *Aberdeen Journal*, 16 Apr. 1892.
[33] Joseph Sharples, David W. Walker and Matthew Woodworth, *Aberdeenshire South and Aberdeen (The Buildings of Scotland)*, New Haven, CT, Yale University Press, 2015: 130–131.
[34] Sharples, Walker and Woodworth, *Aberdeenshire South and Aberdeen*: 394–395; 'Restoration of 12 Windows from Breda House, Alford', Morning Glass, 27 June 2007, www.morningglass.co.uk/news/2007/6/27/restoration-of-12-windows-from-breda-house-alford.html, accessed 15 Nov. 2019.
[35] Jim Fiddes, *The Granite Men: A History of the Granite Industries of Aberdeen and North-East Scotland*, Stroud, The History Press, 2019: 10, 51.
[36] 1901 Census.
[37] 1911 Census.
[38] *Java-Bode*, 28 Apr. 1871.
[39] *Java-Bode*, 23 Dec. 1871, 26 Mar. 1872.
[40] Margot Finn, 'The Female World of Love & Empire: Women, Family & East India Company Politics at the End of the Eighteenth Century', *Gender & History*, 31/1 (2019): 7– 24.
[41] *Aberdeen Journal*, 28 July 1897.
[42] Clare Midgley, 'Bringing the Empire Home: Women Activists in Imperial Britain, 1790s–1930s', in Catherine Hall and Sonya O. Rose (eds), *At Home with the Empire: Metropolitan Culture and the Imperial World*, Cambridge, Cambridge University Press, 2006: 230–250; C. A. Bayly, 'Ireland, India and the Empire: 1780–1914', *Transactions of the Royal Historical Society*, 10 (2000): 377–397.
[43] e.g. 'Primrose League. Central Aberdeen Habitation. Letter from the Prime Minister. Speech by the Lord Chancellor', *Aberdeen Journal*, 27 Aug. 1896.
[44] 'Primrose League Picnic at Balgowan', *Dundee Courier*, 30 Aug. 1888.
[45] *Aberdeen Journal*, 27 Aug. 1896.
[46] Midgley, 'Bringing the Empire Home': 242.
[47] Colin McLean [Jnr] to Isobel McLean, 25 Dec. 1914, in Ian Macpherson, *Colin McLean 1873–1915* [privately printed, Inverness, c.2015]: 36 (copy kindly given to the author by the late Mr Macpherson, October 2016).
[48] Electoral Register, 1939; Probate, 1950, McLean, Godfrey Neil.
[49] J. A. Venn, *Alumni Cantabrigienses*, pt. 2, vol. 4, Cambridge, Cambridge University Press, 1957: 277–278. Probate, 1937, McLean, Lachlan; Passenger Lists Leaving UK (Destination Buenos Aires), 19 Sept. 1936; *Hampstead News*, 7 Oct.1937.

[50] Guy L'Estrange to Margaret L'Estrange née McNeill (1874–1946), 2 Apr. 1935. Crickhowell Papers (in private possession, UK).
[51] *Sumatra Post*, 26 Apr. 1911.
[52] Bevolkingsregister A'dam for Carel Gijsbert de Beus.
[53] *Bataviaasch Handelsblad*, 17 Feb. 1885, 16 Feb. 1885.
[54] *Directory and Chronicle for China, Japan, Corea, Indo-China, Straits Settlements, Netherlands India, Borneo, the Philippines, &c.*, Hong Kong, Hongkong Daily Press Office 1912: 1414.
[55] John O'Brien, *Conflicts of Laws*, 2nd edn, London, Cavendish Publishing, 1999: 68.
[56] *Sumatra Post*, 27 Sept. 1924.
[57] *Het Nieuws van den Dag voor Nederlandsch-Indië*, 18 June 1924, 20 Sept. 1924, 24 Sept. 1924.
[58] Electoral Registers 1926–1929; *The Bystander*, 2 Feb. 1927: *Java Gazette*, June 1934.
[59] *Java Gazette*, Sept. 1932.
[60] *The Sketch*, 22 Aug. 1934; Brett Rogers and Adam Lowe, *Madame Yevonde: Be Original or Die*, London, The British Council, 1998.
[61] *Java Gazette*, Jan. 1935.
[62] *Java Gazette*, Jan. 1935.
[63] *Java Gazette*, Feb. 1935.
[64] *Aberdeen Press and Journal*, 10 and 20 Dec. 1934.
[65] *Weekly Dispatch*, 15 Mar. 1936.
[66] 'Tag Archive: Terence Skeffington-Smyth', *Cocktails With Elvira*, 17 March 2012, https://elvirabarney.wordpress.com/tag/terence-skeffington-smyth, accessed 14 Nov. 2019; D. J. Taylor, *Bright Young People: The Rise and Fall of a Generation*, London, Chatto & Windus, 2007: 2–3, 226–227.
[67] *The Bystander*, 19 June 1935; *Tatler*, 4 Sept. 1935.
[68] *The Bystander*, 1 Jan. 1936.
[69] *Nottingham Evening Post*, 24 Mar. 1936; 'Terence Skeffington-Smyth', Wikipedia, https://en.wikipedia.org/wiki/Terence_Skeffington-Smyth, accessed 14 Nov. 2019; *Straits Times*, 20 Mar. 1936; 'Broadway Mansions', Wikipedia, https://en.wikipedia.org/wiki/Broadway_Mansions, accessed 15 Nov. 2019.
[70] Passenger Lists, California Arrivals, 1936; United States Marriages, 1936, Los Angeles, California, 26 May 1936.
[71] Incoming Passengers, UK, June 1937; Electoral Roll, 1938.
[72] *Aberdeen Press and Journal*, 11 Jan. 1937.
[73] UK Outward Voyages, 1931; 'Eduardo de Crempien', in 'Cadet scandal', Wikipedia, accessed 27 Feb. 2024; New York State Passenger Lists, Oct. 1962.
[74] Outgoing Passengers, UK, 1954, Isobel F. de Crempien.
[75] Electoral Registers, 1939; Probate, 1969, McLean, Catherine Francina E. F; England and Wales Deaths 1837–2007.
[76] *Kent and Sussex Courier*, 30 Aug. 1940.
[77] Probate, 1956, McLean, Loudon MacNeill.
[78] *Vogue*, 15 Apr. 1972: 84.
[79] Probate, 2002, De Crempien, Isobel Florence, 19 Sept. 2002.
[80] Xan Fielding, *One Man in His Time: The Life of Lieutenant-Colonel N. L. D. ('Billy') McLean, DSO*, London, Macmillan, 1990: 2–9 and 146.
[81] 1911 Census.

[82] New York Passenger Lists, 1922.
[83] Electoral Register, 1930.
[84] Fielding, *One Man*: 3.
[85] *Aberdeen Press and Journal*, 21 May 1937.
[86] e.g. the entries for 16 and 18 Sept. 1940 in Simon Heffer (ed.), *Henry 'Chips' Channon: The Diaries 1938–1943*, London, Hutchinson, 2021: 404–408.
[87] Probate, 1964, McLean, Neil Gillean.
[88] Fielding, *One Man*: 146.
[89] Probate, 1969, McLean, Grace Audrey.

10. A House Built from Sugar

[1] Donna Brewster, *The House that Sugar Built*, Wigtown, [GC Books], 1999; Database, Centre for the Study of the Legacies of British Slavery, www.ucl.ac.uk/lbs/claim/view/4441, accessed 11 Feb. 2020.
[2] Brewster, *House*: 90–189.
[3] Brewster, *House*: 190–221.
[4] Mary Miers, *Highland Retreats: The Architecture and Interiors of Scotland's Romantic North*, New York, Rizzoli, 2017: 45–67, 77–93, 126–147.
[5] 'Clifford, Henry Edward', *Dictionary of Scottish Architects 1660–1980*, www.scottisharchitects.org.uk/architect_full.php?id=200235, accessed 11 Aug. 2017.
[6] *Sumatra Courant*, 2 Feb. 1876.
[7] Henri Bernard van Davelaar (1833–1891) and Gijsbertina Maria Starck (1833–1902). See BS Huwelijk 1857 Haags Gemeente Archief; Bevolkingsregisters van de gemeente Nijmegen 1880, Regionaal Archief, https://studiezaal.nijmegen.nl/detail.php?id=2279151740, accessed 1 Jan. 2023; Stamboomonderzoek Uitgebreid onderzoek naar de voorouders van Hans en Mark van Otterlo en aanverwanten, https://jmvanotterlo.nl/002/e10.04.htm, accessed 13 Dec. 2020.
[8] *Amsterdamsch handels- en effectenblad*, 10 Oct. 1859; *Nieuws van den Dag voor Nederlandsch-Indië*, 27 Dec. 1915; *Nieuwe Courant* [Netherlands], 29 Dec. 1915.
[9] *Bataviaasch Nieuwsblad*, 27 June 1896.
[10] *The Scotsman*, 8 July 1911.
[11] 'Etie van Rees', Wikipedia (Dutch edition), https://nl.wikipedia.org/wiki/Etie_van_Rees, accessed 18 Feb. 2020; *Het Louche Maliepaard en Ander Werk van Etie van Rees (1890–1973)*, Leeuwarden, Museum van het Princessehof, 1990.
[12] *Bataviaasch Handelsblad*, 1 Dec. 1894; see Delpher, www.delpher.nl: 8 references to lawn tennis in major Indies newspapers in the 1870s; 130, ditto in 1880s (almost all from 1885 onwards); 925, ditto in the 1890s.
[13] *Bat. Nieuwsblad*, 10 Sept. 1887.
[14] *Soerabaijasch Handelsblad* [hereinafter *SHB*], 3 Apr. 1897.
[15] *SHB*, 10 May 1904; *Nieuws van het Dag voor NI*, 21 Aug. 1905.
[16] e.g. *Bat. Handelsblad*, 1 Dec. 1894.
[17] 'Batavia Lawn Tennis Club/Tennis Tournament . . . 24th November 1888.' Copy of handbill, courtesy of Ann, Lady Crickhowell and the late Lord Crickhowell.
[18] 1881 Census.

[19] *Bat. Nieuwsblad*, 7 Aug. 1888; *Bat. Handelsblad*, 20 Aug. 1890; *De Locomotief*, 10 Apr. 1895; *Bat. Nieuwsblad*, 9 Feb. 1898; India, Select Births and Baptisms, 1786–1947; 1911 Census; Probate, 1946, Robertson, Henriette Anna Philippine.

[20] 'Batavia Lawn Tennis Club/Tennis Tournament . . . 24th November 1888.'

[21] *SHB*, 14 Apr. 1897; See *De Locomotief*, 22 Apr. 1899.

[22] *SHB*, 3 Apr. 1897.

[23] 1901 Census.

[24] George Roche, *Childhood in India: Tales from Sholapur* (ed. Richard Terrell), London, I.B. Tauris, 1994: 20–21, as quoted in Elizabeth Buettner, *Empire Families: Britons and Late Imperial India*, Oxford: Oxford University Press, 2004: 199.

[25] 'Queen Anne's Mansions', Wikipedia, https://en.wikipedia.org/wiki/Queen_Anne%27s_Mansions, accessed 1 Mar. 2020; S. E. Mangeot, 'Queen Anne's Mansions: The Story of "Hankey's Folly"', *Architect & Building News*, 13 Jan. 1939: 77–79.

[26] 1911 Census.

[27] Kerr-McNeill 21 Apr. 1906, St Johns-at-Hampstead, London, England, Church of England Marriages and Banns, 1754–1938.

[28] *Illustrated Sporting and Dramatic News*, 19 Oct. 1907.

[29] A. G. Austin (ed.), *The Webbs' Australian Diary 1898*, Melbourne, Pitman, 1965: 106–107; David Dunstan, 'McEacharn, Sir Malcolm Donald (1852–1910)', *Australian Dictionary of Biography*, vol. 10, Melbourne, Melbourne University Press, 1986: 263–264, https://adb.anu.edu.au/biography/mceacharn-sir-malcolm-donald-7350, accessed 21 Sept. 2024.

[30] Louise Carpenter, *An Unlikely Countess: Lily Budge and the 13th Earl of Galloway*, London, Harper Perennial, 2005: 30–32.

[31] P. E. Razzell, 'Social Origins of Officers in the British Indian and British Home Army, 1758–1962', *British Journal of Sociology*, 14 (1963): 248–260, at 259.

[32] *The Scotsman*, 10 Nov. 1930.

[33] MacNeill, William Loudon (Wills and testaments Reference SC19/41/33, Wigtown Sheriff Court), 1924: 55–75, ScotlandsPeople, www.scotlandspeople.gov.uk, accessed 24 Apr. 2021.

[34] *Berwickshire News and General Advertiser*, 11 Nov.1930.

[35] https://en.wikipedia.org/wiki/Sir_Herbert_Maxwell,_7th_Baronet, accessed 9 June 2023.

[36] *Berwickshire News and General Advertiser* 11 Nov. 1930; *The Scotsman*, 10 Nov. 1930.

[37] Gillian Maclaine to Hector Maclaine, 8 Feb. 1837. Greenfield MSS.

[38] Peter Christiaans, 'Een Schotse Familie in Indie: Gegevens voor de samenstelling van een genealogie van de Indische tak van de familie Mac Neill', unpublished MSS [c.2012] in possession of the author. Christiaans cites Neil Cameron, 'MacNeils of Ardnacross and Islay', *Scottish Genealogist*, 27 (1980): 115–117, and A. I. B. Stewart, 'MacNeils of Ardnacross', *Scottish Genealogist*, 30 (1983): 14–15.

[39] Daniel Maudlin, 'Tradition and Change in the Age of Improvement: A Study of Argyll Tacksmen's Houses in Morvern', *Proceedings of the Society of Antiquaries of Scotland*, 133 (2003), 360–366.

[40] *Dumfries and Galloway Standard and Advertiser*, 7 Sept. 1918.

[41] MacIndoe-Kerr, 1921 UK, Foreign and Overseas Registers of British Subjects, 1628–1969.

[42] *Surrey Advertiser*, 4 Apr. 1942, 28 Nov. 1942 and 29 Apr. 1944.

[43] *Surrey Advertiser*, 22 July 1939.

[44] Robert Gourlay MacIndoe on *Rootsweb*; Probate 1967 MacIndoe, Robert Gourlay.

⁴⁵ 1861 Scotland Census.
⁴⁶ *Edinburgh Evening News*, 3 Nov. 1875.
⁴⁷ 1891 and 1901 Censuses.
⁴⁸ 'John McKenzie', Legacies of British Slave-ownership Database, http://wwwdepts-live.ucl.ac.uk/lbs/person/view/8598, accessed 22 Sept. 2019.
⁴⁹ 1851, 1861, 1881, and 1891 Censuses; Register . . . Deaths at Sea 1844–1890; Roll of Indian Medical Service 1515–1930; conversations with Michael and Charlie McNeill, 8 and 9 Sept. 2019.
⁵⁰ *Dundee Evening Telegraph*, 13 Apr. 1935; *The Scotsman*, 13 Apr. 1935.
⁵¹ 'Argrennan House', Historic Environment Scotland, https://portal.historicenvironment.scot/designation/LB17114, accessed 8 June 2023.
⁵² *Dumfries and Galloway Standard*, 28 June 1939; 'Lidderdale and Gillespie' and 'Hope, Todd & Kirk', in *National Records of Scotland* (formerly *National Archives of Scotland*), *National Archives* [UK], https://discovery.nationalarchives.gov.uk/details/a/A13533032 and https://discovery.nationalarchives.gov.uk/details/a/A13531995, accessed 8 June 2023.; *The Scotsman*, 25 Sept. 1911.
⁵³ MacNeill, 1924 (NRS, SC19/41/33).
⁵⁴ *Dumfries and Galloway Standard*, 28 June 1939.
⁵⁵ Interview, Charlie MacNeill, Shennanton Sawmill, 9 Sept. 2019.
⁵⁶ e.g. *Southern Reporter*, 26 Jan. 1928.
⁵⁷ *Dumfries and Galloway Standard*, 12 Apr. 1939 and 28 June 1939.
⁵⁸ Richard Griffiths, *What Did You Do in the War? The Last Throes of the British Pro-Nazi Right, 1940–45*, New York, Routledge, 2017: 172–191, 329–330; Richard Griffiths, *Patriotism Perverted: Captain Ramsay, the Right Club, and British Anti-Semitism, 1939–1940*, London, Faber & Faber, 2015: 150–154.
⁵⁹ *Dumfries and Galloway Standard*, 21 Mar. 1945.
⁶⁰ Probate 1955, MacNeill, Neil.
⁶¹ Information from Mr Michael MacNeill, Galloway, 8 Sept. 2019.

11. Upper Deck and *Indisch*

¹ *De Locomotief*, 24 Jan. 1890; *Java-Bode* [hereinafter *JB*], 30 Jan. 1890.
² Harald Fischer-Tiné and Susanne Gehrmann, 'Empires, Boundaries and the Production of Difference', in Fischer-Tiné and Gehrmann (eds), *Empires and Boundaries: Rethinking Race, Class, and Gender in Colonial Settings*, New York, Routledge, 2009: 1–22, at 4.
³ Tim Harper, 'The British "Malayans"', in Robert Bickers (ed.), *Settlers and Expatriates: Britons over the Seas*, Oxford History of the British Empire, Companion Series, Oxford, Oxford University Press, 2010: 233–268, at 257; J. G. Butcher, *The British in Malaya, 1880–1941: The Social History of a European Community in Colonial South-East Asia*, Kuala Lumpur, Oxford University Press, 1979: 186–187.
⁴ H. H. Risley and E. A. Gait, *Census of India, 1901*, vol. 1: *India*, pt. 1: *Report*, Calcutta, Superintendent of Government Printing, 1903: 393.
⁵ Petra Boudewijn, '"You Must Have Inherited This Trait from Your Eurasian Mother": The Representation of Mixed-race Characters in Dutch Colonial Literature', *Dutch Crossing*, 40/3

(2016): 239–260; Ann Laura Stoler, 'Re-thinking Colonial Categories: European Communities and the Boundaries of Rule', *Comparative Studies in Society and History*, 31 (1989): 134–161; Stoler, 'Sexual Affronts and Racial Frontiers: European Identities and the Cultural Politics of Exclusion in Colonial Asia', *Comparative Studies in Society and History*, 34 (1992): 514–551.

[6] A. van Marle, 'De Groep der Europeanen in Nederlands-Indië, Iets over Ontstaan en Groei', *Indonesië*, 5 (1951–2): 97–121, 314–341, 481–507.

[7] Donald Maclaine Campbell, *Java: Past and Present: A Description of the Most Beautiful Country in the World, Its Ancient History, People, Antiquities, and Products*, 2 vols, London, Heinemann, 1915, vol. 2: 984, fn. 1.

[8] See Chapter 5: 'Death in Bournemouth and a Surrogate Scotland.'

[9] I am grateful to Dr Henri Chambert-Loir for the suggestion that 'Sienok' is most probably a variant of 'Si Nok, Sinok', a Javanese term of endearment for a little girl, something like 'la petite' or 'the little one'.

[10] McNeill, Alexander (Wills and testaments Reference SC42/20/8, Peebles Sheriff Court), 1867: 34–70, ScotlandsPeople, www.scotlandspeople.gov.uk, accessed 21 Sept. 2024.

[11] W. Wijnaendts van Resandt, 'De Indische tak van de familie Couperus (uitgestorven in 1940)', *De Indische Navorscher* (new series), 5 (1992): 1–8.

[12] G. Roger Knight, *Sugar, Steam and Steel: The Industrial Project in Colonial Java, 1830–1885*, Adelaide, University of Adelaide Press, 2014.

[13] *JB* 28 Nov. 1882.

[14] *JB*, 26 May 1884.

[15] *The First One Hundred Years, 1827–1927, of Maclaine Watson & Co., McNeill & Co. and Fraser Easton & Co.* [n.p., n.d., Batavia, 1927]: 14.

[16] *JB*, 27 Dec. 1886; *Bataviaasch Nieuwsblad*, 12 May 1890; Margaret Leidelmeijer, *Van suikermolen tot grootbedrijf. Technische vernieuwing in de Java-suikerindustrie in de negentiende eeuw*, Amsterdam, Amsterdam University Press, 1997: 231–248.

[17] *Soerabaijasch Handelsblad* [hereinafter *SHB*], 12 Dec. 1882; G. H. von Faber, *Oud Soerabaia. De geschiedenis van Indië's eerste koopstad van de oudste tijden tot de instelling van den gemeenteraad (1906)*, Surabaya, Gemeente Soerabaia, 1931: 170–177.

[18] Louis Couperus's novel *De Boeken der Kleine Zielen* [The Book of the Small Souls] was written in 1901–1902 and published in stages between 1901 and 1903. I have used here the translation [1914–18] of part one by Alexander Teixeira de Mattos, reprinted by Amazon [2017] as part of *Louis Couperus, Collection Novels*. The passage referred to appears on page 137 of this edition; Vilan van der Loo, 'Mensen, Straten en Gebeurtenissen. Zoals Verbeeld in de Haags-Indische Letteren Rond 1900', in Esther Captain, Maartje de Haan and Pim Westerkamp (eds), *De Indische Zomer in Den Haag: Het Cultureel Erfgoed Van de Indische Hoofdstad*, Leiden, KITLV, 2005: 127–158.

[19] Maarten van Doorn, *Het leven gaat er een lichten gang. Den Haag in de jaren 1919–1940*, Zwolle, Waanders, 2002: 39–52; Coos Versteeg, 'Er is maar een echte Indische buurt', in Captain, *Indische Zomer*: 23–40.

[20] Suzanne de Graaf, '"Iets van een Vreemde Vrucht": Indische Verlofgangers in Nederland, 1919–1939', MA thesis, Leiden University, 2009.

[21] Harry A. Poeze, *In het land van de overheerser. Deel I: Indonesiërs in Nederland 1600–1950*, Dordrecht, Foris Publications, 1986: 236–238.

[22] *Nederlandsche Staatscourant*, 15 Nov. 1890.

[23] Information kindly supplied to the author by the membership secretary of De Witte [email, 23 Nov. 2017].

[24] A search [15 Aug. 2018] of the *Ledenlijsten* (a) of the Surabaya '*Vriendschap*' Lodge for the decade of the 1880s (b) of both Lodges extant in The Hague 1890–1915 at Het Cultureel Maçonniek Centrum 'Prins Frederik', The Hague, produced no evidence of Richard Mac Neill's membership. I am grateful for their assistance to the Maçonniek Centrum's Jac. Piepenbrock, and to Tom van den Berg, University of Leiden.

[25] Richard Mac Neill and Family, The Hague, c.1904. Top row left to right: Elisabeth Mac Neill (daughter) Dick Mac Neill (grandson) Folkerus van der Weijde (son-in-law) Georgette Mac Neill-Sluijter (daughter) Euphemia Sluijter (granddaughter) Johan Sluijter (son-in-law) Gijsbert Tienhoven van den Bogaard (son-in-law) Johanna Mac Neil- Bezoet de Bie (daughter-in-law) Wilhelmina Mac Neill (daughter) Alexander Mac Neill (son). Middle row left to right: Willem van der Weijde (grandson) Catherina Mac Neill-Van der Weijde (daughter) Richard Mac Neill (paterfamilias) Arabella Mac Neill-Tienhoven van den Bogaard (daughter). Front row: Richard van der Weijde (grandson) John Mac Neill (grandson) Bella Tienhoven van den Bogaard (granddaughter).

[26] Arjen Taselaar, *De Nederlandse Koloniale Lobby: Ondernemers en de Indische Politiek, 1914–1940*, Leiden, Research School CNWS, School of Asian, African, and Amerindian Studies [CNWS Publications, 62], 1998: 31–98.

[27] *Handboek voor cultuur- en handelsondernemingen in Nederlandsch-Indië* [hereinafter *HCHO*], Amsterdam, J. H. de Bussy, 1888–1940, vol. 5 (1892–3): 500n; Taselaar, *Koniale Lobby*: 77; G. Roger Knight, *Commodities and Colonialism: The Story of Big Sugar in Indonesia, 1880–1942*, Leiden, Brill, 2013: 125–126.

[28] *Bat. Nieuwsblad*, 17 Feb. 1894; *HCHO*, 15 (1903): 579.

[29] 'Cambier', *Nederland's Patriciaat: Genealogieën van Bekende Geslachten*, The Hague, Centraal Bureau voor Genealogie, 1910–, vol. 8 (1917): 88–94.

[30] 'Van Tienhoven', *Nederland's Patriciaat: Genealogieën van Bekende Geslachten*, The Hague, Centraal Bureau voor Genealogie, 1910–, vols 8 (1917): 322–326, and 47 (1962): 320–326; *Algemeen Handelsblad*, 13 Aug. 1889; *De Tijd*, 25 Dec. 1891; *Alg. Handelsblad*, 16 June 1892'; *Alg. Handlesblad*, 17 Nov. 1892; *Alg. Handelsblad*, 23 July 1897; *Ned. Staatscourant*, 9 July 1898; 'Vereenigde Glasfabrieken', Wikipedia (Dutch edition), https://nl.wikipedia.org/wiki/Vereenigde_Glasfabrieken, accessed 14 Aug. 2017; *Alg. Handelsblad*, 5 July 1912; *Alg. Handelsblad*, 15 Feb. 1919; 'Gijsbert van Tienhoven', Wikipedia, https://en.wikipedia.org/wiki/Gijsbert_van_Tienhoven, accessed 14 June 2023.

[31] *Nieuwe Rotterdamsche Courant*, 10 Apr. 1919.

[32] *Alg. Handelsblad*, 19 Aug. 1944.

[33] *De Telegraaf*, 5 Oct. 1915.

[34] *Alg. Handelsblad*, 18 Feb. 1897.

[35] Wijnaendts van Resandt, 'Familie Couperus': 6.

[36] *De Locomotief*, 8 Jan. 1898.

[37] G. Roger Knight, 'Gully Coolies, Weed-Women and *Snijvolk*: The Sugar Industry Workers of North Java in the Early Twentieth Century', *Modern Asian Studies*, 28/1 (1994): 51–76.

[38] Nationaal Archief, The Hague [hereinafter NA]: 2.20.02.03, Archief Cultuurmaatschappij Wonolangan.

[39] Peter A. Christiaans, 'Bezoet de Bie', *De Indische Navorscher*, Jaarboek 21 (2008): 134–140.
[40] Personal communication, Mevrouw Elizabeth del Court Konig van Essen, The Hague, June 2017. (Johanna Mac Neill-Bezoet de Bie was Mevrouw del Court's great-aunt.)
[41] C. M. Vissering, *Een reis door Oost-Java*, Haarlem, Boon, 1912: 78.
[42] Vissering, *Oost-Java*: 178.
[43] NA, Oost-Indische Besluiten, 2.10.30, no. 8377, 1906; 1871 and 1901 Censuses.
[44] *Bat. Nieuwsblad*, 13 July 1903, 5 Apr. 1904.
[45] *Nieuw Adresboek van Geheel Nederlandsch-Indië*, Batavia, Landsdrukkerij, 1903–1930.
[46] A. James Hammerton, *Emigrant Gentlewomen: Genteel Poverty and Female Emigration, 1830–1914*, London, Croom Helm, 1979: 148–186; Kathryn Hughes, *The Victorian Governess*, London, Hambledon Press, 1993: xv–xvi.
[47] Christiaans, 'Bezoet de Bie': 136–137.
[48] NA, Stamboeken Marine, 1813–1940, 2 Dec. 1914, inv. nr. 41. I am grateful to Mrs Debora Luther for kindly supplying crucial information about her Van der Weijde ancestors.
[49] Ulbe Bosma, *Indiëgangers. Verhalen van Nederlanders die naar Indië trokken*, Amsterdam, Bert Bakker, 2010: 87; [H. Ch. C. J. van der Mandere], 'De cultuurmaatschappij Wonolangan (1895–1925)', *Indië. Geïllustreerd tijdschrift voor Nederland en Koloniën*, 9/19 (Dec. 1925): 306–340; Leonard Robinson (with a Foreword by Tom Etty), *William Etty: The Life and Art*, Jefferson, NC, McFarland, 2007: 310; *HCHO*, 6 (1893–4): 222, 434-444; *SHB*, 17 Oct. 1895; P. C. Bloys van Treslong Prins, *Genealogische en Heraldische Gedenkwaardigheden betreffende Europeanen op Java*, 4 vols, Batavia, Albrechts/Koninklijke Drukkerij De Unie, 1934–9, vol. 1: 370–371; *SHB*, 17 Oct. 1895.
[50] G. Roger Knight, 'A Sugar Factory and its Swimming Pool: Incorporation and Differentiation in Colonial Java', *Ethnic and Racial Studies*, 24/3 (2001): 451–471.
[51] *Indische Courant*, 16 Apr. 1935; *SHB*, 11 May 1933.
[52] My thanks to Jac. Piepenbrock of Het Cultureel Maconniek Centrum 'Prins Frederik', The Hague, for kindly facilitating access to archival materials relating to the historic membership of the Veritas lodge and to Dr Tom van den Berge, formerly of the KITLV, Leiden, for his sage advice and assistance in this, as in so many other respects.
[53] *Indische Courant*, 11 Jan. 1928; L. Th. Vossenaar, 'Herinnerigen en Mijmeringen over Herinneringen', Leiden, Koninklijk Instituut voor Taal-, Land- en Volkenkunde [KITLV], H 852.
[54] Wijnaendts van Resandt, 'Familie Couperus': 6.
[55] 'Paul Antoine Renardel de Lavalette', *Geni*, https://www.geni.com/people/Paul-Antoine-Renardel-de-Lavalette/6000000060824446927, accessed 6 July 2023; 'Parenteel Gebhard, Ternate (Nederlands-Indië)', *Homepage of Henri van Asten and Irene Gerverdinck*. http://daktari.antenna.nl/gebhard.htm, accessed 6 July 2023.
[56] 'Abraham Eliza Soesman', *Geneanet*, https://gw.geneanet.org/mmeisenbacher?lang=&n=soesman&oc=0&p=abraham+eliza, accessed 6 July 2023.
[57] Caroline Drieënhuizen, 'Objects, Nostalgia and the Dutch Colonial Elite in Times of Transition ca.1900–1970', *Bijdragen tot de Taal-, Land-en Volkenkunde*, 170 (2014): 504–529, at 509.
[58] *Nieuws van den Dag*, 25 Oct. 1911.
[59] 'Wilhelm van der Weijde (1898–1959)', www.genealogieonline.nl/genealogie-weits/I3529. php.
[60] Dolf Welling, *Floris Arntzenius*, The Hague, Heemhave Holding BV/Van Voorst van Beest Galerie, 1992: 16.

[61] G. Roger Knight 'An "Indies" Couple: Colonial Communities and Issues Surrounding Identity in the Dutch East Indies, ca. 1890–1930s', *Archipel*, 99 (2020): 153–188, at 182–184.

[62] *Sumatra Post*, 3 June 1920.

[63] A. Mac Neill, 'Mechanische grondbewerking met den kabelploeg der firma John Fowler & Co., met illust.', *Archief voor de suikerindustrie NI*, 1923, no. 1: 343–367.

[64] Henk Schulte Nordholt (ed.), *Het dagelijks leven in Indië 1937–1947. Brieven van O. Schulte Nordholt-Zielhuis*, Zutphen, Walburg Pers, 1999: 9–11.

[65] *Indische Courant*, 20 May 1937.

12. Expatriates and Survivors

[1] *Soerabaijasche Handelsblad* [hereinafter *SHB*], 14 Oct. 1940.

[2] Steven Henry Roberson, *Lili Kraus: Hungarian Pianist, Texas Teacher, and Personality Extraordinaire*, Fort Worth, TX, TCU Press, 2000.

[3] *Aberdeen Press and Journal* [hereafter *APJ*], 2 Feb. 1923.

[4] For Clark, see the obituary in *APJ*, 25 Feb. 1930 (Obituary: 'Captain Ian Clark'); 'Planters Registry', History of Ceylon Tea, www.historyofceylontea.com/tea-planters/planters-registry, accessed 8 Jun. 2023.

[5] *APJ*, 17 Jul. 1923.

[6] 'Alford Death', *APJ*, 18 Mar. 1975.

[7] J. A. Venn, *Alumni Cantabrigienses*, pt. 2, vol. 4 Cambridge, Cambridge University Press, 1957: 277–278; Probate, 1937, McLean, Lachlan, and e.g. Passenger Lists Leaving UK (Destination Buenos Aires), 19 Sept. 1936.

[8] I am grateful for this information to Dr Genny Silvanus, College Archivist and Records Manager, Corpus Christi College, University of Cambridge; 1921 Census.

[9] *Het Nieuws van den Dag*, 2 May 1927; *Bataviaasch Nieuwsblad*, 2 May 1927.

[10] Howard W. Dick, *Surabaya, City of Work: A Socioeconomic History, 1900–2000*, Athens, OH, Ohio University Press, 2002: 52.

[11] Dick, *Surabaya*: 253–280.

[12] G. H. von Faber, *Nieuw Soerabaia. De geschiedenis van Indië's voornaamste koopstad in de eerste kwarteeuw sedert hare instelling 1906–1931*, Surabaya, Van Ingen, 1937: 35; Dick, *Surabaya*: 414–425.

[13] Faber, *Nieuw Soerabaia*: 35.

[14] Faber, *Nieuw Soerabaia*; Sophie Junge, 'Old Soerabaja—New Soerabaja? Circulating the Emptiness of the Colonial City', *PhotoResearcher*, 30 (2018): 48–62.

[15] Johny A. Khusyairi and Freek Colombijn, 'Moving at a Different Velocity: The Modernization of Transportation and Social Differentiation in Surabaya in the 1920s', in Freek Colombijn and Joost Coté (eds), *Cars, Conduits, and Kampongs: The Modernization of the Indonesian City, 1920–1960*, Leiden, Brill, 2015: 251–271.

[16] Joshua Chia Yeong Jia, 'Whiteaway Laidlaw', Singapore Infopedia, National Library Board Singapore, www.nlb.gov.sg/main/article-detail?cmsuuid=a3edc99d-1cfc-46d6-9198-cfc4bd51edda, accessed 8 Nov. 2025.

[17] Faber, *Nieuw Soerabaia*: 37.

[18] Faber, *Nieuw Soerabaia*: 37; *Bat. Nieuwsblad*, 13 May 1932. For his parentage see 1861, 1901 and 1911 Censuses. I am grateful for information about the Revd Cribb kindly supplied by his distant descendant, Professor Robert Cribb of the Australian National University.

[19] *Nieuws van den Dag voor Nederlandsch-Indië*, 22 Sept. 1930; *SHB*, 1 June 1931.
[20] For example, the pages of the contemporaneous *Java Gazette* (see below) are replete with instances of the term's use.
[21] Khusyairi and Colombijn, 'Moving at a Different Velocity': 261.
[22] e.g. Henk Schulte Nordholt (ed.), *Het dagelijks leven in Indië 1937–1947: Brieven van O. Schulte Nordholt-Zielhuis*, Zutphen, Walburg Pers, 1999: 9–10.
[23] *Nieuws van den Dag*, 12 May 1937; *SHB*, 13 May 1937.
[24] Malcolm Falkus, *The Blue Funnel Legend: A History of the Ocean Steam Ship Company, 1865–1973*, Basingstoke, Macmillan, 1990: 207.
[25] e.g. *Java Gazette*, July 1935.
[26] Elizabeth Buettner, *Empire Families: Britons and Late Imperial India*, Oxford, Oxford University Press, 2004: 110–145.
[27] Antoinette de Coningh, 'A European Woman's Life in Java', *Java Gazette*, Nov. 1932.
[28] *SHB*, 23 June 1939; *Indische Courant*, 2 Feb. 1935.
[29] *Nieuws van den Dag*, 19 May 1925.
[30] *Nieuws van den Dag*, 24 Feb. 1939.
[31] 'Vertrek G. J. D. R. Cruden. Vooraanstaand Lid der Britische Gemeente', *SHB*, 23 Mar. 1939; Incoming/Outgoing Passenger Lists under 'Cruden' for 1922, 1927, 1928, 1930, 1934 and 1938; *Bat. Nieuwsblad*, 2 Feb. 1935; *Algemeen Handelsblad NI*, 19 Feb. 1935; *SHB*, 29 Apr. 1935; *Indische Courant*, 19 Apr. 1936; *SHB*, 15 Jan. 1938; *SHB*, 23 Mar. 1939.
[32] *APJ*, 6 Jan. 1930; *Sumatra Post*, 22 Feb. 1930; *Java Gazette*, May 1933; *APJ*, 25 Nov. 1935; New York Passenger Arrivals from UK, 22 Dec. 1938; *Nieuws van den Dag*, 13 Jan. 1939.
[33] *Java Gazette*, May 1935; *APJ*, 20 June 1935, 22 July 1935.
[34] Guy L'Estrange to [his mother] Margaret L'Estrange née MacNeill (1874–1946), 2 Apr. 1935. Crickhowell Papers (in private possession, UK). I am deeply grateful to Lady Ann Crickhowell and the late Lord Nicolas Crickhowell for granting me access to these papers.
[35] Edward Lydall (Betty Lydall's cousin), *Enough of Action*, London, Jonathan Cape, 1949: 77.
[36] 'Charles Hawthorne Lydall', Grace's Guide To British Industrial History, www.gracesguide.co.uk/Charles_Hawthorne_Lydall, accessed 19 Aug. 2024.
[37] Robin Jackson, 'The Origins of Camphill: The Haughtons of Williamston, Part 1: Theodore Haughton' Camphill Research Network, 2019, https://research.camphill.edu/wp-content/uploads/2019/12/The-Origins-of-Camphill-1-R-Jackson-1.pdf, accessed 29 Nov 2023; Robin Jackson, 'The origins of Camphill: The Haughtons of Williamston, Part 2: Emily Haughton', Camphill Research Network, 2019, https://research.camphill.edu/wp-content/uploads/2019/12/The-Origins-of-Camphill-2-R-Jackson-1.pdf, accessed 29 Nov. 2023.
[38] *APJ*, 25 Nov. 1935.
[39] *APJ*, 16 Dec. 1935.
[40] Robin Jackson, 'The Origins of Camphill: The Haughtons of Williamston, Part 1: Theodore Haughton' Camphill Research Network, 2019, https://research.camphill.edu/wp-content/uploads/2019/12/The-Origins-of-Camphill-1-R-Jackson-1.pdf, accessed 29 Nov 2023; Robin Jackson, 'The origins of Camphill: The Haughtons of Williamston, Part 2: Emily Haughton', Camphill Research Network, 2019, https://research.camphill.edu/wp-content/uploads/2019/12/The-Origins-of-Camphill-2-R-Jackson-1.pdf, accessed 29 Nov. 2023.
[41] *APJ*, 6 Jan. 1930.
[42] *APJ*, 16 Dec. 1935.

[43] *APJ*, 12 Dec. 1935.

[44] John Darwin, *Unlocking the World: Port Cities and Globalization in the Age of Steam, 1830–1930*, London, Allen Lane, 2020: 333–341.

[45] J. A. de Moor, '"A Very Unpleasant Relationship": Trade and Strategy in the Eastern Seas: Anglo-Dutch Relations in the Nineteenth Century from a Colonial Perspective', in C. J. A. Raven and N. A. M. Rodger (eds), *Navies and Armies: The Anglo-Dutch Relationship in War and Peace, 1688–1988*, Edinburgh, John Donald, 1990: 49–69.

[46] Heather Streets-Salter, *World War One in Southeast Asia: Colonialism and Anticolonialism in an Era of Global Conflict*, Cambridge, Cambridge University Press, 2017: 95.

[47] Streets-Salter, *World War One*: 88–141; Kees van Dijk, *The Netherlands Indies in the Great War, 1914–1918*, Leiden, KITLV Press, 2007: 317–352.

[48] Dijk, *Netherlands Indies*: 221.

[49] Nicholas Tarling, '"A Vital British Interest": Britain, Japan, and the Security of Netherlands India in the Inter-War Period', *Journal of Southeast Asian Studies*, 9/2 (1978): 180–218, at 187–188.

[50] *Java Gazette*, Sept. 1933.

[51] *Java Gazette*, Dec. 1937.

[52] *Java Gazette*, Dec. 1935.

[53] Faber, *Nieuw Soerabaia*: 35; Howard Dick, 'Japan's Economic Expansion in the Netherlands Indies between the First and Second World Wars', *Journal of Southeast Asian Studies*, 20/2 (1989): 244–272, at 251.

[54] Peter Post, '*Indonesianisasi* and Japanization: The Japanese and the Shifting Fortunes of *Pribumi* Entrepreneurship', in J. Thomas Lindblad and Peter Post (eds), *Indonesian Economic Decolonisation in Regional and International Perspective*, Leiden, KITLV Press, 2009: 59–86, at 60.

[55] Dick, 'Japan's Economic Expansion': 251.

[56] Sevinc Carlson, *Indonesia's Oil*, Boulder, CO, Westview Press, 1977, reprint, New York, Routledge, 2018: 14 (Table 1: Proven Oil Reserves in Selected Countries).

[57] Neil Malcolm McLean and Elizabeth Hawthorne McLean, *Normandie*, Arrival New York from UK 22 Dec. 1938, Passenger Lists; Neil M. McLean, *Deutschland*, 6 Jan. 1939, UK Arrivals Passenger Lists; *Nieuws van den Dag*, 13 Jan. 1939.

[58] e.g. *SHB*, 2 Dec. 1940, 3 Feb. 1940, 10 Feb. 1940, 5 Mar. 1940, 11 June 1941.

[59] Albert E. Kersten and Marijke van Faassen, 'Goodbye Mr Churchill', in Nigel Ashton and Duco Hellema (eds), *Unspoken Allies: Anglo-Dutch Relations since 1780*, Amsterdam, Amsterdam University Press, 2001: 155–178, at 156.

[60] Hubertus van Mook, *Netherlands Indies and Japan: Their Relations, 1940–1941*, London, George Allen & Unwin, 1944: 7–8, 14–15, 112–113.

[61] *SHB*, 16 June 1939.

[62] Justin Corfield, *Historical Dictionary of Ho Chi Minh City*, London, Anthem Press, 2013: 171; *Edinburgh Gazette*, 7 July 1899; *SHB*, 5 Feb. 1941.

[63] See under Katherine de Montclos in M. J. Girard Family Tree; Probate, 1965, Meiklereid, Ernest William Frederick.

[64] *SHB*, 29 Aug. 1941.

[65] *SHB*, 14 Oct. 1940.

[66] Roberson, *Kraus*: 65.

[67] e.g. *Bat. Nieuwsblad*, 6 May 1940 and 11 Oct. 1941.

68 Tarling, '"A Vital British Interest'": 180–218; Dick, 'Japan's Economic Expansion'; Nicholas Tarling, *Britain, Southeast Asia and the Onset of the Pacific War*, Cambridge, Cambridge University Press, 1996; Antony Best, *Britain, Japan and Pearl Harbor: Avoiding War in East Asia, 1936–41*, London, Routledge, 1995; Frances Gouda, *American Visions of the Netherlands East Indies/Indonesia*, Amsterdam, Amsterdam University Press, 2002.

69 *Bat. Nieuwsblad*, 3 Feb. 1942.

70 Dick, *Surabaya*: 74–75.

71 *Indische Courant*, 25 Oct. 1940; Diane Collins, 'Robert Pikler (1909–1984)', *Australian Dictionary of Biography*, vol. 18, Melbourne, Melbourne University Press, 2012, https://adb.anu.edu.au/biography/pikler-robert-15463, accessed 19 Aug. 2024.

72 Roberson, *Kraus*: 54, 70–93.

73 Roberson, *Kraus*: 96–99.

74 New Orleans Passenger Lists 1813–1963. Arrivals United States/SS *Tjinegara*, 19 Apr. 1942.

75 For the reconstruction in this and the following paragraph, see: Neil Malcolm McLean, Archive Reference WO417/004, Forces War Records, www.forces-war-records.co.uk; 'Mukaishima (Hiroshima 4) Prisoner of War Camp', Mansell POW Resources, www.mansell.com/pow_resources/camplists/hiroshima/Hiro_4_mukaishima/mukaishima.html (especially the Forbes Diary extracts); POW Research Network Japan, www.powresearch.jp/en/archive/camplist/index.html. For events in Amboina, December 1941–February 1942, see 'Battle of Ambon', Wikipedia, https://en.wikipedia.org/wiki/Battle_of_Ambon, accessed 27 Sept. 2019.

76 Michael Sturma, 'Japanese Treatment of Allied Prisoners During the Second World War: Evaluating the Death Toll', *Journal of Contemporary History*, 55/3 (2020): 514–534.

77 Border Crossing Canada to USA, 1946, Neil Malcolm McLean; UK and Ireland, Incoming Passenger Lists, 1878–1960, 1947, Neil Malcolm McLean.

78 *De Vrij Pers*, 16 Apr. 1951; *Nieuwe Courant*, 2 May 1951.

79 *APJ*, 10 Sept. 1971.

80 *Nieuwsblad voor Sumatra*, 3 Dec. 1951.

81 J. Thomas Lindblad, 'British Business and the Uncertainties of Early Independence in Indonesia', *Itinerario*, 37/2 (2013): 147–164; Nicholas J. White, 'Surviving Sukarno: British Business in Post-Colonial Indonesia, 1950–1967', *Modern Asian Studies*, 46/5 (2012): 1277–1315; Bambang Purwanto, 'Economic decolonization and the rise of Indonesian military business', in J. Thomas Lindblad and Peter Post (eds), *Indonesian Economic Decolonization in Regional and International Perspective*, Leiden, KITLV Press, 2009: 39–58; William A. Redfern, 'Sukarno's Guided Democracy and the Takeovers of Foreign Companies in Indonesia in the 1960s', PhD thesis, University of Michigan, Ann Arbor, MI, 2010.

Bibliography

Manuscript and Archival Sources

Arsip Bank Indonesia, Jakarta, De Javasche Bank Archive.

Crickhowell Papers, in private possession, UK.

Cultureel Maçonniek Centrum 'Prins Frederik', The Hague, Ledenlijsten.

Gemeentearchief, Gouda, Burgerlijke Stand.
Gemeentearchief, The Hague, Burgerlijke Stand; Huwelijksregister.
Gemeentearchief, Wedde, Huwelijksregister.

Gloucestershire Archives, Gloucester, Osborne-Maclaine MSS.

Greenfield Papers, in private possession (National Records of Scotland, NRAS1285).

Koninklijk Instituut voor Taal-, Land- en Volkenkunde [KITLV], Leiden, H 52.

Macpherson Papers, in private possession, UK.

Nationaal Archief [NA], The Hague
   Archief Cultuurmaatschappij Wonolangan.
   Archief James Loudon.
   Archief Ministerie van Koloniën.
   Archief Nederlandsche Handel-Maatschappij.
   Stamboeken Marine.

National Archives, Kew (UK)
   Court of Chancery, Clerks of Records and Writs Office.
   Former British Colonial Dependencies, Slave Registers, 1813–1834.
   Foreign Office Records.

National Records of Scotland [NRS], Edinburgh
Wills and Testaments.

School of Oriental and African Studies [SOAS], University of London
Mackinnon Papers.

Stadsarchief Amsterdam
Archief Handelshuis Van Eeghen.
Bevolkingsregister.

Stadsarchief Rotterdam, Adresboeken.

State Records of South Australia, Adelaide.

Government and Official Publications

Almanak van Nederlandsch-Indië.

Bijblad van de Nederlandsche Staats-Courant.

Census of India.

Edinburgh Gazette.

London Gazette.

Nieuw adresboek van geheel Nederlandsch-Indië.

Official Records of the Union and Confederate Navies in the War of the Rebellion.

Parliamentary Papers GB

Regerings-almanak voor Nederlandsch-Indië.

Report from the Select Committee on Sugar Duties [London, House of Commons, 1862].

Stukken betreffende het onderzoek der (bij besluit van den Gouverneur-Generaal van Nederlandsch Indië van 8 December 1853, no. 10) benoemde commissie voor de opname der verschillende suikerfabrieken op Java.

Victoria Government Gazette.

Periodicals and Newspapers
Dutch Language

Metropolitan Netherlands
Algemeen Handelsblad (Amsterdam); *Amsterdamsch Handels- en Effectenblad; De Avondbode* (Amsterdam); *Maandbulletin van het Nationaal Bureau voor Vrouwenarbeid* (The Hague); *Nieuwe Courant* (The Hague); *Nieuwe Rotterdamsche Courant; Het Nieuws van den Dag* (Amsterdam); *Provinciale Overijsselsche en Zwolsche Courant* (Zwolle); *Rotterdamsche*

Courant; *De Standaard* (Amsterdam); *De Telegraaf* (Amsterdam); *De Tijd* (Amsterdam); *Zutphensche Courant* (Zutphen).

Java

Bataviaasch Handelsblad; *Bataviaasch Nieuwsblad*; *De Indische Courant* (Surabaya/Batavia); *Java-Bode* [JB] (Batavia); *Java Gazette* (Batavia); *Javasche Courant* [JC] (Batavia); *De Locomotief* (Semarang); *Het Nieuws van den Dag voor Nederlandsch-Indië* (Batavia); *De Oostpost* (Surabaya); *Soerabaijasch Handelsblad* [SHB]; *De Vrij Pers* (Jakarta).

Sumatra

Nieuwsblad voor Sumatra (Medan); *Sumatra Courant* (Padang); *Sumatra Post* (Medan).

English Language

Scotland

Aberdeen Journal; *Aberdeen Press and Journal* [APJ]; *Aberdeen Weekly Journal and General Advertiser*; *Berwickshire News and General Advertiser* (Berwick-upon-Tweed); *Blackwood's Magazine* (Edinburgh); *Caledonian Mercury* (Edinburgh); *Dumfries and Galloway Standard* [*and Advertiser*]; *Dundee Courier*; *Dundee Evening Telegraph*; *Edinburgh Evening Courant*; *Edinburgh Evening News*; *Elgin Courant and Morayshire Advertiser*; *Elgin Courier*; *Forres Gazette*; *Glasgow Constitutional*; *Glasgow Herald*; *Greenock Telegraph and Clyde Shipping Gazette*; *Inverness Advertiser*; *Inverness Courier*; *Kelso Chronicle*; *North British Agriculturalist* (Edinburgh); *Southern Reporter* (Selkirk); *The Scotsman* (Edinburgh).

England

Bayswater Chronicle and West London News (London); *Bedfordshire Mercury* (Bedford); *Berks and Oxon Advertiser* (Abingdon); *Boston Spa News* (Yorkshire); *Buckingham Advertiser and Free Press*; *Cheltenham Chronicle*; *City Press* (London); *Clifton Society* (Bristol); *Daily Mirror* (London); *Daily News* (London); *Daily Telegraph* (London); *Diss Express* (Norfolk); *Evening Mail* (London); *The Field* (London); *The Gentlewoman* (London); *The Globe* (London); *Gloucestershire Echo* (Cheltenham); *Hampstead News* (London); *Hearth and Home* (London); *Home News from India, China and the Colonies* (London); *Illustrated London News*; *Illustrated Sporting and Dramatic News* (London); *Isle of Wight Observer* (Ryde); *Kent and Sussex Courier* (Tunbridge Wells); *Lancashire Evening Post* (Preston); *Liverpool Mercury*; *Lynn Advertiser* (King's Lynn); *Morning Advertiser* (London); *Morning Post* (London); *Norfolk News* (Norwich); *Norwich Mercury* (Norwich); *Nottingham Evening Post* (Nottingham); *Oxford Weekly News* (Oxford); *Pall Mall Gazette* (London); *Portsmouth Evening News* (Portsmouth); *Public Ledger and Daily Advertiser* (London); *Reading Mercury* (Reading); *St James's Gazette* (London); *Sevenoaks Chronicle and Kentish Advertiser* (Sevenoaks); *Shipping and Mercantile Gazette* (London); *The Sketch* (London); *Sporting Gazette* (London); *The Standard* (London); *The Sun* (London); *Surrey Advertiser* (Guildford); *Sussex Agricultural Express* (Lewes); *Tatler* (London); *The Times* (London); *Vogue* (London); *Weekly Dispatch* (London); *Western*

Gazette (Yeovil); *Yarmouth Independent* (Great Yarmouth); *Yorkshire Evening Post* (Leeds).

Wales
Western Mail (Cardiff).

Ireland
Belfast Telegraph; Northern Whig (Belfast); *Waterford Standard*.

Overseas
The Argus (Melbourne); *Geelong Advertiser; Kingston Gleaner* (Jamaica); *Singapore Free Press and Mercantile Advertiser; South Australian Register* (Adelaide); *Straits Times* (Singapore); *Sydney Morning Herald*.

Published Sources

A. J. [Alexander Johnston], *A Short Memoir of James Young, etc.*, Aberdeen, J. Craighead & Co., 1860, https://archive.org/details/ashortmemoirjam00youngoog, accessed 23 Sept. 2022.

Abell, Lesley and G. Roger Knight, '"So Like Home": Angus Maclaine (1799–1877), Sheep Farmer and Sojourner in South Australia', *Journal of the Historical Society of South Australia*, 33 (2005): 40–55.

Akenson, Donald Harman, 'Ever more "Diaspora": Advances and Alarums', *Journal of Irish and Scottish Studies*, 4/1 (2010): 1–15.

Alston, David, *Slaves and Highlanders: Silenced Histories of Scotland and the Caribbean*, Edinburgh, Edinburgh University Press, 2021.

Askew, W. D., *Angelica Patience Fraser: The Story of Her Life with Pages from Her Diary*, London, The John Williamson Company, 1923.

Austin, A. G. (ed.), *The Webbs' Australian Diary 1898*, Melbourne, Pitman, 1965.

Baillie, Charles, *The Call of Empire: From the Highlands to Hindostan*, Montreal, McGill-Queen's University Press, 2017.

Baker, T. F. T., Diane K. Bolton and Patricia E. C. Croot, 'Hampstead: Frognal and the Central Demesne', in *A History of the County of Middlesex*, vol. 9: *Hampstead, Paddington*, ed. C. R. Elrington, London, Victoria County History, 1989, *British History Online*, www.british-history.ac.uk/vch/middx/vol9/pp33-42, accessed 24 May 2022.

Baker, T. F. T., Diane K. Bolton and Patricia E. C. Croot, 'Paddington: Bayswater', in *A History of the County of Middlesex*, vol. 9: *Hampstead, Paddington*, ed. C. R. Elrington, London, Victoria County History, 1989, *British History Online*, www.british-history.ac.uk/vch/middx/vol9/pp204-212, accessed 20 June 2021.

Baker, T. F. T., Diane K. Bolton and Patricia E. C. Croot, 'Paddington: Tyburnia', in *A History of the County of Middlesex*, vol. 9: *Hampstead, Paddington*, ed. C. R. Elrington, London, Victoria County History, 1989, *British History Online*, www.british-history.ac.uk/vch/middx/vol9/pp90-198, accessed 18 Jan. 2021.

Banck, Geert, *Van de Javaanse suikercultuur naar de Nederlandse elitecultuur. Twee generaties in de 19e eeuw. Johann Erich Banck en John Eric Banck*. Diemen [Amsterdam]: AMB Uitgeverij, 2016.

Bankes, Viola, *A Kingston Lacy Childhood: Reminiscences of Viola Bankes Collected by Pamela Watkin*, Wimborne Minster, Dorset, Dovecote Press, 2017, originally published 1986.

Basu, Paul, 'Roots Tourism as a Return Movement: Semantics and the Scottish Diaspora', in Marjory Harper (ed.), *Emigrant Homecomings: The Return Movement of Emigrants, 1600–2000*, Manchester, Manchester University Press, 2005: 131–150.

Basu, Paul, *Highland Homecoming: Genealogy and Heritage Tourism in the Scottish Diaspora*, London, Routledge, 2007.

Baud, Jhr. Mr W. A., *De semi-officiële en particuliere briefwisseling tussen J. C. Baud en J. J. Rochussen, 1845–1851*, 3 vols, Assen, Van Gorkom, 1983.

Bayly, C. A., 'Ireland, India and the Empire: 1780–1914', *Transactions of the Royal Historical Society*, 10 (2000): 377–397.

Beck, Ulrich, *Cosmopolitan Vision*, translated by Ciaran Cronin, London, Polity, 2006.

Beckert, Sven, *Empire of Cotton: A Global History*, New York, Alfred A. Knopf, 2015.

Beekman, E. M., 'Preface' and 'Introduction' to Rob Nieuwenhuys, *Mirror of the Indies: A History of Dutch Colonial Literature*, trans. Frans van Rosevelt, ed. E. M. Beekman, Amherst, MA, University of Massachusetts Press, 1982: i–xxiv.

Beinart, William, and Lotte Hughes, *Environment and Empire*, Oxford, Oxford University Press, 2007.

Belich, James, *Replenishing the Earth: The Settler Revolution and the Rise of the Anglo-World, 1783–1939*, Oxford, Oxford University Press, 2009.

Berg, Norbert van den, and Steven Wachlin, *Het album voor Mientje. Een fotoalbum uit 1862 in Nederlandsch-Indië*, Bussum, Thoth, 2005.

Berge, Tom van den, *Karel Frederik Holle. Theeplanter in Indië 1829–1896*, Amsterdam, Bert Bakker, 1998.

Besant, Walter, and James Rice, *The Seamy Side: A Story*, London, Chatto & Windus, 1880.

Best, Antony, *Britain, Japan and Pearl Harbor: Avoiding War in East Asia, 1936–41*, London, Routledge, 1995.

Bettany, G. T., 'Locock, Sir Charles, first baronet (1799–1875)', rev. Anne Digby, *Oxford Dictionary of National Biography*, Oxford, Oxford University Press, 2004, online edition, www.oxforddnb.com/view/article/16915, accessed 26 May 2022.

Bhabha, Homi K., 'Of Mimicry and Man: The Ambivalence of Colonial Discourse', *Discipleship: A Special Issue on Psychoanalysis*, 28 (1984): 125–133.

Bickers, Robert, 'Shanghailanders and Others: The British Communities in China, 1843–1957', in Robert Bickers (ed.), *Settlers and Expatriates: Britons over the Seas*, Oxford, Oxford University Press, 2010: 269–301.

Bindoff, S. T., *The Scheldt Question to 1839*, London, Allen & Unwin, 1945.

Blackburn, Robin, *The Reckoning: From the Second Slavery to Abolition, 1776–1888*, London, Verso, 2024.

Bloys van Treslong Prins, P. C., *Genealogische en Heraldische Gedenkwaardigheden betreffende Europeanen op Java [GHG]*, 4 vols, Batavia, Albrecht/Koninklijke Drukkerij De Unie, 1934–39.

Bloys van Treslong Prins, P. C., 'Genealogie Van Motman', *Indische Navorscher*, 5/11 (1939): 114–117, and 6/1 (1940): 1–3.

Boets, Henk, Jenny de Jong and C. A. Tamse (eds), *Eer en fortuin. Leven in Nederland en Indië 1824–1900. Autobiografie van gouverneur-generaal James Loudon*, Amsterdam, De Bataafsche Leeuw, 2003.

Bosma, Ulbe, 'Sailing through Suez from the South: The Emergence of an Indies-Dutch Migration Circuit, 1815–1940', *International Migration Review*, 41/2 (2007): 511–536.

Bosma, Ulbe, *Indiëgangers. Verhalen van Nederlanders die naar Indië trokken*, Amsterdam, Bert Bakker, 2010.

Bosma, Ulbe, and Remco Raben, *Being 'Dutch' in the Indies: A History of Creolisation and Empire, 1500–1920*, trans. Wendie Shaffer, Singapore, NUS Press, 2008, originally published in Dutch as *De oude Indische wereld* [The Old Indies World] *1500–1920*, Amsterdam, Bert Bakker, 2003.

Boudewijn, Petra, '"You Must Have Inherited This Trait from Your Eurasian Mother": The Representation of Mixed-race Characters in Dutch Colonial Literature', *Dutch Crossing*, 40/3 (2016): 239–260.

Braun, Marianne, 'De ware beginselen van het staatskrediet. Louis Drucker, een leven lang in de oppositie', *De Moderne Tijd* [Amsterdam], 7/1 (2023): 78–102.

Brewster, Donna, *The House that Sugar Built*, Wigtown, [GC Books], 1999.

'Brodie, Alexander', in R. Thorne (ed.), *The History of Parliament: The House of Commons, 1790–1820*, 1986, online edition, www.historyofparliamentonline.org/volume/1790-1820/member/brodie-alexander-1748-1818, accessed 9 June 2022.

Broeze, F. J. A., 'The Merchant Fleet of Java (1820–1850). A Preliminary Survey', *Archipel*, 18 (1979): 251–269.

Brown, Keith M., and Allan Kennedy, 'Land of Opportunity? The Assimilation of Scottish Migrants in England, 1603–ca. 1762', *Journal of British Studies*, 57/4 (2018): 709–735.

Brown, Keith M., and Allan Kennedy, '"Their Maxim is *Vestigia Nulla Restrorsum*": Scottish Return Migration and Capital Repatriation from England, 1603–c. 1760', *Journal of Social History*, 52/1 (2018): 1–25.

Brown, Keith M., and Allan Kennedy, 'Becoming English: The Monro Family and Scottish Assimilation in Early-Modern England', *Cultural and Social History*, 16/2 (2019): 125–144.

Buckley, Charles Burton, *An Anecdotal History of the Old Times in Singapore*, 2 vols, Singapore, Fraser & Neave, 1902.

Bueltmann, Tanja, *Clubbing Together: Ethnicity, Civility and Formal Sociability in the Scottish Diaspora to 1930*, Liverpool, Liverpool University Press, 2014.

Bueltmann, Tanja, 'Ethnic Associational Culture in the Scottish Diaspora: Definitions, Approaches and Perspectives', in Bueltmann, *Clubbing Together: Ethnicity, Civility and Formal Sociability in the Scottish Diaspora to 1930*, Liverpool, Liverpool University Press, 2014: 1–26.

Bueltmann, Tanja, Andrew Hinson and Graeme Morton, *The Scottish Diaspora*, Edinburgh, Edinburgh University Press, 2013.

Bueltmann, Tanja, and Graeme Morton, 'Partners in Empire: The Scottish Diaspora since 1707', in Donald, MacRaild, Tanja Bueltmann and J. C. D. Clark (eds), *British and Irish Diasporas: Societies, Cultures and Ideologies*, Manchester, Manchester University Press, 2019: 209–243.

Buettner, Elizabeth, 'Haggis in the Raj: Private and Public Celebrations of Scottishness in Late Imperial India', *Scottish Historical Review*, 81/2 (2002): 212–239.

Buettner, Elizabeth, *Empire Families: Britons and Late Imperial India*, Oxford, Oxford University Press, 2004.

Buettner, Elizabeth, *Europe after Empire: Decolonisation, Society and Culture*, Cambridge, Cambridge University Press, 2016.

Butcher, J. G., *The British in Malaya, 1880–1941: The Social History of a European Community in Colonial South-East Asia*, Kuala Lumpur, Oxford University Press, 1979.

Caddick, Alison, 'Where Does Value Lie?', review of *Cannibal Capitalism* by Nancy Fraser, *Arena Quarterly* (Melbourne) 16 (2023): 87.

Cahir, Fred, Alison Inglis and Anne Beggs Sunter (eds), *Scots under the Southern Cross* [Ballarat, Victoria]: Ballarat Heritage Services, 2015.

'Cambier', *Nederland's Patriciaat: Genealogieën van Bekende Geslachten*, The Hague, Centraal Bureau voor Genealogie, 1910–, vol. 8 (1917): 88–94.

Cameron, Neil, 'MacNeils of Ardnacross and Islay', *Scottish Genealogist*, 27 (1980): 115–117.

'Campbell, Walter Frederick (1798–1855), of Islay House, Argyll and Woodhall, Lanark', *History of Parliament: The House of Commons, 1820–1832*, ed. D. R. Fisher, Cambridge, Cambridge University Press, 2009, online edition, www.historyofparliamentonline.org/volume/1820-1832/member/campbell-walter-1798-1855, accessed 21 June 2022.

Campo, J. N. F. M. à, *Koninklijke Paketvaart Maatschappij. Stoomvaart en staatsvorming in de Indonesische archipel, 1888–1914*, Hilversum, Verloren, 1992.

Carey, Peter, *The British in Java, 1811–1816: A Javanese Account*, Oxford, published for The British Academy by Oxford University Press, 1992.

Carey, Peter, *The Power of Prophecy: Prince Dipanagara and the End of an Old Order in Java, 1785–1855*, Leiden, Brill, 2008.

Carlson, Sevinc, *Indonesia's Oil*, Boulder, CO, Westview Press, 1977, reprint, New York, Routledge, 2018.

Carpenter, Louise, *An Unlikely Countess: Lily Budge and the 13th Earl of Galloway*, London, Harper Perennial, 2005.

Chapman, Stanley, *The Rise of Merchant Banking*, London, Routledge, 1984.

Chapman, Stanley, *Merchant Enterprise in Britain: From the Industrial Revolution to World War I*, Cambridge, Cambridge University Press, 1992.

Christiaans, P. A., 'De belangrijkste ambtenaren te Batavia anno 1837, alsmede een aantal geïnteresseerde officieren', *De Indische Navorscher* (new series), 6 (1993): 122–136, 175–180.

Christiaans, Peter, 'Van Beusechem', *Indische Navorscher* (new series), 16 (2003): 1–7.

Christiaans, Peter A., 'Bezoet de Bie', *De Indische Navorscher*, Jaarboek 21 (2008): 134–140.

Clancy-Smith, Julia, and Frances Gouda (eds), *Domesticating the Empire: Race, Gender, and Family Life in French and Dutch Colonialism*, Charlottesville, VA, University of Virginia Press, 1998.

Clark, Ian D., *Scars on the Landscape: A Register of Massacre Sites in Western Victoria, 1803–1859*, Canberra, Aboriginal Studies Press, 1995.

Claver, Alexander, *Dutch Commerce and Chinese Merchants in Java: Colonial Relationships in Trade and Finance, 1800–1942*, Leiden, Brill, 2014.

Claver, Alexander, and G. Roger Knight, 'A European Role in Intra-Asian Commercial Development: The Maclaine Watson Network and the Java Sugar Trade c.1840–1942', *Business History*, 60 (2018): 202–230.

Close, Francis, *An Indian Retrospect, or what has Christian England done for Heathen India?* London, Hatchard, 1858.

Coclanis, Peter A., 'Southeast Asia's Incorporation into the World Rice Market: A Revisionist View', *Journal of Southeast Asian Studies*, 24/2 (1993): 251–267.

Cohen, Deborah, 'Love and Money in the Informal Empire: The British in Argentina, 1830–1930', *Past and Present*, 245 (2019): 79–115.

Collins, Diane, 'Robert Pikler (1909–1984)', *Australian Dictionary of Biography*, vol. 18, Melbourne, Melbourne University Press, 2012, https://adb.anu.edu.au/biography/pikler-robert-15463, accessed 19 Aug. 2024.

Corfield, Justin, *Historical Dictionary of Ho Chi Minh City*, London, Anthem Press, 2013.

Coté, Joost, 'Romancing the Indies: The Literary Construction of *Tempo Doeloe*, 1880–1930', in Joost Coté and Loes Westerbeek (eds), *Recalling the Indies: Colonial Culture and Postcolonial Identities*, Amsterdam, Aksant, 2005: 133–172.

Cottrell, P. L., *Investment Banking in England 1856–1881: A Case Study of the International Financial Society*, vol. 1, London, Routledge, 2012.

Couperus, Louis, *The Book of the Small Souls*, 4 vols, trans. Alexander Teixeira de Mattos, reprint of the London, William Heinemann, 1914–18 edition, originally published in Dutch as *De Boeken der Kleine Zielen*, 4 vols, Amsterdam, L. J. Veen, 1901–3, Amazon, 2017.

Cressy, David, *Shipwrecks and the Bounties of the Sea*, Oxford, Oxford University Press, 2022.

Currie, Jo, *Mull: The Island and its People*, Edinburgh, Birlinn, 2000.

Curry-Machado, Jonathan, 'Global Histories, Imperial Commodities, Local Interactions: An Introduction', in Jonathan Curry-Machado (ed.), *Global Histories, Imperial Commodities, Local Interactions*, Basingstoke, Palgrave Macmillan, 2013: 1–14.

Dakers, Caroline, *A Genius for Money: Business, Art and the Morrisons*, New Haven, CT, Yale University Press, 2011.

Dale, Leigh, 'Empire's Proxy: Sheep and the Colonial Environment', in Helen Tiffin (ed.), *Five Emus to the King of Siam: Environment and Empire*, Leiden, Brill, 2007: 1–14.

Darwin, John, *The Empire Project: The Rise and Fall of the British World-System, 1830–1970*, Cambridge, Cambridge University Press, 2009.

Darwin, John, *Unlocking the World: Port Cities and Globalization in the Age of Steam, 1830–1930*, London, Allen Lane, 2020.

Daukes, Wilfred Hicks, *The 'P. & T.' Lands: An Agricultural Romance of Anglo-Dutch Enterprise*, [London], [E. Fisher], [1943].

Davidoff, Leonore, and Catherine Hall, *Family Fortunes: Men and Women of the English Middle Class, 1780–1850*, revised edition, London, Routledge, 2002, originally published Chicago, University of Chicago Press, 1987.

Devine, T. M., *To the Ends of the Earth: Scotland's Global Diaspora, 1750–2010*, London, Allen Lane, 2011.

Devine, T. M. (ed.), *Recovering Scotland's Slavery Past: The Caribbean Connection*, Edinburgh, Edinburgh University Press, 2015.

Devine, T. M., *The Scottish Clearances: A History of the Dispossessed*, London, Penguin/Random House, 2019.

Devine, T. M., and John M. MacKenzie, 'Scots in the Imperial Economy', in MacKenzie and Devine (eds), *Scotland and the British Empire*, Oxford, Oxford University Press, 2011: 227–254.

Devine, T. M., and Angela McCarthy (eds), *The Scottish Experience in Asia, c. 1700 to the Present*, Basingstoke, Palgrave Macmillan, 2016.

Dick, Howard, 'Japan's Economic Expansion in the Netherlands Indies between the First and Second World Wars', *Journal of Southeast Asian Studies*, 20/2 (1989): 244–272.

Dick, Howard W., *Surabaya, City of Work: A Socioeconomic History, 1900–2000*, Athens, OH, Ohio University Press, 2002.

Dijk, Kees van, *The Netherlands Indies in the Great War, 1914–1918*, Leiden, KITLV Press, 2007.

Directory and Chronicle for China, Japan, Corea, Indo-China, Straits Settlements, Netherlands India, Borneo, the Philippines, &c., Hong Kong, Hongkong Daily Press Office, 1912.

Dobson, David, *Scots in Latin America*, Baltimore, MD, Clearfield, 2003.

Doorn, Maarten van, *Het leven gaat er een lichten gang. Den Haag in de jaren 1919–1940*, Zwolle, Waanders, 2002.

Drieënhuizen, Caroline, 'Objects, Nostalgia and the Dutch Colonial Elite in Times of Transition ca.1900–1970', *Bijdragen tot de Taal-, Land-en Volkenkunde*, 170 (2014): 504–529.

Drucker, J. C. J., *Some correspondence concerning a British passport confiscated by H.B.M.'s minister in the land of Guillaume Tell*, Montreux, Société de l'Imprimerie et Lithographie, [1919?].

Dunstan, David, 'McEacharn, Sir Malcolm Donald (1852–1910)', *Australian Dictionary of Biography*, vol. 10, Melbourne, Melbourne University Press, 1986: 263–264, https://adb.anu.edu.au/biography/mceacharn-sir-malcolm-donald-7350, accessed 21 Sept. 2024.

Earl, G. W., *The Eastern Seas* (with an introduction by C. M. Turnbull), Singapore, Oxford University Press, 1971, originally published London, W. H. Allen & Co., 1837.

Elson, R. E., *Javanese Peasants and the Colonial Sugar Industry: Impact and Change in an East Java Residency, 1830–1940*, Singapore, Oxford University Press, 1984.

Engel, E. P., 'Het ontstaan van de verzameling Drucker-Fraser in het Rijksmuseum', *Bulletin van het Rijksmuseum*, 13/2 (1965): 45–66.

Etherington, Norman, 'Introduction', in Etherington (ed.) *Missions and Empire*, Oxford, Oxford University Press, 2005: 1–18.

Faber, G. H. von, *Oud Soerabaia. De geschiedenis van Indië's eerste koopstad van de oudste tijden tot de instelling van den gemeenteraad (1906)*, Surabaya, Gemeente Soerabaia, 1931.

Faber, G. H. von, *Nieuw Soerabaia. De geschiedenis van Indië's voornaamste koopstad in de eerste kwarteeuw sedert hare instelling 1906–1931*, Surabaya, Van Ingen, 1937.

Falkus, Malcolm, *The Blue Funnel Legend: A History of the Ocean Steam Ship Company, 1865–1973*, Basingstoke, Macmillan, 1990.

Fasseur, C., 'Gemengd onthaal. De weerklank op Money's "Java" in Nederland', *Bijdragen en Mededelingen betreffende de Geschiedenis der Nederlanden*, 105/3 (1990): 368–378.

Fasseur, Cees, *Indischgasten. Indische levensgeschiedenissen*, Amsterdam, Bert Bakker, 1997.

Ffolliott, Pamela, and E. L. H. Croft, *One Titan at a Time: The Story of John Paterson of Port Elizabeth, South Africa, and His Times*, Cape Town, H. Timmins, 1960.

Fiddes, Jim, *The Granite Men: A History of the Granite Industries of Aberdeen and North-East Scotland*, Stroud, The History Press, 2019.

Fielding, Xan, *One Man in His Time: The Life of Lieutenant-Colonel N. L. D. ('Billy') McLean, DSO*, London, Macmillan, 1990.

Finn, Margot, 'Anglo-Indian Lives in the Later Eighteenth and Early Nineteenth Centuries', *Journal for Eighteenth-Century Studies*, 33/1 (2010): 49–65.

Finn, Margot C., 'Material Turns in British History: I: Loot', *Transactions of the Royal Historical Society*, 28 (2018), 5–32.

Finn, Margot, 'The Female World of Love & Empire: Women, Family & East India Company Politics at the End of the Eighteenth Century', *Gender & History*, 31/1 (2019): 7–24.

Finn, Margot C., 'Material Turns in British History: IV: Empire in India, Cancel Cultures and the Country House', *Transactions of the Royal Historical Society*, 31 (2021): 1–21.

Finn, Margot, and Kate Smith (eds), *The East India Company at Home, 1757–1857*, London, UCL Press, 2018.

The First One Hundred Years, 1827–1927, of Maclaine Watson & Co., MacNeill & Co. and Fraser Easton & Co., [n.p., n.d., Batavia, 1927].

Fischer-Tiné, Harald, and Susanne Gehrmann, 'Empires, Boundaries and the Production of Difference', in Fischer-Tiné and Gehrmann (eds), *Empires and Boundaries: Rethinking Race, Class, and Gender in Colonial Settings*, New York, Routledge, 2009: 1–22.

Fletcher, Anthony, and Ruth M. Larsen, *Mistress: A History of Women and their Country Houses*, New Haven, CT, Yale University Press, 2025.

Fortuin, Egbert, *Indische adel. De koloniale lotgevallen van de Indische familie Van Braam*, Zutphen, Walburg Pers, 2024.

Foster, B. Walter, and J. Tatham, 'On the Influenza Epidemic of 1892 in London', *British Medical Journal*, 2/1650 (13 Aug. 1892): 353–356.

Foster, Stephen, *A Private Empire*, Millers Point, Sydney, Pier Nine, 2010.

Fraser, Eugenie, *A Home by the Hooghly: A Jute Wallah's Wife*, London, Corgi Books, 1991.
Fraser, Nancy, *Cannibal Capitalism: How Our System Is Devouring Democracy, Care, and the Planet— and What We Can Do About It*, London, Verso, 2023.
Fraser, W. Hamish, 'Urban Society. 5. Urbanization, 1800 onwards', in Michael Lynch (ed.), *The Oxford Companion to Scottish History*, Oxford, Oxford University Press, 2001: 628–629.

Gaastra, Femme, 'The Experience of Travelling to the Dutch East Indies by the Overland Route, 1844–1869', in Gordon Jackson and David M. Williams (eds), *Shipping, Technology, and Imperialism: Papers Presented to the Third British-Dutch Maritime History Conference*, Brookfield, VT, Ashgate, 1996: 120–137.
Gammage, Bill, *The Biggest Estate on Earth: How Aborigines Made Australia*, Crows Nest, NSW, Allen & Unwin, 2011.
Gaskell, Philip, *Morvern Transformed: A Highland Parish in the Nineteenth Century*, Cambridge, Cambridge University Press, 1996, originally published 1968.
Geikie, Archibald, *Life of Murchison*, 2 vols, London, John Murray, 1875.
GHG. See: Bloys van Treslong Prins, P. C., *Genealogische en Heraldische Gedenkwaardigheden betreffende Europeanen op Java*.
Gill, Peter, *Cheltenham Races*, Stroud, Sutton Publishing, 1997.
Gorham, Deborah, *The Victorian Girl and the Feminine Ideal*, London, Routledge, 2012.
Gouda, Frances, 'Nyonyas on the Colonial Divide: White Women in the Dutch East Indies, 1900–1942', *Gender & History*, 5/3 (1993): 318–342.
Gouda, Frances, *Dutch Culture Overseas: Colonial Practice in the Netherlands Indies, 1900–1942*, Amsterdam, Amsterdam University Press, 1995, reprint, Sheffield, Equinox, 2008.
Gouda, Frances, *American Visions of the Netherlands East Indies/Indonesia*, Amsterdam, Amsterdam University Press, 2002.
Graaf, Suzanne de, '"Iets van een Vreemde Vrucht": Indische Verlofgangers in Nederland, 1919–1939', MA thesis, Leiden University, 2009.
Graaf, Ton de, *Voor handel en maatschappij. Geschiedenis van de Nederlandsche Handel-Maatschappij, 1824–1964*, Amsterdam, Boom, 2012.
Grace, Richard J., *Opium and Empire: The Lives and Careers of William Jardine and James Matheson*, Montreal, McGill-Queen's University Press, 2014.
Greenberg, Michael, *British Trade and the Opening of China 1800–42*, Cambridge, Cambridge University Press, 1969, originally published 1951.
Griffiths, Richard, *Patriotism Perverted: Captain Ramsay, the Right Club, and British Anti-Semitism, 1939–1940*, London, Faber & Faber, 2015.
Griffiths, Richard, *What Did You Do in the War? The Last Throes of the British Pro-Nazi Right, 1940–45*, New York, Routledge, 2017.
Gust, Onni, 'Remembering and Forgetting the Scottish Highlands: Sir James Mackintosh and the Forging of a British Imperial Identity', *Journal of British Studies*, 52/3 (2013): 615–637.

Haan, F. de, 'Personalia der periode van het Engelsch bestuur over Java 1811–1816', *Bijdragen van het Koninklijk Instituut voor Taal-, Land- en Volkenkunde*, 92 (1935): 477–681.
Hadley, Tessa, 'The Italianness of It All: Iris Origo', *London Review of Books*, 10 May 2018: 19.
Hainsworth, D. R., *The Sydney Traders: Simeon Lord and his Contemporaries, 1788–1821*, Melbourne, Cassell Australia, 1971.
Hall, Catherine, *Civilising Subjects: Metropole and Colony in the English Imagination, 1830–1867*, Cambridge, Polity Press, 2002.
Hamilton, Thomas, 'Macleod, Norman (1812–1872)', rev. H. C. G. Matthew, *Oxford Dictionary of National Biography*, Oxford, Oxford University Press, 2004, online edition, Jan. 2007, www.oxforddnb.com/view/article/17679, accessed 5 May 2022.

Hammerton, A. James, *Emigrant Gentlewomen: Genteel Poverty and Female Emigration, 1830–1914*, London, Croom Helm, 1979.

Hammerton, A. James, 'The Late Twentieth-Century "British" Diaspora: Last Gasp or Robust Revival?', in Philip Payton (ed.), *Emigrants and Historians: Essays in Honour of Eric Richards*, Adelaide, Wakefield Press, 2016: 39–57.

Hammerton, A. James, *Migrants of the British Diaspora since the 1960s: Stories from Modern Nomads*, Manchester, Manchester University Press, 2017.

Handboek voor cultuur- en handelsondernemingen in Nederlandsch-Indië [*HCHO*], Amsterdam, J. H. de Bussy, 1888–1940.

Harper, Marjory, *Adventurers and Exiles: The Great Scottish Exodus*, London, Profile Books, 2003.

Harper, Marjory (ed.), *Emigrant Homecomings: The Return Movement of Emigrants, 1600–2000*, Manchester, Manchester University Press, 2005.

Harper, Marjory, 'Introduction', in Marjory Harper (ed.), *Emigrant Homecomings: The Return Movement of Emigrants, 1600–2000*, Manchester, Manchester University Press, 2005, 1–14.

Harper, Tim, 'The British "Malayans"', in Robert Bickers (ed.), *Settlers and Expatriates: Britons over the Seas* (Oxford History of the British Empire, Companion Series), Oxford, Oxford University Press, 2010: 233–268.

Hart, Gwen, *A History of Cheltenham*, Leicester, Leicester University Press, 1965.

Hazareesingh, Sandip, 'Interconnected Synchronicities: The Production of Bombay and Glasgow as Modern Global Ports c.1850–1880', *Journal of Global History*, 4/1 (2009): 7–31.

Hedinger, Daniel, and Nadin Heé, 'Transimperial History – Connectivity, Cooperation and Competition', *Journal of Modern European History*, 16/4 (2018): 429–452.

Hedrick, Marie C., 'Australia's Colonial Wool Industry: A Sheep-Walk for the Benefit of British Imperialism, 1788–1851', MA thesis, University of Hawai'i at Mānoa, 1998.

Heffer, Simon (ed.), *Henry 'Chips' Channon: The Diaries 1938–1943*, London, Hutchinson, 2021.

Heijbroek, J. F., and E. L. Wouthuysen, *Portret van een kunsthandel. De firma Van Wisselingh en zijn compagnons 1838–heden*, Zwolle, Waanders and Amsterdam Rijksmuseum, 1999.

Hembry, Phyllis, *British Spas from 1815 to the Present: A Social History* (edited and completed by Leonard W. Cowie and Evelyn E. Cowie), London, Athlone Press, 1997.

Hodges, Andrew, *Alan Turing: The Enigma*, London, Penguin Random House, 2014, originally published London, Burnett Books, 1983.

Holcomb, Janette, *Early Merchant Families of Sydney: Speculation and Risk Management on the Fringes of Empire*, Melbourne, Australian Scholarly, 2013.

Hopkins, Harry, *The Long Affray: The Poaching Wars, 1760–1914*, London, Secker & Warburg, 1985.

Houben, Vincent J. H., *Kraton and Kumpeni: Surakarta and Yogyakarta, 1830–1870*, Leiden, KITLV Press, 1994.

Hughes, Kathryn, *The Victorian Governess*, London, Hambledon Press, 1993.

Hunter, James, review of *Opium and Empire* by Richard Grace, in *Northern Scotland*, 8/1 (2017): 109–110.

Hunter, Jim [James], 'Opium, Hong Kong and Long Memories', *Aberdeen Press and Journal*, 1 Apr. 2021.

Hyslop, Jonathan, 'Making Scotland in South Africa: Charles Murray, the Transvaal's Aberdeenshire Poet', in David Lambert and Alan Lester (eds), *Colonial Lives Across the British Empire: Imperial Careering in the Long Nineteenth Century*, Cambridge, Cambridge University Press, 2004: 309–334.

Jack, Kenneth C., 'The 6th Duke of Atholl', *Square Magazine*, online, 10 (Oct. 2021), www.thesquaremagazine.com/mag/article/202110the-6th-duke-of-atholl/, accessed 2 Feb. 2023.

Jones, Charles A., *International Business in the Nineteenth Century: The Rise and Fall of a Cosmopolitan Bourgeoisie*, Brighton, Wheatsheaf Books, 1987.

Jordaan, Roy, and Peter Carey, 'Thomas Stamford Raffles' Masonic Career in Java: A New Perspective on the British Interregnum (1811–1816)', *Journal of the Malaysian Branch of the Royal Asiatic Society*, 90/2 (2017): 1–34.

Junge, Sophie, 'Old Soerabaja – New Soerabaja? Circulating the Emptiness of the Colonial City', *PhotoResearcher*, 30 (2018): 48–62.

Junghuhn, Franz Wilhelm, *Java, zijne gedaante, zijn plantentooi en inwendige bouw*, 4 vols, The Hague, Mieling, 1853–4, accessed via Delpher, 1 Jan. 2022.

Kal, P., 'Genealogie van het geslacht Du Puy in de Oriënt', *De Indische Navorscher* (new series), 9 (1996): 49–56, 108.

Karras, Alan L., *Sojourners in the Sun: Scottish Migrants in Jamaica and the Chesapeake, 1740–1800*, Ithaca, NY, Cornell University Press, 1992.

Kelly, Serena, 'Fraser, Angelica Patience (1823–1910)', *Oxford Dictionary of National Biography*, online edition, https://doi.org/10.1093/ref:odnb/59507, accessed 1 May 2024.

Kemp, P. H. van der, and D. A. Overbeek, 'De jaren 1817–1825. Der Nederlandsche factorijen aan Hindostans Oostkust. Naar onuitgegeven stukken', *Bijdragen tot de Taal-, Land- en Volkenkunde van Nederlandsch-Indië*, 74, no. 1–2 (1918): 1–13.

Kerkhoven, Marga C. (ed.), *Eduard Julius Kerkhoven. 20 Indische brieven 1860–1863 verzameld uit de Hunderensche Courant*, Renkum, Theefamilie Archief, 2010.

Kerr's Melbourne Almanac and Port Phillip Directory for 1842: A Compendium of Useful and Accurate Information Connected with Port Phillip, Melbourne, Kerr and Thompson, 1842.

Kersten, Albert E., and Marijke van Faassen, 'Goodbye Mr Churchill', in Nigel Ashton and Duco Hellema, eds, *Unspoken Allies: Anglo-Dutch Relations since 1780*, Amsterdam, Amsterdam University Press, 2001: 155–178.

Khusyairi, Johny A., and Freek Colombijn, 'Moving at a Different Velocity: The Modernization of Transportation and Social Differentiation in Surabaya in the 1920s', in Freek Colombijn and Joost Coté, eds, *Cars, Conduits, and Kampongs: The Modernization of the Indonesian City, 1920–1960*, Leiden, Brill, 2015: 251–271.

Kiddle, Margaret, *Men of Yesterday: A Social History of the Western District of Victoria, 1834–1890*, Melbourne, Melbourne University Press, 1961.

Kinloch, Walter, *De Zieke Reiziger; or, Rambles in Java and the Straits in 1852 by 'Bengal Civilian'*, London, Simpkin, Marshall & Co., 1853, reprint, Singapore: Oxford University Press, 1987.

Klein, P. W., '"Little London": British Merchants in Rotterdam during the Seventeenth and Eighteenth Centuries', in D. C. Coleman and Peter Matthias (eds), *Enterprise and History: Essays in Honour of Charles Wilson*, Cambridge, Cambridge University Press, 1984: 116–134.

Knight, G. Roger, 'Gully Coolies, Weed-Women and *Snijvolk*: The Sugar Industry Workers of North Java in the Early Twentieth Century', *Modern Asian Studies*, 28/1 (1994): 51–76.

Knight, G. Roger, 'A Case of Mistaken Identity? *Suikerlords* and Ladies, *Tempo Doeloe* and the Dutch Colonial Communities in Nineteenth Century Java', *Social Identities*, 7/3 (2001): 379–391.

Knight, G. Roger, 'A Sugar Factory and its Swimming Pool: Incorporation and Differentiation in Colonial Java', *Ethnic and Racial Studies*, 24/3 (2001): 451–471.

Knight, G. Roger, *Commodities and Colonialism: The Story of Big Sugar in Indonesia, 1880–1942*, Leiden, Brill, 2013.
Knight, G. Roger, 'Rescued from the Myths of Time: Toward a Reappraisal of European Mercantile Houses in Mid-Nineteenth Century Java, c. 1830–1870', *Bijdragen tot de Taal-, Land- en Volkenkunde*, 170 (2014): 313–341.
Knight, G. Roger, *Sugar, Steam and Steel: The Industrial Project in Colonial Java, 1830–1885*, Adelaide, University of Adelaide Press, 2014.
Knight, G. Roger, 'Neglected Orphans and Absent Parents: The European Mercantile Houses of Mid-Nineteenth-Century Java', in Ulbe Bosma and Anthony Webster (eds), *Commodities, Ports and Asian Maritime Trade since 1750*, Basingstoke, Palgrave Macmillan, 2015: 127–143.
Knight, G. Roger, *Trade and Empire in Early Nineteenth-Century Southeast Asia: Gillian Maclaine and his Business Network*, Woodbridge, The Boydell Press, 2015.
Knight, G. Roger, 'An "Indies" Couple: Colonial Communities and Issues Surrounding Identity in the Dutch East Indies, ca. 1890–1930s', *Archipel*, 99 (2020): 153–188.
Knight, G. Roger, and William Woods, 'Ancestral Voices, Highland Homecomings and High Society: The Lochbuie Family of Mull, ca. 1855–1920', *Journal of Scottish Historical Studies*, 42/2 (2022): 217–242.
Kobayashi, Atsushi, 'The Role of Singapore in the Growth of Intra-Southeast Asian Trade, c.1820s–1852', *Southeast Asian Studies* (Kyoto), 2/3 (2013): 443–474.
Kroon, Andréa Angela, 'Masonic Networks, Material Culture and International Trade: The Participation of Dutch Freemasons in the Commercial and Cultural Exchange in Southeast Asia (1735–1853)', PhD thesis, Leiden University, 2015.
Kynaston, David, *The City of London*, vol. 1: *A World of its Own, 1815–1890*, London, Pimlico (Random House), 1995.

Laidlaw, Zoë, 'National Biographies and Transnational Lives: Tracing Connections between Slavery and Settler Colonialism', *Australian Journal of Biography and History*, 6 (2022): 143–170.
Laurence, A. E., 'Karl Marx on the Isle of Wight', *Society* (New Brunswick), 23 (1985): 54–60.
Leidelmeijer, Margaret, *Van suikermolen tot grootbedrijf. Technische vernieuwing in de Java-suikerindustrie in de negentiende eeuw*, Amsterdam, Amsterdam University Press, 1997.
Lindblad, J. Thomas, 'British Business and the Uncertainties of Early Independence in Indonesia', *Itinerario*, 37/2 (2013): 147–164.
Locher-Scholten, Elsbeth, *Women and the Colonial State: Essays on Gender and Modernity in the Netherlands Indies 1900–1942*, Amsterdam, Amsterdam University Press, 2000.
Loo, Vilan van der, 'Mensen, Straten en Gebeurtenissen. Zoals Verbeeld in de Haags-Indische Letteren Rond 1900', in Esther Captain, Maartje de Haan and Pim Westerkamp (eds), *De Indische Zomer in Den Haag: Het Cultureel Erfgoed Van de Indische Hoofdstad*, Leiden, KITLV, 2005: 127–158.
Loos, Wiepke, Marijn Schapelhouman and R. J. A. te Rijdt, *Aquarellen van de Haagse School. De collectie Drucker-Fraser*, Amsterdam, Rijksmuseum; Zwolle, Waanders, 2002.
Het Louche Maliepaard en Ander Werk van Etie van Rees (1890–1973), Leeuwarden, Museum van het Princessehof, 1990.
'Loudon', in *Nederland's Patriciaat: Genealogieën van Bekende Geslachten*, The Hague, Centraal Bureau voor Genealogie, 1910–, vols 21 (1933–4): 240–249, and 53 (1967): 158–167.
Lydall, Edward, *Enough of Action*, London, Jonathan Cape, 1949.

MacDonald, William, and John Murdoch, *Descriptive and Historical Sketches of Islay*, Glasgow, 1850, reprinted with an introduction by John Newton, Bowmore, Celtic House, 1997.

MacKenzie, John M., 'Foreword', in Andrew Mackillop and Steve Murdoch (eds), *Military Governors and Imperial Frontiers c. 1600–1800: A Study of Scotland and Empires*, Leiden, Brill, 2003: xiii–xxi.

Mackillop, Andrew, 'The Political Culture of the Scottish Highlands from Culloden to Waterloo', *Historical Journal*, 46/3 (2003): 511–532.

Mackillop, Andrew, 'The Highlands and the Returning Nabob: Sir Hector Munro of Novar, 1760–1807', in Marjory Harper (ed.), *Emigrant Homecomings: The Return Movement of Emigrants, 1600–2000*, Manchester, Manchester University Press, 2005: 233–261.

Mackillop, Andrew, 'Europeans, Britons, and Scots: Scottish Sojourning Networks and Identities in Asia, c. 1700–1815', in Angela McCarthy (ed.), *A Global Clan: Scottish Migrant Networks and Identities since the Eighteenth Century*, London, I. B. Tauris, 2007: 19–47.

Mackillop, Andrew, 'Locality, Nation and Empire: Scots and the Empire in Asia, c.1695–c.1813', in John M. MacKenzie and T. M. Devine (eds), *Scotland and the British Empire*, Oxford, Oxford University Press, 2011: 54–83.

Mackillop, Andrew, *Human Capital and Empire: Scotland, Ireland and Wales and British Imperialism in Asia, c. 1690–c. 1820*, Manchester, Manchester University Press, 2021.

Mackillop, Andrew, 'Scotland, Scots and the Boundaries of the Indian Ocean World', *Journal of Indian Ocean World Studies*, 5/2 (2021): 150–157.

MacKinnon, Iain, and Andrew Mackillop, 'Plantation Slavery and Landownership in the West Highlands and Islands: Legacies and Lessons. A Discussion Paper', Glasgow, University of Glasgow, 2023: 1–23, https://eprints.gla.ac.uk/321913, accessed 1 July 2025.

Maclaine Campbell, Donald, *Java: Past and Present: A Description of the Most Beautiful Country in the World, Its Ancient History, People, Antiquities, and Products*, 2 vols, London, Heinemann, 1915.

Maclaine of Lochbuie, Lorne (ed.), *Siol Eachainn: The Race of Hector*, Sydney, Amazon, 2019.

Maclean-Bristol, Nicholas, 'Lieutenant Hector Maclean 14th Regt. of Foot: A Cadet of Coll?', *Scottish Genealogist*, 18/1 (1971): 11–12.

MacLean, John Patterson, *Renaissance of the Clan MacLean: Comprising also a History of Dubhaird Caisteal, and the Great Gathering on August 24, 1912: Together with an appendix containing letters of Gen'l Allan MacLean, etc.*, Columbus, OH, F. J. Heer Printing Company, 1913.

Macmillan, David S., *Scotland and Australia, 1788–1850: Emigration, Commerce and Investment*, Oxford, Clarendon Press, 1967.

MacMillan, Margaret, *Women of the Raj: The Mothers, Wives, and Daughters of the British Empire in India*, new edition, London, Thames & Hudson, 2018, originally published 1988.

Mac Neill, A., 'Mechanische grondbewerking met den kabelploeg der firma John Fowler & Co., met illust.', *Archief voor de suikerindustrie NI*, 1923, no. 1: 343–367.

Macpherson, Ian, *Colin McLean 1873–1915* [privately printed, Inverness, c.2015].

MacRaild, Donald, Tanja Bueltmann and J. C. D. Clark (eds), *British and Irish Diasporas: Societies, Cultures and Ideologies*, Manchester, Manchester University Press, 2019.

Magee, Gary B., and Andrew S. Thompson, *Empire and Globalisation: Networks of People, Goods and Capital in the British World, c. 1850–1914*, Cambridge, Cambridge University Press, 2010.

[Mandere, H. Ch. C. J. van der], 'De cultuurmaatschappij Wonolangan (1895–1925)', *Indië. Geïllustreerd tijdschrift voor Nederland en Koloniën*, 9/19 (Dec. 1925): 306–340.

Mangeot, S. E., 'Queen Anne's Mansions: The Story of "Hankey's Folly"', *Architect & Building News*, 13 Jan. 1939: 77–79.

Mansvelt, W. M. F., *Geschiedenis van de Nederlandsche Handel-Maatschappij*, 2 vols, Haarlem, De Erven F. Bohn, 1924–1926.

Markovits, Claude, *The Global World of Indian Merchants, 1750–1947: Traders of Sind from Bukhara to Panama*, Cambridge, Cambridge University Press, 2000.

Marle, A. van, 'De Groep der Europeanen in Nederlands-Indië, Iets over Ontstaan en Groei', *Indonesië*, 5 (1951–2): 97–121, 314–341, 481–507.

Martin, Bonnie, 'Slavery's Invisible Engine: Mortgaging Human Property', *Journal of Southern History*, 76/4 (2010): 817–866.

Mate, Charles Henry, *Bournemouth: 1810–1910, the History of a Modern Health and Pleasure Resort*, London, W. Mate, 1910.

Matthews, Derek, Malcolm Anderson and John Richard Edwards, *The Priesthood of Industry: The Rise of the Professional Accountant in British Industry*, Oxford, Oxford University Press, 1998.

Maudlin, Daniel, 'Tradition and Change in the Age of Improvement: A Study of Argyll Tacksmen's Houses in Morvern', *Proceedings of the Society of Antiquaries of Scotland*, 133 (2003), 360–366.

McCarthy, Angela, and John M. MacKenzie (eds), *Global Migrations: The Scottish Diaspora since 1600*, Edinburgh, Edinburgh University Press, 2016.

McCrae, Hugh (ed.), *Georgiana's Journal: Melbourne 1841–1865*, Sydney, William Brooks, 1978.

McCrorie, Ian, *Steamers of the Highlands and Islands: An Illustrated History*, Greenock, Orr, Pollock & Co., 1987.

McCullough, Katie Louise, 'Building the Highland Empire: The Highland society of London and the Formation of Charitable Networks in Great Britain and Canada, 1778–1857', PhD thesis, University of Guelph, 2014.

McGilvery, George, 'Return of the Scottish Nabob, 1725–1833', in Mario Varricchio (ed.) *Back to Caledonia: Scottish Homecomings from the Seventeenth Century to the Present*, Edinburgh, John Donald, 2012: 90–108.

McKean, Charles, 'Edinburgh: 3. 1750 onwards', in Michael Lynch (ed.), *The Oxford Companion to Scottish History*, Oxford, Oxford University Press, 2001: 220–224.

'McLachlans of Salachan', *Notes and Queries*, 171/11 (12 Sept. 1936): 192.

Melville, Elinor G. K., *A Plague of Sheep: Environmental Consequences of the Conquest of Mexico*, Cambridge, Cambridge University Press, 1994.

Merrillees, Scott, *Batavia in Nineteenth Century Photographs*, Richmond, Surrey, Curzon, 2000.

Midgley, Clare, 'Bringing the Empire Home: Women Activists in Imperial Britain, 1790s–1930s', in Catherine Hall and Sonya O. Rose (eds), *At Home with the Empire: Metropolitan Culture and the Imperial World*, Cambridge, Cambridge University Press, 2006: 230–250.

Miers, Mary, *Highland Retreats: The Architecture and Interiors of Scotland's Romantic North*, New York, Rizzoli, 2017.

Mijers, Esther, 'Scotland, the Dutch Republic and the Union: Commerce and Cosmopolitanism', in Allan I. Macinnes and Douglas J. Hamilton (eds), *Jacobitism, Enlightenment and Empire, 1680–1820*, London, Pickering & Chatto, 2014: 93–109.

Miyata, Toshiyuki, 'Tan Kim Ching and Siam "Garden Rice": The Rice Trade between Siam and Singapore in the Late Nineteenth Century', in A. J. H, Latham and Heita Kawakatsu (eds), *Intra-Asian Trade and the World Market*, London, Routledge, 2006: 114–132.

Money, J. W. B., *Java, or, How to Manage a Colony: Showing a Practical Solution of the Questions Now Affecting British India*, 2 vols, London, Hurst and Blackett, 1861.

Mook, Hubertus van, *Netherlands Indies and Japan: Their Relations, 1940–1941*, London, George Allen & Unwin, 1944.

Moor, J. A. de, '"A Very Unpleasant Relationship": Trade and Strategy in the Eastern Seas: Anglo-Dutch Relations in the Nineteenth Century from a Colonial Perspective', in C. J. A. Raven and N. A. M. Rodger, eds, *Navies and Armies: The Anglo-Dutch Relationship in War and Peace, 1688–1988*, Edinburgh, John Donald, 1990: 49–69.

Moore, D. T., 'Falconer, Hugh (1808–1865)', *Oxford Dictionary of National Biography*, Oxford, Oxford University Press, 2004, online edition, www.oxforddnb.com/view/article/9110, accessed 26 May 2022.

Morrison, John, *Painting the Nation: Identity and Nationalism in Scottish Painting, 1800–1920*, Edinburgh, Edinburgh University Press, 2003.

Morton, Graeme, 'Caledonian societies', in Michael Lynch (ed.), *The Oxford Companion to Scottish History*, Oxford, Oxford University Press, 2001: 60.

Muirhead, Stuart, *Crisis Banking in the East*, Aldershot, Scholar Press, 1996.

Munden, A. F., 'Close, Francis (1797–1882), dean of Carlisle', in *Oxford Dictionary of National Biography*, online edition, Oxford, Oxford University Press, 2004, https://doi.org/10.1093/ref:odnb/5703, accessed 26 Feb. 2023.

Munro, J. Forbes, *Maritime Enterprise and Empire: Sir William Mackinnon and his Business Network, 1823–1893*, Woodbridge, The Boydell Press, 2003.

Mutch, Alistair, 'Agriculture and Empire: General Patrick "Tiger" Duff and the Shaping of North-East Scotland', *Review of Scottish Culture*, 22 (2010): 85–98.

Mutch, Alistair, *Tiger Duff: India, Madeira and Empire in Eighteenth-Century Scotland*, University of Aberdeen Press, 2017.

Nath, Ipshita, *Memsahibs: British Women in Colonial India*, London, Hurst Publishers, 2022.

Nenadic, Stana, 'Introduction', in Nenadic (ed.), *Scots in London in the Eighteenth Century*, Lewisburg, PA, Bucknell University Press, 2010: 13–45.

Neve, R. G. de, and D. van Duijn, 'De Vrijmetselarij in Oost-Indië: De Oprichters van de Loge "De Ster in het Oosten" te Batavia', *Indische Navorscher* (new series), 7/3 (1994): 194–220.

Newman, R. K., 'Opium Smoking in Late Imperial China: A Reconsideration', *Modern Asian Studies*, 29/4 (1995): 765–794.

Nieuwenhuys, Rob, *Komen en blijven. Tempo doeloe—een verzonken wereld*, Amsterdam, Querido, 1982.

Noble, Frederick Harwood, and Robert Morgan, *Speed the Plough: A History of the Royal Agricultural Society of Victoria*, [Melbourne], Royal Agricultural Society of Victoria, 1981.

Nussbaum, Felicity A., 'Introduction', in Nussbaum (ed.), *The Global Eighteenth Century*, Baltimore, MD, Johns Hopkins University Press, 2003: 1–18.

O'Brien, John, *Conflicts of Laws*, 2nd edition, London, Cavendish Publishing, 1999.

O'Hagan, Andrew, 'Bournemouth', *London Review of Books*, 42/10 (21 May 2020): 7.

Okubo, Shohei, 'An Armenian Opium Revenue Farmer in Java: His Business Partnerships with British and Chinese Entrepreneurs under the Dutch Colonial Regime ca. 1820–1835', *Acta Asiatica: Bulletin of the Institute of Eastern Culture*, 123 (2022): 67–85.

'Pahud de Mortanges', in *Nederland's Patriciaat: Genealogieën van Bekende Geslachten*, The Hague, Centraal Bureau voor Genealogie, 1910–, vols 2 (1911): 388–389, and 39 (1953): 222–227.

'Papworth Everard: Manors and other estates', in *A History of the County of Cambridge and the Isle of Ely*: vol. 9, *Chesterton, Northstowe, and Papworth Hundreds*, ed. A. P. M. Wright and C. P. Lewis, London, Victoria County History, 1989: 359–361, www.british-history.ac.uk/vch/cambs/vol9/pp359-361, accessed 26 May 2022.

Pharand, Michel W. (ed.), *Benjamin Disraeli Letters*, vol. 10: 1868, Toronto, University of Toronto Press, 2014.

Pless, Mary Theresa Olivia, *Daisy Princess Daisy of Pless, by Herself*, ed. Desmond Chapman-Huston, New York, Dutton, 1928, https://archive.org/stream/daisyprincessofp017081mbp/daisyprincessofp017081mbp_.txt, accessed 21 Aug. 2022.

Poeze, Harry A., *In het land van de overheerser. Deel I: Indonesiërs in Nederland 1600–1950*, Dordrecht, Foris Publications, 1986.

Pope, David, 'The Wealth and Social Aspirations of Liverpool's Slave Merchants in the Second Half of the Eighteenth Century', Appendices 1 and 2, in David Richardson, Suzanne Schwarz and Anthony Tibbles (eds), *Liverpool and Transatlantic Slavery*, Liverpool, Liverpool University Press, 2007: 194–208, 288.

Porter, Andrew, 'Religion and Empire: British Expansion in the Long Nineteenth Century, 1780–1914', *Journal of Imperial and Commonwealth History*, 20/3 (1992), 370–390.

The Port Phillip Almanac and Directory, for 1847, Melbourne, [n.p.], 1847.

Post, Peter, '*Indonesianisasi* and Japanization: The Japanese and the Shifting Fortunes of *Pribumi* Entrepreneurship', in J. Thomas Lindblad and Peter Post, eds, *Indonesian Economic Decolonization in Regional and International Perspective*, Leiden, KITLV Press, 2009: 59–86.

Prentis, Malcolm, *Scots in Australia: A Study of New South Wales, Victoria and Queensland, 1788–1900*, Sydney, UNSW Press, 2008.

Purwanto, Bambang, 'Economic decolonization and the rise of Indonesian military business', in J. Thomas Lindblad and Peter Post, eds, *Indonesian Economic Decolonization in Regional and International Perspective*, Leiden, KITLV Press, 2009: 39–58.

Ramsay, Freda, *John Ramsay of Kildalton J.P., M.P., D.L.: Being an Account of His Life in Islay and including the Diary of His Trip to Canada in 1870*, Toronto, Peter Martin, 1969.

Rappaport, Erika, *A Thirst for Empire: How Tea Shaped the Modern World*, Princeton, NJ, Princeton University Press, 2017.

Razzell, P. E., 'Social Origins of Officers in the British Indian and British Home Army, 1758–1962', *British Journal of Sociology*, 14 (1963): 248–260.

Redfern, William A., 'Sukarno's Guided Democracy and the Takeovers of Foreign Companies in Indonesia in the 1960s', PhD thesis, University of Michigan, Ann Arbor, MI, 2010.

Reid, Anthony, *An Indonesian Frontier: Acehnese and Other Histories of Sumatra*, Singapore, National University of Singapore Press, 2004.

Reid, Anthony, '"Slavery so Gentle": A Fluid Spectrum of Southeast Asian Conditions of Bondage', in Noel Lenski and Judith Cameron (eds), *What is a Slave Society? The Practice of Slavery in Global Perspective*, Cambridge, Cambridge University Press, 2018: 410–428.

Reitsma, S. A., *Korte geschiedenis der Nederlandsch-Indische spoor- en tramwegen*, Batavia, G. Kolff, 1928.

Reynolds, Henry, *Forgotten War*, Sydney, NewSouth, 2013.

Richards, Eric, 'The Highland Scots of South Australia', *Journal of the South Australian Historical Society*, 4 (1978): 33–64.

Richards, Eric, 'The Highland Passage to Colonial Australia', *Scotlands*, 2 (1995): 28–44.

Richards, Eric, 'Scottish Voices and Networks in Colonial Australia', in Angela McCarthy (ed.), *A Global Clan: Scottish Migrant Networks and Identities since the Eighteenth Century*, London, I. B. Tauris, 2007: 150–182.

Richards, Eric, 'Afterword', in Angela McCarthy and John M. MacKenzie (eds), *Global Migrations: The Scottish Diaspora since 1600*, Edinburgh, Edinburgh University Press, 2016: 272–280.

Roberson, Steven Henry, *Lili Kraus: Hungarian Pianist, Texas Teacher, and Personality Extraordinaire*, Fort Worth, TX, TCU Press, 2000.

[Robertson, James], *The Mull Diaries: The Diary of James Robertson, Sheriff Substitute of Tobermory, 1842–1846*, transc. and ed. Joseph Buist Loudon, Lochgilphead, Argyll and Bute Library Service, 2001.

Robinson, Jane, *A Force to Be Reckoned With: A History of the Women's Institute*, London, Virago, 2011.

Robinson, Leonard (with a Foreword by Tom Etty), *William Etty: The Life and Art*, Jefferson, NC, McFarland, 2007.

Rock, David, 'The British in Argentina', in Robert Bickers (ed.), *Settlers and Expatriates: Britons over the Seas*, Oxford, Oxford University Press, 2010: 117–145.

Rogers, Brett, and Adam Lowe, *Madame Yevonde: Be Original or Die*, London, The British Council, 1998.

Rogge, J., *Het Handelshuis Van Eeghen. Proeve eener geschiedenis van een Amsterdamsch handelshuis*, Amsterdam, Van Ditmar, 1949.

Rothschild, Emma, *The Inner Life of Empires: An Eighteenth-Century History*, Princeton, NJ, Princeton University Press, 2011.

Rush, James R., *Opium to Java: Revenue Farming and Chinese Enterprise in Colonial Indonesia, 1860–1910*, Ithaca, NY, Cornell University Press, 1990.

Schär, Bernhard C., 'Introduction: The Dutch East Indies and Europe, ca. 1800–1930: An Empire of Demands and Opportunities', *BMGN – Low Countries Historical Review*, 134/3 (2019): 4–20.

Schmiedell, J. H., *Gedenkblatter zum 50-Jahrigen Bestehen der Firma Erdmann & Sielcken in Java, 1875–1924*, np. nd. [1924].

Schmitz, Christopher, 'The Nature and Dimensions of Scottish Foreign Investment, 1860–1914', *Business History*, 39/2 (1997), 42–68.

Schoute, D., *De geneeskunde in Nederlandsch-Indië gedurende de negentiende eeuw*, The Hague, Kolff, 1935.

Schulte Nordholt, Henk (ed.), *Het dagelijks leven in Indië 1937–1947. Brieven van O. Schulte Nordholt-Zielhuis*, Zutphen, Walburg Pers, 1999.

Sebba, Anne, *The Exiled Collector: William Bankes and the Making of an English Country House*, Wimborne Minster, Dorset, Dovecote Press, 2009, originally published London, John Murray, 2004.

Sens, Angelie, *De kolonieman. Johannes van den Bosch (1780–1844), volksverheffer in naam van de koning*, Amsterdam, Balans, 2019.

Serville, Paul de, *Port Phillip Gentlemen: And Good Society in Melbourne before the Gold Rushes*, Melbourne, Oxford University Press, 1980.

Sharples, Joseph, David W. Walker and Matthew Woodworth, *Aberdeenshire South and Aberdeen*, The Buildings of Scotland, New Haven, CT, Yale University Press, 2015.

Smeaton, George, *Memoir of Alexander Thomson of Banchory*, Edinburgh, Edmonston & Douglas, 1869.

Stenton, Michael, *Who's Who of British Members of Parliament*, vol. 1: 1832–1885, Hassocks, Harvester Press, 1976.

Stevenson, David, 'Four Hundred Years of Freemasonry in Scotland', *Scottish Historical Review*, 90/2 (2011): 280–295.

Stevens, Th., *Vrijmetselarij en samenleving in Nederlands-Indië en Indonesië 1764–1962*, Hilversum, Verloren, 1994.

Stewart, A. I. B., 'MacNeils of Ardnacross', *Scottish Genealogist*, 30 (1983): 14–15.

Stoler, Ann Laura, 'Re-thinking Colonial Categories: European Communities and the Boundaries of Rule', *Comparative Studies in Society and History*, 31 (1989): 134–161.

Stoler, Ann Laura, 'Sexual Affronts and Racial Frontiers: European Identities and the Cultural Politics of Exclusion in Colonial Asia', *Comparative Studies in Society and History*, 34 (1992): 514–551.

Stoler, Ann Laura, 'Sexual Affronts and Racial Frontiers: European Identities and the Cultural Politics of Exclusion in Colonial Southeast Asia', in Frederick Cooper and Ann Laura Stoler (eds), *Tensions of Empire: Colonial Cultures in a Bourgeois World*, Berkeley, CA, University of California Press, 1997: 198–237.

Storrie, Margaret, *Islay: The Biography of an Island*, Islay, OA Press, 2nd edition, 1997.

Streets-Salter, Heather, *World War One in Southeast Asia: Colonialism and Anticolonialism in an Era of Global Conflict*, Cambridge, Cambridge University Press, 2017.

Sturma, Michael, 'Japanese Treatment of Allied Prisoners During the Second World War: Evaluating the Death Toll', *Journal of Contemporary History*, 55/3 (2020): 514–534.

Tagliacozzo, Eric, *Secret Trades, Porous Borders: Smuggling and States Along a Southeast Asian Frontier, 1865–1915*, New Haven, CT, Yale University Press, 2005.

Talbott, Siobhan, 'Diasporic or Distinct? Scots in Early Modern Europe', in Donald M. MacRaild, Tanja Bueltmann and J. C. D. Clark (eds), *British and Irish Diasporas: Societies, Cultures and Ideologies*, Manchester, Manchester University Press, 2019: 100–135.

Tarling, Nicholas, '"A Vital British Interest": Britain, Japan, and the Security of Netherlands India in the Inter-War Period', *Journal of Southeast Asian Studies*, 9/2 (1978): 180–218.

Tarling, Nicholas, *Britain, Southeast Asia and the Onset of the Pacific War*, Cambridge, Cambridge University Press, 1996.

Taselaar, Arjen, *De Nederlandse koloniale lobby. Ondernemers en de Indische politiek, 1914–1940*, Leiden, Research School CNWS, School of Asian, African, and Amerindian Studies [CNWS Publications, 62], 1998.

Taylor, D. J., *Bright Young People: The Rise and Fall of a Generation*, London, Chatto & Windus, 2007.

Taylor, Jean Gelman, *The Social World of Batavia: Europeans and Eurasians in Dutch Asia*, Madison, WI, University of Wisconsin Press, 1983.

Teulié, Gilles, 'Monarchy, Spirituality & Britishness: The Anglican Diaspora in Grasse 1880–1950', in Claire Davison, Béatrice Laurent, Caroline Patey and Nathalie Vanfasse (eds), *Provence and the British Imagination*, Milan: Ledizioni, 2013: 145–156.

Thompson, F. L. M., *The Rise of Respectable Society: A Social History of Victorian Britain, 1830–1900*, London, Fontana Press, 1988.

Topik, Steven C., and Allen Wells, 'Commodity Chains in a Global Economy', in Emily S. Rosenberg (ed.), *A World Connecting: 1870–1945*, Cambridge, MA, The Belknap Press of the Harvard University Press, 2012: 593–812.

Trocki, Carl A., 'The Rise of Singapore's Great Opium Syndicate, 1840–1886', *Journal of Southeast Asian Studies*, 18/2 (1987): 58–80.

Trocki, Carl A., *Opium and Empire: Chinese Society in Colonial Singapore, 1800–1910*, Ithaca, NY, Cornell University Press, 1990.

Tsolidis, Georgina, 'Introduction: Does Diaspora Matter When Living Cultural Difference?', in Tsolidis (ed.), *Migration, Diaspora and Identity: Cross-National Experiences*, Dordrecht, Springer, 2014: 1–15.

Turnbull, C. M., *The Straits Settlements, 1819–1867: Indian Presidency to Crown Colony*, London, Athlone Press, 1972.

Turnbull, C. M., 'Crawfurd, John (1783–1868)', *Oxford Dictionary of National Biography*, Oxford, Oxford University Press, 2004, online edition, www.oxforddnb.com/view/article/6651, accessed 21 June 2022.

Turner, John D., *Banking in Crisis: The Rise and Fall of British Banking Stability, 1880 to the Present*, Cambridge, Cambridge University Press, 2014.

'Uit de *Regeerings Almanak* van 1824. Engelsche en Armenische namen', *De Indische Navorscher*, 1/4 and 1/5 (1934).

'Van Motman', *Nederland's Patriciaat: Genealogieën van Bekende Geslachten*, The Hague, Centraal Bureau voor Genealogie, 1910–, vol. 40 (1954): 314–324.

'Van Tienhoven', *Nederland's Patriciaat: Genealogieën van Bekende Geslachten*, The Hague, Centraal Bureau voor Genealogie, 1910–, vols 8 (1917): 322–326, and 47 (1962): 320–326.

Varricchio, Mario (ed.), *Back to Caledonia: Scottish Homecomings from the Seventeenth Century to the Present*, Edinburgh, John Donald, 2012.

Veenendaal, G., 'De locomotief van de moderniteit. Aanleg van het net van spoor- en tramwegen', in Wim Ravesteijn and Jan Kop (eds), *Bouwen in de Archipel. Burgerlijke openbare werken in Nederlands-Indië en Indonesië 1800–2000*, Zutphen, Walburg Pers, 2004: 63–91.

Venn, J. A., *Alumni Cantabrigienses*, pt 2, vol. 4, Cambridge, Cambridge University Press, 1957.

Versteeg, Coos, 'Er is maar een echte Indische buurt', in Esther Captain, Maartje de Haan and Pim Westerkamp (eds), *De Indische Zomer in Den Haag: Het Cultureel Erfgoed Van de Indische Hoofdstad*, Leiden, KITLV, 2005: 23–40.

Vissering, C. M., *Een reis door Oost-Java*, Haarlem, Boon, 1912.

Vreede-de Stuers, Cora, 'Adriana: Een Kroniek van haar Indische Jaren, 1809–1840', *Bijdragen tot de Taal-, Land- en Volkenkunde*, 152 (1996): 74–108.

Vries, J. de, ed., *Herinneringen en Dagboek van Ernst Heldring (1871–1954)*, 3 vols, Utrecht, Nederlands Historisch Genootschap, 1970.

Walther, Eric H., *William Lowndes Yancey and the Coming of the Civil War*, Chapel Hill, NC, University of North Carolina Press, 2006.

Walther, Heidrun (ed.), *Aus dem Leben von Theodor Adolf von Möller: Nach unvollendet hinterlassenen Aufzeichnungen über die Jahre 1840–1890*, Neustadt an der Aisch, Verlag Degener, 1958.

Watson, Don, *Caledonia Australis: Scottish Highlanders on the Australian Frontier*, Sydney, Collins, 1984.

Webster, Anthony, *The Richest East India Merchant: The Life and Business of John Palmer of Calcutta, 1767–1836*, Woodbridge, The Boydell Press, 2007.

Webster, Anthony, 'The Development of British Commercial and Political Networks in the Straits Settlements 1800 to 1868: The Rise of a Colonial and Regional Economic Identity?', *Modern Asian Studies*, 45/4 (2011): 899–929.

Welling, Dolf, *Floris Arntzenius*, The Hague, Heemhave Holding BV/Van Voorst van Beest Galerie, 1992.

Westendorp Boerma, J. J. (ed.), *Briefwisseling tussen J. van den Bosch en J. C. Baud, 1829–1832 en 1834–1836*, 2 vols, Utrecht, Kemink en Zoon, 1956.

White, Daisy, *Daisy in Exile: The Diary of an Australian Schoolgirl in France (1887–1889)*, introduced and annotated by Marc Serve Rivière, Canberra, National Library of Australia, 2003.

White, Nicholas J., 'Surviving Sukarno: British Business in Post-Colonial Indonesia, 1950–1967', *Modern Asian Studies*, 46/5 (2012): 1277–1315.

Wijnaendts van Resandt, W., 'De Indische tak van de familie Couperus (uitgestorven in 1940)', *De Indische Navorscher* (new series), 5 (1992): 1–8.

Wilkie, Benjamin, *The Scots in Australia, 1788–1938*, Woodbridge, Boydell & Brewer, 2017.

Withers, Charles, 'The Historical Creation of the Scottish Highlands', in Ian L. Donnachie and Christopher Whatley (eds), *The Manufacture of Scottish History*, Edinburgh, Polygon, 1992: 143–156.

Young, Thomas, *Pioneer Station Owners of the Wimmera* [n.p., n.d., c. 1930]: 11, copy in State Library of Victoria, Melbourne.

Websites

Ancestry.com.au, www.ancestry.com.au
    1841–1911 England, Wales and Scotland Censuses.
    1850 United States Federal Census.
    Australia Birth, Marriage and Death Indexes, 1788–1985.
    Border Crossings: Canada to U.S., 1895–1960.
    California, Passenger and Crew Lists, 1882–1959.
    England & Wales, National Probate Calendar (Index of Wills and Administrations), 1857–2002.
    England and Wales, Civil Divorce Records, 1858–1918.
    England and Wales, Civil Registration Death Index, 1837–2007.
    England and Wales, Electoral Registers, 1832–1939.
    England, Church of England Marriages and Banns, 1754–1938.
    England, Oxford Men and Their Colleges, 1880–1892.
    England, Select Marriages, 1538–1973.
    England, United Grand Lodge of England Freemason Membership Registers, 1751–1921.
    Gloucestershire, England, Burials, 1813–1988.
    India, Select Births and Baptisms, 1786–1947.
    Kelly's Directory for Oxfordshire, London, Kelly & Co., 1901 and 1911.
    London City Directories, 1890–1905.
    New Orleans, Passenger Lists, 1813–1963.
    New York, Passenger Lists, 1820–1957.
    Register of Deaths at Sea, 1844–1890.
    Roll of the Indian Medical Service, 1515–1930.
    Scotland, Select Births and Baptisms, 1561–1910.
    UK and Ireland, Find a Grave Index, 1300s–Current.
    UK and Ireland, Incoming Passenger Lists, 1878–1960.
    UK and Ireland, Outgoing Passenger Lists, 1890–1960.
    UK, Foreign and Overseas Registers of British Subjects, 1628–1969.
    UK, Officer Service Records, 1764–1932.
    United States Marriages, 1733–2016.
    Victoria, Australia, Outward Passenger Lists, 1852–1915.
    World Book of Maclaines.
The British Newspaper Archive, www.britishnewspaperarchive.co.uk
Gale Primary Sources: Newspaper / Periodical databases, https://go.gale.com/ps
NewspaperSG, https://eresources.nlb.gov.sg/newspapers

Findmypast.com.au, www.findmypast.com.au
    1841–1921 England, Wales and Scotland Censuses.
    Great Western Railway Shareholders, 1835–1932.
    The Lands and People of Moray series.
    Middlesex, Harrow School Photographs of Pupils & Masters, 1869–1925.
    Morayshire Ordnance Survey Name Books, 1868–1871.
    Passenger Lists Leaving the United Kingdom, 1890–1960.

ScotlandsPeople, www.scotlandspeople.gov.uk

All Saints Jakarta, www.allsaintsjakarta.org
Canmore, www.canmore.org.uk
Centre for the Study of the Legacies of British Slavery, University College London, Legacies of British Slavery Database, www.ucl.ac.uk/lbs
Cocktails With Elvira, https://elvirabarney.wordpress.com
Companion to Tasmanian History, www.utas.edu.au/library/companion_to_tasmanian_history
Delpher, www.delpher.nl
Dictionary of Scottish Architects 1660–1980, www.scottisharchitects.org.uk
Digitaal Vrouwenlexicon van Nederland, Huygens Instituut voor Nederlandse Geschiedenis, https://resources.huygens.knaw.nl/vrouwenlexicon
Donald Historical Society, http://donaldhistory.org.au
Forces War Records, www.forces-war-records.co.uk
Genealogie Online, www.genealogieonline.nl
Grace's Guide to British Industrial History, www.gracesguide.co.uk
Historic England, https://historicengland.org.uk
Historic Environment Scotland, https://portal.historicenvironment.scot
History of Ceylon Tea, www.historyofceylontea.com
Islay Blog, www.islay.blog
Islay History, http://islayhistory.blogspot.com
Landed Families of Britain and Ireland, https://landedfamilies.blogspot.com
Library of Nineteenth-Century Photography, www.19thcenturyphotos.com
LocalWiki Adelaide Hills, https://localwiki.org/adelaide-hills/
Mansell POW Resources, www.mansell.com/pow_resources
Morning Glass, www.morningglass.co.uk
National Archives [UK], https://discovery.nationalarchives.gov.uk
National Records of Scotland, www.nrscotland.gov.uk
Open Archieven, www.openarchieven.nl
POW Research Network Japan, www.powresearch.jp
Singapore Infopedia, National Library Board Singapore, www.nlb.gov.sg/main
WieWasWie, www.wiewaswie.nl
Wikipedia, www.wikipedia.org and https://nl.wikipedia.org (English and Dutch editions consulted)

Index

Italic page numbers indicate illustrations.

A. Persons

Albert, Prince Consort *47*, 48
Anderson, Thomas (1797–1839) 17
Arntzenius, Floris (1864–1925) 259
Audsley, Maclaine Fraser (b. 1863) 121
Audsley, William James (1833–1907) 121

Baldwin, Stanley (1867–1947) 210
Ballingal, Robert (1827–1876) 89
Ballingal, Robert Rennie (1867–1928) 87
Bankes, Frances. See Woodley, Frances, later Bankes (1760–1823)
Bankes, Henriette. See Fraser, Henriette Jenny (1867–1953)
Bankes, Ralph, Jnr (1902–1981) 166
Bankes, Walter Ralph (1854–1904) *136*, 164–166
Barugh, Margaret (1816–1856) 43
Battenberg, Victoria Eugenie of, Queen of Spain 144
Baud, Jean Chrétien (1789–1859) 24, 158
Be Biauw Tjoan (1824–1904) 159
Beaver, Hugh Rowland (1842–1879) 119
Beckett, Walter Ralph Durie (1864–1917) 276
Berg, Norbert Pieter van den (1831–1917) 39
Beus, Anna de (b. 1871) *209*
Beus, Carel Gijsbert de (1833–1885) 209
Beusechem, Catharina van (1814–1840), aka Catherine Maclaine 11, 19–25, 26–27, 29, 32
Beusechem, Jan Michiel van (1775–1847) 14, 19
Beusechem, Nicolaas Philippus van (1778–1839) 21
Bezoet de Bie, Hermann (1844–1915) 252, 259
Bezoet de Bie, Johanna Elisabeth (1873–1957), aka the *nyonya besar* of Oemboel *236*, 249–260, *250*, *251*, *254*, *255*, *256*, *257*, *261*
Bhabha, Homi Kharshedji 42
Blackman, Emma Augusta (1847–1924) *136*, 160–161
Blackman, William Moies (1798–1875) 161
Blanckenhagen, Johannes Jacobus (1813–1885) 86
Bogaardt, Catharina Johanna Wilhelmina (1807–1839) 153–154
Bogaardt, Frederick (1835–1902) 86
Bogaardt, Louisa Isabella (1798–1871) 153–154
Bonhote, John Lewis (1804–1867) 32, 39
Borradaile, John (1815–1902) 127
Bosch, Johannes van den (1780–1844) 14, *14*, 19, 22–23, 36
Bouman, Cornelie Louise (b. 1883) *218*
Brodie, Alexander (1748–1818) 114
Brodie, James (fl. 1680s) 114
Buminata, Pangeran (fl. 1826) 26, 41
Burns, Robert ('Rabbie') (1759–1796) 11, 13, 198

Cambier, Jacob Carel Laurens (1835–1923) 246

Cameron, Alexander, Revd (1788–1872) 83, 86–87
Cameron, Alexander Patrick (1842–1919) 83, *96*, 109–111, *218*
Cameron, Elizabeth (1845–1935) *82*, 83, 84, 86, 89–90, 91–94, *93*, *94*, 95
Campbell, Catherine Matilda (1815–1847) *96*
Campbell, Frederick (1844–1926) 70
Campbell, John, 1st Baron Campbell of St Andrews (1779–1861) 155
Campbell, John Francis (1821–1885) 101
Campbell, Thomas (1777–1844) 15
Campbell, Walter Frederick (1798–1855) *74*, 80–81, 88
Cheere, Maria Ellen (1859–1938) *112*, 134
Chijs, Wilhelmina van der (1864–1921) *136*
Citters, Jan Willem Frederik van (1785–1836) 153
Citters, Julia Hermina van (1819–1879), aka Nonya Fraser *136*, 152–155, *153*, 157, 159
Clark, Ian Hugh Mackay (1890–1930) *218*, 266, 272
Clark, Isabel. See MacNeill, Isabella ('Isabel') Gijsberta Maria (1880–1975)
Clifford, Henry Edward (1852–1932) 222
Close, Francis, Revd (1797–1882) 189
Cobden, Richard (1804–1865) 71
Cochrane, Blair Onslow, Capt. (1853–1928) 144–145
Cochrane, Edith Hamilton (1858–1949) *136*
Cochrane, Joan (1884–1973) *136*
Coleman, Charles (1854–1907) *112*
Colijn, Hendrikus ('Hendrik') (1869–1944) 276
Conrad, Doda (1905–1997) 281
Cornwallis-West, Daisy, Princess of Pless (1873–1947) 164–165
Couperus, John (1855–1889) 251
Couperus, Louis (1863–1923) 242–243
Couperus, Petrus Theodorus (1815–1872) 241
Couperus, Wilhelmina Johanna (1849–1874) *236*, *240*, 241, 246
Coxworthy, Agnes Edith Fanny (1843–1880) 130
Craik, Jane (1835–1913) 105
Crawfurd, John (1783–1866) *74*, 80
Crempien-Velásquez, Eduardo de (b. 1907) *196*, 213
Cribb, Charles Theodore, Revd (1888–1976) 269
Cruden, George James David Ramsay (1889–1957) 269, 270–271
Cruden, Penelope Ann (1918–2008) 271

Cumming, Ann (1811–1888) *112*, 121–122, 123–124, 129
Cumming, James Bannerman (1819–1889) 122
Cumming, John (1781–1837) 121–122
Cumming, Marjory (1828–1849) 122
Cumming, Simon Fraser (1823–1874) 120
Cumming, Sophia (1826–1876) *112*, 113, 122–124, *124*, 128–129, 132, 134

Darlot, James Monckton (1811–1903) 176, 177
Davelaar, Anna Elisabeth van (1859–1917) *96*, 104, 223, 225, 226–227, 229
Davelaar, Jacobus van (1859–1915) 223–224
Davidson, Anne (1826–1880) 147
Davidson, Duncan (1773–1849) 147
Davidson, John (1791–1841) 13, 16, 17
Davidson, Margaret Jane (1820–1905) *136*, *146*, 147, 148–150
Davidson, Walter Stevenson (1785–1869) 147
Deans, John (1786–1868), later Deans-Campbell 16, 17, 20, *74*, 77, 78
Denne, Thomas (1829–1887) 44
Dickens, Charles (1812–1870) 117
Dingwall Fordyce, Agnes (1781–1834) 138
Dingwall Fordyce, Arthur (1745–1834) 138
Dolder, Henriette Anna Philippine van (1863–1945) 225
Donald, William (1825–1877) *172*, 185–186
Drucker, Jean Charles ('Carel') Joseph (1862–1944) *136*, 167–169, *168*, 170
Drucker, Louis (1805–1884) 167
Drucker, Wilhelmina (1847–1925) 169
Duff, Alexander, Dr (1806–1878) 152
Duff, Patrick ('Tiger'), Gen. (1742–1803) 102

Eaton, William (fl. 1835–1843) 145
Edward VII, King of Great Britain 91, 106, 166
Eeghen, Samuel Pieter van (1853–1934) 246
Elgar, Sir Edward (1857–1934) 227
Essen, Jan Lodewijk Frederik van, Dr (1902–1962) 248
Evans, Frances Elizabeth Florence ('Flossie') (1890–1969) *196*, 209, *210*, 210–211, 214
Evans, Lloyd (1864–1944) 209–210

Falconer, Alexander (1797–1856) 115
Falconer, Hugh (1808–1865) 115
Firebrace, Samuel, Judge (1800–1849) 176

Forbes, William ('Danzig Willie') (c.1566–1627) 274
Forbes-Sempill, Lady Gwendolen Emily Mary. See Sempill, Gwendolen Emily Mary, Lady
Forrest, John, Dr (1804–1865) 186
Forrest, John, Jnr (1842–1910) *172*, 186–187, *187*
Fraser, Adelaide (1850–1929) *112*, 129, 130–131, 135
Fraser, Alexander ('Alec') (1816–1904) *136*, 149, *150*, 150–161, *151*, *154*, *160*, 170, 199
Fraser, Alexander (1854–1897) *112*, 131
Fraser, Alexander Caspar (1835–1916) *136*, *141*, 141–143, *142*, 167
Fraser, Alexander Christian (1873–1959) *136*
Fraser, Angelica Patience (1823–1910) *136*, 147–148
Fraser, Anna Maria (1846–1903) *112*, 132
Fraser, Annie (1829–1904) 121
Fraser, Arthur (1811–1881) *136*, 137, 145–149, *146*, 152
Fraser, Arthur Abraham (1845–1935) 162, 167
Fraser, Arthur Hyde (1884–1944) *136*
Fraser, Bernard Norman (1876–1955) *136*, 144–145
Fraser, Clive Stuart (1887–1974) 36
Fraser, Duncan Davidson (1857–1931) *136*
Fraser, Edward Seymour (1846–1893) *112*
Fraser, Ellen Allan (1862–1942) *112*, 132
Fraser, Emily (c.1859–1945) *112*, 132
Fraser, Emma J. (b. 1860) 131
Fraser, George John (1846–1887) *112*, 132–133
Fraser, Henriette Jenny (1867–1953), aka Henriette Bankes *136*, 162–167, *163*, *164*, *165*, 170–171
Fraser, James (1801–1872) *112*, 113–129, *115*, *123*, 132–135
Fraser, James (b. 1856) *112*, 132
Fraser, James Maclaine (1831–1878) 121
Fraser, Jean Steuart (1804–1870) 1–2, 5, 7–8, *136*, 137–139, 147
Fraser, Jessy (1799–1870) *136*, 147–149
Fraser, John Ellis (1833–1845) 121
Fraser, John Mathison, Snr (1805–1885) 64, *136*, 139–141, 142, 143, 145, 152
Fraser, John Mathison, Jnr (1867–1950) *136*, 143–144
Fraser, John Thomson (1869–1936) 163
Fraser, Lewis, Snr (1811–1868) *112*, 113–115, *115*, 117–129, *124*, *125*, *127*, 131–132, 133–135
Fraser, Lewis, Jnr (1852–1906) *112*, 132

Fraser, Lewis James (1841–1906) *112*, 132–135
Fraser, Margaret Amy (1847–1909) *112*, 131
Fraser, Margaret Still (1825–1904) 39
Fraser, Marjorie Read (1849–1929) *112*, 132
Fraser, Mary Lydia (1862–1944) *136*, 167–169, *168*, 170–171
Fraser, Matilda Maria (1844–1914) *112*
Fraser, Sophia Cumming (1839–1904) *112*, 130, 133–134
Fraser, Sophia Cumming (1848–1916) *112*, 132
Fraser, William Thomson (1841–1880) *136*, 161–162
Fyfe, Jane (fl. 1832) 43

Gehne, Amalie Frederika (1821–1902) *172*, 180–181, *180*, 183–184, 190
Gehne, Augusta Carolina (1824–1891) 181
Gehne, Carl Friedrich (1792–1843) 180
Gehne-Klamberg, Sara Hester Catharina (1789–1858) 180–181
George VI, King of Great Britain 269
Gijselman, Catharina Maria Hermina Alexandrina (1870–1943) 191
Gill, Francina Henriette (1872–1957) 93–94
Gillespie, Grace Marjorie ('Boe') (1914–1990) 218, 231–232, *232*, 233, 234
Goldberg, Szymon (1909–1993) 281
Goldney, Alfred (1834–1890) *112*
Granpré Molière, Charles Antoine (1803–1876) *52*, 55, 56, 59, 145–146
Gregorson, John (1776–1845) 25, *65*, 66
Gregorson, Marjorie (1778–1836) xi
Groll, Elisabeth Johanna van (1789–1861) *52*, 55
Groll, Gerhardus van (1748–1821) 55
Groll, Sara Wilhelmina van (1787–1855) *52*, 54–59
Gurney, Sir Henry Lovell Goldsworthy (1898–1951) 133
Guthrie, James (1814–1900) *112*, 133–134

Hackblock, John (1804–1877) 127
Hall, Catherine 38, 39
Harbord-Hammond, Richard Morden, Adm. (1865–1951) 107
Hare, Sir Thomas Leigh (1859–1941) 107
Haughton, Emily (1881–1971) 272–273
Haughton, William Theodore (1886–1973) 272
Haydn, Joseph (1732–1809) 263
Herbert, Arthur Colthurst, Capt. (1867–1933) 190–191
Hofland, Anna Catharina (1824–1884) 57
Holle, Adriaan Walraven (1832–1871) *41*

Holle, Karel Frederik (1829–1896) 40
Howard, George Percy (1862–1936) 92
Hubner, Johanna Maria Louisa (1796–1872) 201
Hubner, Margaretha Augusta (1869–1910) *236*, 248, *249*
Hucht, Wilhelmina ('Mientje') Françoise van der (1841–1903) *172*, 181–183, *182*, 184, 184–185, 188, 189, 191, 193
Hucht, Willem van der (1812–1874) 35, 40, 41, *41*, 182
Hulstijn, Sam van (1830–1879) 158–159
Hunter, Robert (1813–1878) *74*, 87

Iida, Nobuo (1903–1991) 282
Innes-Ker, James, 6th Duke of Roxburghe (1816–1879) 155
Israëls, Jozef (1824–1911) 169

Jackson, Eugenie (b. 1867) 254, *254*
James, Charles Deere, Capt. (1832–1878) *112*, 130
Jongh, Coenraad Alexander de (1803–1873) 181

Kasminah (fl. 1908) 107–108
Kearns, Grace Audrey (1893–1969) *196*, 214–215
Kerr, George (1867–1918) *218*, 227–228, 230
Kraus, Lili (1903–1986) 262, 263–265, *264*, 280–282

Landseer, Sir Edwin (1802–1873) 205
Lange, Johanna Wilhelmina de (1840–1888) *236*, 241–242
Lange, Louise Cornelia de (1850–1918) 246
Larsen, Rasmus Samuel Thal (1837–1928) 258
Lavers, Adela Mary (1863–1930) *112*
Le Souef, Charles Henry Bouillard (1818–1891) 186
Levert, Johanna Bernardina (1842–1926) 258
Levyssohn Norman, Henry David (1836–1892) 158–159
Lightfoot, Pamela Cecil (1910–1974) *218*
Limburg Stirum, Johan Paul, graaf van (1873–1948) 276
Locock, Sir Charles (1799–1876) 130
Locock, Herbert, Lt-Col. (1837–1910) *112*, 130–131
Loon, Willem Hendrik van, Jhr (1855–1935) 246
Loudon, Agnes (1827–1906) *96*, 100
Loudon, Alexander (1789–1840) 23–24, 36, 42–43, 65–66, 100, 158

Loudon, Isabella Maria (1825–1877) *96*, *98*, 100–101, *101*, 103
Loudon, James (1824–1900) 24, 158, 159, 161
Loudon, William, Lt (1782–1870) 100
Lydall, Charles Hawthorne (1878–1945) 272
Lydall, Elizabeth ('Betty') Hawthorne (1903–2000) *196*, 272–274, *273*, 278, 283

McCrae, Georgiana Huntly (1804–1890) 176
McEacharn, Sir Malcolm Donald (1852–1910) 228
McGregor, Archibald (1809–1863) 201–202
McGuffie, John (1785–1861) 219–222, *221*
McGuffie, Margaret (1812–1896) 221–222
MacIndoe, Flora. See MacNeill, Flora (1884–1964)
MacIndoe, Robert Gourlay (1890–1967) 230–231, 269
MacIntyre, Donald (1782–1836) 17, 79, 115
MacIntyre, John, Gen. (1750–1828) 79
Mackenzie, Alexander Marshall (1848–1933) 205
Mackenzie, Emma (1887–1959) *218*, 231, 233–235
Mackenzie, Gilbert Proby (1847–1890) 231
Mackey, Hugh Allen, Capt. (1840–1877) *112*, 130
McKie, John Hamilton (1898–1958), later Mackie 233–234
Mackillop, Andrew 6
Mackinnon, Sir William (1823–1893) 157
McLachlan, Alexander, Capt. (1859–1898) 190
McLachlan, Alfred Francis (1865–1901) 191
McLachlan, Amelia Ross (1818–1865) 186
McLachlan, Ann (1810–1842) *172*, 186
McLachlan, Annie Constance (1876–1951) 190–191
McLachlan, Archibald (1814–1879) *172*, 185
McLachlan, Archibald Sawers, Maj. (1857–1932) 190
McLachlan, Arthur Cecil (1872–1953) 192
McLachlan, Donald (1812–1893) 40, *74*, 76, 79, 152, *172*, 173–174, 178–181, *180*, 183–184, *183*, 187, 190
McLachlan, Donald, Capt. (1778–1863) *172*, 175–177, 186, 194
McLachlan, Donald Maxwell (1867–1940) 190

McLachlan, Duncan (d. after 1831) 17
McLachlan, James (1825–1903) 40, 74, 79, *172*, 173, 178–185, *181*, 184, *186*, 187–189, 190, 191, 193
McLachlan, James Douglas, Lt-Col. (1869–1937) 189–190
McLachlan, Mary Anne (1833–1901) *172*, 185–186
McLachlan, Patrick (d. 1825) 17, 79
McLachlan, Ronald (1828–1904) *172*, 185, 191, 192–193
McLachlan, William John (1864–1948) 191–192
Maclaine, Alexander Campbell (1827–1885) 64, 67, 68–69
Maclaine, Allan (1822–1878) 68
Maclaine, Angus, Revd (1800–1879) xi–xii, 28, 59, 64–68, *66*, 113, 117
Maclaine, Anthony Vincent (1846–1887) 70
Maclaine, Colquhoun (1828–1853) 69
Maclaine, Donald, of Lochbuie (1816–1863) 15, 45–46, *52*, 53–54, *54*, 56, 58–64, *58*, 67–70, *70*, 72
Maclaine, Gillian (1798–1840) xi–xii, xiii, 8, 11–13, *12*, 15, 16, 17–27, 29, 32, 36, 38, 39, 41, 42, *43*, 49, 50, 53, 59, 64, 65–66, *74*, 77, 78, 79, 80, 99, 100, 107, 115, 119–120, 121, 125, 137, 139, 145, 146, 147, 158, 202, 216, 229, 265, 287, 289, 290–291
Maclaine, Hector (1785–1847) 33
Maclaine, John Campbell (1818–1885) 67–68
Maclaine, Kenneth Douglas Lorne, of Lochbuie (1880–1935) 52
Maclaine, Margaret Maxwell (1832–1861) 34, *52*, 62–64, *63*
Maclaine, Murdoch, Snr, of Lochbuie (1791–1844) *52*, 60–61, 67
Maclaine, Murdoch, Jnr ('Little Murdie'), of Lochbuie (1814–1850) *52*, 61
Maclaine, Murdoch Gillian, of Lochbuie (1845–1909) *52*, 70–72, *71*
McLean, Alexander (1869–1929) 93–94
McLean, Alexander Ellister (1875–1907) *196*
McLean, Anna Elizabeth (1902–2000) 283
McLean, Annabella (1832–1867) 87
McLean, Billy. See McLean, William ('Billy') (1918–1986)
McLean, Callum. See McLean, Neil Malcolm ('Callum') (1903–1992)
McLean, Christina, of Kinlochleven (1796–1873) *52*, 60–61
McLean, Colin Alexander, Maj. (1866–1937) 87, 92, 94
McLean, Colin, Jnr, Lt.-Col. (1873–1915) *196*, 203, 208–209, 265–266
McLean, Colin, Snr (1792–1861) 74, 75–78, 80–82, *81*, 87, 95, 101, 199, 265
McLean, Elizabeth Marjorie (1897–1933) *196*
McLean, Elizabeth Nora (1878–1959) 92–93
McLean, Flora (b. 1840) 87
McLean, Godfrey Neil, Maj. (1880–1950) *196*, 209
Maclean, Hector, Lt (1792–1812) 16
McLean, Isobel Agnes Loudon (1888–1953) *196*, 209
McLean, Isobel Florence (1912–2002) *196*, *210*, *211*, 211–214, *212*
McLean, Lachlan (1830–1880) 74, 75–77, 76, 82–91, *82*, *88*, 95, 199
McLean, Lachlan, Jnr (1877–1937) *196*, 209, 266
McLean, Loudon MacNeill (1885–1956) *196*, 209–211, 214, 215
McLean, Lucy (1829–1877) 74, 87
McLean, Lucy Campbell (1877–1953) 94
McLean, Mary Stiles (1871–1952) 92
McLean, Neil (1836–1923) 74, 89, 103, *196*, 197–208, *198*, *200*, *204*, *206*, 212, 213, 215–217, 265
McLean, Neil Gillean (1881–1964) *196*, 209, 214–215, 265
McLean, Neil Malcolm ('Callum') (1903–1992) *196*, *262*, 263–285, *273*, *279*
McLean, William ('Billy') (1918–1986) *196*, 214–215
McLennan, Alexander (1821–1898) 202
McLennan, Anna Frederika (1818–1913) 201–202
McLennan, Donald (1784–1865) 44, 201
Macleod, Norman, Revd (1812–1872) 125
McMaster, John (1799–1825) 26
MacNeill, Agnes Webster (1858–1892) *96*, 104
MacNeill, Alexander, Jnr (1862–1947) *96*, 104–105, 107–109
Mac Neill, Alexander, Jnr (1871–1937), aka the *tuan besar* of Oemboel *236*, 244, 246, 249–260, *250*, *251*, *252*, *256*
MacNeill, Alexander, Snr (1810–1867) 74, 78, *96*, 97–103, *98*, *99*, *101*, 104, 105, *218*, 223, 229, 235, *236*, 239–241
MacNeill, Alexander ('Sandy') Henry, Col. (1883–1930) *218*, 228–230, 231
Mac Neill, Ann Jeanne (b. 1898) 107
Mac Neill, Arabella (1872–1944) *236*, 246–248, *247*
Mac Neill, Catharina Rica (1870–1945) *236*, 255
Mac Neill, Edward Henry (1895–1990) 107

MacNeill, Eila (1867–1954) *96*, *108*, 109–110
Mac Neill, Elisabeth (1878–1933) *236*
MacNeill, Elizabeth (1851–1926) *96*, *196*, 203–208, *206*, 215–216, *218*
MacNeill, Flora (1861–1932) *96*, 109–111, *218*
MacNeill, Flora (1884–1964) *218*, 227–228, 230–231, 272
Mac Neill, Georgette (1868–1964) *236*, 255
MacNeill, Isabella ('Isabel') Gijsberta Maria (1880–1975) *196*, 208, *218*, 230, 266, 272
MacNeill, Isabella Gillis (1857–1892) *96*, 104
MacNeill, John (1800–1857) 25, *74*, 78–79, *79*, *96*, 99–100, 102, 223, 229
MacNeill, John Godfrey (1859–1882) *96*
MacNeill, Loudon (1915–1990) *218*, 231–233, 232, 234–235
MacNeill, Margaret (1803–1877) *74*, 78, 87–88, 197
MacNeill, Michael Loudon Lorne (b. 1945) 235
MacNeill, Neil, 'the first' (1766–1848) 229–230
MacNeill, Neil, Jnr (1885–1955) *218*, 224–225, 235, 266–267
MacNeill, Neil, Snr (1853–1935) *96*, 104–107, *105*, 109, 237
Mac Neill, Richard (1842–1915) *236*, 237–249, *238*, *244*, *245*, 255
Mac Neill, Richard ('Dick') (1898–1963) 259
MacNeill, Sandy. See MacNeill, Alexander ('Sandy') Henry, Col. (1883–1930)
Mac Neill, Wilhelmina (1876–1904) *236*
MacNeill, William Loudon (1854-1923) *96*, 104, 107, *218*, 219–229, *220*, *224*, *232*, 235, 237
Malcolm, John Wingfield, Lt-Col. (1833–1902) 89
Marx, Karl (1818–1883) 184
Mary of Teck, Queen of Great Britain 166
Maxwell, Sir Herbert (1845–1937) 229
Maxwell, John Argyll (1790–1857) 118, 119
Meiklereid, Ernest William Frederick (1899–1965) 279
Menzies, Alexander Anderson (1830–1847) 43
Menzies, Mary (b. 1832) 43–44
Menzies, Robert (1795–1859) 43
Menzies, Robert Bunn (1826–1868) 44
Menzies, William (1791–1854) 17, 18, 21, 43, 44
Miesegaes, Gerhard Hermann (1833–1913) 201

Mina (fl. 1832) 21
Mojzer, Louis (1906–1986) 282
Möller, Theodor Adolf von (1840–1925) 155
Money, James William Bayley (1818–1890) 36
Monteux, Pierre (1875–1964) 280
Morgan, Daisy Ruth (1890–1982), 270–271
Morison, Janet (1747–1831) 138
Morrison, James (1789–1857) 88
Motman, Jan Casimir Theodorus van (1819–1865) 40
Munro, Sir Hector, Gen. (1760–1807) 102
Murchison, Robert Impey (1792–1871) 45, 46

Nash, John (1752–1835) 123
Nata di Laga (fl. c.1861) 41, *41*
Nickerson, Pliny Marshall (1845–1879) 160–161
Nicol, William (1790–1879) 126–127
Nottebohm, Caspar André (1816–1888) 141
Nottebohm, Gertrude Eleonore ('Emilie') (1814–1887) *136*, 139–141, 142, 143

Onnen, Anna (1844–1885) *136*, 161–162, 164
Oudraad, Barend Nicolaas (1890–1970) 282
Overgaauw, Elisabeth (1814-1887) 142, 143

Padday, Henry James Duncan (1832–1916) *112*
Pahud, Antoinette Catharina (1828–1898) 57
Pahud, Charles Ferdinand (1803–1873) 56–57
Palmer, John (1767–1836) 77
Paston-Bedingfeld, Sir Henry Edward (1860–1941) 106
Paston-Bedingfeld, Sybil, Lady (1883–1985) 109
Paterson, John (1822–1880) 127
Paull, Henry (1824–1898) 128
Pérouse de Montclos, Katherine (1895–1958) 279
Pikler, Robert (1909–1984) 282
Pirie, Frances Mary (1786–1859) 147
Pless, Hans Heinrich XV, Prince of (1861–1938) 164–165
Pless, Princess of. See Cornwallis-West, Daisy, Princess of Pless (1873–1947)
Pryce, John (1819–1891) 34–35, *34*, 40, *52*, 63–64
Puy, James du (1792–1881) *52*, 55–56, 58

Puy, Pieter James Gerhard du (1828–1897) 56

Radin (fl. 1832) 21
Ramsay, Archibald Maule, Capt. (1894–1955) 233
Ramsay, John, of Kildalton (1815–1892) 79
Read, William Henry Macleod (1819–1909) 122
Rees, Eecoline ('Etie') Adrienne van (1890–1973) *218*, 224–225
Rees, Otto van (1823–1892) 224
Renardel de Lavalette, Gerrit Christiaan (1849–1926) 258
Renardel de Lavalette, Jean Guillaume (1828–1918) 258
Renardel de Lavalette, Margaretha Johanna Cornelia (1849–1939) 258
Renaud, Sara Justina (1781–1840) 21
Rennie, William (1820–1887) 126–127
Robertson, Mrs C. H. E. See Dolder, Henriette Anna Philippine van
Rochussen, Jan Jacobus (1797–1871) 57–58, *57*
Rodger, Eveline (1850–1905) 187
Rodocanachi, Michel Emmanuel (1821–1901) 128
Rothschild, Emma 9

St Clair, Margaret Helen, Hon. (1873–1939) *136*
Saleh, Raden (c.1811–1880) 151, *151*, 161
Salis-Schwabe, Julie (1818–1896) *52*
Sands, David (1808–1881) 68
Sands, Marian Palmer (1831–1889) 68
Sarinah (fl. 1849) 241
Sawers, John, of Bellfield (1761–1839) 176
Sawers, Mary Anne (1792–1854) *172*, 176
Schumann, Robert (1810-1856) 263
Schwabe, Catherine Marianne (1850–1934) *52*, 71–72
Schwabe, Salis (1800–1853) *52*
Scott, Jane (1851–1926) 231
Scott, Sir Walter (1771–1832) 13
Sebo, Dorothea Elisabeth (1812–1880) 86
Sedgwick, Adam (1785–1873) 45
Semmes, Raphael, Capt. (1809–1877) 119
Sempill, Gwendolen Emily Mary, Lady (1869–1944) 274
Shaw, Elizabeth (1815–1891) *172*, 185
Sie Poddie (d. 1909) 258
Sienok (fl. 1842) *236*, 240
Sijthoff, Sarah (1849–1934) 252, 259
Silvy, Camille (1834–1910) 129
Skeffington-Smyth, Terence George Randall (1905–1936) *196*, 212–213, *212*
Sluijter, Johannes (b. 1869) *236*, 255

Sminia, Catharina Maria Rolina, jonkvrouw van (1875–1955) 276
Soesman, Robert Erland Nicolai (1868–1919) 258
Spruytenburg, Hendricus (1830–1878) 202
Stewart, Randolph Algernon Ronald, 12th Earl of Galloway (1892–1978) 233–234
Stewart, Randolph Henry, 11th Earl of Galloway (1836–1920) 228
Stiles, Mary (1807–1894) 83, 86–87
Stuers, Louise de (1835–1915) 159
Sturler, Rudolphina Wilhelmina Elisabeth de (1798–1873) 22–23, *22*
Suharto (1921–2008) 285
Sukarno (1901–1970) 284–285
Sutton, Mary Evelyn (1860–1934) 144
Sutton, Sir Richard (1821–1878) 144

Tan Kim Ching (1829–1892) 120
Tan Tock Seng (1798–1850) 120
Tennyson, Alfred, Lord (1809–1892) 189
Thaden, Bernard Antoine Louis (1802–1882) 142
Thaden, Maria Johanna (1835–1907) *136*, *141*, 142–143
Thomas, Theresa Anne (1828–1908) *172*, 192–193
Thomson, Alexander (1798–1868) *136*, 147–149
Thompson, Dora Georgina Rivers (1866–1963) 92
Tienhoven van den Bogaard, Gijsbert van (1871–1919) *236*, 246–248, *247*
Tienhoven, Gijsbert van (1841–1914) 248
Todd, Helen Marjorie (1887–1970) 231
Turing, Alan (1912–1954) 2
Turing, John Robert (1793–1828) 1, 7, *136*, 137
Turquand, William (1818–1894) 128

Valck, Susanna Gaspardina (1801–1828) 24
Victoria, Queen of Great Britain *47*, 48, 130, 144, 150
Villiers-Stuart, John Patrick, Col. (1879–1958) 107
Vincent, Anthonij (1792–1828) 54–55
Vincent, Anthonij Willem Adriaan (1817–1852) 57
Vincent, Catharina Sara Elisabeth (1815–1894) *52*, 55
Vincent, Edward James Elize (1822–1877) 57
Vincent, Elisabeth Charlotte (1827–1851) 57–58
Vincent, Emilie Guillaumine (1826–1882) *52*, 54, 56, *58*, 69–70
Vincent, Rosalie Antoinette (1824–1902) 56

Vissering, Cornelia Margaretha (1859–1942) 253

Walsh, Henry Francis Chester (1891–1976) 281
Watson, Edward (1799–1873) xi, 18, *19*, 43–44
Waugh, Evelyn (1903–1966) 213
Webb, Beatrice (1858–1943) 228
Webb, Sidney (1859–1947) 228
Weijde, Folkerus Karel van der (1863–1951) *236*, 255
Weijde, Willem van der (1896–1957) 259
Wellerson, Eugenia (1910–2011) 282
Wheeler, Alice Burbank (1849–1931) 157
White, Gwendolyn Mabel (1878–1959) 190
White, Henry Charles (1837–1905) 194
Wilhelm II, German Emperor 165, 166
Wilhelmina, Queen of the Netherlands 278
Winterbottom, Marie Austier (1811–1874) 68
Woodhall, Harold Whiteman, Lt-Col. (1872–1951) 92–93
Woodley, Frances, later Bankes (1760–1823) 166

Yancey, William Lowndes (1814–1863) 156
Yevonde, Madame (Yevonde Middleton) (1893–1975) 211
Young, James (1777–1834) 138–139

B. Places

Aberdeen 1, 2, 7, 46, 102, 137–139, 145, 147, *150*, 152, 167, 170, 199, 205, 212, 216, 265, 266, 273, 291; Marischal College 13, 205
Aberdeenshire 48, 205, 206, 207, 212, 233, 283
Aceh 159, 224
Adelaide xii, xiv, 64, 65, *66*, 67–68, 69
Africa 55; southern 2, 127, 207, 290
Alabama 156
Alas Bezoeki 107
Alexandria 59
Alford 205, 266
Ambarawa 260
Ambon 282–283
Americas 4, 55, 114, 140, 161

Amsterdam xiv, 40, 86, 167, 168, 169, 182, 242, 246, 248, 289
Antipodes xii, 40, 65, 66, 68, 69, 85, 135, 173, 174, 175, 176, 178, 179, 184, 186, 190, 191, 192, 194, 228, 280, 282. See also Australia; New Zealand
Antwerp 1, 64, 138, 139, 140, 141, 152
Archipelbuurt. See The Hague
Ardgay (Easter Ross) 215
Ardnacross (Mull) 100, 230
Ardnamurchan 67
Ardsheal House (Lochaber) 110
Ardtornish (Morvern) 25, *60*, *65*, 66
Ardtornish (South Australia) 66–67, *66*
Argentina 7, 92, 232
Argrennan House (Kirkcudbrightshire) 232
Argyll 71, 80, 203, 229
Arjuna (mountain) 201
Arnhem 244, 246, 248
Asia 4–5, 7–8, 11, 35, 37, 39, 42, 50, 55, 77, 83, 85, 114, 118, 126, 156, 231, 268, 270, 276, 277, 281, 288, 292
Atlantic Ocean 60
Atlantic Zone 5, 36, 288
Auchintoul (Aberdeenshire) 208, 265, 272
Australia xi, xii, 29, 64, 65, 132, 147, 158, 175–178, *175*, 179, 179, 185, 191–194, 228; south-eastern 173, 178, 192, 282
Australasia 2–3, 173, 290

Backhill House (Midlothian) 100
Bahamas 214
Bahia (Brazil) 139
Balgowan Park (Perthshire) 208
Ballachulish 110
Balmoral Castle *47*, 48
Banchory House (Aberdeenshire) 147, 148
Bandungan 260, *261*
Bangkok 119, 120, 279
Barbados. See Wigtown
Barbreck House (Argyll) 203
Batavia 1, 4, 7, *10*, 11, 13–22, 25, 27, 29, *30–31*, 32–35, 36, 39, 40, 41, 43, 45, 46, 54, 55, 56, 57, 58, *58*, 59, 62, 63, *78*, 84–85, 86, 105, 115, 116, 118, 121, 137, 139, 145, 147, 152, *153*, 158, 160, 161, 181, 182, 191, 199–200, 201, 202, 203, 204, 207, 210, 214, 225–226, 237, 241, 242, 267, 268, 271, 279, 281, 282, 287, 289; Koningsplein 29, *34*, 58, 63, 152; Tanah Abang 27, 29, 58; Willemskerk *57*, 58
Bath 206, 270
Battleby House (Perthshire) 204–205, 207
Bayswater. See London

Beachamwell (Norfolk) 107
Belgium 59, 139, 210, 258
Belgravia 163
Ben Nevis 21, 25, 110
Bengal 17, 18, 92, 146
Benham Park (Berkshire) 144
Berkshire 140, 141, 144
Bexhill-on-Sea 132
Billiton 182
Blackheath. See London
Bladnoch (river) 222
Bogor. See Buitenzorg
Bombay 1, 13
Bordlands (Peeblesshire) 100–102, *101*, 103
Borneo 277
Boston 161
Bournemouth 72, 92, 97, *98*, 107, 206
Bowmore (Islay) 230
Brantas River 145, 267
Brazil 35, 36, 139
Breda House (Aberdeenshire) *204*, 205–207, 212, 215, 265, 272, 274, 283
Bridgend (Islay) 87, 88
Brighton 214
Brisbane 158
Bristol 50
Britain 2, 5, 17, 18, 43, 76, **82**, **88**, **89**, 105, 108, 109, 110, 114, 119, 120, 137, 147, 154, 155, 156, 158, 162, 173, 193, 194, 205, 228, 231, 239, 271, 283, 284, 290, 291
British Guiana 176, 231
British Empire 3, 7, 103, 114, 118, 151, 178, 198, 207, 208, 216, 231, 239, 275, 290, 291
British Isles 2, 4, 237, 265, 270
British Malaya 238, 266
Buckinghamshire 187
Buenos Aires 213
Buitenzorg *10*
Bukit Fraser. See Fraser's Hill (Pahang)
Burma 283

Cairo 59
Calcutta 17, 18, 32, 77, 87, 115, 127, 152, 268
California 280, 282
Cambridge 2, 266, 272
Cambridgeshire 134
Canada 69, 90, 109, 131, 198, 232
Cannes 86, 150
Canton 119, 147
Cape of Good Hope 1, 59, 75, 271
Cape Town 55, 186
Capri 131
Caribbean 4, 39, 55, 61, **84**, 139, 166, 175, 176, 185, 219
Castle Douglas (Kirkcudbrightshire) 231
Castle Forbes (Aberdeenshire) 208

Cepiring. See Tjepiring
Ceylon 190–191, 266, 272
Charleston (South Carolina) 139
Charleton Manor. See Cheltenham
Chelsea. See London
Cheltenham 50, 184–186, 187–190, 191, 192, 193, 194; Charleton Manor 190; Cheltenham College 188–189, 191; Cheltenham Ladies' College *188*, 189; Holland House *184*, 185, 188; Lisle House 186
China 1, 5, 7, 78, 105, 114, 116, 118, 119, 146, 147, 269, 277, 278, 281, 292
Chios 128
Christchurch (New Zealand) 69
Cipanas *10*, 22–23, *23*
Clyde 46
Clydeside 46
Coleraine (Victoria) 68
Côte d'Azur 150
Cotswolds 193
Covent Garden. See London
Craigievar Castle 274
Croydon 130, 254
Cuba 5, 35, 36, 84
Cumberland 127, 166
Cumloden (Kirkcudbrightshire) 228
Curzon House. See Mayfair

Dartmouth College 265
Dauphiné 279
Dee (river) 147
Delft 247
Demerara 176, 231
Devon 149
Dorchester 93
Dorset 92, 93, 165, 166
Dover 127
Downpatrick 160
Duart Castle 197
Dumfries 229
Dundee 23, 46
Dutch East Indies. See Indies.
Dutch empire 1, 4, 7, 11, 99, 114, 151, 239, 263, 275, 289. See also Indies.

Eastbourne 70
Edinburgh 15, 46–47, 61, 63, 64, 69, 94, 97, 100, 102, 107, 148, 149, 174, 190, 203, 215, 223, 229, 231, 235, 240; Holyrood Palace 47; New Town 46–47, 102
Egypt 189, 223, 229
Elgin 114
Ellister (Islay) 78, 100
Emden 142
England xiii, 2, 3, 38, 48, 49, 70, 91, 102, 103, 104, 106, 107, 109, 110, 114, 129, 133, 143, 149, 162, 163, 165, 166, 169, 170, 183–185, 187, 188,

191, 213, 214, 215, 216, 270; Home Counties 137, 141, 167, 170, 187, 214, 292; South Coast 50, 70, 72, 93, 97, 132, 184, 206, 225; southeast 254, 263; southern 135; West Country 92, 130, 164, 270
English Channel 263
Europe xiii, 2, 40, 50, 81, 86, 114, 118, 122, 139, 162, 163, 166, 203, 225, 233, 240, 242, 244, 252, 263, 264, 272, 275, 278; Western 35, 46, 59, 174, 237
Eton 166
Exeter 130

Farnham 131
Folla Rule 273
Formosa 277
Forres 114–115, 121, 122, *124*
Fort William 110
France 150, 190, 208, 246, 263
Fraser's Hill (Pahang) 133, 134
French Indochina 263–264, 279
French Riviera 86
Frensham Grove (Surrey) 131
Friesland 276
Frognal. See Hampstead

Gallipoli 229
Galloway 233, 234, 235
Galloway Forest Park 219
Galloway House (Wigtownshire) 228
Genoa 59, 203
Germany 137, 142, 165, 273
Gippsland 68
Glasgow 45, 46, 62, 76, 101, 102, 118, 155, 157, 203, 222
Glen Calvie Lodge (Easter Ross) 215
Glensanda (Morvern) 78
Gloucestershire 50, 184, 191–192, 193, 194, 225
Gooderstone (Norfolk) 106, 109
Gouda 21
Great Australian Bight 64
Great Britain. See Britain
Great Post Road (Java) 23
Green Park. See London
Greenwich. See London
Groningen 108
Guildford (Surrey) 230
Guyana. See British Guiana

The Hague xiii, xiv, 24, 153, 158, 159, 223, 243–245, 247–249, 254, 255, 258–259, 260, 276, 284; Archipelbuurt 244; Koninginnegracht 244–245, *244*, 247; Scheveningen 244, 249; Willemspark 244
Hamburg 139
Hampshire 131

Hampstead. See London
Hampstead Heath. See London
Harrow 143, 163, 208
Hartrigge House (Roxburghshire) *154*, 155–156
Hatton Garden. See London
Havilah (New South Wales) 193
Hebrides, Inner xi, 16, 25, 45, 76, 79, 80, 87, 99, 102, 103, 111, 197, 221, 227; Southern 230
Hemel Hempstead 44
Henley-on-Thames 143
Hobart 65
Holland 56, 86, 154, 157, 158, 159, 169. See also Netherlands
Holland House. See Cheltenham
Holyrood Palace. See Edinburgh
Hong Kong 231
Horsham (Victoria) 68, 177, 192
Hove 206, 225
Hyde Park. See London

Inchmarlo (Aberdeenshire) 147, 148
Indian Ocean xi, 5, 64
Indian subcontinent 1, 5, 7–8, 17, 25, 32, 78, 79, 114, 115, 118, 119, 153, 155, 161, 188, 189, 190, 208, 231, 232, 238, 266, 270, 275
Indies xii, xiii, 1, 4–5, 7–8, 11–14, 16–17, 19, 21, 22, 24, 25, 33, 34, 35, 37, 38, 39, 40, 42, 43, 44, 50, 54, 55, 56, 59, 62, 64, 65, 67, 68, 70, 71, 72, 73, 75–80, 82–84, 86, 87, 88, 89, 93, 95, 97, 100, 105, 106, 110, 120, 137–139, 142, 143, 145–146, 149, 151, 152, 154, 157, 158, 159, 162, 164, 174, 178, 179–184, 187, 190, 192, 193, 194, 197, 199, 202, 203, 209, 210, 211, 214, 216, 222, 223–226, 230, 235, 237–242, 243, 243, 246, 247, 248, 249–258, 259–260, 263–265, 267–272, 274–282, 284–285, 287–292
Indochina. See French Indochina
Indonesia 235, 284–285
Inveresk (Midlothian) 100
Inverness 90, 114, 138, 215
Inverness-shire 94
Ireland 2, 82, 92, 127, 165, 192, 207, 208, 233
Islay 25, 73, 76–83, *77*, 86–91, 93, 95, 99, 100, 101, 110, 111, 197, 199, 203, 204, 230, 239, 265
Islay House (Islay) 80, 88–89, *88*, 90–91, 230
Isle of Wight 125, 144, 184
Italy 131

Jakarta 282. See also Batavia
Jamaica 38, 130, 176

Japan 105, 213, 263, 276–279, 283
Java xi, xii, xiii, 1, 2, *10*, 11–13, 16–18, 20–24, 26, 29, 32–37, 38, 40, 41, 42, 43, 44, 45, 53, 55, 56, 57, 60, 62, 64, 65, 67, 68, 69, 77–78, 83–85, 86, 87, 88, 95, 97, 99, 100, 104, 105, 107, 108, 110, 113, 116, 117, 119, 120, 137, 138, 145, 151, *151*, 152, 154, 155, 157, 158, 159, *160*, 162, 164, 173, *174*, 179, 181–182, 184, 186, 187, 191, 193, 200–203, 204, 207, 209, 211, 214, 216, 219, 222, 223–224, *226*, 230, 237, 240–242, 246, 249–254, 257, 258, 260, 265, 267, 269–272, 274, 276, 277, 280–283, 285, 287, 288, 290–291; Central Java 24, *37*, 68, 69, 100, 157, 179, 239, 252, 260; East Java 44, 56, 84, 99, 107, 145, 146, 173, 179, 223, 242, 252–254, 263, 265, 267, 269, 280; Eastern Salient, see Oosthoek; South-Central Java 16, 18, 25, 27, 57, 99; West Java 21, 41, *41*, 84, 182
Java Sea 57
Jedburgh 155
Jersey 215

Kayun. See Surabaya
Kalimantan. See Borneo
Kensington Gardens. See London
Kent 133
Kentallen (Lochaber) 110
Kentish Weald 134
Kilchoman (Islay) 80, *82*, 83, 86
Kildalton (Islay) 79
King's Lynn 106
Kingston Lacy (Dorset) 165–166, *165*, 292
Kinloch (Mull) 62
Kinlochleven (Lochaber) 61
Kintail (Wester Ross) 44, 201
Kirkcudbrightshire 229, 233
Kleve 59
Koninginnegracht. See The Hague
Koningsplein. See Batavia

Laggan (Islay) 80–82, *81*, 87, 89
Lake Geneva 169, 214
Lambeth. See London
Lausanne 224
Leiden xiii
Lisle House. See Cheltenham
Liphook (Hampshire) 131
Liverpool 92, 118, 140, 156, 185, 213, 214, 219, 221
Loch Gilp (Argyll) xii
Loch Indaal (Islay) 83
Loch Linnhe 110
The Lodge, Gooderstone (Norfolk) 106, 109

Lochbuie (Mull) 15, 45, 60–61, *60*, *61*, 62, 64, 72
Loemadjang 258
Lombok 255
London 17, 18, 32, 43–44, 48–50, 70–72, 79–80, 83, 85, 87, 92, 94, 95, 102, 103–104, 105, 106, 108, 109, 110, 111, 113–114, 115, 120, 123–133, 134–135, 137, 138, 140, 141, 142, 143, 144, 148, 149, 150, 151, 152, 157, 158, 160, 161, 162, 163, 164, 166, 167, 169, 170, 185, 187, 190, 191, 192, 199, 209, 210, 211, 213, 214, 215, 216, 227, 230, 231, 235, 254, 266, 267, 269, 270, 275, 276, 278, 279, 281, 283, 284, 289, 291; Bayswater 104, 110, 149, 162, 163, 167, 185; Blackheath 92; Chelsea 133; City of London 49, 87, 103, 125–129, 133, 140, 142, 156, 157, 160, 184, 192; Covent Garden 213; East End 269; Curzon House 212; Green Park 214; Greenwich 92; Hampstead 44, 92, 94, 209, 228; Frognal 227, 228; Hampstead Heath 227; Hatton Garden 49; Hyde Park 49, 103, 104, 110, 124, 140, 149, 160, 160, 162, 167, 185; Kensington Gardens 162; Lambeth 43; Marylebone 94, 150; Mayfair 105, 106, 108, 109, 110, 167, 210, 212, 276; North London 209; Oxford Square *125;* Paddington 94, 103, *160*; Putney 43; Regent's Park 123, *123*; Roehampton 94; St James's 192, 214; Shoreditch 127; South Kensington 130–131, 149; South London 132; West End 49, 83, 105, 108, 190, 209, 210; West London 110; Westminster 212, 227; Westminster Abbey 269
Loretto School. See Musselburgh
Los Angeles 213
Low Countries 7, 39, 137–139, 141, 144, 152, 157, 170
Lumajang. See Loemadjang

Maas 247
Macao 147
Madras 32, 33, 114
Maiden Bradley House (Wiltshire) 164
Maidenhead 254
Makassar 181
Malay Peninsula 119, 133, 134, 238
Malaysia 284
Manchester 71, 118
Marischal College. See Aberdeen
Marseille 59, 203
Marylebone. See London

Massachusetts 69, 161
Mauritius 29
Mayfair. See London
Medan 284
Mediterranean Sea 33, 83, 109
Melambong *10*, 25–27
Melbourne xiii, xiv, 68, 158, 173, 175, 177, 179, 185, 186, 191, 192, 193; South Yarra 193
Mongewell Park (Oxfordshire) *140*, 141, 142, 143
Montevideo 139
Montreal 69
Montreux 169, 214
Moray Firth 114
Morvern 25, *60*, 66, 67 , 78, 202
Morvern (Melambong) 25
Mull, Isle of xiii, 12, 45, 46, 53, 60, *60*, 63, 67, 72, 197, 230
Mull, Sound of 45, 60
Musselburgh 100, 231; Loretto School 107

Nassau (Bahamas) 214
Neidpath (Peeblesshire) 101
Netherlands 13, 14, 20, 21, 29, 38, 40, 42, 43, 55, 56, 59, 86, 97, 108, 116, 139, 141, 143, 145, 147, 153, 157, 167, 168, 169, 170, 180, 182, 183, 185, 201, 223, 224, 225, 237, 238, 239, 240, 242–248, 253, 254, 258–259, 260, 263, 275, 276, 278, 279, 281, 284, 290
Netherlands East Indies. See Indies.
New England 69, 161
New Orleans 139, 282
New South Wales 66, 147, 173, 177, 193
New York 72, 213, 278
New Zealand 69, 193
Newton House (Islay) 87
Newton Stewart (Wigtownshire) 227, 228, 229
Nice 86, 203
Nile 59, 189, 207
Norfolk 92, 104–105, 106, 107, *108*, 109, 110
Normandy 81
North Brabant 246
North Sea coast 248
Northamptonshire 214
Norway 2
North America 2, 35, 118, 156, 161, 174, 197

Oban 45, *60*, 62
Oemboel 251–257, *252, 254, 255, 256, 257*
Ohio 197
Oosthoek (Java) 56, 84, 145, 200, 241, 246, 249, 251, 258, 260, 267
Overland Route 59, 83

Oxburgh Hall (Norfolk) 106
Oxford 92, 107, 166, 213
Oxfordshire 141

Pacific Islands 193
Padang 54, 55
Paddington. See London
Palestine 229
Pamanoekan and Tjiasem 57
Paris 59, 211, 272, 281
Pasuruan *10*, 44, 200–202, 241
Pearl Harbour 281
Pearl River 147
Peebles 233
Peeblesshire 100
Pekalongan *10*, 24
Penang 132, 225
Perth 18
Perthshire 204, 208
Philippines 232
Plantungan 69
Poland 278
Poole 92
Port Charlotte (Islay) 83, 86
Port Phillip (Australia) 173, 176, 192
Port Phillip Bay 175, 193
Portsmouth 184
Portugal 109
Preanger Mountains 21, 57
Priangan. See Preanger Mountains
Probolinggo *10*, 200, 242, 251, 257–258, 260
Provence 150
Putney. See London

Quebec 283
Queensland 158

Red Sea 59, 83
Regent's Park. See London
Rendcomb Manor (Gloucestershire) 191
Rhine 139
Rhinns Peninsula (Islay) 78, 100
Rich Avon 177, 186, 192
Rich Avon East sheep station 177, 185, 192
Rio de Janeiro 113
Riviera. See French Riviera
Roehampton. See London
Rotterdam 1, 19, 58, 75, 138, 139, 141–142, *141*, 144, 145, 147, 167, 170, 246, 247, 252, 264, 278, 280
Roxburghshire 155
Rugby 272
Ryde 144

Saigon 120, 279
St James's. See London
St Moritz 169
Salachan (Morvern) 78

Salatiga 26
Sale (Victoria) 68
Salzburg 134, 213
San Francisco 213, 280
Sandringham 106, 107
Sandhurst 208
Scheldt 139
Scheveningen. See The Hague
Scotland xi, xii, xiii, 2–6, 8, 11–13, 15, 19–20, 23, 25, 32, 38, 39, 44, 45, 47, 48, 49, 51, 59, 60, 61, 62, 63, 65, 66, 68, 69, 71, 72, 77–85, 87, 91, 93, 94, 95, 99, 100, 101, 102, 107, 109, 110, 116, 121, 122, 124, 125, 132, 135, 137, 138, 140, 144, 145, 149, 152, 177, 183, 186, 187, 189, 197, 202, 204, 205, 207, 208, 215, 216, 222, 231, 235, 239, 240, 268, 271–274, 278, 283, 287, 288, 290–291; Highlands and Islands 45, 46, 47, 48, 62, 71, 72, 81, 88, 90, 91, 103, 109, 110, 174, 175, 202, 205, 206, 222, 234, 265; Lowlands 46, 47, 90, 205; north 44, 103, 114, 147, 215; north-east 13, 170, 205, 274; Scottish Borders 46, 91, 155, 222, 223, 234, 235; south-west 219, 227, 228, 229, 232, 233, 234; Western Highlands 20, 23, 25, 62, 78, 88, 125, 201, 203; Western Isles, see Hebrides, Inner.
Semarang 10, 18, 24, 26, 62, 69, 75, 78, 99, 100, 139, 157, 159, 180, 181, 209, 223, 230, 239–241, 248, 257, 260, 276
Semeru (mountain) 201
Shanghai 213, 268
Shennanton (Wigtownshire) 219, 220, 221, 222–223, 227–228, 229, 230–235
Shoreditch. See London
Silesia 165
Singapore 29, 33, 58, 59, 80, 113–122, 115, 125, 126, 129, 131–134, 135, 235, 238, 268, 281, 283
Singapore Cottage (Forres) 124
Skye, Isle of 233
Solent 184
South Africa 208, 225, 266, 271, 275
South Australia xii, 32, 64, 65, 66, 67, 68
South Carolina 139
South Island (New Zealand) 69
South Kensington. See London
South Yarra. See Melbourne
Southampton 59, 271
Southeast Asia 1, 4, 11, 36, 78, 79, 80, 97–98, 99, 116, 119, 120, 126, 137, 146, 151, 158, 162, 263, 267, 275, 281, 288
Spain 144
Sri Lanka. See Ceylon

Stirling 174, 176
Stow Hall (Norfolk) 107
Suez Canal 59, 271
Sukapura 253
Sumatra 54, 56, 159, 224, 241, 277, 280; West Coast 54, 55–56
Sumira. See Semeru (mountain)
Surabaya 10, 39, 44, 75, 76, 99, 99, 107, 145, 152, 162, 173, 181, 187, 191, 199, 201, 202, 209, 223–225, 226, 227, 241–242, 252, 262, 263–265, 267–272, 274–281, 280, 283, 284; Kayun 225, 279, 280
Surakarta 10, 25, 26
Suriname 55
Surrey 131, 254
Sussex 143, 272
Switzerland 169, 213, 214, 258
Sydney 65, 132, 173, 193

Taiwan. See Formosa
Tanah Abang. See Batavia
Tasmania 177
Tengger Mountains 107, 253
Thailand 120, 283
Thames 17, 127, 140, 141
Tjepiring 37
Torquay 149
Tras Lahang (Pahang) 134
Trieste 59
Trinity College, Dublin 143
Tunbridge Wells 134

Umbul. See Oemboel.
United Kingdom. See Britain
United States 69, 105, 160, 161, 198, 213, 277, 278, 283
United States, southern states 34, 36, 118

Victoria (Australia) 68, 103, 193
Vietnam. See French Indochina
Vlaardingen 247

Wallingford 141, 143
Washington, D.C. 190, 281
Werkendam 246
West End. See London
West Indies 26, 127, 128, 176
Western Front (First World War) 190, 229, 265, 266
Western New Guinea 284
Westminster. See London
Westminster Abbey. See London
Wigtown 219, 221, 222, 228; Barbados 219, 221–222, 221
Wigtownshire xiii, 219, 227, 229, 233, 234
Willemskerk. See Batavia
Willemspark. See The Hague
Williamstown (Aberdeenshire) 273
Wiltshire 164

Wimborne Minster (Dorset) 165
Wimmera 177–178, 185–186, 192
Wonolangan 255, 257
Worcester (Massachusetts) 161

Yogyakarta *10*, 16
Yokohama 213

Zeeland 153, 278
Zwolle 55

C. Themes

Anglo-Dutch cooperation 13, 275–276
architecture 32, 34, 205–206, 222
archival challenges, diaspora history 8–9
Armenian merchants 77–78
arms trade 118, 156
assimilation, Scottish migrants 2, 50, 287

Balmoralism 47, 274. See Also Highlandism
banking 85–86, 103, 126–128, 140, 145–146, 156–157, 160, 162, 167, 226, 259, 267
bankruptcy 1, 61, 70, 80–81, 133. See Also financial decline
British imperial presence 4, 17, 116–118, 151–152, 155–156, 158, 173, 177–178, 189–191, 199, 207–209, 216, 223, 263–264, 270, 276, 278–283, 285. See Also consuls
business investments 232, 245–247; Scotland 62, 72, 102–103, 106

Calvinism 19, 38. See Also Presbyterianism
capital accumulation 77, 85–86, 110, 219, 221–222, 232; Asian 4, 85
career emigrants 5, 44, 173, 223–224, 267, 287. See Also sojourning
Celtic fringe 76, 78–79, 90
Celtic isolationism 3
chinchona 107
Chinese 17, 24, 116, 118–120, 159, 277
Chinese trade 77–78. See Also Sino-Indonesian trade
clan revivalism 47, 49, 62, 197, 216, 265
coercive labour regimes 35–36, 84, 151, 179, 194, 200, 219–222, 251–252, 283, 288. See Also corvée labour, slavery

coffee 18, 24–26, 107, 139, 248, 257–258
colonial bureaucracy 54–57, 80, 145, 153–154, 158–159, 181, 221, 223–224, 238, 240–242, 255, 267, 279–281
colonial churches 33, 58, 67
colonial domestic life 32–34, 38–39, 42, 89, 159, 194, 200, 225–227, 240–241, 243, 249, 251–255, 257–260, 263–264, 268–272, 281, 289–291
colonial integration, Dutch Indies 11–15, 18–19, 21–27, 29, 32, 35–37, 39–43, 53, 93, 99, 151–152, 157, 179–182, 202, 223–225, 237–239, 249, 251–252, 257–258, 263–264, 266, 268–270, 275, 277–278, 282, 289, 291, 292
commercial networks 54, 62, 64, 66, 70, 75–77, 83–86, 99–100, 107, 115–120, 126–128, 139–140, 146, 151–153, 156–162, 179, 181–182, 187, 191, 199–202, 209, 219, 223–226, 241–242, 246, 257–259, 265, 267, 270–271, 275–278, 281, 285
commodity chains 4, 17–18, 23–25, 35–36, 83–84, 117–120, 125–126, 133, 140, 151, 156–158, 170, 173–174, 176, 178–179, 182, 190–191, 194, 219–224, 235, 241–242, 248–249, 251–252, 255, 257–258, 267, 275, 277–278, 285, 292. See Also chinchona, coffee, cotton, indigo, oil, opium trade, rice, rubber, sheep farming, sugar, tea, textiles, tin, tobacco
comparative colonialism 34–36, 38, 42–43, 84, 174, 219, 221, 238–239, 255, 275–278, 292
consuls 62, 149, 152, 181, 207, 267, 276, 281. See Also British imperial presence
corvée labour 25, 35–36, 151, 194, 220, 288. See Also Cultivation System (Cultuurstelsel)
cotton 17–18, 25, 36, 79, 118–119, 139, 156, 173, 277–278. See Also textiles
creolisation 42, 56, 121, 237–239, 243, 289, 292
Cultivation System (Cultuurstelsel) 36, 84, 151, 179, 194, 219–222, 288. See Also corvée labour
cultural difference 19–21, 25–27, 29, 32–33, 37–39, 41–42, 67, 69, 116, 238, 251–254, 268, 289, 292

cultural identity 62, 170, 238–240, 243, 245, 253–255, 259, 264–265, 290–291; Europeans 33–34, 39, 42, 75, 169, 247–248; Scottish 66–67, 69–70, 72, 88–89, 100–101, 106, 110, 117, 169, 189, 198, 216; Scottish diaspora 12, 15, 47, 49, 53, 63, 94–95, 97–98, 103–104, 108–109, 116, 120–121, 144, 246

diaspora 4, 116, 128, 170, 260; critiques of 2, 6, 9, 50, 239, 243, 287–288, 291, 292; Scottish 2, 6, 8–9, 50, 72, 76, 98, 113–114, 122, 126, 128, 135, 137–140, 142–143, 147, 152, 157–158, 170, 181, 193–194, 197–198, 202–203, 210, 219, 223, 237, 245–246, 259, 264–265, 276, 285, 287–290, 292. See Also Islay diaspora
Dutch East India Company (VOC) 54–55
Dutch families 21–22, 24, 54–59, 104, 152–154, 180–182, 209, 223–225, 240, 279, 290
Dutch governors 18, 22, 24, 157–159, 283

East India Company (EIC) 17, 114
economic development, Highlands 62, 81–82, 102
education 43–44, 56, 92, 107, 121, 163, 180, 188–190, 208, 224–225, 244, 246–247, 253, 266, 270, 290
equestrianism 26, 32–33, 39–40, 193–194, 222, 271
estate management 1, 100, 102
Eurasian communities 41–43, 97, 107, 121, 179, 191, 200–202, 223, 237–246, 251–253, 255, 257–259, 268, 289–290

family migration strategies 2, 4, 6, 9, 21, 29, 32, 54–60, 62–64, 66–69, 82–83, 86–87, 89–90, 92–94, 97, 103, 120–122, 131–135, 137–144, 149, 152–153, 162–163, 170, 173–176, 178, 180–186, 188, 191, 193, 199, 203, 208, 222–223, 228–231, 237, 239–242, 244, 246–249, 251–252, 254–255, 257–260, 265–266, 270–274, 281, 283, 287–288, 290–291, 292
financial decline 72, 80, 131–135, 184, 202, 215, 222, 232–235, 275. See Also bankruptcy

Fraser Eaton & Co. 107, 145, 152, 201, 223, 241, 267, 270, 271, 275
Freemasonry 13–14, 38, 99–100, 122, 125, 191, 257

Gaelic 25–26, 202
Gaelic cultural revival 72
gender relations 120–121, 132, 147. See Also women
genealogical sources, use of 9
glocalisation 6, 77, 99

health 18, 26, 97, 104, 130–131, 201, 266. See Also illness
health migrations 50, 59, 97
Highlandism 47, 49, 60–62, 70, 72, 89–91, 100, 103, 106, 109, 155, 197, 199, 202–207, 215–216, 222, 265, 274, 288. See Also Balmoralism, clan revivalism
household arrangements, Dutch Indies 34, 38, 42, 62, 75–76, 179, 254; England 70, 92, 94, 97, 104, 124, 129–132, 149, 165–167, 183–186, 188, 194, 206, 227; Europe 244–245; Scotland 64, 87–89, 101, 155, 203
hunting 40, 63, 72, 90–91, 100, 106, 109, 155, 204–205, 215, 222, 233–234, 265, 273–274
hybridity 13, 42, 243

identity transformation 50, 72, 95, 109–110, 135, 144, 149, 159, 161, 163–164, 169–170, 187, 189–190, 198, 203–208, 210, 212–216, 223, 237–240, 251–253, 259–260, 268–271, 288–291, 292
illness 18, 69, 97, 266. See Also health
Indigenous dispossession 66, 177–178, 194
indigo 23
Indonesian society 24–26, 34, 40–42, 107, 201, 219–220, 251–255, 258, 260, 268, 277–278, 285
inheritance, disputes and debt 61–62, 68, 70, 72, 80–82
Islay diaspora 77–79, 82, 89–90, 95, 197, 265

kin-based networks 76–79, 83, 145, 147–148, 167, 199
kinship 7, 25, 29, 32, 38, 40–41, 43–45, 47, 53, 100, 138–139, 239–240

landed estates, Australia 64, 66, 174, 176–178, 191, 193; Dutch Indies 57; England 103, 106, 141–144,

164–166, 185; Scotland 60–62, 72, 80, 88, 100, 110, 155, 203–206, 219, 221–222, 227–229, 232–234, 265, 274
London High Society 72, 103–104, 129, 160, 162–169, 210–214, 216, 288

Maclaine Fraser & Co. 117, 133
Maclaine Watson 4–8, 11, 13, 18, 24, 27, 32, 36–37, 39–41, 43–44, 46–48, 50, 53, 56, 64, 68, 76–79, 82–86, 93–94, 97, 105–106, 113, 115–116, 119, 126, 146, 152, 157, 173, 182, 187, 191, 199–203, 209, 216, 219–220, 223, 225–226, 231, 235, 242, 265, 267, 270, 275–276, 283, 285, 287, 291, 292
MacNeill & Co. 25, 78–79, 99, 239, 241
marriage alliances 1, 7, 11–12, 18–22, 24, 38, 54, 56–58, 62, 68, 70, 78, 82–83, 92–95, 97, 100, 103, 107, 110, 120–122, 129–131, 138–144, 147, 149, 152–154, 160–167, 170, 180–183, 185–187, 191, 193, 203, 209, 212–214, 216, 223–225, 228, 230–232, 241, 245–249, 255, 266, 272–274, 289–291, 292
mercantile families 1, 4, 7, 11–13, 15–18, 20–25, 27, 29, 32, 34, 36–37, 39–40, 43–45, 54, 82–83, 99, 113–115, 118, 137–144, 146–147, 158–162, 168, 183, 203, 219, 265, 291
migration 4, 6, 13, 16–18, 25, 29, 33, 37–40, 43–46, 48–50, 59, 68–69, 75, 80, 82, 87, 90, 97, 99, 107–108, 114–116, 120–123, 127, 129–130, 132–135, 150, 152, 157–158, 160, 173–179, 183–184, 186–187, 189–191, 193, 199, 201–203, 214–215, 219, 258, 267–271, 285, 287
military service 26, 130–131, 163, 189–190, 195, 208–209, 228–229, 231, 265–266, 281–283
mortality 69, 91, 97, 104, 110, 113, 149–150, 162, 186, 191, 202, 209, 223, 230–231, 241–242, 249, 266, 282–283

near diaspora, Scots in England 48–50, 87, 92–94, 106, 110, 123, 129–135, 141, 144, 149–150, 160–167, 183–191, 194, 198, 211–212, 214–216, 227, 235; Scots in Netherlands 242–248, 259–260, 279

Netherlands India Steam Navigation Company (NISM) 157–159
Netherlands Trading Society (NHM) 55–56, 145–146, 181

oil 277–278, 281–282, 285
opium trade 4, 16, 77–78, 117, 119, 147, 159, 213

peasant agriculture 36, 84, 220
political influence 89, 143, 149, 158, 160, 207–208, 216, 224, 229, 232–234, 248, 275–276, 279–281, 283, 285
Presbyterianism 18–19, 33, 83, 150, 152, 160, 189, 269
Primrose League 207–208, 216
proto-globalisation 6, 72, 77, 114, 277

race attitudes 42–43, 238–240, 268, 289
railways 46, 59, 62, 85, 91, 101–102, 110, 127–128, 154, 157, 232
religion 18–19, 33, 38, 83, 152, 189. See Also Calvinism, colonial churches, Presbyterianism
repatriate afterlives 45–50, 59–62, 72, 83, 85–86, 95, 97, 102–103, 106, 108–110, 114, 121, 123–124, 126–135, 137–138, 141–143, 149–151, 155–158, 160–162, 183–189, 191, 194, 197, 199, 203–211, 214–216, 221–223, 225–232, 234–235, 243–245, 247–249, 258–260, 265–266, 270–274, 281–283, 285, 287–288, 290–291, 292
repatriation 2, 5–6, 18, 44–45, 83, 85–86, 95, 98, 100, 113–114, 121, 137–138, 145–146, 149, 154–156, 158–161, 183, 197, 199, 203, 210, 221–223, 245, 258–260, 271, 282–283, 285, 287–288, 290
return migration 5–6, 18, 82–83, 121, 132–134, 145, 147, 183, 191, 194, 216, 222, 258–260, 271, 283, 285, 290–291
rice 26, 36, 65, 120, 126, 255
Royal Dutch Shell 24
rubber 235, 279

Scottish, community abroad 2, 4, 7, 11–17, 23–26, 29, 33, 37–39, 80, 83, 99–100, 113–117, 120, 122, 124–125, 127–128, 133, 149–151, 157, 181–182, 198, 263–269, 292; distinctiveness debates 3, 38; identity 3, 12–15, 18–21, 25–27, 127, 129, 144, 198, 202–

203, 205–207, 222, 237, 274, 288–290; in Australia 64, 66–68, 175; in Dutch Indies 4, 7–8, 11–13, 16, 18, 21–27, 29, 32–34, 37–42, 44–45, 53–54, 62, 64, 68–69, 75–76, 83, 99–100, 107, 146, 152, 263–265, 267, 279; industry 46, 62, 82, 102

Scottish landscape, transformation of 45–47, 72, 81, 89–91, 100

Scottish returnees in England 2, 4, 48–50, 70, 72, 83, 91, 95, 97, 103–106, 108–110, 123–126, 141–144, 188, 288

Scottish returnees in Scotland 46–47, 60–64, 68–69, 72, 80, 83, 86, 88–89, 100–103, 110, 147–148, 197, 228–231, 233–235, 265–266

servants 89, 101, 104–105, 110, 124, 129–131, 143–144, 149–150, 162, 243

sheep farming 29, 60, 66–68, 80–81, 173–175, 177–178, 191, 193–194

Sino-Indonesian trade 17, 119, 159, 277–278. See Also Chinese trade

slavery 25, 118, 128, 140, 176, 185, 219, 222, 231; Dutch Indies 34–36, 179; Scottish debates on 4, 176

sojourning 5–6, 24–25, 29, 38, 44–45, 59, 64, 75–76, 82–83, 86, 95, 99–100, 105, 114–115, 120, 133–135, 137–138, 146, 150, 152, 155–157, 159, 173, 179, 183, 191, 193–194, 199–202, 216, 223–226, 237, 258, 260, 265–271, 275–276, 282, 285, 287, 290–291, 292. See Also career emigrants

St Andrew's Day 11–12, 15, 117, 198, 283, 288

sugar 83–84, 86, 127–128, 139, 145, 151, 162, 173–174, 179, 194, 200–201, 219, 221–224, 237, 241–242, 244, 249, 251–252, 255, 257, 267, 275, 277–278, 285, 292; export trade 4, 23–24, 35–36, 64, 68, 95, 100, 146, 219–221, 237, 244, 267, 275

tea 107, 191, 235, 266
Tempo Doeloe 33–34
textiles 17–18, 24, 79, 117–118, 121. See Also cotton
tin 182, 235
tobacco 139
trans-imperial networks 7, 11, 15, 17–18, 23–24, 29, 32–33, 38–40, 43–44, 54–56, 59, 72, 78–79, 83–84, 86, 95, 97–99, 113–120, 126–128, 133–135, 138–142, 146–147, 151–154, 156–159, 161, 168–170, 173, 194–195, 209–210, 213–214, 216, 219, 223–224, 235, 237, 242–243, 246, 255, 257–258, 265, 267–270, 275–281, 283, 285, 288–289, 292

transportation, colonial 59, 75, 82, 158, 267–269, 271, 281–283

voyages, long-distance 1, 29, 58–59, 82–83, 105, 108, 114, 155, 213, 237, 267, 269–271, 280–283

wages and salaries, colonial 75–76, 83, 199–200

wealth, diasporan 4, 6, 16, 18, 20, 24, 27, 29, 32, 36, 72, 82–89, 93, 95, 98, 100, 102–104, 106, 108–110, 114, 116, 121, 126–127, 129, 134–135, 140–146, 149–150, 152, 155–157, 159, 161–170, 176–177, 179, 183–186, 188–191, 194, 203–206, 209–216, 219, 221–222, 226–230, 232, 265, 274, 287, 290, 292

widowhood 91, 103, 130–134, 149–150, 161–162, 215, 230–231, 248, 266; financial hardship 2, 87, 137

women, agency of 7, 87, 89, 97, 104, 129–130, 138, 144, 161–170, 180–181, 183, 190, 207–208, 210–214, 216, 225, 230–231, 233–234, 245, 253–254, 259–260, 266, 272–273, 279–283, 291, 292; in colonial settings 1, 7, 20–22, 26, 29, 54–57, 121, 129, 153, 159, 180–181, 183, 191, 223–225, 230, 253–254, 272, 279–280, 282–283, 289, 291, 292; later-life trajectories 72, 91, 94, 104, 109–110, 129–130, 132, 134, 161–166, 183, 207–208, 213–216, 221–222, 245, 266, 282–283

Photo © Jarran Zen

Born in rural Shropshire, **G. Roger Knight** has been living and teaching in Adelaide, Australia, since the late 1960s. He gained his PhD from London University's School of Oriental and Asian Studies, where his mentors included John Bastin and C. D. Cowan. He is an internationally recognised authority on the sugar industry of colonial Indonesia, with many publications to his name. Among the latest is *Commodties and Colonialism: The Story of Big Sugar in Indonesia, 1880-1940* (Brill 2013), *Sugar, Steam and Steel: The Industrial Project in Colonial Java, 1830-1885* (University of Adelaide Press 2015), and *Trade and Empire in Early Nineteenth-Century Southeast Asia: Gillain Maclaine and his Business Network* (Boydell Press 2015).